D0535542

MODERN EUROPE IN THE MAKING

From the French Revolution to the Common Market

MODERN EUROPE IN THE MAKING

From the French Revolution to the Common Market

GEORGE FASEL
University of Missouri–Columbia

DODD, MEAD & COMPANY
New York / 1974

Riverside Community College
Library
4800 Magnolia Avenue
Riverside, California 92506

Copyright © 1974 by Dodd, Mead & Company, Inc.
All rights reserved
No part of this book may be reproduced in any form
without permission in writing from the publisher
ISBN 0-396-06895-2
Library of Congress Catalog Card Number: 73-15381
Printed in the United States of America
Designed by EMILY HARSTE

Index by SALLY GERSHMAN

This investigation was supported
by a grant from the University of
Missouri-Columbia Research Council.

For
Kimberley
Marion
&
Mason

Preface

College history teachers often teach, as a regular part of their offerings, an introductory course taken by large numbers of students—large enough that the historian has frequently become inseparable from his microphone. Although such courses are sometimes required in the prevailing curriculum structure, the teacher is unusual if more than a small fraction of his students go on to become majors in history, much less professional historians.

At the same time, most introductory books—at least in the area of modern European history—appear to be written for future professionals. These accounts are largely factual narratives filled with the sort of information which specialists alone are liable to find of use: details of the treaty of Unkiar Skelessi, the development of British technology from the flying shuttle to the slubbing billy, the fortunes of the Sanjak of Novi-Bazar, points of contention between Schopenhauer and Nietzsche. A teacher may legitimately expect that aspirant historians will eventually command such knowledge. But can he reasonably demand that all college graduates be capable of summoning up this sort of information?

Without professional specialization, most teaching would be impossible. But we do not teach only to produce specialized professionals. If professional historians have become a social necessity, it is primarily because historically minded nonprofessionals are a necessity too. We study the past—and require its study—because it can tell us things worth knowing, because responsible citizens ought to know something of the past which has shaped their lives and the world around them. But how much ought they to know, and what? The problem is especially acute for the student whose first college history course will also be his last—in other words, most students.

This book was conceived from two premises. First, I believe that beginning students will benefit more and retain more from introductory history courses if those courses are topically organized within a broad chronological framework. Narrative history is valuable—or, rather, invaluable—but it is neither the only nor in all circumstances the best teaching approach. An approach which emphasizes issues over factual narrative may be the best means of making large blocs of time and information intelligible to students unfamiliar with them and unlikely to pursue them in depth in the future. Such an approach implies neither a defiance of chronology nor a refusal to communicate significant historical information. It simply attacks those traditional tasks of the discipline in different ways.

Second, I am not persuaded that a beginning student's grasp of history is best measured through his ability to cite names, dates, or other assorted "facts" of the kind demanded on examinations to be graded by machines. Without a study of issues or problems, the facts are meaningless and will in any case be swiftly forgotten. If a student is going to become a history major, he or she will learn the "facts" in due time. Surely we would prefer that the vast majority of students who do not become history majors be exposed to some major problems, even if this exposure comes at the expense of factual knowledge of dubious significance.

Accordingly, this book has been highly selective in its relation of discrete facts and has concentrated on some of the chief problems which have characterized modern European history and how those problems relate to one another. Similarly with the problems themselves, I have not attempted to include a discussion of every subject which might be of interest or even some importance. In general, my principle of selection has been to respond to a single question: does a person who is not a professional historian need to know something about this subject in order to make some sense out of modern European history? Individual teachers will regret the absence in these pages of certain indubitably important subjects—the Crimean War, existentialism, Stresemann's foreign policy, for example. In one sense, I share this regret (though I am also mindful of Voltaire's observation that "The best way to be boring is to leave nothing out"). Yet I also hope that the treatment of what *is* in the book will at least partially justify my conviction that professional historians must find new ways to talk about the past with nonprofessionals.

GEORGE FASEL

Contents

ix

Maps

MAPS BY DAVID ROBERTS

Part One
THE BIRTH
OF THE
NINETEENTH
CENTURY

Historical study always begins with a choice: one selects a point in past time at which to start, and then moves steadily toward the present. In the case of nineteenth-century European history, that point is usually the year 1815. On the other hand, "background" is the historian's stock-in-trade. When you say that you wish to begin your study with 1815, historians will probably respond that you cannot possibly understand that year without understanding what went on in the year—or decade, or generation—preceding. But if we cannot understand 1815 without understanding, say, 1789, can we hope to understand 1789 without grasping the significance of the 1770's or even the 1760's? Clearly, we need something like a statute of limitations to protect us from infinite regress.

It may be a reasonable compromise—between beginning abruptly in 1815 and tracing (as it were) the entire family tree of that very important year—to limit ourselves to an account of its gestation period. Chapters 1–3 examine, from three different but interrelated perspectives, the period from roughly the 1780's into the second decade of the nineteenth century. They focus upon the changes in political institutions, in economic and social relationships, and in cultural attitudes during these transitional years. They describe both the conditions in which the nineteenth century was born and the legacy of problems passed on by its predecessor.

1 / *French Politics*

Historians have widely regarded the passing of the Old Regime in France as symbolic of its demise throughout all of Europe. The French Revolution thus becomes a sort of watershed between two large expanses of historical terrain—the Old Regime and modern Europe. It is convenient to have such disjunctions: they provide handy jumping-off places for academic courses and for books such as this one, and they make it easy for professional historians and their students to establish neatly defined areas of specialization. But if the human past is a story of change, close inspection of it reveals that such abrupt changes and clean severances are the exception rather than the rule. They happen, as we shall see, but with a frequency more akin to that of earthquakes and tidal waves than to the less dramatic but equally decisive processes of erosion which reshape the land. The revolutionary-Napoleonic era did not dispatch the Old Regime—in France or elsewhere—either so quickly or so completely as the watershed metaphor suggests. Even though the revolution did level a few prominent outcroppings, of which the most notable was the head of King Louis XVI of France, in general new configurations tended to emerge less suddenly. Nor were events in France alone in generating erosive forces (see Chapter 2). Moreover, just as much of the Old Regime stubbornly persisted well beyond the French Revolution, counter to all the imperatives of tidy historical periodization, the French Revolution itself had its energizing sources deep in the Old Regime.

Absolutism and Its Critics

Government in eighteenth-century Europe was not a public affair. Hereditary monarchs ruled the major states through large, growing bureau-

3

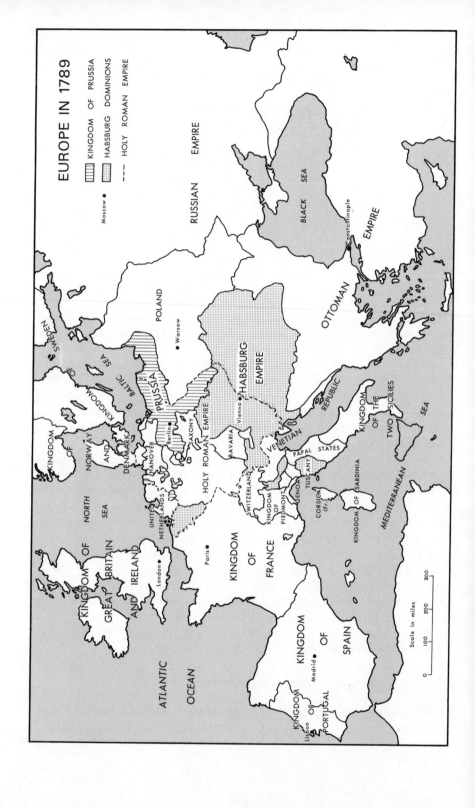

EUROPE IN 1789

||||| KINGDOM OF PRUSSIA
::::: HABSBURG DOMINIONS
– – – HOLY ROMAN EMPIRE

Moscow •

RUSSIAN EMPIRE

POLAND

• Warsaw

KINGDOM OF SWEDEN

BALTIC SEA

KINGDOM OF NORWAY AND DENMARK

PRUSSIA

Berlin •

HANOVER

SAXONY

HOLY ROMAN EMPIRE

BAVARIA

Vienna •

HABSBURG EMPIRE

VENETIAN REPUBLIC

BLACK SEA

Constantinople •

OTTOMAN EMPIRE

NORTH SEA

KINGDOM OF GREAT BRITAIN AND IRELAND

London •

UNITED NETHERLANDS

SWITZERLAND

PAPAL STATES

TUSCANY

GENOA

KINGDOM OF PIEDMONT

KINGDOM OF SARDINIA

CORSICA (Fr.)

KINGDOM OF THE TWO SICILIES

MEDITERRANEAN SEA

ATLANTIC OCEAN

Paris •

KINGDOM OF FRANCE

Madrid •

KINGDOM OF SPAIN

Lisbon •

KINGDOM OF PORTUGAL

Scale in miles

0   100   200   300

cracies, and "politics" was largely a matter of administration. Outside of Great Britain, there were few legislative institutions which could rival the power of the throne. In a few lesser kingdoms, such as Sweden, the prince was little more than a decorative figurehead. In most places, however, political initiative—though not uncontested political supremacy—lay with the monarchy. Royalty argued that its powers were "absolute"; and though this claim was not so much an accurate description of reality as an aspiration, its fulfillment appeared to be within the realm of possibility.

Absolute monarchy was a relatively recent creation, the product of widespread dissatisfaction with the extensive civil upheavals of the sixteenth and early seventeenth centuries. Medieval monarchs had tended to share political power with the nobility, with its considerable landed wealth, social prestige, and control of large private armies upon which the monarch was frequently dependent. Besides exercising many important administrative and judiciary functions, the nobility largely dominated the various pseudo-representative institutions—semilegislative and semiconsultative—which sprang up in the middle ages. These bodies made no pretense of democratic representation and were mostly composed of nobles elected by their peers, though they claimed to guard the interests of all subjects. Often, they had some version of a right to consent over taxation, as well as a limited legislative role.

The distinction between political partnership and political rivalry in these arrangements was hard to draw. Increasingly, monarchs complained that nobles were using their positions of responsibility to frustrate "legitimate" royal prerogative and amass what was simply private power. Noblemen in their turn regarded royal ambitions to independent authority with deep suspicion, and some of them sought to establish further constitutional limitations upon the throne. The rivalry for power between dynasty and nobility periodically erupted into civil war; with the Protestant Reformation of the sixteenth century, religious violence intersected these struggles and escalated them into international conflicts. Spiritual and secular motives intermingled in wars which set nobles against their king, state against state, and sometimes one faction of the nobility against another.

The political chaos into which western and central Europe had descended by the mid-seventeenth century formed the context for renewed royal claims to increased power. Monarchy alone, of all institutions, appeared capable of guaranteeing public order and a return to domestic tranquility. To do so, however, the monarch had to be free of three traditional restraints. First, he needed something like a monopoly on coercion so that he was no longer dependent upon the privately recruited armies of the nobility either to keep the public peace or to defend against foreign attack. As a result, most states witnessed the expansion of standing armies, loyal to the king rather than being paid and commanded by one of his potential competitors. Next, he needed an instrument of government responsive to his own will, one which was not infested by nobles whose sense of responsibility to the crown was often vague. Therefore, most monarchs began to elaborate the royal administration into a larger and more efficient institution and to staff it with professional bureaucrats obligated to the king for their position and advancement. Finally, the monarch who would command such a bureaucracy, as well as a standing army, had to be able to pay for it all. In other words, he needed independence from the pseudo-representative bodies and their rights of approval over taxation. The public temper was so overwhelmingly in favor of restoring civil order, however, that most monarchs could simply ignore—rather than going to the trouble to abolish—these bodies and could proceed to collect taxes without any formal consent to them.

Thus the political synthesis known as absolute monarchy grew from the development of standing armies, bureaucracy, and fiscal independence. European princes approached the fulfillment of absolute power in widely varying degrees, though none of them exercised uncontested political supremacy. Whatever progress absolutism made, however, was almost everywhere accomplished at the expense of the nobility and of their pseudo-representative institutional strongholds.

Two structural faults in absolutism condemned it to a relatively short life. To begin with, the gap between the nobility's continued high social status and its political powerlessness could not persist for long. Power may not always coincide with high social status, but those with high social status will usually try to see that it does. Aristocrats refused to accept the role of mere social ornaments to the throne, and once the immediacy of civil turmoil had abated they launched a campaign to reconquer the political responsibilities which they deemed commensurate with high birth. Had absolute monarchs successfully shorn their nobles of prestige and wealth in addition to power, the socio-political discrepancy would not have existed. But far from attempting such a revolution, most monarchs profoundly believed in the necessity of a hierarchical society, ordered from the top downwards by decreasing degrees of prestige and privilege. Thus, while concentrating political authority, they sought to fortify aristocratic social domination, and also thereby to compensate for the nobles' loss of a significant political role. Reinforced noble privilege —sometimes honorific, but often enough material, as with the French nobility's exemption from the main direct tax—was supposed to take the place of power. In other words, nobility still occupied a strategic social position from which it might mount an assault upon absolutism. The special prestige of the nobility, the deference it commanded, made it the only social group which could plausibly challenge the throne and mobilize opposition to absolutism behind its leadership.

The second fault lay in the fact that most princes did not see the structure of absolute government as serving exclusively domestic ends. Standing armies, centralized administration, and the relatively uninhibited disposition of money combined to create more effective war machines. It was a rare dynasty which was not internationally ambitious, seeking new territories to be chiseled off one's neighbor and added to one's own domain, seeking weak or soon-to-be vacant thrones which might be reoccupied by representatives of one's own line, seeking new reservoirs of wealth overseas. Louis XIV of France, the very model of an absolute monarch, ruling from 1661 to 1715, was a relentless expansionist whose territorial ambitions involved him in war for nearly twenty-nine of his fifty-four years in power. The crowned heads of the eighteenth century proved scarcely less belligerent; and major wars involving most or all of the large states raged from 1733 to 1735, 1740 to 1748, and again from 1756 to 1763, the latter war spreading from Europe to India and North America.

These conflicts were massively expensive. All governments were therefore forced to enlarge their revenues in order to pay for wars past, present, and future. Frequently, this imperative meant increasing the financial exactions upon their respective populations, and it was at this point that the structural faults of absolutism joined, as it were, to create a dangerous weakness at a vital point. Nobles objected to new taxes—especially when their own traditional exemptions were threatened—and began to argue that taxation could only be legitimate if approved by the old "representative" institutions. European aristocrats began to shriek about a "despotism" which ran roughshod over "traditional liberties" and "natural rights." In hopes of exerting some leverage upon financially desperate monarchs, nobility took its case before larger segments of the public, trying to create a broad front of resistance to new, unilateral levies.

Aristocratic motives in this movement were complex, and it is difficult to sort out the selfish from the altruistic ones. Some noblemen doubtless saw themselves as the guardians of public liberties being threatened by the monarchy, as the necessary checks or balances which kept royal prerogative from degenerating into unrestrained tyranny. But it was equally true that the revivification of the faltering pseudo-representative institutions would be an important step toward restoring the nobility to a position of political authority, not to mention that it would make any violations of noble privileges and exemptions considerably more difficult. However that may be, the issue of royal finances became almost identical with the issue of the allocation of political responsibilities. If the monarchs surrendered the exclusive power of the purse and admitted any significant degree of prerogative to aristocratically dominated bodies, they compromised the principle of absolutism at its very core.

In the aftermath of the dreadfully expensive Seven Years War, which ended in 1763, Europe's aristocrats and monarchs attacked and counterattacked one another over this dual issue. Although each side could claim victories, it was clear by the 1780's that absolute monarchy was conducting a sort of strategic withdrawal. Whether by assertion of right or by prudent royal concessions, the pseudo-representative bodies had begun to reappropriate some of their historical jurisdictions and prerogatives. Few princes renounced their claims to absolute and undivided authority, but absolutism at this time plainly occupied a position slightly closer to pretension than to practice.

The resurgence of European nobility in the late eighteenth century not only deflected the process of absolutism, it also inspired a variety of political activities which sometimes supported, sometimes enlarged, and even sometimes contradicted aristocratic conceptions of how government ought to be organized and operated. When titled spokesmen of the pseudo-representative institutions demanded that their rights be restored, they frequently presumed to speak on behalf of *all* the people whom their institutions supposedly represented. Rebellious grandees were not above appealing to well-to-do commoners when they tried to round up a following against "despotism." In so doing, however, they only further awakened the political interests of people who did not customarily concern themselves with politics. Financiers and merchants and professional men had habitually regarded government as the preserve of a tiny elite; middle-class civil servants in the provincial or local administration had hitherto resigned themselves to the fact that important decisions would be made by the centralized bureaucracy. Aristocratic agitation in the second half of the century invited them to imagine a politics more public, to express themselves in favor of a government open to a broader range of influence and opinion.

It can be dangerous to posit a uniquely middle-class political program and mentality—in part because the social groupings we refer to by the term "middle class" were in fact bewilderingly diverse and in part because well-to-do commoners followed no single political line.* Indeed, exclusively non-noble political movements were rare in the late eighteenth century, and even those commoners who came to oppose both absolutism and its aristocratic alternatives generally found themselves joined—and sometimes led—by like-minded nobles. The majority of the nobility in

---

* Strictly speaking, "middle class" is a term which could apply to all urban commoners from a fabulously wealthy banker to the corner greengrocer. In the present context, it refers to the educated and at least relatively well-off strata of non-nobles who were liable to take an interest in politics.

most countries urged a return to the arrangement whereby the pseudo-representative bodies would share power with the throne and block any intrusion upon the traditional rights, privileges, prerogatives, and autonomies of various social groups, institutions, or regions. Although this was a program which generated noteworthy backing outside the aristocracy, some commoners thought that aristocratic talk about "liberties" too readily translated into a reality which confined participation in politics to the bearers of noble titles. Accordingly, they began to talk of expanding the old bodies so as to include some meaningful representation of non-noble elements. Such suggestions occasionally went even further and posed the ideal of a representation so much more equitable—though still very far from truly egalitarian—that the influence of the privileged orders would dwindle to a level somewhat closer to their actual numbers in the society at large. Again, however, although these daring schemes had little support from the majority of aristocrats, neither did they have anything like the unanimous support of politically interested commoners. Moreover, the aristocracy experienced some fragmentation in the political ferment of the late eighteenth century, and certain of its members began to think in terms of recasting the state on more solid and rational foundations than of merely establishing the rule of a single class. Each of the reformist camps therefore included both aristocrats and delegates from the middle classes, though not in equal numbers.

Origins of the French Revolution

From one perspective, this selective sketch of eighteenth-century politics, emphasizing but one set of characteristic problems, may seem to make the eruption of revolution in France more intelligible. The French crown's flirtation with financial calamity and its struggle with a politically ambitious aristocracy reached crisis proportions in the 1780's. Reluctantly, King Louis XVI conceded that his destitute regime could no longer survive on its existing tax base and also could not summon the legitimacy to demand new taxes without seeking approval from a consultative assembly. After backing and filling for a few years, in 1788 he finally authorized elections to the Estates-General, a pseudo-representative institution which had last convened in 1614. But the Estates-General was a medieval institution, ill adapted to cope with eighteenth-century problems. Of its three Estates, the first represented only the clergy, so that 300 deputies would speak for roughly 130,000 clerics—out of a total population of perhaps 26 million souls. The Second Estate represented solely the nobility; another 300 men would stand for the approximately 210,000 parents and children in France's titled families. The Third Estate represented *everyone* else. However, since political responsibility was bound to flow toward people of means and education and some social standing, the deputies of the Third Estate—of whom there were also 300—were preponderantly drawn from the more comfortable layers of the middle classes. But the Estates-General voted "by order" (which is to say that each Estate cast one vote, determined by a majority ballot within its own ranks) and not "by head."

Historically, therefore, the First and Second Estates had been able to count on domination of the Estates-General by virtue of the combination of their two votes, since—as privileged orders—their interests tended to coincide.* However, the Third Estate, politicized by the aristocratic activities of a generation, rejected this traditional organization of the Estates-General. A number of prominent aristocrats, like the Marquis de Lafayette and the Duc de la Rochefoucauld-Liancourt, also deemed this form of representation outdated and joined the commoners in agitating for its reform.

The crux of the reformist position was that the monarchy, by virtue of its financial straits, had demonstrated that France needed a new instrument of government. The Estates-General, moreover, at least as traditionally organized, was not equal to the task. The accident of birth conveyed a wildly disproportionate share of power upon the nobility; privileged tax exemptions made no sense in a time of government bankruptcy. The reformers sensed that the time was right for constructing a government in which power was more rationally and more equitably distributed, in which access to positions of political influence and responsibility was open to more than those of noble lineage. Consequently, advocates of reform demanded that the Third Estate should number 600 delegates (equal to the First and Second Estates combined) and that votes within the Estates-General be by "head" rather than by "order." They also called for change in the tax structure, the administration of justice, the system of internal economic tariffs which impeded the free circulation of goods from one province to another, and so forth.

The winter of 1788–89 was one of unprecedented political activity in France. Delegates to the Estates-General were to be chosen by a complicated process of indirect election which began at the village level and involved a remarkably large number of commoners. (Suffrage was extended to all persons paying *any* direct taxes, which meant that a good many peasants of distinctly modest circumstances were enfranchised.) But the king had also asked that each electoral assembly submit a list of grievances (the *cahiers de doléances*) for his consideration. In other words, be-

* The Roman Catholic Church of France owned between 6 and 10 percent of all land, yet still enjoyed exemption from direct taxation. The harmony of interests between at least the upper clergy and the Second Estate may be suggested by the fact that, after 1783, all 135 bishops of the French church were also titled noblemen.

sides simply nominating candidates, voters were given an opportunity to verbalize their discontents, to focus upon the abuses which most troubled them, and (at least implicitly) to hold out some hope for reform. The *cahiers* ranged from complaints about aristocratic privilege and the crushing burden of taxes which lay upon the peasantry (who made up perhaps four-fifths of the population) to grumblings about rural bridges in need of repair. They are principally important because the very process of drawing them up helped politicize the great mass of people, literally forcing them to think in political terms, and sparked expectations that their grievances would be remedied.

But when the Estates-General finally convened in May 1789 at Versailles, just outside of Paris, the advocates of change quickly discovered that Louis XVI neither planned any major restructuring of the Estates-General nor envisaged any substantive role for it. Rather, the king apparently expected the Estates merely to rubber-stamp a disappointingly modest program of royal reforms and to vote approval of new taxes. A timely offer of meaningful reform would probably have won Louis solid support in the Third Estate. Instead, his intransigence forced the reformers into demands which were truly radical by eighteenth-century standards. With considerable justification, the Third Estate claimed that it alone of the three orders truly represented the nation and therefore renamed itself the National Assembly. Along with sympathizers among the other two orders, the National Assembly refused to disband until it had produced a written constitution for France, one which would redefine the nature of government and redistribute political power. Formerly fractious aristocrats now realized that their assault upon absolute monarchy had gotten badly out of hand, that their talk of restoring narrowly representative institutions had excited visions of broadly representative ones in which the influence of nobility would be submerged. The blue-blooded rebels suddenly became arch-royalists and urged the king to concede nothing to the National Assembly.

Violence ultimately shattered this political deadlock. In mid-July, Louis dismissed a government minister popular with the National Assembly, Jacques Necker; rumors bristled through heavily pro-reform Paris that this was the overture to a royal coup d'état. Bad crop harvests had sent food prices soaring, and the Paris poor—goaded by hunger and holding authority responsible—began to riot. On the 14th, they turned their fury against the Bastille, a fortified prison thought to house arms; with some aid from defecting army units, they conquered it and slaughtered some of its defenders. When order resumed on the next day, the Paris delegation to the National Assembly asserted control over the capital through a hastily concocted municipal government. But violence was not confined to Paris. There had been scattered peasant rioting throughout 1789. When wild stories of a violent revenge being planned by noble landlords began to spread, huge numbers of peasants in several major regions responded defensively with attacks upon the lords' castles, destruction of tax records, and a generally successful defiance of authority. By early August, no one could doubt that the old order was dead, that absolute monarchy no longer ruled in France, and that it would not be replaced by aristocratic government. What precisely would replace it was a matter of far less certainty.

Major revolutions are uncommon occurrences; detached from their context, they may appear so strange that there is an inclination to attribute them to accident, to odd quirks of historical development. When the French Revolution is seen as arising from certain typical issues of eighteenth-century politics, issues which troubled most European states, then it may become somewhat more comprehensible. Yet if this approach is useful, it hardly confers omniscience. Indeed, the fact that Frenchmen engaged in political contentions which were anything but unique in their time only makes it *more* difficult to deal with the question: why was there revolution in France and not elsewhere? There is no dearth of answers, several of which are plausible and none of which has commanded anything remotely approaching consensus. It has been suggested that the burden of oppression and want was so great in France that it could simply no longer be borne. Conversely, it has been argued that conditions in France were not only better than elsewhere, but also improving distinctly —yet not fast enough to satisfy the expectations of improvement which the first stirrings of reform (like the calling of the Estates-General) had generated. In these terms, France may have undergone the first major "revolution of rising expectations." Others have insisted that the French monarchy was more financially strapped—and thus politically weaker— than its counterparts, so that it was more easily toppled. Still others maintain that the explanation is to be found not in the vanquished but in the victors—that is, that France alone had a middle class sufficiently large and sufficiently conscious of its interests and potential to move beyond the aristocratic alternative to absolutism.

Most recently, certain historians have tried to change the terms of this inconclusive debate by pointing out that political change was no more confined to France after 1789 than political conflict had been confined to France before that date. They point to the considerable ground gained by opponents of absolutism in several places and urge us to agree that the French Revolution was actually but the most dramatic instance of a broad—though admittedly not comprehensive—European revolution. This interpretation, though provocative, still overlooks the fact that absolute monarchy suffered numerous setbacks, but few routs. Moreover, its adversary was most commonly aristocracy, which preferred the sort of pseudo-representative institutions and caste politics which French reformers were trying to render obsolete. The French Revolution emerged from general circumstances which most other politically literate Europeans would have found familiar. But the rest of Europe did not follow France into revolution; even more striking than the continued retreats of absolutism is the fact that French politics appeared to give the rest of Europe some pause. Pro-French reformers doubtless dreamed of following in the footsteps of the National Assembly, and sometimes they made a small start. But monarchs and rebellious aristocrats alike, while hardly reconciling their differences, could reflect that the French version of their rivalry had led to the superseding of them both.

Events in France at the end of the eighteenth and the beginning of the nineteenth century surely inspired revolutionaries elsewhere in Europe, but they did not inspire successful revolution. Rather, they provided a set of models or examples. Other revolutionaries would try to emulate the French models, or perhaps adapt them to fit local conditions. Reactionaries would reject them, especially when the French tried to export their politics by force of arms. Conservatives, who favored stability but not stagnation, sought to appropriate certain features of the French political models without profoundly dislocating the status quo. Curiously, the proponents of a strong monarchy and those of aristocratic government fell into both of the latter categories. In short, the French Revolution did not exactly revolutionize Europe, but rather marked out for other countries forms of change they might accept, modify, or repudiate.

Europe and French Politics

The French Revolution was far too complex an upheaval to be narrated here. For the purposes of studying *European* history, it may be most useful to consider the political models which the revolution built and presented to Europe. By far the most important was the system of constitutional and parliamentary government which the National Assembly hammered out and substituted for absolute monarchy. The constitution which went into operation in 1791—the first written constitution in a major European state—did more than define and guarantee such fundamental political rights as freedom of expression and assembly. It also redefined sovereignty, which it removed from the crown and placed in "the nation," while a major share of political responsibility passed to the nation's elected representatives. A "civic oath," or pledge of allegiance, contained in the constitution suggests the new institutional priorities: "I swear," it read, "to be faithful to the nation, to the law, and to the King, and to maintain with all my power the Constitution. . . ." The king himself was obliged to swear loyalty to the nation, the law, and the constitution. Legislative authority appertained solely to a Legislative Assembly, and though its decisions were submitted for royal approval, the king could not flatly quash them, but only exercise a suspensive veto which might delay enactment. Neither could he dissolve the Assembly.

Yet if the revolutionaries of 1789–91 determined to destroy absolutism, they were still not republicans; and they reserved for monarchy real, though sharply reduced, powers. The king alone selected government ministers; he directed the bureaucracy, the armed forces, and was primarily responsible for the conduct of foreign relations. On the other hand, "royal justice" disappeared in the sense that, as the constitution put it, "Under no circumstances may the judiciary power be employed by the legislative body or the King."

Besides disdaining republicanism, the early revolutionaries disdained democracy. The constitution guaranteed political *rights* to all Frenchmen, but political *responsibilities* it reserved to those who did not fall into the illiterate majority of the population. The vote went to those who paid a certain amount annually in direct taxes, on the assumption that such assessments were indicative of a level of income likely to be accompanied by education and a certain social standing. The constitution struck down privileges which discriminated against citizens before the law: "Neither privilege nor exception to the law common to all Frenchmen exists for any part of the nation or for any individual," declared the Preamble, which also disallowed nobility, "hereditary distinctions," and "distinctions of birth." Beyond this, however, no attempts were made to level the social hierarchy.*

The constitution of 1791 provided a clear alternative to both absolute monarchy and aristocratic government, whose respective advocates generally treated it like some savage beast—to be destroyed if possible, to be domesticated if not. The constitution, and variant versions of it, was a central issue in European politics for another generation or two. Yet it had become unworkable in France within a year of its enactment. Part of the problem was that Louis XVI and much of his nobility failed to regard the constitution as the quintessence of political wisdom. Their resistance sometimes took extreme forms—as when numerous aristocrats took up residence outside France in hopes of creating a counterrevolutionary force which would overthrow the new regime, or when the king tried unsuccessfully to flee the country in June 1791 and join them. Royal and

* In 1790, the Assembly nationalized church land and put it up for sale. It is by no means certain, however, that this redistribution of property drastically altered French social structure. Indeed, it would appear that in most cases church land was purchased by persons of some means—from the middle classes or at least the well-to-do strata of the peasantry. The measure did little by way of closing the gap between the very rich and the very poor.

aristocratic resistance to the revolution prompted some pause among certain revolutionaries, who began to argue that change had gone too far. Among others, it stirred doubts about the necessity for monarchy itself.

But the very existence of the throne was only truly endangered when war broke out in the spring of 1792 between France and two conservative monarchies, the Austrian Habsburg Empire and Prussia. The war had its origins in French expansionist impulses, in the desire of certain French politicians to generate patriotic enthusiasm and then ride what wave of feeling into office, and perhaps in a dash of missionary zeal as well—for the most ardent advocates of the revolution yearned to extend its benefits to their oppressed brethren elsewhere on the continent. The Habsburg Emperor Leopold, brother of the French queen, Marie Antoinette, helped mobilize European resistance to the revolution; ultimately, the coalition he initiated embraced all the major powers (including Great Britain). Clearly, the defeat of France would mean not merely a halt to the spread of revolutionary infection; it would mean destruction of the revolution itself, as the émigré French nobles who joined the foreign armies made unmistakable.

The war went badly for France at first, and by the summer of 1792 coalition forces were advancing steadily upon Paris. Moreover, the war placed Louis XVI in an impossible position. A French defeat would reverse the revolution and free him of the shackles imposed by the constitution, so that he could hardly give the French war effort unqualified support. By the same token, many of his subjects sensed the paradox of fighting under a supreme commander whose sympathies lay with the enemy, who stood to gain from the coalition's victory, and who (it was widely rumored) had been engaging in a host of secret treasons designed to weaken the French cause. The closer to Paris the invaders marched, the more unbearable these contradictions became; at last, in August 1792, armed crowds successfully executed a planned invasion of the royal palace and dethroned the king. The Legislative Assembly dissolved, and elections to a new body—the National Convention—followed. The Convention met in September, when it officially proclaimed France a republic and, within a few months, had Louis executed on charges of treason.

The French republic was born of circumstances rather than of philosophical preference. A year prior to its abrupt appearance, few persons thought the republic a desirable or practicable form of government. It owed its creation to the fact that the alternative, monarchy, had allowed itself to become thoroughly identified with the counterrevolution. Yet there were also growing sentiments—in Paris, at least—that a monarchy would no longer square with the more democratic sort of government which was increasingly finding advocates. The urban poor, and those middle-class politicians who sought a following among them, found the constitution of 1791 too conservative—especially when it reserved the franchise to the more well-to-do strata. Besides, although the constitution was firm in its protection of the rights of property owners, it said little of the needs of manual laborers. Arbitrary distinctions based upon wealth went down no better with the poor than had arbitrary distinctions based upon birth with the comfortable middle classes. The Paris poor, stimulated to far greater political involvement and awareness, argued that the revolution would not have occurred in the first place without their contribution, as on July 14, 1789. They demanded a more literal application of the constitution's doctrine of sovereignty of the people and a government which would not simply defend the revolution from foreign reversal, but would extend its libertarian and egalitarian benefits to the lower reaches of society.

In the abstract, there is nothing which compels republicanism to be democratic. In the concrete circumstances of the 1790's, however, the model of republicanism which Frenchmen created became inextricably associated in the European mind with democracy—and with a great deal else besides. The National Convention had been elected by universal manhood suffrage (though in fact the distractions of war and revolution led to extremely high abstentionism). It soon prepared a new constitution, which announced that "All men are equal by nature and before the law" and which vested power largely in a democratically elected legislature. Adopted in June 1793, this constitution remained a virtual dead letter for the two years of its existence; under the pressure of foreign and civil war, the Convention and the executive committees it elected ruled France by decree.

Support for the war and for the drastic political changes it had entailed was hardly unanimous. Fighting against massive odds, the republican government had to resort to extreme measures to supply its armies, feed the civilian population, and keep its swelling ranks of critics at bay. The execution of the king horrified much of the peasant population, which continued to regard monarchy as near sacred, if not exactly infallible. Confiscations of food and price controls alienated some rural areas, and the wartime dislocations of the economy intensified suffering everywhere. Provincial observers came increasingly to feel that the Paris mob was ruling France, and in mid-1793 civil war erupted in parts of the west and south.

Civil war, when added to foreign invasion (though the French armies had for the moment staved off the threat to Paris), prompted a strenuous response from the government. The Convention granted its chief executive organ, the Committee of Public Safety, broad exceptional powers to repress insurrection and eliminate persons thought to be threatening the republic and the revolution. It is important to recall that this so-called reign of terror was not designed merely to satiate the blood lust of mad-men, though it sometimes degenerated into that. Rather, it grew from pa-triotic determination to protect a France which the Committee and the Convention saw as endangered by foreign agents, reactionary monarch-ists, and political opportunists. It is indisputable that some of the esti-mated 14,000 persons executed during the terror of 1793–94 fell into at least one of those categories; most of the victims were open insurgents against the republic, and it is hard to imagine that they would have had a gentler fate under any other government. But there was also a broad streak of paranoia in the terror, not to mention a dose of cynicism, so that innocent persons were killed because someone thought them royal-ists or perhaps because someone in power held a grudge against them. Some of the most sensational executions came in March and April 1794, when Maximilien Robespierre, who had dominated the Committee of Public Safety since the previous autumn, dispatched some thirty of his political opponents—including two former members of the Committee. For a half-century thereafter, it was difficult to pronounce the word "re-public" in Europe without evoking Robespierre and the guillotine as well as "democracy."

Most of those who supported the terror had thought it a strictly tem-porary expedient, a means of self-defense against domestic treachery. Once civil war had been ended and the foreign armies repulsed from French soil, the terror therefore seemed less justifiable, and many of its original advocates feared Robespierre would continue to employ it to build a largely personal regime. In July 1794, the Convention overthrew Robespierre, and along with 70 supporters he perished under the guillo-tine in the bloodiest single day of the terror.

However, enemies of the revolution—which included a large number of former friends appalled by the lengths to which it had gone—claimed to detect some intimate relationship between republican democracy (or even revolution) and terror. They argued that to tamper with the re-straints imposed by traditional authority was to summon the basest human instincts to the surface. Government existed to check those in-stincts, to protect men from one another; and history had delivered gov-ernment into the hands of a few because most people—"ordinary" people —were bound to abuse its powers and privileges, to exercise it for per-sonal ends rather than for the general welfare. Rule by the majority could also lead to the tyrannical oppression of minority groups, especially where the majority was ignorant, politically inexperienced, and suscepti-ble to the urgings of republican demagogues. Reformers who endorsed something like the constitution of 1791 were convinced that to go further, into republicanism and democracy, was to issue an invitation to terror. Even more implacable opponents of the revolution insisted that any serious tampering with the status quo was bound to lead directly and inevitably to something like a reign of terror rather than settle down into the moderate constitutionalism of 1791. Ignoring the impact of the war upon revolutionary politics, they quoted freely from the English parliamentarian and political writer Edmund Burke. For Burke, political change had to proceed by slow, "natural" processes which did not threaten to fracture the delicate and intricate structure of government in the course of refining it. "A spirit of innovation," wrote Burke in his *Reflections on the Revolution in France* (1790), "is generally the result of a selfish temper and confined views. People will not look forward to posterity who never look backward to their ancestors." The fact that Burke combined this conservatism with an accurate prediction that the revolution would go on to greater violence and disorder gave his work a profound influence.

The model of republican democracy held up by France was therefore too widely associated with the terror to inspire much enthusiasm elsewhere in Europe, and future generations of republicans found it difficult to overcome their inherited reputations as political murderers.* One might even consider the model of parliamentary and constitutional monarchy compromised to the extent that one thought it cleared the path for republicanism and terror. Reformers of the early nineteenth century were constantly dogged by charges that they would end up plunging the nation into revolutionary chaos.

The Napoleonic Era

After the fall of Robespierre and the abolition of the Committee of Public Safety, something like a power vacuum existed at the center of the French republic. Once a new constitution of 1795 had established a two-house legislature and reattached suffrage to a property qualification, a variety of political factions sought control of the new five-man executive council, known as the Directory. Beyond cracking down on democrats and alleged ex-terrorists, the Directory never expressed a coherent domestic policy, nor even effectively exercised its authority over most of the nation. It did continue the war, now conducted largely on foreign soil, though with no clear-cut set of aims and goals. The Directory was neither so corrupt nor so inept as it was painted by Napoleon Bonaparte, the thirty-year old army general who overthrew it by a coup d'état at the end

* The terror had also had a conspicuous anti-Christian streak which horrified the faithful in other countries. The abolition of church privileges and the nationalization of church lands in 1790 had driven into opposition even those clerics who had supported the early policies of the National Assembly. Assaults upon Church property and upon priests who failed to swear allegiance to the new regime were increasingly common under the Convention.

of 1799. But because it stood for so little, it could be blamed for much, and few persons lamented its passing.

Bonaparte swiftly converted the republic he had conquered into a personal dictatorship and, in 1804, an empire with himself upon the hereditary throne. It was an impressive achievement for the little Corsican whose cosmic ambitions had propelled him rapidly up through the ranks of the French army and whose luck had enabled him to survive the numerous political turnabouts and purges of the revolution. Bonaparte's political support after 1799 lay in the hope he offered of strong leadership guaranteeing order after a decade of internal convulsion and in the clever promise that he would "save" the revolution—that is, consolidate its most popular accomplishments and protect them from the dangers of foreign assault and domestic disorder. In point of fact, the Napoleonic episode represented nothing like the revolution's essence, in part because the revolution meant too many different things to too many different people for anyone to have distilled a recognizable "essence" from it. But even if one could get agreement that the French Revolution had something to do with establishing a more libertarian political atmosphere than that of the Old Regime, it is obvious that Napoleon had no intention of saving even a moderate version of constitutional and parliamentary government.

Although Napoleon allowed parliamentary institutions to exist, he allowed them no meaningful constitutional function. Thus, if all adult males had the vote, there was nothing of significance they could vote upon. In any event the constitution deprived universal suffrage of vital force by an elaborate process of indirect election and by reserving to Napoleon personally the right to appoint part of the legislature. The constitution and the legislature were thus mere fig leaves over an autocracy which Napoleon exercised through a centralized bureaucracy. All potentially competitive institutions were reduced to complete subordination; public criticism was thoroughly strangled by official censorship; the legal system, the church, the schools were all made into extensions of the imperial will. Napoleon did sanctify the partial redistribution of property which had occurred in the 1790's and, although he recreated a titled nobility, he also opened the bureaucracy to talent rather than simply to high birth. In general, however, his regime amounted to a return to the absolutism which the revolutionaries had overthrown—though an absolutism distinguished by a degree of efficiency and central control of which few eighteenth-century princes could boast.

Napoleon largely established his rule upon a broad desire for order, and maintained it through repression and coercion. But much of his astonishing popularity grew from his military exploits. He had achieved prominence prior to 1799 as the youthful director of some spectacular campaigns, and thereafter he depended heavily upon the patriotic and militaristic passions which his battlefield victories stimulated. Napoleon's continuation of the war which had been raging with few pauses since 1792 was, of course, far more costly of human life than the terror had been, yet somehow more respectable (to many historians as well as to contemporaries). People electrified with outrage at terrorism thrilled to the thunder of Napoleonic cannons, even though the state of scientific knowledge in the early 1800's strongly suggested that bullets might be entirely as fatal as the guillotine. But the Emperor's determination to stop at nothing less than French hegemony over all of Europe, frequently replacing existing sovereigns with members of his own family (which sprang from a modest strain of Corsican nobility), stirred deep springs of French national pride and ambition. Glory gained in combat has lost some of its glitter in the twentieth century, but no one will ever comprehend an important part of Napoleon's appeal if he fails to appreciate its powers of attraction in the nineteenth century.

Even under the republic, French conquest of foreign countries had often meant the imposition upon that country of some version of French institutions (whatever they might be at that moment). Napoleon continued this practice, at least with the lesser states that he overwhelmed. Conquest was frequently followed by the substitution of efficient (if authoritarian) administrations, for ramshackle governments riddled with outmoded survivals and weakened by recent aristocratic counteroffensives. Napoleonic rule was thus a mixed blessing for Europe. Although it represented military humiliation and foreign occupation, it also brought streamlined government and the elimination of numerous annoyances which local reformers considered intolerable. Patriotic impulses thereafter dictated that one reject Napoleonic influences; the impulses of domestic reformism urged that one accept any benefits that defeat brought with it. From one perspective, a nation vanquished by Napoleon might be able to overlap France's decade of upheaval, acquiring a more modern and efficient—though also autocratic—government without paying the price in civil discord.

The Napoleonic preference for rational and efficient order did not stop with bureaucracy; it extended to boundaries as well. The map of Europe in 1789 was the product not of a controlling intelligence, but of helter-skelter historical development. The Italian peninsula, for instance, was politically divided into a fistful of sovereign states ranging in size from the Kingdom of Naples (which included nearly half the peninsula and the island of Sicily) to petty dukedoms and independent city states. Central Europe in the eighteenth century (a nightmare for historical cartographers) contained hundreds of principalities between larger Prussia to the north and the Habsburg Empire to the south. The larger dynastic states were not always compact units: the Habsburgs ruled Austrians,

Magyars, and Slavs in central Europe, but also parts of Italy and what is now Belgium; Protestant Prussia also held territories in the Catholic Rhineland. Napoleonic conquest drastically simplified all this, annexing large chunks of neighboring territory to France and, more important, consolidating micro-states into far larger units. The Emperor never meant creations like the Kingdom of Italy, the Kingdom of Westphalia, or the Confederation of the Rhine to be more than his satellites; and of course French invasion and occupation stirred local patriotism profoundly. But the brief experience of unity also provided another political model, the national one, which posed the ideal of political unification and independence for culturally common people.

Napoleon, for all his military genius, ultimately proved himself an incorrigible overreacher. Even prior to his invasion of Russia in 1812, there were signs that his grip on the rest of the continent was weakening. By the time his shattered army was in full retreat westward, having failed to subdue the Russian behemoth, guerrilla resistance to his brother Joseph's rule in Spain threatened his rear and provided the opening for British invasion. Within two years, Napoleon had been sent packing and the Bourbon dynasty restored in the person of Louis XVI's brother (who took the title of Louis XVIII). In 1815, Napoleon briefly returned, rallied enough popular backing to frighten Louis into exile, and took one last fling at the coalition armies. Defeated at Waterloo, he was now consigned to definitive exile on a bleak south Atlantic island.

The Restoration

The conclusion of this quarter-century of conflict stirred up by French politics inaugurated a period known as the Restoration. The name can be misleading, however, if it is taken to imply either a faithful reconstruction of prerevolutionary Europe—in the way that one can restore a decrepit antique automobile to its original working condition—or a clean break between the revolutionary-Napoleonic episode and the succeeding generation. Pure and simple reaction was impossible, although that did not dissuade a few rulers from attempting it. The victorious statesmen who formalized the peace in diplomatic conference at Vienna determined to undo much that the French had wrought. But the European map they redrew by treaty clearly demonstrated that 1788 was not to be resurrected in 1815.

The diplomats nominally restored the old order, but they also recognized that it would face new challenges. Napoleonic consolidations in Italy had prompted renewed yearning there for genuine unification and independence. The appeal launched by petty German princes in 1812–13, to "free the fatherland" of foreign invaders, quickened hopes

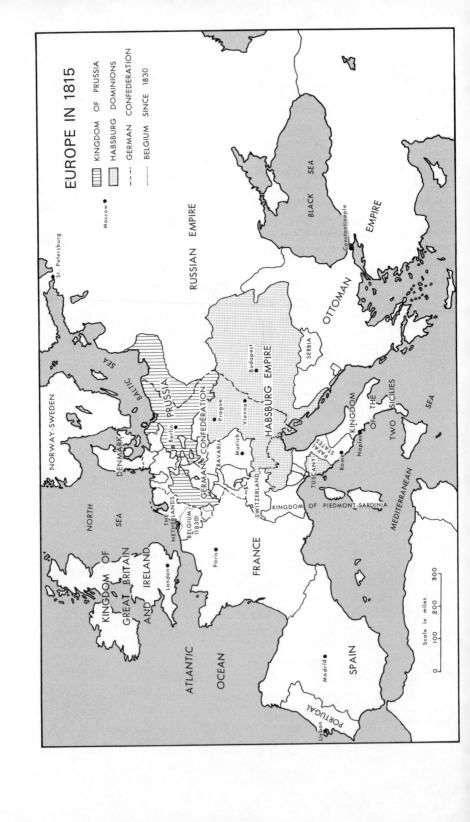

EUROPE IN 1815

KINGDOM OF PRUSSIA
HABSBURG DOMINIONS
GERMAN CONFEDERATION
BELGIUM SINCE 1830

ATLANTIC OCEAN

KINGDOM OF GREAT BRITAIN AND IRELAND

London

NORTH SEA

NORWAY-SWEDEN

St. Petersburg

Moscow

BALTIC SEA

DENMARK

THE NETHERLANDS

BELGIUM (1830)

PRUSSIA

Berlin

GERMAN CONFEDERATION

Prague

BAVARIA

Munich

Vienna

Budapest

HABSBURG EMPIRE

RUSSIAN EMPIRE

Paris

FRANCE

SWITZERLAND

KINGDOM OF PIEDMONT-SARDINIA

TUSCANY

PAPAL STATES

Rome

KINGDOM OF THE TWO SICILIES

Naples

SERBIA

OTTOMAN EMPIRE

BLACK SEA

Constantinople

MEDITERRANEAN SEA

SPAIN

Madrid

PORTUGAL

Lisbon

Scale in miles
0   100   200   300

that a genuine German fatherland might be born. The creation of large, unified nation-states in these areas threatened not only the swarm of lesser sovereigns who ruled there but the traditional interests of the great powers—and especially the Austrian Empire, long accustomed to a dominant influence in both central Europe and the Italian peninsula. Thus, the Habsburgs ceded their Belgian territories to the Dutch and acquired in turn more defensible holdings in adjacent northern Italy. The Congress of Vienna also rejected literal restoration when it decided to let most of the lesser German princes survive as nothing more than quaint historical memories. A new German Confederation appeared, containing but thirty-seven small and middling independent states grouped together loosely under the dominance of its other two members, Prussia and Austria. The Confederation was not designed as a step toward unity; it was a device for frustrating the national model. Its very creation, however, acknowledged the impact of that model and admitted that French politics had rendered the Europe of 1788 obsolete.

The members of the coalition defeating Napoleon even went so far as to experiment with a new version of foreign policy. Between 1818 and 1822, the foreign ministers of the Quadruple Alliance (that is, Britain, Prussia, Russia, and Austria) met in a total of four diplomatic congresses to ensure execution of the peace settlement and to discuss matters of common interest. When the settlement appeared threatened, the continental members of the alliance were not above armed intervention into the affairs of independent states. Revolutions in Spain, Naples, and the Kingdom of Piedmont-Sardinia were all snuffed out by foreign troops which intervened on allied authorization. It was a frank admission that the French Revolution had helped knit European politics closer together; murmurs of reform in Madrid now set off quivers of panic in Vienna. Allied cooperation soon foundered on mutual suspicions and rivalries, however, and the British decided to revert to their traditional aloofness from European entanglement. But the brief heyday of the so-called congress system still implied a new community of conservative interests.

Restoration monarchies paid lip service to the sanctity of prerevolutionary structures, but in fact they were eager to assimilate selected features of at least the Napoleonic regime. In exile, Napoleon boasted: "I have saved the revolution, which was on the point of death; I have washed off its crimes, I have held it up to the eyes of Europe resplendent with glory." The monarchs who defeated him knew better. They appreciated that his rule had reactivated the centralizing tendencies of absolutism which had faltered in the period of aristocratic and liberal attack. Although there was a certain revulsion from things French early in the Restoration, Napoleonic institutions which rationalized and modernized central government frequently persisted where they had been installed and were copied where they had not. Even Louis XVIII of France, who missed few opportunities to refer to Napoleon as "the usurper," saw no reason to dismantle the administrative structure or law codes which he inherited in 1814 or to alter the imperial arrangements which had so firmly placed the church and the educational system under the central authority.

When it came to the liberal model of politics, however, the instinctive reflex of most Restoration governments was resistance and repression. There were exceptions: France and a few small states in the German Confederation experimented with limited versions of parliamentary and constitutional government. In all these cases, the constitutions guaranteed certain minimal civil liberties, although the executive was still free to crack down on overly broad interpretations of them; the parliaments, all elected on a highly restricted suffrage, exercised some degree of control over the royal budget. It was indicative of the conservative nature of these experiments that the constitutions were royally authored and granted to the nation out of princely generosity—"handed down," in the phrase of the time, which implied that the monarch might just as quickly snatch them back. No monarch actively sought limitations on his own prerogatives, and the ones who accepted them did so because they felt that liberal sentiment in their realm was too powerful to ignore. Those who thought they could crush constitutionalism usually tried. Spanish liberals had patched together a constitution after Joseph Bonaparte's departure; but when King Ferdinand VII returned to Spain from his wartime captivity in France, he successfully reimposed absolute rule. Louis XVIII reasoned, however reluctantly, that to follow a similar line in France was to invite a reenactment of the events which had destroyed his brother. The coalition powers agreed, just as reluctantly—and determined to quarantine parliamentary and constitutional government to those few preserves in which the alternatives to it seemed even worse.

This expedient, if grudging and watchful, toleration did not extend to more radical recrudescences of French politics. Democratic republicanism had developed such a sinister reputation that it scarcely dared show its face during the Restoration. Yet its presence was felt all the same. Though the few actual republicans (mostly French and Italian) rarely surfaced from the underground secret societies in which they tended to group, the very fact that they could not be seen and counted led to an exaggeration of their numbers and influence. When authorities on occasion ferreted out a republican cell, most people assumed that only a tiny fragment of a huge conspiracy had been unearthed. Liberal reformers suffered the consequences of this mentality nearly as much as revolutionaries, since—by Burkean logic—to meddle with the structure of authority at all was to give the lurking swarms of terrorists an opening just wide enough for them to wheel through the guillotine.

The Restoration is customarily depicted as a reactionary epoch in European history, a period in which rulers tried to ignore the preceding twenty-five years and pick up where they had left off when the French Revolution erupted. But the image of the political pendulum swinging to the extreme right is accurate only if we can establish that it had already swung to the extreme left. Only in France itself had home-grown revolutionaries destroyed the Old Regime; and the Restoration government there demonstrated that total reaction was impossible—however much a few persons who "had learned nothing and forgotten nothing" from the revolutionary-Napoleonic experience may have desired it. Elsewhere, nobody was exactly trying to put Humpty-Dumpty back together again because he had not been smashed to smithereens in the first place. French politics posed a threat to traditional European political institutions, a few of which buckled under the strain; but the revolution did not dismantle the whole structure. The Restoration makes more sense as adaptation than as reaction. Traditional institutions met the challenge of French politics not only by repression and a reassertion that the old ways were best, but also by incorporating certain elements of French political models designed to make the established order stronger, more efficient, and even (now and then) a bit more palatable to reformers.

This interpretation may puzzle those accustomed to thinking of the French Revolution as a savage riptide upending anyone who tried to stand his ground in its path. The revolution was part of a broad movement of protest against absolutism, but only in France did that movement become revolutionary—a fact that retarded rather than stimulated reform elsewhere. To be sure, it inspired liberal reformers all across the continent; but they were of little political consequence prior to 1830. In the middle of the nineteenth century, the French political writer Alexis de Tocqueville noted that although the French Revolution had been directed in part against the absolutism of the Old Regime, it ended up by hastening the progress of administrative centralization. In fact, the paradox holds true for Europe in general, for at least in the short run, the events of 1789–1815 enhanced royal power. Though there were certain institutional changes, they did not betoken any substantial redistribution of political power (except where aristocrats resurgent in the 1780's suffered a post-Napoleonic setback). Rather, the role of the French Revolution in early nineteenth-century politics was to suggest some models for achieving such redistributions.

This introductory essay has ignored two important issues which merit some attention. First, its sketch of Old Regime politics has focused exclusively upon the continent, deliberately neglecting the somewhat special case of Great Britain. Since the late seventeenth century, British politics had been edging gradually (if unevenly) toward parliamentary dominance. By 1789, the king was still very far from being a figurehead, yet absolutism was unmistakably dead. No single written constitution existed, yet a series of constitutional acts—bolstered by powerful traditions rooted in the system of common law—served to restrain royal prerogatives. There was nothing remotely democratic about Parliament: all hereditary nobles sat by right in the House of Lords, which exercised a veto on measures proposed by the House of Commons (elected on a narrow suffrage and dominated by wealthy landed interests). To a degree, then, British institutions anticipated the liberal model of French politics and even, it should be noted, owed an important part of their development to revolution—both violent (in the 1640's and 1650's) and nonviolent (in 1688). Such defenders of the British system as Burke, however, liked to portray it as the product of long and cautious evolution over centuries. Besides, Great Britain had been the mainstay of the anti-French coalition. Few continental supporters of the Restoration status quo therefore regarded British parliamentarism as an immediate danger, however much they may have disliked it in principle.

In the second place, this chapter has largely neglected the social dimension of politics and has perhaps misleadingly suggested that political change is an exclusively institutional matter. As a matter of fact, European social structure altered about as much between 1789 and 1815 as did the structure of political institutions. In France, legal privilege disappeared; and the church and (to a lesser degree) the nobility had much of their property confiscated. Again, however, such wealth as shifted hands *tended* to pass from the elite to adjacent strata, and not to the great mass of peasant poor. Outside of France, social change was even more restrained; the most notable development came with the abolition of legal serfdom in Prussia, although this reform of 1808 was carried out on terms which strengthened noble landlords and even further depressed the conditions of their peasants. The social consequences of French politics were confined largely to France.

The society of the Old Regime survived the era of the French Revolution with even less damage than had been done to political institutions. But just as the models of French politics posed a continuing threat to those institutions, British machines were generating forces which would gradually undermine traditional society.

2 / *British Machines*

The French Revolution was an abrupt, dramatic upheaval, concentrated into a few years and full of conspicuous shifts in power and institutional changes. The industrial revolution consisted of no such neatly focused and easily visible events. It began toward the end of the eighteenth century in Great Britain, with innovations in the mode of industrial production, innovations which were not widely emulated on the continent until the 1850's. But it did not stop there. The industrial revolution ultimately accomplished a radical renovation in economic and social structures everywhere and served as an engine of political transformation as well. It was not so much an event as a process, and evidence of its workings appears throughout this book. The present chapter deals with its British origins and with its early, halting progress in continental Europe.

The First Industrial Revolution

In the twentieth century, industrial revolution takes place by imitation. Economically "underdeveloped" nations in Asia, Africa, and Latin America attempt to "modernize" by simply copying the industrial structures of more "advanced" nations. Under the direction of central planning agencies, they seek to leap directly into economic viability by patterning themselves after those nations which have already achieved it. In the eighteenth century, no such models existed. Change came by trial and error, by response to local and immediate needs, and not in pursuit of articulated national goals. In retrospect, it is plain that the process of industrial revolution in Britain was under way—though very far indeed from completion—by 1800. But the British people at that time were not *consciously* trying to create the first "modern industrial state," since that was a goal no one could begin to understand for another half-century. The British built the first model of industrialized society without knowing that they were doing so, for the obvious reason that the concept would make no sense until the thing itself existed.

Contemporary industrial revolution is a misleading guide to the British experience in yet another respect. Although the existence of clear and successful models facilitates rational planning, making industrialization less haphazard, the so-called third-world nations presently aspiring to modernize usually have to build on an economic base which is largely agrarian and which has been undermined by recent imperial exploitation. The chasm between them and industrially modernized states is vast and murderously expensive to bridge; delays in narrowing the distance between economic "backwardness" and the visible affluence of the model nations generate deep frustrations. Since the British did not, as it were, know where they were going, they were spared the pain of thwarted ambitions (though they suffered a great deal else along the way). More important, Britain in the late eighteenth century was already the most prosperous nation in the world. Then appropriate metaphor for its industrial revolution is not, therefore, a mighty vault from poverty to plenty, but rather, in the term of one economist, a "takeoff"—a sharp acceleration accomplished only after a running start.

Britain's preeminent economic position in the eighteenth century helps to explain why the industrial revolution began there rather than elsewhere. The thriving British economy, which depended largely upon overseas trade, generated both the demand which made innovations in production necessary and the resources which made them possible. It is worth emphasizing that the industrial revolution marked the transformation of industry, but not its birth. Small-shop manufacturing with simple manually powered machinery had for centuries been producing goods for export, especially textiles. The woolen trade loomed largest in this industry, though in the mid-eighteenth century, cotton cloth came into its own. The British began to import raw cotton from India (a recent colonial acquisition), convert it into cloth, and then sell it abroad. The demand for cotton—cheaper than wool, better suited to warmer seasons and climates, and washable besides—quickened perceptibly in both the domestic and colonial markets. The traditional spinning wheel was not producing cotton fiber fast enough for it to be woven and finished; to keep up with demand, technological improvement in spinning was necessary. A series of mechanical inventions introduced (though by small stages) machinery which spun cotton faster. Toward the end of the century, steam power replaced human power as the motive force, and the long and agonizing transition into modern industrial production had begun, if only barely.

But the critical point is that innovation, and all that followed from it, sprang from the stimulation of a mature and prosperous economy. Without the existence of a large textile industry, however structurally different from its successor, and without the large and growing colonial markets for its goods, change would not have come when and where it did. Moreover, change was possible because there was at hand the engineering experience to effect it and the money to finance it. Technological advances, and even occasional breakthroughs, were not the product of some mysterious mechnical ingenuity lodged in the collective British psyche. It was rather that Britain had long been in the textile business, and had a considerable number of persons who lived by making, repairing, and generally tinkering about with manufacturing equipment. Commerce had also prompted the elaboration of a reasonably effective banking system accustomed to paper transactions and capable of providing the credit for promising business ventures. Prosperity created ready capital in abundance—more than actually proved necessary for the very earliest stages of industrial advance, which were accomplished at a relatively low cost. Finally, a long tradition of colonial trade meant that the British possessed both a large merchant fleet for getting products to overseas markets quickly and a navy powerful enough to protect the merchant vessels.

In the twentieth century, industrial revolution is the response to economic backwardness; in the eighteenth, it was the result of economic growth. In the latter, the expansion of the traditional economy, and especially of overseas trade after mid-century, provided what the historian E. J. Hobsbawm has called "the runway for the industrial 'takeoff'."

The industrial revolution was at bottom an attempt to employ new technology and business organization in the pursuit of greater profits. The maximization of profit and business activity in general were more or less acceptable forms of social conduct in Britain, carrying less of the stigma of vulgarity than they did in continental countries. In France, for example, the nobility considered trade mere money-grubbing, beneath the dignity of noble blood. Such attitudes did not keep numerous aristocrats from investing in commercial ventures, but they persisted strongly enough to prevent high status from attaching to mercantile enterprises. In Britain, as on the continent, the political and social elite were large landowners—an hereditary nobility and a lesser strata of untitled gentry —and the preferred form of wealth was therefore land. But in Britain, nobility and property passed only to the eldest son; the rest of the nobleman's family had to make its own way in the world (though usually with the benefit of excellent family connections). Younger sons of noblemen often headed toward army commissions, government service, the church, and the legal profession. But commerce also absorbed a share, which both demonstrated that trade and gentle birth were compatible and conferred a certain degree of social legitimacy upon commercial life.

The social flow also operated in the other direction. Eighteenth-century Britain was a highly stratified society, but the lines of stratification signified different levels of status, not closed and rigid castes. Advancement through the hierarchy was the exception rather than the rule, and yet it was easier and more common than anywhere else in Europe. The best vehicle for upward mobility was money; and with the remarkable economic expansion of the eighteenth century, one of the best sources of money was commerce (and therafter, of course, industry). If a man made enough money, he could hope to invest it in a landed estate; assume the life style of the gentry; and even, perhaps, reasonably expect that his heir might be granted (or purchase) a title. Older, better established noble houses were not above contemptuous remarks about the pretensions of newly rich merchants; but neither were they above replenishing their order with liberal injections of mercantile wealth.

Besides, the commercial spirit was not absent in the landed aristocracy. On the continent, noble landlords were generally content to lease their holdings to tenants (and live off the rental income) or have the land worked by serfs (and live off a combination of feudal dues and profits from sale of the produce). In neither case did the lord see his estate as an improvable resource whose capacity for profits might be increased; rather, it was considered the source of a constant and certain income.* From the end of the seventeenth century, however, British landlords increasingly showed a greater interest in the productivity of their estates and began to bring them even more under direct cultivation—working them, that is, through hired rather than tenant labor, and living off the sale of the harvest rather than rents. The nobility and the gentry alike began to experiment with various means (many of which originated in the Netherlands) of increasing the yield of their lands; in contrast, few continental landlords went beyond trying to increase the yield of the peasants who worked their land. By using fertilizers, crop rotation, and a variety of other methods, British lords successfully enlarged their harvests and their profits from them. Nor was it unusual for some of these profits to find their way into commercial investments or even industrial enterprises. In such an atmosphere, the quest for profits in business suffered little serious disrepute. British social structure and social values thus furnished an enabling framework for industrial revolution, just as British economic growth furnished it the stimuli of demand and resource.

Rapid increases in population are customarily regarded as an economic bane in the nations presently undertaking industrial modernization. Often, the economy simply cannot keep pace with a rampaging birth rate, and gains are literally eaten up. Yet Britain also experienced a

---

* One exception was if mineral resources should be discovered on the estate. In such circumstances, it was common for the lord to mine and market the product like any industrial entrepreneur.

sharp surge in population growth concurrent with its industrialization, as the following estimates (in millions of persons) show:*

	1700	1750	1800	1850
England & Wales	5.8	6.5	9.0	17.9
Scotland	1.0	1.3	1.6	2.9
Ireland	2.7	3.1	5.0	6.5
Total	9.5	10.9	15.6	27.3

The sudden population leap after 1750 might have staggered a less vigorous economy, and it did entail profound misery and social dislocation. But from a purely economic point of view, it provided infant industries with two important advantages. First, it meant an expanding domestic market which was far more stable than the overseas market, itself subject to wild gyrations when disrupted by war or colonial revolt (as in North America during the 1770's and 1780's). In this respect, the growth of the British population backstopped foreign trade. Second, it meant cheap labor. With so many people in need of work, employers could be certain of attracting sufficient labor even though they kept wages hovering around the subsistence level. The glut on the labor market not only kept overhead low, it strengthened the industrialist's hand in other ways: he could, for example, dispense with workers who complained of wages or working conditions in full confidence that their place would be taken by men desperate for work under any circumstances.

One final contrast with present-day patterns demonstrates the unplanned character of British industrialization. It is a rule of thumb that underdeveloped nations must begin with heavy industry—metallurgy, which produces the steel for other machines, and energy, which produces the fuel (like petroleum) to power them. Once this foundation is firmly laid, then the elaboration of "light' consumer industry may follow. In Britain, the pattern was reversed. Technological innovation had penetrated deeply into textile production long before it began to reshape—indeed, to create—capital industry. Steam power was driving textile machinery years in advance of its use to power vehicles on land and sea. In a sense, heavy industry grew out of consumer industry, or rather out of its effects.

Industrial revolution was marked not only by technological innovations, but by new forms of enterprise to accommodate them. Cotton spinning had hitherto been conducted in small shops and, even more commonly, in the homes of rural families. A middleman would bring fibers

---

* Since the first British census was taken in 1801, the figures for earlier dates can only hope to convey an order of magnitude.

to be spun on the family reel, pick them up when finished, and take them to a home weaver. Mechanization rendered these procedures obsolescent (though not overnight); larger, more efficient machines were owned by entrepreneurs rather than by the producers themselves. The spinner now came to the machine, which could mean moving to the town in which it was located. He was often joined by other immigrants from the countryside in search of work—surplus agricultural laborers, small farmers who had been squeezed off the land by the expansion and rationalization of large aristocratic estates, or (in the early nineteenth century) refugees from Ireland, where overpopulation left little choice between immigration and starvation. Industrial boom towns sprouted like ugly, irrepressible weeds. In 1750, there were in all England but two cities counting over 50,000 persons; fifty years later, there were six more; by the middle of the nineteenth century, nearly one of three Britons lived in towns of 50,000 or more.

This incredible convulsion, initiated by textiles but reinforced by other urbanizing industries, set off a massive social crisis, several features of which receive attention below. For present purposes, its result was to create a massive demand for coal to heat urban dwellings and fuel their stoves. To supply this burgeoning market, it was not enough for the coal industry to explore the application of steam power to mining. It also had to get the mined coal to the towns faster. It was in this sense that—as Professor Hobsbawm has put it—coal mining "invented" the railroad. The railroad both synthesized the new technology (it carried coal, but also burned it to power its steam engine) and pushed it forward by necessitating the refinement and drastic enlargement of metallurgical industry. When the steel industry began to shift into high gear, around the middle of the nineteenth century, the British industrial revolution had completed its first, formative stage, and could prepare to move on into maturity.

Workers and the New Industry

From the strictly economic point of view, the British industrial revolution clearly signified progress: steam-powered machines in factories produced more goods cheaper and faster than ever before. But the industrial revolution had consequences far beyond the enhancement of the gross national product. From the broadly social point of view, it is a matter of debate whether industrialization brought progress (in the sense of improvement).

It is generally accepted that, over the long run, industrialization measurably improved the standard of living for the great mass of people: by the end of the nineteenth century, that convenient fiction, the average

British worker, ate better, was better clothed and sheltered, and was paid more for his labor than his counterpart at the end of the eighteenth century. But what of the short run? If one could graph social improvement beginning in the 1780's, would the result be a steadily ascending line? Or would there be meaningful irregularities—perhaps even, as some historians have argued, a noticeable decline in the standard of living from the beginning of the industrial revolution until around the middle of the nineteenth century? Did the first two or three generations of laborers in the industrial era pay with their sufferings for the improvements which their descendants enjoyed? For all the brainpower that has been applied to these questions, no conclusive answers have emerged.

Part of the difficulty is the absence of reliable data—particularly for the mid-eighteenth century—so that one cannot be confident whether later developments represent progress, decline, or no significant change at all. Moreover, the industrial revolution did not proceed evenly through all sectors of the economy and all regions of the country: laborers in some trades clearly suffered; others benefited from steadier work and perhaps even increased purchasing power; and still others went untouched by the new manufacturing. Handloom weavers undercut by factory competition were driven to economic extinction and starvation. Some home textile workers, however, who spun or wove cotton supplied them by a middleman, were able to embezzle enough raw material to set themselves up as modest entrepreneurs and turned a tidy profit, thanks to the booming demand.

Although most statistical generalizations for the period 1780–1850 are therefore liable to be suspect, it seems clear that in many of the new industries, at least, the workers' lot was not particularly enviable (though it was doubtless preferable to starvation if unemployment was the alternative). The hours were long, the wages were low, and the work often exhausting, even though humans did not power the machines. The new industrial boom towns were unequipped to absorb the new labor force: housing and sanitation conditions were usually wretched at their best, and the absence of any recreational facilities meant that workers had little to occupy their off-hours besides alcohol. Observers could not help being struck by the contrast between industrial progress and social misery; when the French political writer Alexis de Tocqueville visited Manchester—northern England's most prodigious industrial center—in 1835, he marveled that "From this foul drain the greatest stream of human industry flows out to fertilize the whole world. From this filthy sewer pure gold flows. Here humanity attains its most complete development and its most brutish; here civilization works its miracles, and civilized man is turned back almost into a savage."

Whether or not the industrial revolution improved the situation of working people, it certainly *changed* it in some important ways—though in ways which do not always submit to precise measurement. Technological innovation had been a response to the need for more efficient production; the ethos of "more, and faster" had also to be imposed upon those who worked in the factory. Waste of time and motion meant a loss of advantage in the marketplace for the owner—the longer it took to produce something, then the more it cost him, and the greater the delay before the product could be sold. It had not always been so. Before the growing market stimulated mass production, the imperatives of efficiency were less stringent, and wages were often linked to the job to be done. A domestic spinner might be paid a certain wage to work a certain amount of cotton and have it ready when the middleman made his rounds a week hence; how many hours were spent on the work in the interim concerned no one, since the payment was a factor of the amount of cotton to be spun. An agricultural laborer might be paid a set sum to clear a small field; though whether it took him two days or three to finish was probably not a part of the transaction.

The industrial revolution not only hastened the economic rhythms; it demanded as well a new work-discipline, one which emphasized regularity and temporal thrift. To compete effectively, an industrialist had to produce as much as possible as quickly as possible. Workers were therefore paid by the day, or the week, and expected to keep pace with the tireless machines. Rest breaks, except for the midday meal, were largely unheard of; the worker who dared to take one on his own or otherwise idled about during working hours was subject to penalty—either by fine or by corporal punishment at the hands of factory overseers. With labor unions officially prohibited (prior to 1825) and in the absence (prior to 1833) of any legal restrictions upon employers, factory managers were free to demand a rigorous work discipline. Workers who failed, or refused, to internalize that discipline could be replaced from the oversupply of labor. Increasingly, industrial entrepreneurs turned to female and child labor, and not solely because women and children would work for lower wages than adult males; it was also widely supposed that they were more pliant and thus more readily adaptable to the new factory regimentation.

Even if it could be convincingly demonstrated that the factory workers' standard of living improved during the industrial revolution, the fact remains that the new work-discipline was a harsh and unpleasant regime. The transplanted agricultural worker was suddenly deprived not only of fresh air, but also of the more varied pace of work in the fields; whether or not he found factory employment more remunerative, he was likely to find it more strenuous. There may have been little to covet in the circumstances of a home cotton spinner, but at least within certain confines he set his own pace and was not assaulted for any irregularities in it.

Where pride in craftsmanship may have existed before, artisans whom mechanized competition drove into the mills now dealt with only one phase of production and were enjoined to concentrate on quantitative rather than qualitative goals. In sum, though it may well be mistaken to glamorize preindustrial labor—it could be mean, backbreaking, ill-compensated toil—it is just as mistaken to suppose that the transition to modernized industrial production was smooth and painless. The new industry had numerous enthusiasts who sang its praises as a superior productive mechanism; but few of them came from the working classes.

If, in fact, workers were better off in the first half of the nineteenth century than before, their gratitude was not conspicuous. To the contrary, the strikes, rioting, and machine breaking which greeted industrialization in several regions suggest that more than one worker failed to be moved by arguments regarding "progress." Machine breaking and violent agitation reached such proportions in parts of northern England during 1811–13 that the government actually dispatched more troops there than it had fighting Napoleon in Spain—the main theater of British infantry operations at the time. These disturbances were both attempts to apply pressure for higher wages and outright resistance to the new machines themselves, which would displace traditional manual labor. Moreover, machine breakers commanded surprisingly broad support from the local community. The reason was not that most people approved of disorder and condoned the destruction of property, but rather that industrialization itself was clearly a disruptive force, destroying the structure of the traditional economy and violating widely accepted practices.

Paternalism and Laissez Faire

The first half-century of the industrial revolution, from the 1780's to the 1830's, marked not only the appearance of power-driven machines and factories, but also witnessed the ascendancy of a new economic ideology —laissez faire. The idea that the economy functions best when freed from all external regulation—that unhindered competition in a perfectly free market will ensure that prices and wages find their proper, "natural" level—was a new one. For centuries past, the prevailing ethos had sanctioned special advantages, legalized privileges, trading monopolies, and the like; people routinely expected to be at least partially protected, and sometimes wholly exempted, from the rigors of competition. Economic paternalism did not prevent poverty, but it was widely regarded— especially among the poor—as a necessary buffer against the worst forms of exploitation and as a guarantee of some livelihood, however modest. Controls upon wages, prices, production, and working conditions were therefore an integral part of the traditional economy.

The first major assault on the paternalistic ethos came from the countryside. As large landlords sought to modernize their estates, they consolidated their holdings into single, more easily workable units, and fenced off areas historically subject to free access and usage by the whole community. Open fields and common lands, where virtually landless peasants had grazed the family cow or gathered fallen branches for fuel, became part of the lord's domain. This "enclosure movement" was a clear-cut violation of traditional rights to use of common land—so clear-cut, in fact, that acts of Parliament were required to legitimate enclosures. (This proved no serious obstacle, since Parliament was dominated by the very landlords who were engaged in enclosing.) Enclosures were part of a larger process whereby noble and gentry estates expanded, virtually eliminating small farmers and helping to create the surplus labor force upon which industry drew. For present purposes, however, it should be emphasized that the enclosure movement represented a blow to the paternalistic economy. It deprived many people of benefits which may seem trivial now but which loomed large in a marginal existence.

Even so, the principal offensive against economic controls came from the new manufacturing interests, for whom the maximization of profit meant (among other things) the minimization of overhead. The manufacturers insisted that success in the expanding trade markets demanded competitive prices, which in turn entailed the lowest possible production costs. While manufacturers found it difficult to control the cost of their raw materials and their machinery, the question of wages for their employees was another matter. The labor surplus made it possible for manufacturers to keep wages at the bare subsistence level; but they could justify their wage policies with arguments more compelling than simply the need to keep costs down.

In 1798, an Anglican clergyman named Thomas Malthus had published an *Essay on Population* which drew attention to the increasing number of human beings in the world. According to Malthus, the growth of population was fast outstripping the growth of food resources, so that for the great mass of (poor) people, extinction was not merely a regrettable possibility, it was an unavoidable law of nature. Population could only be reduced by famine, disease, or war. Even more relevant for present purposes, to improve the lot of the poor by higher wages or the large-scale establishment of social services was only to encourage their irrepressible propensity to breed. Therefore, the best way to keep huge numbers of people from starving to death was to discourage the masses from reproducing by holding them at the subsistence level. Malthus' arguments received powerful support from David Ricardo's *The Principles of Political Economy and Taxation* (1817). Ricardo maintained that an "iron law" held wages at a point just sufficient for survival: any higher wage would prompt population growth, and thus a labor surplus, which would pull wages back down again. Needless to say, both Malthus and Ricardo found a receptive audience in the community of industrial entrepreneurs.

Industrialists also insisted that the government did more harm than good by interfering with "natural" economic processes; a wholly free market would allocate resources at peak efficiency, so that wages, prices, and production would find their "natural" level. The producer who overpriced his goods would inevitably be driven from the market. Therefore, let the market also determine wages, and the worker who overpriced his labor would run the same risk. To tamper with the infallible mechanisms of the market was sheer folly and openly invited economic catastrophe. Besides, a man's business was his property, and how he ran it was no affair of government.

It was not merely because government found these arguments cogent that it began to accept them around the end of the eighteenth century. It was also that working-class agitation against wage cuts, against machine competition, against deteriorating working conditions, and (vaguely) against factory work discipline often dovetailed with radical political agitation. Once the French Revolution had begun, official repression of British radicalism became particularly energetic. The authorities interpreted (and sometimes with justice) industrial protest as just another version of radical political protest and repressed it with equal verve. Abruptly, what remained of the paternalistic economy's scaffolding (and there was a fair amount) was dismantled. The working man—and woman and child—were deprived of the protection afforded by the benevolent paternal state, as slight and theoretical as that protection often was, and were left to the mercy of their employers.

Nor were these masters cognizant of any obligations to their employees. In the small workshop characteristic of the preindustrial era, the employer was as often as not an artisan who worked alongside his employees. This sort of fraternization did not spell instant brotherhood, but it did create certain subtle human bonds which now and then extended beyond the workshop itself. Shop employers were expected to harbor some sense of responsibility for the interests of their employees, who were not so very far beneath them on the scale of status. Needless to say, factory production transformed this relationship. For the person who had worked in a small shop, and for those who had worked at home, it substituted the overseer and the clock for the artisan master or the middleman and his weekly visits.

Those changes wrought by the industrial revolution in the lives of working people which will not admit of statistical formulation are still the most important ones. They cut across the debate about measurable improvements in the standard of living and raise questions instead about improvements in the quality of life. Not that workers traded idyllic circumstances for dismal ones: preindustrial labor suffered exploitation too, and paternalism promised only to place limits on it (which it did not always do). Textile artisans in the north smashed machines not because mechanical competition reduced them from comfort to beggary. They did so because they had for centuries enjoyed legal protection from mechanical competition of any sort, because industrialization threatened to destroy them as independent artisans and turn them into mere factory "hands." Modern industry may or may not, during its first few generations, have brought some increased prosperity. But it undeniably brought, for those who worked in it, the regimentation and the monotony of the factory, dwindling self-respect occasioned by the decline in status, and a master likely to regard his employees as no more human than the machines they tended.

The Captains of Industry

It is, at the least, debatable whether the industrial revolution created a higher standard of living for working people. It is not debatable whether (collectively) their employers' standard of living improved: it did, and at a rate far exceeding that by which the poor became less poor. Industrialization can hardly be accused of creating the gap between the poor and the rich; but it certainly broadened it. This fact was more obvious to poor people than were any gains *they* might have made, and it rendered the conditions of the new industrial labor all the more intolerable. For it could easily be argued that the entrepreneur's enhanced wealth had been acquired at the cost of his employees' degradation. When an employer's income increases conspicuously and his employee's does not, the employee may perhaps be forgiven for suspecting that something has gone wrong. That suspicion was at the root of much of the extensive violence and discontent which troubled British society during the early industrial age.

Modern industry caused far less disorganization in the upper reaches of society than in the lower. Ultimately—by, say, the early twentieth century—it had helped dislodge large landowners from their elite rank. But by the middle of the nineteenth century, the aristocracy and the gentry had found no serious difficulty in accommodating themselves to industrializing society. They profited from their own investments in industry, and they obviously benefited from the growing demand for agricultural produce stimulated by population growth and from the rise in food prices and in rents. Reluctantly, and under intense pressure, they relaxed their monopoly upon political power, and in 1832 admitted some representatives of the new industrial interests into the oligarchy which dominated Parliament. (See Chapter 4.) Industrial wealth might now provide the same access into the landed elite as commercial wealth had done before.

Although the industrial revolution vastly enlarged the numbers of well-to-do businessmen, it did not create overnight a class of entrepreneurs prepared to restructure the social hierarchy. The new captains of industry, as the writer Thomas Carlyle called them in 1843, were naturally anxious that their interests be recognized and secured; but they were in no position as yet to do much more. The industrialization of society had unmistakably begun by the 1840's, but it was still only a beginning. Once the question of industrial wealth's political representation had been resolved, the principal issue of contention between agriculture and manufacturing was that of tariffs. Briefly, landed proprietors supported the high duty on cheap food imports to hold up domestic prices on their own produce. Industrialists sought to abolish these duties, in part because high food prices forced wages up, and in part because they hoped for reciprocal tariff cuts by other nations which would thus open new foreign markets to British goods. The victory of the "free trade" forces in 1846 was accomplished only after widespread political agitation against the resistance of the landed interests. Yet it signified only the general direction of social change, and certainly not a social revolution.

The expanded opportunities for making money afforded by the new industry combined with individual initiative to create some impressive new fortunes during the industrial revolution. The career of the "self-made man" was held up as a model for the ambitious poor and as evidence of the excellence and justice of a social system which permitted talent, energy, and ingenuity their due rewards. Typically, however, the self-made man rose to wealth from obscurity, but only rarely from extreme poverty. Most of those who climbed high on the social ladder had begun at least several rungs from the bottom, frequently in small business. Just as the industrial revolution built upon the economic growth of the eighteenth century, the new industrialists were not created from a vacuum. As a group, they had their nucleus in the eighteenth-century business class, the manufacturers and merchants who comprised the largest and most prosperous "middle class" grouping in the world and who possessed the experience and the capital (or access to it) to make the new industrial ventures successful. Wealth, that is to say, ran to wealth. The industrial revolution greatly expanded and enriched the middle classes, which grew increasingly more conscious of their interests and more confident of their power and rightful place in society; but it did not give birth to them. Something closer to the opposite is nearer the truth.

Britain underwent an industrial revolution in the years between (roughly) 1780 and 1850, not in the sense that its economy and society had been revolutionized by the middle of the nineteenth century but rather in the sense that revolutionizing forces were unleashed during those years. Again, it is necessary to observe that the industrial revolution was a process. By about 1850, the new industry had still failed to displace agriculture as the economic activity which occupied the great bulk of the population. But it had struck its roots, and they were spreading. Mechanized factory production was still but a small part of total economic production; yet it was rapidly increasing its share. The diffusion of technological change was transfiguring production beyond the cotton mill. The number of persons who worked in factories was growing, as were the number and size of factories themselves, the rate of investment in them, and the dependence of other sectors of the economy upon their demands. The throb of the new machines was becoming the economic pulse beat of the nation.

Continental Industrialization

As partial as British industrialization was by 1850, it still far exceeded that of any other European nation. Continental Europe was rapidly coming to the realization that modern industry was going to be a prerequisite to international power. But the continent not only lacked large colonial markets and the commercial demand from them which had been so vital in stimulating the British industrial revolution, it also faced a number of structural impediments to industrialization.

Forced to rely on domestic markets in the absence of substantial foreign ones, continental nations clearly suffered from the economic fragmentation of their territories. Provinces or groups of provinces frequently retained rights to commercial autonomy long after political autonomy had been lost to a centralizing monarchy. Internal tariffs were common, as were high tolls on roads and bridges, all of which tended to limit the circulation of goods outside the customs zone in which they were produced. In other words, economic fragmentation discouraged expanding production which had an eye to capturing markets elsewhere in the realm. The revolution eliminated internal trade barriers in France and, by example, called them into question elsewhere; but sometimes political fragmentation—as on the Italian peninsula or in the new German Confederation—created comparable obstacles. In 1834, Prussia took the lead in building a customs union (or *Zollverein*) in the Confederation, which eliminated most tariffs between member states; but it was another decade before most of the German principalities had joined.

Moreover, legal restrictions on production and wages persisted where the guild system survived. Artisan craft guilds had, among other things, fostered an ethos not of cutthroat competition and efficient mass production, but of security and stability. Organized by crafts—for example, all the cabinet makers in a given town, whether employers or employees, belonged to a single guild—and chartered by the government, the guilds monopolized production and markets. By agreement, they kept prices high by holding down production and restricted entry into a craft so as to keep skilled labor scarce and wages up. Such regulations obviously militated against the sort of technological innovations and the price and wage policies characteristic of the industrial revolution. Though the guilds were in decay in the late eighteenth century and though the revolution abolished them in France, their structure and their conservative, paternalistic spirit proved remarkably tenacious in many places.

Indeed, matters of "spirit" are relevant in more than one way to an explanation of the continent's relatively slow industrial start, though they are sometimes difficult to document. It is easier to identify concrete obstacles—the absence of voracious foreign demand, economic and political fragmentation, or deficiencies in critical raw materials such as (known) coal and iron deposits. But many continental nations also harbored attitudes which discriminated against trade. The idea that noble status was inconsistent with the grubby business of making money frequently found its way into laws which threatened to punish nobles who engaged in trade, thereby sullying the gentility of their order. Although such laws did not prevent some French nobles from discreetly investing in certain commercial ventures, they were hardly even necessary in most of central and eastern Europe, where the landed aristocracy regarded urban commerce as the domain of grasping commoners. Such attitudes did little to attract men of talent and ambition into business.

The role of the state in early industrialization was complex. In Britain, government enthusiastically fostered trade—even to the point of waging wars to conquer colonial markets—and abstained from interfering in the new industry until the first, limited social legislation of the 1830's. On the continent, the governments of the eighteenth century were lavish in their subsidies of private manufacturing enterprises and frequently established state-owned industries as well. Moreover, government officially demanded technological improvement and often financed it. Secondarily, the state served as market; in particular, the armies of Europe—busy throughout the eighteenth century and especially active from 1792 to 1815—had to be clothed and armed.* But government on the continent was not a uniformly positive force for economic modernization. State-owned industries were often paragons of inefficiency which did

---

* It should also be noted, however, that this chronic warfare posed a physical threat (which the British avoided) and can hardly have created confidence that one would live to enjoy the fruits of investment and labor.

more to retard than to stimulate development. Governments perennially in need of instant cash sold trade monopolies, thus reducing such benefits as competition might bring. Policy toward the guilds and their system of restrictions varied, but in general, governments (excepting the French) were reluctant to stage a frontal assault upon them prior to the middle of the nineteenth century—even though the most impressive industrial advances were manifestly being made in nonguild manufacturing.

It is hardly surprising, then, that industrialization and its by-products were far more conspicuous in Great Britain by about 1850 than on the continent. The British had no meaningful competition in the production of textiles, coal, and steel. There were 6,600 miles of railroad track laid in the British Isles, but only 1,800 in all of France and 3,500 in the sprawling lands of the German Confederation. Moreover, the British population was urbanizing at an astounding rate—by mid-century, fully 20 percent of the people resided in the 28 towns that numbered more than 100,000 inhabitants each. France, the most urbanized of the major states on a still rural and agrarian continent, could count but five cities that size. But all the explanations for the economic distance between the continent and Britain—and we have only sketched the major ones here —ought not to obscure the fact that change was beginning, that the continental nations were alive to the challenge and the opportunity posed by British machines.

One way in which those nations tried to close the gap was by transplanting British machines to their own industrial soil. Lacking technological expertise, continentals imported technicians from Britain or, when the British authorities tried to halt the sale of mechanical secrets and talent to foreigners, by industrial espionage. Some important nuclei of the new continental industry got their start with British personnel, who installed modern machinery and trained local mechanics in its operation and repair. However, the continent was not bereft of ingenuity, only experience, and in time it created its own corps of engineers. Nevertheless, factories and factory towns were relatively slow in springing up. In Britain, the consolidation of large landed estates had reduced the small-farmer class to one of negligible size. On the continent, the growing population—and thus the labor surplus—was still in the countryside; cheap rural labor sustained domestic manufacture, with peasants (or "semi-peasants") spinning and weaving cloth in their own homes for middlemen suppliers. Yet factory production was making inroads by 1850— especially in Belgium, parts of northern France, and a few German cities. The progress toward industrial "takeoff" was wildly uneven, not only from state to state but from region to region within states; in much of central, eastern, and southern Europe, it had not even begun. But Britain's successful industrialization was both a model and a prod to action.

To summarize, economic modernization was only incipient in Europe as of 1850, so that the social impact of industrial revolution had been felt in but a few scattered places. The social structures of the old regime survived largely intact, dominated by noble landowners whose prestige and power far exceeded that of the small urban middle classes. Although the European revolutions of 1848 threatened to alter the distribution of political power, the industrial revolution had by that date raised no comparable challenge.

In January 1848, Karl Marx and Friedrich Engels announced in *The Communist Manifesto:* "Modern industry has converted the little workshop of the patriarchal master into the great factory of the industrial capitalist." A continental reader of the time could be excused for regarding that statement as pure rubbish: it was simply a false description of mid-century Europe. But if we regard the statement not as description, but as a version of prophecy, an extrapolation from processes actually at work, then it has a certain truth. The steady hum of British machines had already set off vibrations, however faint, in continental Europe.

3 / The Romantic Revolt

European thought in the nineteenth and twentieth centuries has been largely characterized by the delicate interplay of two intellectual dispositions, one dating from the so-called Age of Enlightenment and the other from the era of romanticism. Great expanses of modern history are unlikely to make much sense unless one has some familiarity with these two dispositions. For present purposes, it is more useful to concentrate primarily upon the romantic revolt. But it is equally important to emphasize that the birth of the nineteenth century did not witness the complete superseding of Enlightenment attitudes by romanticism—nor is any age liable to do so.

The Enlightenment

The dramatic developments in seventeenth-century science reshaped philosophical attitudes not only toward nature, but toward man as well. The revelations of Galileo, Kepler, and especially Newton helped fortify that confidence in human powers of reasoning which had been growing since the Renaissance. The fact that mere mortals could discover the laws which governed the functioning of the universe raised questions about the point of traditional Christian intellectual humility. Increasingly in the Age of Enlightenment (the name historians of thought have bestowed upon the eighteenth century), man's reason was taken as his defining characteristic, rather than his immortal soul or his inherent flaws—that is, original sin.

Christianity had long preached that God was both the author and master of the world, and that the Christian faith (denominational rivalries aside) was the worldly repository of divine wisdom. If, however, rather than accepting Christianity without question, one applied critical reason to various of its tenets, then problems began to arise. Newton, whose prestige was enormous in the Enlightenment, had shown that the world operated in a regular, systematic fashion, according to rational laws. What, then, was one to make of miracles—parting seas, virgin births, resurrections, and the like? The Bible was said to be the word of God. How, then, was one to account for the manifest contradictions and flat-out errors revealed by rational analysis and historical scholarship? For many eighteenth-century intellectuals, reason and Christian faith were incompatible, with the latter often equivalent to error at best and superstition at worst.

In Catholic Europe, the apostles of reason went even further in their critique of Christianity, focusing upon the Church as well as upon its creeds. In France, for example, the Church was not merely a sacramental institution, but an integral part of the social and political system. Advocates of reform under the Old Regime usually found themselves embroiled with clerical defenders of the status quo, as well as with government authorities, and the Church was an important part of the bureaucracy of censorship which tried to throttle all manner of critics. It seemed to François-Marie Arouet, better known by his pen name of Voltaire, that the ecclesiastical hierarchy was filled both with men of substantial means trying to protect their privileged position and fanatics trying to perpetuate their grotesque views by silencing dissent. Voltaire never seemed to tire of reciting instances in which agents of the God of Love disemboweled those of differing views.

The *philosophes* * of the eighteenth-century Enlightenment were generally convinced that the rigorous exercise of human reason did not lead to Christian faith. For that matter, it did not lead to any single all-embracing thought system. Although the *philosophes* felt that reason pointed the way to truth, they were still suspicious of the concept of Truth. They urged the systematic scrutiny of orthodox values, but they did not seek to replace them with a coherent philosophy. An important part of their approach was negative: the Enlightenment, as one recent historian has put it, saw philosophy as "the organized habit of criticism." The task of the *philosophes* was therefore to subject the received wisdom of their age to the litmus test of reason.

Yet criticism not only revealed superstition and error, it could also suggest alternatives. Toward the middle of the eighteenth century, after a generation of critical writing which spanned a vast range of subjects, the

* Literally, this French word means "philosopher." In practice, however, the men to whom the name applied were not formal academic philosophers, but something more like free-lance intellectuals—men of letters who wrote not only philosophical treatises but novels, drama, poetry, history, and all manners of essays as well.

French *philosophes* began to feel the need for synthesis. Under the general editorship of Denis Diderot, the best minds of the era contributed to a multivolumed *Encyclopedia,* which began to appear in 1749. The *Encyclopedia* was nothing if not ambitious; Diderot described it as an effort "to change the general way of thinking." But it did not confine itself to arcane disquisitions on purely abstract subjects. The whole point of critical reason was that it was *useful* to all men. Thus, articles on Christianity and on logic found themselves nestled up against pieces on how to plow a field.

The synthesizing bent of the *Encyclopedia* can be misleading, however. Although the *philosophes* shared the critical temperament, they had little programmatic unity. Some, like the Frenchmen Turgot and Condorcet, were convinced that there were no limits upon the benefits which reason might bring and spoke in terms of boundless future progress for the human race. Others, like Voltaire, were more skeptical about human perfectibility, more pessimistic, and while thoroughly committed to reform, they held out no hope of a heaven on earth. While some *philosophes* argued that man, by his very nature, possessed certain rights (to freedom of speech, freedom of religion, self-government, and so forth), others distrusted the notion of "natural rights" and tried to justify reform in terms of social utility.

Although the *philosophes* achieved no consensus on what ought to be changed and why, still the thrust of their work (in France, at least) was in the direction of reform. Consequently, they have been supposed—by contemporaries and many historians alike—to have provided the intellectual inspiration for the French Revolution. It is true that the revolutionaries generally spoke in the language of the Enlightenment and quoted approvingly from such advocates of change as Voltaire and Jean-Jacques Rousseau, the eighteenth century's sole prominent proponent of political democracy. On the other hand, it is almost impossible to establish some firm empirical connection between the Enlightenment and the revolution. Although the revolutionary politicians read the *philosophes,* can we be certain that they *therefore* became revolutionaries? However that may be, the fact remains that most observers at the end of the eighteenth and beginning of the nineteenth centuries simply assumed that the connection was there. Whatever the substance of Enlightenment thought, its reputation was for a long time linked with the revolution.

The premises and predilections of the Enlightenment surfaced again and again in modern European thought. Nineteenth-century science and positivism were direct outgrowths of eighteenth-century empiricism; liberals and socialists alike were the children of the Age of Reason. On the other hand, the Enlightenment heritage was immediately and vigorously challenged at the end of the eighteenth century by romanticism—in large part because the *philosophes* were firmly ensconced in the classical tradition which was the target of the romantic revolt. Frequently, as we shall see, the romantics misread the *philosophes*, charging them with an arid and unfeeling rationalism which was scarcely the distinguishing characteristic of their work. There was far more complexity in the Enlightenment (and its version of classicism) than either the romantics realized or this brief sketch has revealed. Still, the conflict between the classical tradition of the Enlightenment and romanticism was real enough.

Classicism and Romanticism

It has become almost obligatory to preface discussions of romanticism with a *caveat lector* that the word has no single generally accepted definition. This elastic term has been stretched to fit so many different things that it retains little of its original shape (if, indeed, it had one). One is tempted to agree with the French poet Alfred de Musset, who wrote in 1836 that "we came to believe that this word *romanticism* was only a word. We found it to be beautiful, and it seemed unfortunate that it meant nothing." In fact, the problem is not that the word "meant nothing," but that it meant—and means—too many things, many of them mutually incompatible or contradictory.

The "ism" of romanticism is deceptive; it suggests a coherent body of thought, a tightly formulated doctrine. Rather, romanticism was a set of dispositions which deliberately rejected neat categorization. The problem of definition arises from the fact that the early romanticists consciously exalted the unique, the peculiar, the individual over the typical, the universal, the classifiable. Romanticism was meant to defy precise definition because that, argued its partisans, was what life itself did.

The classical tradition in European culture, which suffused the Age of Enlightenment, is easier to define. For most *philosophes*, the culture of classical antiquity supplied both the models and the standards of art. The classical tradition valued order, clarity, and discipline. Above all, it was didactic: it sought to extract timeless truths from the welter of human detail. A Greek statue of a warrior was also a *lesson*, conveying the "essence" of courage, or strength, or manly beauty, as the case may be. In this sense, classical art tended to idealize its subject matter, to depict edifying types rather than the vulgar worldly reality in which no such types might be readily found.

The classical tradition could be useful and stimulating; it is difficult to think of men like Dante or Michelangelo or Milton apart from it. But it could also be shallow and suffocating, encouraging imitation rather than innovation, faithfulness to classical models rather than imaginative exploration of new possibilities. In the seventeenth and eighteenth centuries, classicism became increasingly austere and abstract, emphasizing formal grandeur and drawing increasingly remote from human feelings. There were, to be sure, clear intimations of dissatisfaction with these tendencies prior to the appearance of romanticism. Beginning in the early eighteenth century, the rococo style reveled in ornamentation and exotic colors. The adjective "romantic" began to signify something more than "amorous" when it was applied to English landscape gardens, in which the geometrical patterns popular in France were broken up and a less rigorous organization was experimented with. Sentimental novels came into vogue, and one of the most popular—*La Nouvelle Héloïse* (1761) —was written by a leading *philosophe*, Rousseau. In 1774, the twenty-five-year-old writer Johann Wolfgang von Goethe won instant fame with *The Sorrows of Young Werther*, a novel of frustrated passions which ends in suicide.

The romanticists placed a high value on what the eighteenth century called "sensibility," the capacity for *feeling*. Had romanticism been nothing more, however, than an emotional tempest, it would soon have blown itself out. But the revolt against classicism went farther, challenging its universalizing and idealizing bent, and calling attention instead to the uniqueness of reality. This particular aspect of the revolt had its most significant beginnings in the German states, where the last third of the century witnessed the stirrings of "cultural nationalism."

Eighteenth-century Europe shared an international culture dominated by France. French was *the* language of the Enlightenment; the prestige of French artists and men of letters was unrivaled; and of course French culture was predominantly classicist. The idea of several distinct national cultures had few adherents, mainly because most states were dynastic agglomerations rather than culturally coherent nations. The revolt against classicism and the revolt against French cultural dominance were thus two sides of the same coin, two movements bound to reinforce one another. From about the 1770's, those German intellectuals who were seeking an alternative to classicism were also seeking something non-French, and those in search of a uniquely German cultural personality could hardly expect to find it in classicism. The quest for "German-ness" led not so much into high art, so heavily under French influence, as into popular culture—the folk tales and songs of the common people, untainted by foreign tastes. What the historians of German popular culture found, or thought they found, was a unique cultural heritage created not by the Greeks and Romans nor even by single, identifiable authors, but rather by the collective German soul. Furthermore, since folk culture was "common" and since it abounded in tales of magic and eerie spiritual forces, it served as a useful contrast to the "elevated" rationalism of the classical tradition.

The gradual discovery and celebration of a unique German culture became of special importance as the French escalated from cultural to political tyranny. When Napoleon's armies occupied German soil and tried to plant French institutions in it, the repudiation of things Gallic and the glorification of things German became a patriotic duty. At the same time, it could hardly be ignored that Napoleon—while personally addicted to the trashiest of sentimental novels—had firmly identified his regime with the classical style, complete with the construction of Roman victory arches and official paintings by the arch-classicist Jacques-Louis David. The so-called Imperial style was the high-water mark of neoclassical sterility, and consequently was a powerful stimulus to romanticist reverence for sensibility and individuality.

On the aesthetic level, cultural nationalism translated into a rejection of the didactic representation of universals in preference to the peculiarities of the real world. Not that romanticism was above smuggling moral lessons into its art, but they were lessons in feeling and not in cerebration, lessons extolling differentiation rather than generalization, lessons for people seeking identity. They were also lessons in reality, which was both more complex and also simpler than the classical tradition made out. In the romanticists' eyes, classicism considered only Man; *they* would consider men.

Thus romanticism began as a revolt against Enlightenment classicism, an ode to the unique, a rediscovery of sensibility. The German vanguard of the romantic revolt inspired widespread interest—in Great Britain at the end of the eighteenth century, and even in France at the beginning of the nineteenth—though early German romanticists also had a number of independent counterparts in these countries. Most of these early romanticists praised individuality and exulted in the rediscovery of sensibility; however these activities hardly exhausted romanticism. We may get a better sense of its breadth and complexity by investigating romanticist attitudes toward several subjects: nature, religion, history, and art.

Romantic Nature

For the eighteenth century, nature was above all knowable. It was complex, sometimes puzzling and unpredictable; but still it functioned according to natural laws which could be understood by the human mind. Not all the laws were known as yet; nevertheless, there was general confidence—especially after the major breakthroughs made by Newton —that science would dispel the remaining mysteries. When eighteenth-century classical writers sought a metaphor for nature, they often turned to machinery, and especially the clock—an elaborate, intricate, but still logical meshing of gears, difficult but ultimately possible to comprehend.

Dissent from these views generally arose more from skepticism about man's reasoning powers than from the belief that nature was random chaos.

The romantic revolt rejected this vision of nature as a giant machine capable of rational analysis. In the first place, it was too simplistic, a prime example of the classicist proclivity for idealizing. If you look at nature, said an increasing number of writers toward the end of the eighteenth century, *real* nature—and not nature as imagined by the rationalist mind—you see infinite variety, a rich catalogue of phenomena some of which are difficult to explain. You see paradoxes and contradictions: the British poet William Blake pondered a savage beast such as the tiger and could only ask, "Did He who made the Lamb make Thee?" You see powerful, uncontrollable forces most unmachinelike in their irregularity and unpredictability. In short, romanticism found in nature depths unplumbed by scientific investigation and liable to remain impenetrable to rational comprehension. Many romanticists preferred it that way, preferred a nature that one appreciated and experienced rather than analyzed coolly; and this was their second major objection to the classicist vision of nature.

Classicism perceived nature intellectually, romanticism perceived nature sensually; for the former, nature was orderly, for the latter, beautiful. The intellectual approach not only missed the beauty; it sometimes mangled nature in the name of science. William Wordsworth, an early apostle of the sensual approach to nature, wrote in 1798:

> Sweet is the lore which Nature brings;
> Our meddling intellect
> Mis-shapes the beauteous forms of things:—
> We murder to dissect.

For Wordsworth, nature communicated not rational knowledge, but ". . . sensations sweet,/ Felt in the blood, and felt along the heart. . . ." Goethe's hero Werther wrote of "the holy fire which animates all nature, and filled and glowed within my heart." Machines were cold and impersonal; nature was warm, full of color and graceful rhythms and inspiring forms. Indeed, while convinced that nature was a complexity often beyond rational apprehension, romanticists could also argue that nature's essence was simplicity—the simple beauty of a flower, a soft breeze, a bird's song. Nature spoke in simple words, and it spoke directly to the heart.

Romantic nature was first of all the countryside, away from the city, from the brittle and barren conventions of human "civilization." The countryside as a retreat from urban woes was not an invention of romanticism; in the 1770's, Queen Marie Antoinette of France had had a tiny rustic hamlet constructed in the forest of Versailles to which she could repair, to frolic about in peasant costume when the ritual etiquette of the court threatened to overwhelm her. For the romanticists, however, nature was more than an occasional frisk around the maypole. It was a spring unpolluted by human evil from which a man might drink to cleanse his soul. Wordsworth described nature as a "counterpoise"—"Which, when the spirit of evil reached its height,/ Maintained for me a secret happiness." He who could escape into the countryside could reinvigorate himself, sharpen his perceptions, taste the pleasures of simplicity, let himself be astonished by natural (as opposed to artificial) sounds and sights and smells. Ludwig van Beethoven expressed the experience musically in his sixth symphony, the "Pastoral Symphony" (1810), of which the lyrical first movement is entitled "Awakening of Cheerful Feelings upon Arrival in the Country."

Nature provided enjoyment, awakened "natural" feelings, heightened sensibility—and it did more. It was a source both of spiritual and aesthetic values. Nature was freedom, wild beauty uncluttered by the restraints of the classical tradition or of artificial social mores. It was purity, untainted (as Wordsworth put it) by "human ignorance and guilt" or "spectacles of woe"; it was the embodiment of childlike innocence— and romanticism much preferred the unaffected innocence of children to the worldly sophistication of the "reasonable" man. Nature was an integrated, satisfying whole, an organic unity which stirred total human response and did not appeal merely to the intellect. Nature was, lastly, *real;* it was unique and original, and not an artful imitation. Although "romanticizing" has come to mean mere prettifying, the distortion of reality in order to make it more attractive, romanticism in fact regarded the reality of nature as superior to classicism's idealizations and recognized there no discrepancy between "is" and "ought." In commenting upon John Constable's painting "The Hay Wain," one historian has spoken of the artist's refusal "to be more impressive than nature."

While the countryside served as romanticism's principal contrast to European classical civilization, non-European cultures played a similar— if less important—role. Here the romanticists enlarged upon eighteenth-century tastes rather than rejecting them outright. The Sagacious Mandarin and the Tolerant Brahmin had been stock characters in eighteenth-century literature, though basically only as devices for pointing up defects in the European character; eighteenth-century artists and designers who became dissatisfied with severe classical forms experimented with Oriental ornamentation. Romanticism turned even more eagerly to the Near East after the exposure provided by Napoleon's invasion of Egypt. The French painter Eugène Delacroix did some of his most exciting work inspired by the lush colors and violent rhythms of Near Eastern life. North America performed a similar function for the writer François-René de Chateaubriand, whose popular story *Atala* (1801) was a celebration of unspoiled Indians and "primitive fields of nature." Samuel Taylor Coleridge's "Kubla Khan" (1798), a standard anthology piece of romantic poetry, evokes the sensuous mysteries of the East. In short, an English meadow and a Turkish harem had at least one thing in common: neither had been infected by classical culture.

Religion

For classicists and romanticists alike, apart from a handful of skeptics in each camp, nature was God's creation. Just as their respective visions of nature differed, however, so too did their visions of nature's architect: the God who fashioned a machine could scarcely resemble the God responsible for a mountain brook. In any age, of course, divinity is bound to assume several shapes; in the eighteenth century, there was little similarity between the God of the Quakers and that of the Calvinists, between the God of Roman Catholicism and that of rationalist deism. Since deism had the closest connections with classicism, romanticists identified the deists as their spiritual enemies.

Deism was not an organized religion, but rather a persuasion, a cluster of religious ideas which comprised a noninstitutionalized, nondenominational theism, mainly attractive to educated people. Seventeenth-century rationalist philosophy and the beginnings of higher Biblical criticism had acted as a solvent upon the faith of numerous educated persons. Religious persecution and civil wars between rival Christian factions raised doubts about the morality of those who claimed to worship a God of Love; miracles seemed less credible in an Age of Reason. In these circumstances, deism was an attempt to salvage religion by making it simpler, more reasonable, more humane. The deist could have begun reciting the Nicean Creed with the Christian: "I believe in one God the Father Almighty, Maker of heaven and earth. . . ." He could rarely go beyond that, however, into the divinity of Jesus and the mysteries of the trinity and the resurrection and baptism (although there was disagreement among deists on the question of an afterlife). Deism made no claims to absolute knowledge, to a monopoly upon religious truth, and therefore its principal counsel was toleration. According to the American deist Benjamin Franklin, "the most acceptable service we can render to [God] is doing good to his other children." Voltaire pleaded, "We must tolerate each other, for we are all weak, inconsistent, subject to change and error." Deism's impulses were ethical rather than metaphysical, and it distrusted elaborate bodies of doctrine and ritual. For Voltaire, the best religion was clearly "the simplest one."

Although the God of deism was, for some persons, a personal and im-

HISTORICAL PICTURES SERVICE, CHICAGO

Above, a typical contemporary depiction of August 10, 1792, when Parisian revolutionary crowds stormed the Tuileries palace to remove Louis XVI from the throne and turn France into the first major European state with a republican government. Twelve years later, the French exchanged a republic for an Empire, governed by Napoleon Bonaparte, whose coronation, below, was portrayed by the arch-classicist painter Jacques-Louis David.

NEW YORK/FLORENCE

HISTORICAL PICTURES SERVICE, CHICAGO

The illustration above, dated 1851, captures some of the monotony and dreariness of an English textile mill. Note the presence of the overseer at the right. (Below) Robert Owen was an industrialist turned social reformer who hoped that labor might be more agreeably organized. Owen and his followers were constantly sketching out plans for model villages like the one shown in a woodcut of 1828.

HISTORICAL PICTURES SERVICE, CHICAGO

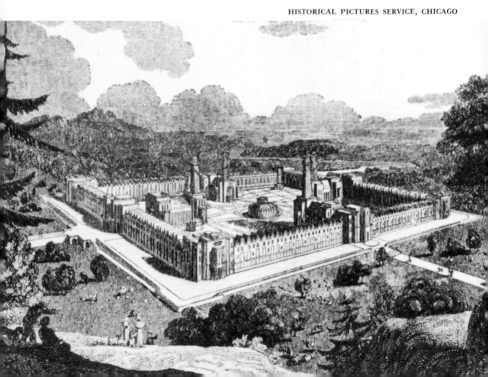

NEW YORK PUBLIC LIBRARY PICTURE COLLECTION

In 1851, the British government sponsored an impressive show of modern industrial products and the machines which made them. A massive new building, the Crystal Palace, was constructed to house this Great Exhibition, which drew admirers from all over Europe. But when the French illustrator Gustave Doré visited London two decades later, he saw a different dimension of industrial society. Below, see his version of the Houndsditch quarter of the city.

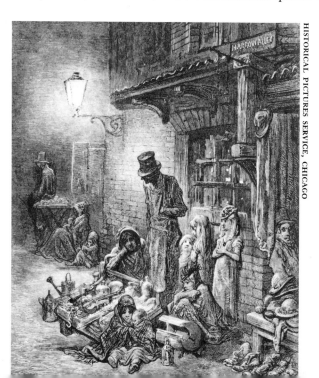

HISTORICAL PICTURES SERVICE, CHICAGO

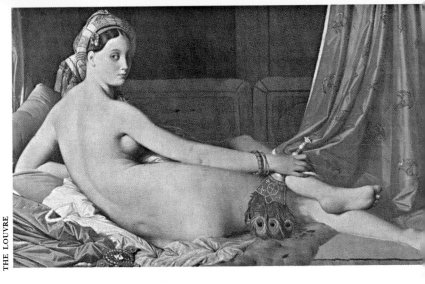

THE LOUVRE

French classicists and romanticists who visited the same exotic Near East saw different worlds. Jean-Auguste-Dominique Ingres, who studied with David, brought back the cool, detached, wholly classicist study in form titled "Odalisque" (1814). Eugène Delacroix's "The Abduction of Rebecca" (1846) betrays the romanticist taste for movement, pictorial drama, and rich color tones.

THE METROPOLITAN MUSEUM OF ART, WOLFE FUND, 1903

LAING ART GALLERY AND MUSEUM, NEWCASTLE UPON TYNE

To capture the spirit of a movement, it is sometimes necessary to investigate its more obscure participants. John Martin was a minor English painter who happened to express a great many of romanticism's themes in his work "The Bard" (1817). Here the glorified artist is an integral part of nature, virtually growing out of a great stone crag, and perched high above the seething human throng (fittingly clad in medieval garb).

SCALA NEW YORK/FLORENCE

historians, the French revo-
on of 1848 was a complex
of social and political forces.
contemporaries, however, it
class war, pure and simple,
ching its awful climax in the
l war of June. Jean-Louis
issonier's painting, "The Bar-
de," commemorates the
kers who attempted to hold a
ition on the Rue de la Mor-
erie against the superior
nbers and firepower of the
ernment.

HISTORICAL PICTURES SERVICE, CHICAGO

In 1878, the statesmen of the great powers of Europe gathered in Berlin to work out the diplomatic implications of a war in the pestiferous Balkans. Bismarck was at the height of his influence, as this official portrait accurately reflects: Bismarck is the tallest man, shaking hands, slightly right of center. At the left, with the cane, is Benjamin Disraeli. Yet life was also becoming perilous for the great at the end of the nineteenth century. Below, see an English depiction of the assassination of Czar Alexander II of Russia in 1881.

HISTORICAL PICTURES SERVICE, CHICAGO

HISTORICAL PICTURES SERVICE, CHICAGO

In the Punch cartoon of 1894, with the legend "What, another!!—Well, I suppose I must take it in!!!" John Bull accepts yet another colonial possession with resignation. The cartoon of 1898, entitled "The Heathen Yields to Christian Influence," suggests a rather different mentality behind imperialism. As France, Germany, and Russia assault China, imperial expansion becomes little more than a mugging.

HISTORICAL PICTURES SERVICE, CHICAGO

Industrialization and the consequent burgeoning of the middle classes vastly enlarged the numbers of those who would patronize art, or that which aspired to be art. One of the beneficiaries of this development was the popular English painter John Everett Millais. In "The Woodman's Daughter," Millais managed to combine classicist concern for formal proprieties with romanticist taste for "common" subjects without in any way capturing what was best in either movement.

GUILDHALL ART GALLERY CORPORATION OF LONDON

THE METROPOLITAN MUSEUM OF ART, THE THEODORE M. DAVIS COLLECTION. BEQUEST OF THEODORE M. DAVIS, 1955

The French painter Claude Monet was one of the most prolific and talented of the Impressionists. In 1894, he set out to capture the effects of light on solid forms, and painted several studies of the massive medieval cathedral of Rouen at different times of day. His work here of the cathedral at noontime is a superb example of the effort to catch personal "impressions" of reality, and forms a striking contrast to David, Delacroix, and Millais alike.

mediate spirit, for others he was little more than an extrapolation from nature. The clock had to have a clock-maker, in a popular metaphor of the time, and it stood to reason that the creation would reflect the creator. Thus, God was the embodiment of order, rationality, and all the other intellectualized qualities which classicism saw in nature. Moreover, a mechanical world ran according to its own momentum: God had made the clock, and then wound it up, but had thereafter left its gears to turn by themselves. It was this mechanistic strain in deism to which romanticists objected.

In 1802, Chateaubriand published in France a book entitled *The Genius of Christianity*. It was, unmistakably, romanticism's counterblast to deism. "Every religion has its mysteries," wrote Chateaubriand. "All nature is a secret." Against eighteenth-century rationalism (which he was, unjustly, prone to label "atheism"), Chateaubriand posed Roman Catholic Christianity—full of spiritual feeling, grand and moving ceremony, rich cultural traditions. He appealed directly to aesthetic sentiments: "Who is there but must be convinced of the beauty and the grandeur of Christianity?"

Years after the publication of *The Genius of Christianity*, Chateaubriand claimed to have despaired at first that it would have any impact: "What hope could I have, I with no name and no extollers, of destroying the influence of Voltaire . . . ?" The question was disingenuous, since Chateaubriand had already built a huge reputation upon *Atala*. Even so, his fame had less to do with the success of his newest work than did the timeliness of its publication. *The Genius of Christianity* coincided with Napoleon's official reestablishment of Roman Catholicism as "the religion of the majority of Frenchmen" after the separation of church and state in the late years of the revolution. Devout Catholics could surely remember that eight years earlier the arch-fiend Robespierre had tried to erect a version of deism—the Worship of the Supreme Being—as the state religion during the terror. In an atmosphere of political reaction and revival of religious orthodoxy, and in the midst of the official "Imperial style," Chateaubriand's encomium to Catholicism in the name of religious sensibility was bound to find a sympathetic audience.

The religious revival which accompanied romanticism—and which was, in part, stimulated by it—commonly built on two foundations: first, the fact that deism, so fashionable among the eighteenth-century elite, had become closely identified with revolutionary excesses; and, second, the growing hunger for *feeling* in religion. But romanticist religiosity did not always find its way into orthodox channels. Although God was the author of nature, nature could easily become God. Those who most ardently worshipped nature were never far from a kind of pantheism in which divinity suffused every heath and forest. Much of the religious spirit of romanticism remained as nondenominational as deism. The difference was, of course, that to the romantics God was the creator of beauty rather than order, infinite variety rather than mere logical patterns, *real* nature rather than an abstract machine. God spoke to the senses rather than the mind, was immediate and personal and inspirational rather than distant and impersonally beneficent, was a spirit rather than a being. Although the resurgence of a religion of feeling touched most established churches, romanticist spirituality remained difficult to institutionalize.*

History

In many respects, Chateaubriand's case for Christianity rested on arguments which were historical as well as aesthetic or emotional. He stressed the long Christian tradition which put the contemporary believer in touch with ages past, and particularly with that era of supreme Christian cultural achievement, the middle ages. Consciousness of history was hardly unique to romanticism; classicism glorified Greek and Roman antiquity, and many prominent eighteenth-century intellectuals had written history as well as philosophy and literature (indeed, they scarcely distinguished among the three pursuits). Indeed, the idea of history as "progress," as a process leading somewhere, had its roots in the Enlightenment. On the other hand, there was a strong tendency among *philosophe* historians to treat the past as a collection of edifying examples, as stories with a moral. History as *development* really came into its own with romanticism. Moreover, Chateaubriand's enthusiastic and widely shared medievalism was a significant departure.

The Enlightenment did not simply ignore the middle ages, it frequently treated them with disgust and contempt. Voltaire, to choose a representative and influential example, identified Christianity with superstition, fanaticism, and intolerance. The period when the Roman Catholic Church's authority was at its zenith was therefore, by definition, an age of barbarism. Those people who agreed with Voltaire quite deliberately overleaped the middle ages as they looked backward for cultural inspiration and settled instead upon *pre*-Christian antiquity. "Gothic" became a term of abuse, signifying obscurantism and hopeless intellectual backwardness.

The romantic revolt regarded the medieval centuries as natural allies. The middle ages (or so romanticist admirers claimed) had valued feeling,

* The most emotional religious movement of the time, John Wesley's evangelical Methodism, far predated romanticism, though it still had its origins in dissatisfaction with the sterile ritualism and lack of immediacy of mid-eighteenth century official Anglicanism.

had appreciated the *mysteries* of nature, man, and God. Medieval art was richly expressive, and romanticism reserved special affection for the great gothic cathedrals with their stained-glass windows and their soaring vaults disclaiming classical measure and balance. Romanticist medievalism was much more than propaganda for Roman Catholicism. The middle ages answered romanticism's need for spiritual vitality, for color, for pageantry and spectacle on a grand scale in a way that classical austerity never could. Nor was this need confined to a few intellectuals. The growing middle-class reading public of the early nineteenth century devoured the medieval "romances" of the Scottish novelist Walter Scott; the fabulously popular French author Victor Hugo frequently exploited medieval subject matter.

It would be convenient if we could say that the middle ages played the same role for romanticism that antiquity had played for classicism— convenient, but also false, since little about romanticism was so simple. Although the romanticists attempted to rehabilitate the middle ages, they did not ignore the sources of classicism itself (romantic tastes, however, appeared to prefer ancient Greek culture to the Roman civilization which had loomed so large in the eighteenth century). The German critic Friedrich Schlegel, writing in 1795, praised the capacity for feeling and the reverence for nature that he found in Greek poetry. Byron, Keats, and Shelley all recognized their spiritual affinities for ancient Greece. Goethe went further, shedding the sentimental romanticism of his youth (which, in later life, he regarded with some embarrassment) and preaching a new, revitalized classicism. Though other romanticists stopped far short of this sort of conversion, they refused to be confined to one epoch in their cultivation of the past and would hardly have thought of themselves as "mere" medievalists.

Romanticist historical-mindedness went beyond enthusiasm for certain historical periods into fascination with history as a process. While romanticism never wholly escaped from classical didacticism, it enlarged the focus from history as teacher to include history as *maker*. In this larger focus the past became a mold in which the present was cast; attention began to shift from the historical example to the historical cause. Cultural nationalism, with its search for unique historical identities, had much to do with the development of this enlarged focus; many intellectuals of the early nineteenth century had been first attracted to the study of history in hopes of revealing their people's proud past and discovering the forces which had shaped national culture.

The themes of growth, development, and change—while far from absent in the Enlightenment—permeated all manner of thought during the time of the romantic revolt. Edmund Burke's assault upon the French Revolution, for example, was fundamentally historical. Political institutions, he argued, were the product of long and subtle evolution, shaping (and being shaped by) the peculiar character of a nation's collective experience; to attempt to refashion those institutions at a single stroke according to current fashions was to suppose that history could be denied or ignored. Addressing a French proponent of the revolution, Burke admonished him that "you chose to act as if you had never been moulded into civil society, and had everything to begin anew." It is worth adding that Burke saw a respect for history as equivalent to "following nature."

The Prussian philosopher G.W.F. Hegel built an enormous reputation in the late Napoleonic and Restoration years upon a historically conscious philosophical system. For Hegel, eighteenth-century thought had examined man's present at the expense of his past (and also of his future, the product of the present). One of the principal tasks of philosophy was therefore to give structure and meaning to history—both to its past course and its future direction. Briefly stated, Hegel saw history as the progress of the collective human mind—the "World-Spirit"—toward absolute knowledge, unencumbered by superstition and error. (See Chapter 5.) The same general tendencies of thought—emphasizing growth, development, and change—were apparent in the sciences, and had been from well back in the eighteenth century. Increasingly, scientists were coming to view nature not as a static "given," but as constantly evolving; geologists and biologists in particular were anticipating most of the arguments which would make Charles Darwin famous, or notorious, later in the nineteenth century.

In addition to enlarging the focus of history, romanticism also gave history a decisive push toward its present status as an independent professional discipline. It is true that romanticist history writing, like that of the eighteenth century, was more akin to popular literature than to the formidably specialized monographs which characterize the discipline today. But the sheer volume of interest in history promoted more, and sometimes more sophisticated, study of the past. The most famous histories were still being written by intellectuals whose interests ranged also outside the study of history; but, for better or for worse, more and more history books came from the pens of men who made their living exclusively from writing and teaching about the past. Historians began more systematically to explore unpublished sources, and while broadening the scope of documentation they also began to broaden the range of their subject matter. History ceased to be only the record of great deeds performed by great men and began to dwell upon the conditions and the behavior of common people. Again, romanticism's belief in the intrinsic value and interest of the unique and the individual exerted its influence.

Romantic Art

The classical tradition had provided art with a defining framework, with models and aesthetic standards from antiquity. The romantic artist proclaimed his freedom from this tradition. His art was not limited to the refinement of tested ideas and images and patterns; it was personal, an expression of his own unique feelings. Thus he often repudiated the standard forms and rules which had guided eighteenth-century classicists. In landscape painting, to take one example, Constable ignored the orthodox wisdom which urged the use of "warm" colors (browns and golds) and painted nature as he saw it. English poets began to discard the rhymed couplet and reexplore the possibilities of blank verse and other forms. Composers increasingly departed from the formal restraint of eighteenth-century music to experiment with flowing, deeply emotional lyricism. Innovation fed upon itself, and the sense of freedom was exhilarating. "The Lord be praised!" cried Victor Hugo. "At last we are delivered from the Greeks and Romans!"

Classicism sometimes came close to arguing that art was in substantial part a craft, whose skills could only be mastered when the wisdom of the classical tradition had been assimilated. In the 1730's, Alexander Pope maintained that

> True ease in writing comes from art, not chance,
> As those move easiest who have learned to dance.

Although the best romanticist poets were usually supreme craftsmen, they refused to define artistic creation as the product of "labor and study," as Percy Bysshe Shelley put it in *A Defence of Poetry* (1821).

> Poetry is not like reasoning, a power to be exerted according to the determination of the will. A man cannot say, "I will compose poetry." The greatest poet even cannot say it; for the mind in creation is as a fading coal, which some invisible influence, like an inconstant wind, awakens to transitory brightness; this power arises from within, like the colour of a flower which fades and changes as it is developed, and the conscious portions of our natures are unprophetic either of its approach or its departure. Could this influence be durable in its original purity and force, it is impossible to predict the greatness of the results; but when composition begins, inspiration is already on the decline; and the most glorious poetry that has ever been communicated to the world is probably a feeble shadow of the original conceptions of the poet. I appeal to the greatest poets of the present day, whether it is not an error to assert that the finest passages of poetry are produced by labour and study. . . .

To the romanticist, art was a matter of inspiration, not calculation, and inspiration proceeded from anything which stirred the feelings.

Classicism, characteristically didactic, had demanded that art be lofty, noble, edifying; romanticism, in its ardor for the "natural," found beauty and moral worth in the plain and the ordinary as well. Words- worth, in his *Lyrical Ballads* (1798), deliberately eschewed convention- ally elevating subjects for "incidents and situations from common life" described "in a selection of language really used by men." His justifica- tion, from the preface to the second edition, ran in part:

> Humble and rustic life were generally chosen, because, in that condition, the essential passions of the heart find a better soil in which they can attain their maturity, are less under restraint, and speak a plainer and more em- phatic language; because in that condition of life our elementary feelings co-exist in a state of greater simplicity, and, consequently, may be more ac- curately contemplated, and more forcibly communicated; because the man- ners of rural life germinate from those elementary feelings, and, from the necessary character of rural occupations, are more easily comprehended, and are more durable; and, lastly, because in that condition the passions of men are incorporated with the beautiful and permanent forms of nature. . . .

This is not of course to say that romantic art was confined to bucolic en- thusiasms, but rather that it refused to recognize any "proper" subject matter: its spirit was expansive; its domain included whatever moved the artist. Whereas the classical tradition had once defined art, now the artist did so.

The best classicists did not simply ape the art of antiquity—more and more artists of the seventeenth and eighteenth centuries were confident that they could rival or exceed their ancient masters—but they still ac- cepted its basic norms. Moreover, they expected their audiences to do the same, just as readers and viewers and listeners expected artists to respect traditional aesthetic values and conventions. Artists might surprise their audiences, but they would rarely shock or confound them. Since romantic art was more personal (the confirmed classicist would say "more idiosyn- cratic"), the artist's relationship to his audience was more complex. Though some romanticists met with great popular favor, artists could not count upon a community of shared tastes with the audience—as was dra- matized when the premier of Hugo's play *Hernani* in 1830 was disrupted by catcalls from traditionalists and brawls in the theater. Fame and for- tune did not prevent a mood of alienation in many artists, a sense of iso- lation even from an admiring public. For the artist was a special sort of person, endowed with unusual sensitivity and expressive powers. "A poet," wrote Shelley, "as he is the author to others of the highest wisdom, pleasure, virtue, and glory, so he ought personally to be the happiest, the best, the wisest and the most illustrious of men." But such qualities could also set the artist apart from his audience. In a remarkable painting, "The Bard" (1817), the Englishman John Martin places the singer high upon a craggy peak, dominating a landscape in which the mere mortals below (outfitted in medieval garb) are dwarfed and insignificant. The bard there pictured is clearly free, but is also alone—a towering genius, perhaps, but solitary as well.

This image of the artist as a voice crying in the wilderness suggests another of which romanticism was fond—the artist as prophet, a man with a message for society. His role, wrote the Hungarian pianist and composer Franz Liszt in 1835, was "to teach the public . . . where we [all] come from, where we are going, what our mission is, what we really are! . . ." Art, by purifying and perfecting itself, would purify and perfect man; thus could Liszt write that the artist has "a great religious and social MISSION. . . ." From there it is not far to the young Richard Wagner, who saw his efforts to fuse opera and theater into a new "music drama" as but part of a broader program for revolutionizing society.

The artist prophesied man's regeneration, and his art was a means to that end. Though romanticists disagreed sharply among themselves on the political and social implications of this vision, in general they saw in art a transforming experience. In this, perhaps, they were not so far from classical didacticism as they believed.

Romanticism and Politics

The politics of romanticism have been much debated, but the search for a single formula expressing them is doomed to failure. The dispositions which made up romanticism were (it should by now be clear) far too diverse to admit of uniform political application. Romanticist intellectuals and artists ranged across the political spectrum or were sometimes indifferent to politics; romanticist influences and ideas are apparent in the thought of bitter political opponents. Sometimes individual figures turned from liberalism to conservatism within a few years, suggesting that romantic sympathies did not determine the shape of political commitments.

In general, romanticists outside of France hailed the early stages of the French Revolution as a liberating, regenerating movement. Wordsworth later recalled that the revolution first inspired in him the hope to see

> All institutes for ever blotted out
> That legalised exclusion, empty pomp
> Abolished, sensual state and cruel power
> Whether by edict of the one or few;
> And finally, as sum and crown of all,
> Should see the people having a strong hand
> In framing their own laws, whence better days
> To all mankind. . . .

Such sentiments became difficult to sustain when the revolution resorted to terror and France to foreign conquest. Wordsworth disavowed his youthful liberalism, and years later a convinced liberal like Byron would still have to admit:

> But France got drunk with blood to vomit crime,
> And fatal have her Saturnalia been
> To Freedom's cause, in every age and clime. . . .

Edmund Burke's denunciation of the revolution proceeded from assumptions which some romanticists must have shared. For Burke, society was rather like nature itself—not a machine to be manipulated at will, but a delicate organism whose workings might be permanently damaged by foolish innovation, whose "natural development" had to be respected.

> The nature of man is intricate; the objects of society are of the greatest possible complexity; and therefore no simple disposition or direction of power can be suitable either to man's nature, or to the quality of his affairs. When, I hear the simplicity of contrivance aimed at and boasted of in any new political constitutions, I am at no loss to decide that the artificers are grossly ignorant of their trade, or totally negligent of their duty. . . .

On the continent, the Swiss writer Joseph de Maistre opposed the revolution not only because of its offenses to Roman Catholicism, but also because it designed constitutions for an abstract Man. There was no such thing, complained de Maistre, as Man: there were only Frenchmen, Englishmen, Spaniards, Russians, and so forth. Nor could they write their own constitutions, which were the product of God working through history to develop rules appropriate to individual peoples. Constitutions were best left unwritten and even somewhat mysterious. The German jurist and legal philosopher Friedrich Carl von Savigny similarly warned that it could be dangerous to codify law, thus making it inflexible. Law, he wrote in 1814, had an "organic connection" with the "being and character of the nation," which was itself created by history and ever evolving.

Nationalism, cultural and otherwise, with which romanticism had such close links, is customarily thought of as a conservative force. Frequently, however, it had the backing of liberals and was stoutly opposed by the conservative powers which organized the Restoration settlement of 1814–15. When it came to domestic politics, a man like Johann Gottlieb Fichte, a German philosopher heavily influenced by early romanticism, was regarded as a conservative; but when it came to international politics, Fichte—an ardent German nationalist—found himself in the liberal camp. It is just this sort of case, of which there were many, that makes romanticist politics so elusive.

Although there were enough politically liberal romanticists about in the late eighteenth and early nineteenth centuries to discourage sweeping generalization, still in its earlier phases romanticism tended more often than not to be partnered with conservative politics. Significant deviation in this pattern only began to occur around 1830—and especially in France—when romanticist artists and intellectuals started reexamining their politics and ultimately made a vital contribution to modern socialist thought (see Chapter 5). All things considered, however, it is safest to see romanticism as a cultural movement and to avoid the temptation to search in it for any coherent political creed.

The Contribution of Romanticism

Romanticist artists often spoke of their careers in bitter, frustrated tones. John Keats, as a friend of his put it, "began life full of hopes . . . expecting the world to fall at once beneath his powers . . ."; instead, he died at twenty-five, "Unable to bear the sneers of ignorance or the attacks of envy. . . ." Despondency and recurring bouts of melancholy were something of an occupational hazard in the romantic revolt; suicide and otherwise premature deaths claimed an alarming number of talented artists. (A classicist would argue that without accepted norms, without notions of proper measure and degree, the artist was groping for the infinite and was bound to end up dejected by his failure.) Though critical appreciation and popular success were not unknown, still many artists experienced rejection—or, even worse, lack of recognition—which only reinforced their sense of alienation from their audience and isolation in their society. Besides, romanticism did not unequivocally triumph, banishing regard for classical restraints and revolutionizing the tastes and sensibilities of the early nineteenth century. Varieties of the classical tradition persisted in all the arts.

If the romanticists sometimes despaired, however, their contribution still helped remodel—if not totally renovate—European culture at the beginning of the nineteenth century. They taught, in Professor Jacques Barzun's words, "that there is more than one layer of experience," a perception which became increasingly central in modern European thought. Their views of art and the artist laid the foundation for the modern artist's relationship to society. Their tolerance for aesthetic diversity, their enthusiasm for spontaneous, personal art opened the way to fruitful creative experimentation. Finally, their passion for the unique and the individual, their role in the quest for authentic identity, did much to promote national self-consciousness and to reinforce the political developments which would remake Europe.

Part Two
THE
NINETEENTH
CENTURY

The birth of the nineteenth century was doubtless traumatic. Yet Europeans of the 1820's had not been orphaned—cleanly severed from their past by the disruptive political, socioeconomic, and intellectual developments discussed in Part One. To the contrary, the past was very much with them. They lived not only with the legacy of the French Revolution, but with the older institutions against which the revolution had been waged and which persisted well into the century. They lived in societies in which industrialization was about to work its massive transformations, but in which the old structures of rural agrarian society still endured and resisted change. In this sense, nineteenth-century European history must be studied not so much in terms of what was new as in terms of how old and new came into conflict, intermingled, achieved a new synthesis.

The first subject at hand is politics. Chapter 4 follows the frequently allied persuasions of liberalism and nationalism from the Restoration through the revolutions of 1848. Chapter 5 examines the origins, theory, and practice of socialism from the French Revolution through the Paris Commune of 1871. The means by which moderates and conservatives responded to challenges from the left—from the early 1850's into the 1880's—are discussed in Chapter 6.

With Chapters 7 and 8, we turn to the spread and the impact of modern industry in the second half of the century. Chapter 7 deals with the growth and increasing sophistication of industry, and with the changing mentalities which accompanied it. Chapter 8 explores some of the social and cultural characteristics of the new industrial age. Political responses to industrialism, from the 1880's to the eve of World War I, are the subject of Chapter 9. The final chapter of this section, Chapter 10, takes up overseas expansion and its relation to European international politics.

4 / Liberalism and Nationalism

In the years before the industrial revolution made its way to the continent, liberalism and nationalism were the principal forces of change. While nationalists often spoke of a great rising of the peoples against the arbitrary obstacles to nationhood, most liberals saw their programs as an alternative to revolution. The old order refused to budge, however, so that liberals—usually against their will—sometimes found themselves enmeshed in revolutionary upheavals. Liberal and nationalist revolt came together in 1848, that remarkable and crucially important year which did so much to change the shape of modern history.

Liberalism

Nineteenth-century European liberalism traced its immediate ancestry to the early, moderate phase of the French Revolution and to the principles embodied in the constitution of 1791. Since legalized social privilege had largely disappeared with the Old Regime, nineteenth-century liberalism concentrated on political questions: the establishment of parliamentary and constitutional government, and of certain fundamental political freedoms. A constitution would provide the legal guarantees of those freedoms; a parliament would protect the constitution and ensure that legislation was consistent with it.

Wherever monarchy survived the revolutionary-Napoleonic era with still substantial powers—which is to say, in virtually all the continental countries—liberalism was likely to find an audience. Just as absolutism was a response to civil disorder, liberalism was obviously a response to an overpowerful executive. Monarchy had shown that it could not be trusted to rule unfettered: it had levied taxes without consulting the taxpayers; it had shown scant regard for freedom of expression and other basic rights; it tended to operate irregularly and arbitrarily, rather than according to rational rules and equitable laws. Much like the aristocratic critics of eighteenth-century absolutism, the nineteenth-century liberals sought to impose checks upon royal prerogative. A constitution would therefore define the limits of the king's authority; a parliament would share power with him and see that he respected constitutional restraints.

Liberal constitutional ideas, which took their lead from the French constitution of 1791 and the short-lived Spanish constitution of 1812, assumed an exemplary form in the Belgian constitution of 1831, which guaranteed equality before the law; individual liberty; the inviolability of private property; and freedom of assembly, expression, and religion. The legislature was composed of two houses, each elected by a restricted suffrage; all financial measures required the approval of the lower house. The king shared legislative initiative with the parliament, commanded the armed forces, appointed and recalled the government ministers, and was in general responsible for the executive branch. However, the parliament could also force dismissal of the ministers and the king's orders needed a ministerial countersignature to be valid.

Clearly, in such a regime, the king is hardly stripped of all power. The Belgian liberals no more wished to abolish the executive power of government than they wished to abolish monarchy itself. Rather, they wished to subordinate the executive to the constitution—that is, to law—and deprive it of a monopoly on legislative functions.

There is a common misconception of nineteenth-century liberalism as a movement antagonistic to government. Nineteenth-century liberals, in this view, believed "that government is best which governs least," or followed Thomas Paine in regarding government as "even in its best state, a necessary evil. . . ." In fact, the liberals' attitude toward the state was much more complex. It is true that they were frequently skeptical about allowing government expansive powers, but only because they had seen so many abuses of such powers. Many liberals felt in principle that there were certain areas into which government ought not intrude: the exercise of property rights, the basic political freedoms, religious worship, and the like. On the other hand, government was plainly necessary to ensure national security and to protect civil order, especially when it appeared to be threatened by the radical left. Liberals (like most people) detested the censorship of their own views, but had few qualms about censoring republicans. Decidedly, nineteenth-century liberals were men of the center. They believed in certain political reforms as a matter of principle, but they often justified those reforms as a means of assuaging popular discontent and thus avoiding revolution. In this sense, the liberal center buffered the conservative right from the radical left.

Just as nineteenth-century liberalism was not truly antagonistic to government, neither was it merely a political version of laissez faire, an attempt by the new industrial bourgeoisie to reshape the state according to their economic ideas. Liberal political economy sometimes bore the distinct traces of selfish class interest—as when industrialists argued out of one side of their mouths against state intervention in the economy to regulate wages and working conditions and out of the other for government prohibition of trade unions or for high tariffs to protect struggling domestic industries from foreign competition. Although this narrow class-interest streak ran through early liberalism, its personnel and its objectives were broader. Landed aristocrats, professional men, journalists, and intellectuals joined with the emergent industrialist group to demand an enlarged degree of political liberty within a constitutional government and an end to the residual absolutism of the Restoration era. Nevertheless, liberalism was clearly a persuasion of the relatively comfortable: it spoke of freedom rather than of justice, of political rights rather than of the right to survival, of reform rather than of thoroughgoing renovation. The poor would have to look elsewhere for the satisfaction of their most urgent material needs. (See Chapter 5.)

Although the liberals insisted that parliamentary and constitutional government would protect the rights of all citizens, they denied that all citizens had an equal right to participate in government. Government would be *representative:* members of parliament would represent, but not be elected by, all their constituents—which was another way of saying that a well-to-do and well-educated elite would rule the vast majority of the nation. Only men of some means, men of some learning—and liberal opinion varied widely over the specific criteria—could be entrusted with the responsibilities of voting and lawmaking; they alone possessed the sophistication to interpret what was and what was not in the nation's interest. Prior to mid-century, most liberals contemplated the idea of political democracy with undisguised horror.

Nationalism

In the first half of the nineteenth century, liberalism and nationalism frequently went hand in hand. Liberals sought to reform Restoration politics; nationalists sought to revise the international settlement of 1815, to free whole peoples from subjection to foreigners, to unite culturally coherent but politically divided areas into a single nation. Born of the search for unique cultural identities at the end of the eighteenth century, nationalism received a vital stimulus from French military expansion and occupation, which served to remind the various ethnic groups of central Europe in particular of their individuality. The nationalist position of the early nineteenth century was simple: if it was wrong for the French to rule Italians, Spaniards, Dutch, or Germans, was it right for Austrians to rule Slavs, Magyars, or Italians? Did it make sense to have Russians, Prussians, and Austrians ruling Poles? * To have Dutch ruling Belgians? To have Turks ruling Greeks? Similarly, Napoleonic consolidations had fueled feelings among many Germans and Italians that their respective fragmentation into several sovereign states was unjust. German and Italian nationalists thus called for an end to petty princelings and arbitrary boundaries; common cultural traditions demanded a single German, a single Italian nation.

Nationalism—as distinct from patriotism or love of fatherland, which was a notion familiar to Greeks of the fifth century B.C.—began in an urge for national independence and national unity. Liberals generally applauded both goals, or rather, to eliminate a confusing distinction, liberals were usually nationalists (and vice versa) during the first half of the nineteenth century. Context determined priority: sympathetic Frenchmen might think of themselves first of all as liberals, since French unification and independence were not at issue while the nature of French government was; Germans might define themselves as nationalists, with the understanding that parliamentary and constitutional government would follow the primary task of unification. The programs of liberalism and nationalism were different, but the advocates of one were often the advocates of the other. It was likewise with their opponents: the same persons who resisted domestic reform largely defended the international features of the Restoration settlement. Prince Klemens von Metternich, Chancellor of the Habsburg Empire and chief architect of the post-Napoleonic repression, treated liberal reformism and national independence movements—wherever they occurred—as symptoms of the same disease, preliminary stages of the virulent republican plague.

Finally, nationalism remained, for the first half of the nineteenth century, nearly as much an affair of the upper and middle classes as liberalism, though not intentionally. Although nationalist agitators often tried to reach a wide audience, to interest "the people" in their movement, only on rare occasions before 1848 did nationalism show signs of stirring the popular imagination. Even literature which sought to locate a unique cultural identity in peasant songs and simple folk poetry was still literature—aimed at the *reading* public, which was but a fraction of the general public. Most Europeans remained sunk in the dailiness of scratching out a life, scarcely conscious of ties that bound them to a larger cultural community. For nationalism to become an issue of mass

* Russia, Prussia, and the Habsburg Empire had simply eliminated the weak independent state of Poland by three separate partitions and annexations in the last third of the eighteenth century.

politics, it would take the intense politicization of 1848 and the advance of modern industry—facilitating transportation and communication, enmeshing people in something like a national market.

Early Stirrings, 1821–32

The liberal and nationalist agitation which punctuated the decade of the 1820's was met at first with successful repression. In 1821, Metternich, intent upon protecting Austrian holdings in northern Italy, quashed liberal revolts in two independent states—Naples and Piedmont—by armed intervention. In 1823, France demonstrated that it had returned to the conservative fold when, under a mandate from the other major powers, French forces snuffed out a constitutionalist rising in Spain. But the war which the Greeks had begun in 1821 for independence from the Ottoman Empire proved more difficult.

Austria opposed any alteration in the status quo on principle, and feared besides that any stirrings of Slavic nationalism might spread to the millions of subject Slavs within its own borders. The Russian Empire, however, supported the Greeks. Russian policy turned not only on the fact that the Greeks were fellow Eastern Orthodox Christians attempting to break away from Muslim rule, but also on the fact that an independent Greece which was obligated to Russia would perhaps afford the Russians the access to the Mediterranean Sea they had sought for so long. At the same time, public sympathy for the insurgents ran high in France and Britain; romantic artists popularized their cause, Lord Byron even going to fight on the Greek side (and dying—rather unheroically, by drowning—near Missolonghi in 1824). In 1828, the Russians attacked the Turks; France and Britain gave moral support. Although the Russian offensive ultimately stalled, a multipower conference of 1829–30 determined that the complete collapse of the Ottoman Empire could only be averted by ending the war and granting Greece total independence.

The first successful nationalist revolt of the post-Napoleonic period was followed quickly by the first successful liberal revolution. Political sentiments were sharply divided in Restoration France, but King Louis XVIII was shrewd enough to recognize that a return to absolutism was out of the question. His brother and heir, who ascended the throne as Charles X in 1824, was less tolerant of parliamentary and constitutional government. His relations with the legislature, however, were relatively untroubled during the first three years of his reign. The Chamber of Deputies, elected by the 90,000 highest taxpayers (out of a population of nearly 30 million), was dominated by the so-called Ultra-Legitimists, a right-wing group with which Charles had been intimately involved before his brother's death.

The Ultras were heavily populated with aristocratic landowners, linked also—though more closely in the liberal imagination than in fact —with the Church. Liberal fears that the Church was conspiring with the Ultras to establish an inquisitorial theocracy were hardly calmed by Charles' own intense religiosity. A sacrilege law of 1825, which prescribed the death penalty for certain infractions, only reinforced the embattled mentality of the liberals. The same year, the Chamber approved another bill partially indemnifying landowners for property lost during the revolution. Although this law had the virtue of legitimizing property redistributions once and for all, liberals were convinced that it was but another attempt to make the calendar read "1788." Apprehension spread sufficiently, even among the very wealthy, so that the electorate returned a liberal majority to the Chamber in 1827. After laboring for a time with a moderate ministry, Charles suddenly appointed a new government in August 1829; at its head was the Prince Polignac, who had the reputation of being an "Ultra-Ultra." Seven months later, in an attempt to bring in a Chamber which would support his ministry, the king called new elections. Again, however, the liberals triumphed.

Charles' response was nothing less than a royal coup d'état. On July 26, 1830, he issued a series of ordinances which would have throttled the press, dissolved the Chamber once more, and established a new electoral law designed to guarantee an Ultra majority. Resistance was immediate and violent. It came from two sources: first, the liberal parliamentarians and journalists, who claimed that they were in fact the conservatives of the hour, defending the Constitutional Charter of 1814 from royal assault; and second, the Parisian working classes, brought to a fighting pitch by an economic crisis which had driven up food prices and unemployment at the same time. The workers, joined by a few enraged bourgeois, manned barricades in the capital, and not only held off royal troops but managed to take the city hall on July 29.

But Charles' abdication quickly revealed the fissures in the impromptu revolutionary coalition. The workers had experienced a reawakening of republican feeling in the last years of the Restoration and were perfectly content to see the throne stay empty. Their champion was the seventy-seven-year-old Marquis de Lafayette, whose revolutionary experiences dated back to America in the 1770's. The liberals refused to shed their monarchism simply because of one intractable monarch, however, and backed the candidacy of Louis-Philippe, Duc d'Orléans, and head of the Bourbon family's younger branch. As a youth, Louis-Philippe had served in the French revolutionary armies before fleeing into foreign exile as the revolution moved left; his father, a member of the Convention, had even voted for the execution of Louis XVI. Needless to say, Louis-Philippe had gravitated to a more conservative position by 1830. But he did agree, in negotiation with liberal politicians, to swear an oath to an only slightly revised constitution and to accept the throne by proclamation from the Chamber (or what was left of it after the Ultras departed in disgust). When Lafayette, to the consternation of the republicans, abruptly rallied to Louis-Philippe, the liberal victory was complete; and the Orléans dynasty replaced the Bourbon.

The peace settlement of 1815 had transformed Roman Catholic, French- and Flemish-speaking Belgium from a province of the Habsburg Empire into a province of the Protestant, Dutch-speaking Kingdom of the Netherlands. However, political and economic issues combined with the conflict of cultural traditions to render the union unworkable. The Dutch totally dominated the state administration. The Belgians were allowed equal representation in the parliament, but then they had a larger population. The Dutch policy of low tariffs furthermore threatened to undercut Belgian industry by allowing an influx of British goods. In August 1830, Belgian liberal nationalists, doubtless encouraged by developments in France, escalated their demands for autonomy. Violence erupted in September and fighting between Belgians and Dutch dragged on into late autumn. At last, an international conference of powers recognized an independent Belgium at the beginning of 1831. In short order, the Belgian liberals put together their constitution and installed a German prince, Leopold of Saxe-Coburg, as their king.

The events of 1830–31 demonstrate clearly that the old conservative coalition of the early Restoration was a dead letter. Austria and Russia had split over the Greek question. Even had the arch-conservative Czar Nicholas I, who came to the throne in 1825, wished to interfere in western affairs, he was fully occupied with a nationalist revolt in Russian Poland in 1831. The British had long since renounced intervention in continental affairs, except as a diplomatic mediator. Metternich was therefore confined to keeping the lid on in the Habsburg sphere of influence alone, a job which kept him busy enough. There were revolts all throughout northern and central Italy in 1831, most of which required suppression by Austrian troops. German nationalist activity prompted Metternich and his Prussian ally to force repressive legislation through the (nonelective) Diet of the German Confederation.

The liberal ferment of the early 1830's reached even to Great Britain, where the threat of royal absolutism had long receded but where pressure for parliamentary reform had been building up gradually. The British Parliament, the oldest and most powerful legislative body in Europe, rested upon a representational basis which had become increasingly obsolescent. Geared to a rural society of centuries past, the House of Commons in 1830 vastly overrepresented the countryside at the expense of urban areas—and especially some of the new industrial colossi which had shot up in the last half-century. Thanks to huge internal migrations and the decline of certain old towns, some constituencies of microscopic population had the same number of representatives as densely-packed regions. Electoral qualifications varied from place to place, and outright purchase of votes—especially where the electorate was small—was not unheard of.

Parliamentary reform developed a broad coalition in its support. Naturally, the new manufacturers expected that it would expand their influence in Parliament. But workers also demonstrated enthusiasm, even though it was not clear how they would benefit from the measure, since no one was proposing anything like a democratic franchise. Probably, working-class democrats hoped to intimidate middle-class and aristocratic reformers into a more generous reform bill. In any event, the continuous and often riotous popular pressure in favor of reform during 1831–32 was vital to the liberals' success. Finally, reform was sponsored by what at first may seem an unlikely group—the Whig party, which was dominated by the same class of country gentlemen who controlled the antireform Tory party, men largely from the overrepresented country districts which reform would trim down to size. While there may not have been much to choose between the Whigs and Tories in terms of ideology or social class, one crucial distinction was that the Tories had been in power for a half-century and the Whigs had not. Whig leaders, some of whom believed in reform on its merits, also recognized that it was a popular issue, one they might well ride into power. Besides, newly enfranchised voters and districts with enlarged representation could not help but be grateful to them.

Reform fever swept the country during the general election of 1830, and the new king, William IV, had little alternative but to appoint a Whig ministry later that year. After two years of parliamentary infighting, intermittent mob demonstrations, and a veto by the House of Lords, Tory opposition finally gave way in June 1832. The Great Reform Bill reorganized representation on a somewhat more up-to-date basis (although certain rural areas were still overrepresented), regularized suffrage requirements, and created an electorate of approximately 620,000, the largest in Europe.* The bill clearly did not replace the old landed elites with the new industrial interests; but it reflected the direction in which power was flowing.

The Revolutions of 1848

The events of 1830–32 in Greece, France, Belgium, and Britain looked, at the time, like the beginnings of a liberal and nationalist offensive

---

* The figure is for England and Wales only, whose total population was 13.8 million. Scotland and Ireland were the subjects of separate reform bills later in 1832.

which would engulf all Europe. As it turned out, there were no major changes in the structure of politics, no alterations in the map of Europe, for another sixteen years. In part, the relative calm was attributable to the vigilance of the authorities in areas such as the German Confederation, the Habsburg Empire, and the Italian peninsula. Secret police were constantly on the prowl for liberal-nationalist plots, in hope of staying a jump ahead of frequently nonexistent conspiracies. In part, the calm grew from the fact that liberals in France, Belgium, and Britain were reasonably satisfied with what they had wrought in the early 1830's and therefore settled down to defend it. In a manner of speaking, they became conservatives.

The events of 1830–32 helped open even wider the political gap between Britain and France on the one hand and central, southern, and eastern Europe on the other. Neither national independence nor constitutional and parliamentary government were any longer issues in the west; democracy and social justice henceforth became the principal subjects of politics. East of the Rhine and south of the Alps, however, absolutism still prevailed, and national unification and independence were urgent issues. It is essential to keep this lag in mind when considering the events of 1848, that remarkable year of revolution when the forces of liberalism and nationalism challenged the old order head on.

The French liberals who had installed Louis-Philippe on the throne strove thereafter to minimize the implications of 1830: there had been no revolution, they argued, only a change of dynasties. As the so-called July Monarchy settled into a conservative groove, the republicans naturally felt that they had been swindled; the republican institutions which Lafayette (who died in 1834) had promised would "surround" the monarchy were conspicuous by their absence. The republican press, though legally denied the right of explicitly calling for a republic, insisted upon a democratic franchise; the government continued to support high property qualifications; and the electorate never exceeded 240,000 (although the population had grown, by 1846, to 35.4 million). Furthermore, the regime showed itself indifferent to the lot of its least fortunate citizens. In the face of mounting poverty and unemployment, especially among urban workers (a phenomenon which was indignantly documented and publicized by social critics on the left), government inaction was nearly total.

In 1846, a poor cereal harvest sent the price of bread—the staple item in the working-class diet—sharply upward. This "subsistence crisis," as the French called it, dragged on into early 1848. At the same time, the left stepped up its agitation for suffrage reform by sponsoring a series of political banquets for middle-class sympathizers across the nation in the second half of 1847. When the reformers attempted to stage a banquet in Paris in February 1848, the government refused permission. The banquet organizers, a coalition of Orléanist liberals and moderate republicans, were anxious to avoid trouble; revolution was the farthest thing from their minds. On February 22, however, pro-reform students demonstrated against the government's decision, and in the highly charged atmosphere of the capital, push came to shove not long after the intervention of the riot police. Spontaneously, barricades sprang up in the working-class districts, where deprivation and a tradition of republican commitment drove people into the streets to do battle with the government. Just how shallowly the roots of the July Monarchy had run was soon clear: the National Guard, a middle-class militia organized for domestic peacekeeping, defected to the revolutionaries in large numbers. By February 24, the insurgents captured the royal palace. Not long before, Louis-Philippe had abdicated and fled into exile, to be replaced a few hours later by a republican Provisional Government acclaimed by the revolutionary crowds.

The French Revolution of 1848 emboldened the partisans of change elsewhere in Europe, but its issues and its course were different from the other revolutions which followed. The "social question"—that is, the condition of the urban poor—dominated French politics in 1848. Laborers and their socialist spokesmen voiced, and the propertied classes resisted, a "right to work," by which the laborers meant a guarantee of employment or, in its absence, adequate welfare provisions. The specter of social revolution mobilized the propertied classes; and when Parisian workers, in frustration and despair, took to the streets again in mid-June, a horrible civil war raged for four days. The forces of order, led by the moderate republican government, crushed the workers' revolt; but in the process they also crippled the republic itself, which limped along in name only for another four years. Power passed increasingly into the hands of conservative monarchists, who used it to repress republicanism wherever it dared show itself. (See Chapter 5.)

To the east and the south, there was also plentiful lower-class misery. Yet the issues of liberal and nationalist politics had not yet been faced there, as they had in France, so that it was perhaps inevitable that conflicts over government and nationhood would overshadow the social question.

It was the Habsburg Empire which felt the first vibrations of the February revolution of 1848. Hard on the heels of the news from France came word of liberal agitation in several south German states. Viennese liberals were soon passing from hand to hand copies of a speech made in Budapest by Lajos Kossuth, a Hungarian nationalist, who called for the immediate enactment of a constitution. Reformist petitions poured in upon the autocratic government, which threatened in turn to prosecute their authors. The government's unflinching posture of resistance held out not the least hope of change, while at the same time political excitement mounted rapidly in the imperial capital. The liberals were unable to give much shape to these feelings. Leaderless and unorganized—the government would, of course, have regarded any hint of political organization as seditious, and acted accordingly—the liberals spoke in rather vague terms about "reform," demanded a constitution, but said little about what would be in it. Thus, the Viennese revolution developed not from reformist planning but, as in Paris, from a spontaneous explosion.

On March 13, 1848, a crowd made up mostly of well-dressed burghers gathered in support of the reform petitions. Imperial troops ordered to clear the square met with some resistance, and they responded by firing into the crowd, killing five persons. Within hours, barricades were up and Vienna was in revolt. Although the insurgents were not as militarily successful as their Parisian counterparts had been, still they were able to extract one concession from the government. On the evening of the 13th, Emperor Ferdinand dismissed Metternich, who had been the personification of repression throughout Europe for more than thirty years. Fighting continued, however, and when left-wing student groups were able to stir the working-class districts outside the city walls into insurrection, the government buckled. Ferdinand lifted the rule of censorship and promised to meet with elected representatives of the realm to discuss the subject of a constitution.

The liberal revolution in Vienna was accompanied by nationalist risings throughout the Empire. Magyars, Czechs, Poles, South Slavs, and Italians called for independence, or at the very least autonomous status within the empire. And, to the north, the revolutionary fever was rising in the German Confederation. In the smaller German states of the south and southwest, the more supple princes were meeting constitutionalist demands with accommodations, hoping that they could preserve much of their power by sacrificing a little of it. But the key to German politics was Prussia, which had combined with Austria for a generation to hold liberalism at bay.

King Frederick William IV had ruled Prussia in conjunction with the noble landlord class known as the Junkers, a class which staffed the officer corps of the army and the upper echelons of the bureaucracy. Given its head, this hard-bitten ruling elite could probably have smashed the reformist movement, which began public demonstrations in early March and which gathered considerable momentum when the news of Metternich's dismissal reached Berlin on March 16. When a large crowd gathered in the courtyard of the royal palace on the 18th to hear the king's response to liberal demands, two gunshots set off panic. Though it was not, and is not, known who fired the shots, and though they struck no one, the crowd assumed that they were an overture to massacre being sounded by the troops guarding the palace. The crowd dispersed, but only to build barricades. Within twenty-four hours, however, the army had scattered most of the insurgents and confined the street fighting to one section of the capital. But Frederick William, deeply distressed at the sight of his soldiers killing his subjects, preferred concession to further bloodshed; therefore, he had the Berlin garrison withdraw from the city. Ten days later, he appointed a new ministry with a middle-class liberal at its head.

With the liberal tide running high, the nationalist current began to follow. The conservative governments of Prussia and Austria had long co-operated to keep the German Confederation weak and divided: Prussia, on the ground that it sought to dominate northern Europe and would be swallowed up in and unable to dominate a unified Germany; the Empire, on the ground that such a state would replace it as the supreme power in central Europe. By late March 1848, however, the revolutions in Vienna and Berlin had apparently removed the major obstacles to forging the German states into a single nation under a liberal constitution. A committee of German liberal nationalists invited some 500 delegates from all members of the Confederation to meet in Frankfurt as a "Pre-Parliament" and implement national unification. The Pre-Parliament called for elections to a constituent assembly which would draft a constitution for the new Germany. Although, in principle, the vote was to be by universal male suffrage, the rulings on voter qualifications were left to the individual states, in which less generous authorities tended to limit the franchise to property owners. In any case, the elected parliament convened in Frankfurt on May 18 and set about its historic task. The nationalist vision appeared close to fulfillment.

There was cause for optimism in Italy, too, where—as in Germany—the liberal assault preceded the nationalist one. Indeed, Sicilian reformers had picked up arms before the French and, after a savage struggle in early 1848, had wrenched a constitution from the king of Naples and Sicily. Liberals elsewhere won similar prizes, most notably in Piedmont—the largest state in northern Italy—and in the Papal States of the center, where Pope Pius IX also ruled as temporal sovereign. Then, on March 16, word of Metternich's dismissal—the same Metternich who had once contemptuously remarked that Italy was nothing more than a "geographical expression"—touched off insurrection in Austria's Italian possessions, Lombardy and Venetia. By March 22, Habsburg forces had been driven out of the two provincial capitals, Milan and Venice.

The dream of Italian unification varied with the dreamer. The great romantic nationalist Giuseppe Mazzini preached unification under a democratic republic. Roman Catholic unificationists looked to the papacy for leadership; they thought their hour had come in 1846 when Pius IX ascended the Holy See, accompanied by vague hints of liberal-nationalist leanings. But Pius proved to be, in the course of 1848, a strict conservative, committed to a preservation of the status quo. Moderate liberals fixed their hopes on Piedmont, where the king, Charles Albert, had granted a liberal constitution in early 1848. The Piedmontese scenario for unification was modest, and not a trifle imperialistic. It envisioned not so much Italian unity as Piedmontese expansion so as to absorb the northern third or so of the peninsula. Anything more, leaders in Turin feared, would see Piedmont submerged in a state too large for it to control. As disappointing as such plans were to more ambitious nationalists, they were nonetheless a start; besides, Piedmont alone of the Italian states was in a position to evict the Austrians from northern Italy. Since Italian independence, in whatever shape, was unthinkable without dispatching the Habsburgs, most nationalists rallied behind Piedmont when it declared war on Austria in March 1848.

The Counterrevolutionary Triumph

The most conspicuous fact about early 1848—and, for the revolutionaries, the most ominous one—was that only one ruler in central Europe lost his throne.* In general, the revolutions had resulted in royally granted constitutions or promises of reform and in the appointment of new liberal ministers. The old conservative institutions—the crown, the landed aristocracy, the bureaucracy, the Church—had not been destroyed. Once they recovered from the shock of revolution, they discovered that they were still in an excellent position to counterattack. The most important thing to be regained was self-confidence. The revolutions of 1848 had struck with incredible speed: within a month, they had apparently liberalized most of Europe, giving the impression of an inexorable force of nature which was not to be turned back.

The key to the revolutions in central Europe was the Habsburg Empire. If liberalism and nationalism triumphed there, the way was open to change in both Germany and Italy; if conservatives regained the upper hand, the Habsburgs would be free to roll back the revolutions to their north and south. In the summer of 1848, counterrevolutionaries in the Empire demonstrated that they had only been stunned—and not defeated—by the events of March. They still maintained control of the army, which they used to crush nationalist revolts in the provinces and eventually turned against liberals in Vienna. In June, Prince Windischgrätz, commander of the imperial garrison in Prague, seized upon the occasion of some popular disorders there to bombard the city, scatter the Czech liberal nationalist movement, and reassert the authority of the old order. The next month, Austrian troops in Lombardy decisively defeated

---

* Ludwig I of Bavaria abdicated in favor of his son on March 19.

Charles Albert at Custozza, thus exploding Piedmontese dreams of a partial Italian unification. Buoyed up by this military resurgence, conservatives at the imperial court cleverly manipulated ethnic hostilities within the Empire in order to meet the challenge of Magyar separatism. Specifically, they were able to set the Croats against the Magyars, and in the autumn Croatian forces invaded Hungary.

By October, the counterrevolutionaries were confident enough of their renewed strength to attempt to win back the capital city. After a siege of nearly three weeks, Vienna fell to Windischgrätz on October 31. Austrian troops then joined the Croatians in Hungary, where nationalist leaders (who would soon proclaim an independent Hungarian republic with Kossuth at its head) had taken to the hinterland. In August 1849, the Austrians finally triumphed—though only after accepting military assistance from neighboring Russia, which was anxious to see an end to liberal nationalist activities on its border.

Meanwhile, conservatives in the Habsburg Empire paid lip service to liberal opinion by granting a constitution for the Empire which would have established a limited version of parliamentary government. However, the new chancellor, Prince Felix zu Schwarzenberg (a brother-in-law of Windischgrätz), refused to allow the constitution to take effect until "order" had been restored—which it never was, to his satisfaction. Yet 1849 was not simply a return to 1847. For one thing, administrative centralization was tightened up appreciably, so that the subject nationalities had hardly the faintest guise of autonomy. For another, there was significant turnover in the upper ranks of government. The men of the Metternich era gave way to younger, tougher, more efficiently repressive rulers. Even the imperial crown itself passed to a new head. In December 1848, Schwarzenberg persuaded the incompetent Ferdinand to abdicate in favor of Franz Joseph, his eighteen-year-old nephew. The new emperor, who ruled for nearly sixty-eight years, was in close agreement with Schwarzenberg on policy matters; together, they determined to reinvigorate an Empire which, just months before, had seemed on the verge of disintegration.

Once the dust had cleared, in the summer of 1848, German conservatives could take some solace from the fact that much of the old order remained intact. Although the Frankfurt Parliament was preparing to unite Germany under a liberal constitution, the parliament's authority was less legal than moral and its political status vis-à-vis the sovereign princes was questionable. Besides, the liberal, middle-class majority was hostile both to the small democratic movement which was calling for a German republic and to the demands of labor, whose representatives wanted the constitution to recognize the need for appropriate social reforms. The liberals were therefore finding themselves increasingly isolated, with no allies in the impending struggle with the right. Finally, the liberals were divided against themselves, unable to agree on just which territories would comprise the new Germany and on certain other features of the constitution as well. Would the new Germany bring together German-speaking peoples only (including those of Austria) or would it also take in, say, the Poles of East Prussia, themselves in revolt for an independent Poland?

Once the authority of the Frankfurt Parliament had been effectively challenged, the counterrevolutionaries could plainly see on what a fragile base the liberal nationalist hopes rested and what little distance the March revolution had actually traveled. A territorial dispute with Denmark over two neighboring duchies of dubious international status, Schleswig and Holstein, led the parliament to authorize Prussian military intervention on its behalf. Frederick William IV of Prussia never had much enthusiasm for this war, since he disliked working at the command of the Frankfurt liberals. Strong diplomatic protests from Great Britain and Russia gave him just the excuse he needed; in August 1848, he concluded peace with Denmark, though without any prior authorization from the Frankfurt Parliament. The parliament howled at this defiance —in vain, for it had no military forces sufficient either for the resumption of the war or for disciplinary action against Prussia. The lesson was unmistakable: the Frankfurt Parliament's authority rested upon consent, not power.

Shortly thereafter, Frederick William moved against liberals in his own kingdom. After having dismissed his liberal ministry with impunity, he exploited middle-class fears of insurrection from the small but vocal radical left in Berlin, and brought royal troops back into the capital in October. In November, the government declared a state of siege in Berlin, thus choking off political opposition. In December, it handed down a constitution which was designed to appease the liberals by establishing a two-house parliament. But the electoral law also ensured that the wealthiest 20 percent of the population elected fully two-thirds of the lower house. Most important, the king remained firmly in control of the army.

With reaction ascendant in Vienna, Berlin, and throughout the lesser German states (where princes were now emboldened to dismiss many of the liberal ministers they had taken on in March), the Frankfurt Parliament's days were clearly numbered. In a last, desperate effort to salvage something from the wreckage, the parliament offered the crown of a united Germany to the very man who had defied its authority the previous summer—Frederick William IV. The Prussian king contemptuously rejected this "swine's crown," as he called it, along with the liberal constitution under which he would have been obliged to rule. In the summer of 1849, what was left of the old Frankfurt Parliament (now meeting in Stuttgart) dispersed ingloriously under the prodding of Prussian bayonets.

To all intents and purposes, the Italian liberal-nationalist movement had been defeated at Custozza on July 23, 1848. What followed was little more than futile resistance against superior odds. In November, a republican revolution in Rome sent Pius IX scurrying into exile. But the Roman republic, which soon placed Giuseppe Mazzini at its head, was virtually isolated against the counterrevolution. When Charles Albert of Piedmont tried to renew the war in the north, the Austrians beat him badly at Novara in March 1849. The Piedmontese king thereupon abdicated in favor of his son, Victor Emmanuel. Habsburg troops meanwhile besieged Venice, where the republic finally buckled in August 1849. Two months earlier, the Roman republic had capitulated to a French expeditionary force. (The French Second Republic had by this time fallen into the hands of reactionaries determined, among other things, to restore the temporal power of the papacy.) The Roman republicans were no match for the French, and Giuseppe Garibaldi's imaginative and heroic defense of the city only delayed the inevitable.

The Impact of 1848

The revolutions of 1848 are most famous for their failure; one historian referred to that eventful year as "the turning point at which European history failed to turn." The hopes of spring had almost everywhere faded by autumn, and the vitality of the counterrevolution by 1849 was undeniable. The explanation for this sharp reversal lay primarily in the revolutionaries' inability, or refusal, to be revolutionary enough, their failure to strike directly at the power of the conservative elites, their assumption that the events of March had rendered the old order impotent rather than merely incapacitated for the moment.

Yet 1848 was no dead end for liberals and nationalists, however swift and impressive the triumph of counterrevolution. In spite of electoral restrictions, for example, Prussian liberals made impressive gains in the new legislature. In spite of the debacles of Custozza and Novara, Piedmontese leaders were within a few years laying plans for ejecting the Austrians from Italy. The counterrevolution had beaten back the liberal nationalist assault, but it had neither destroyed its enemy nor removed the root causes of discontent. Thus, where the remedy for reformist agitation was more repression, the most that the authorities could expect was a temporary abeyance of the symptoms. Moreover, the nationalist ferment of 1848–49 had tended to popularize the issue and, especially where war had erupted, to attract larger segments of the population than ever before into unificationist and independence movements.

Far from being a dead end, 1848 clearly anticipated some of the major political developments of the next generation. It accurately described the ethnic hostilities which would rack the Habsburg Empire and strongly hinted that the Austrians' days of sole dominance were numbered. It demonstrated that Italian unification was unthinkable without war, and that war against the Habsburgs was unthinkable without a powerful ally. Frederick William IV's brief dalliance with the idea of German unification in 1850 was the first crack in the liberal monopoly on nationalism. (See Chapter 6.) Finally, the emergence of a vocal socialist movement in France posed a threat to traditional values beside which liberalism, nationalism, and even republicanism paled by comparison.

5 / *Socialism*

Socialism was a response to industrial capitalism. It was not directed at industrialization per se; mature socialism accepted modern industry but rejected the capitalistic organization in which (it was argued) owners exploited workers. By the same token, capitalism had been present for centuries prior to the industrial revolution without provoking anything like the socialist outcry of the nineteenth century. It was the sudden appearance of a capitalist industrial revolution which prompted critics to search for an alternative form of social organization.

Industrial capitalism made its debut in Britain, but socialism was international in origin. The British provided a social laboratory, as it were, in which the nature of industrial capitalist society could be observed; and they made important contributions to the budding discipline of economics upon which later social critics drew. (One might add that they also provided desk space at the British Museum for Karl Marx to conduct his research.) From France came both the revolutionary working-class political movements which eventually fused with socialism and a number of suggestive theoretical critiques of industrial capitalism. Germany contributed the intellectual structure of socialism, synthesizing selected features of the French and British experiences with ingredients from German philosophy.

Socialism and the French Revolution

There have been several attempts to locate the origins of socialism in the French Revolution. For Karl Marx, the French upheaval was not itself a socialist revolution, but it performed the essential function of creating the framework within which a socialist revolution was possible. In Marxist language, it was a "bourgeois revolution": it marked the replacement of the aristocracy by the bourgeoisie as the dominant social class; it signified the beginning of a transition from a rural, agrarian society of noble landlords and peasant masses to an urban, industrial-capitalist society of middle-class entrepreneurs and of proletarians. Marx argued that socialist revolution, in which the working-class breaks free from the chains of wage slavery, was only possible after the full development of industrial capitalism had polarized class relationships; therefore the French Revolution clearly performed a major service by facilitating that development.

The Marxist interpretation has not gone unchallenged, though there is no room here to do more than hint at some of the points of controversy. Skeptics insist that a dispassionate study of the revolution reveals very little evidence of the sort of simplistic class conflict—aristocracy versus bourgeoisie—that the Marxists profess to see. Moreover, if the revolution in fact gave rise to "bourgeois industrial-capitalist society," it took its time in doing so. It is hard to find traces of such a society before the 1830's; urban population did not outnumber rural population until fully a century after that. The implication is that bourgeois society had its origins in other sources than the revolution, which critics of Marx tend to see as a fundamentally political conflict between socially heterogeneous groups. Defenders of the Marxist interpretation, many of whom are not "Marxists" in any formal sense at all, point to the revolution's sanctification of private property, its legal strictures against workers' associations (that is, proto-labor unions), its abolition of aristocratic privilege. They remind us that the revolutionaries of 1789 were earnestly concerned with rationalizing commercial codes, state administration, weights and measures, and with breaking the stranglehold of internal tariffs and tolls upon domestic commerce. No convincing resolution to this debate is presently in sight; both sides doubtless have a degree of truth in their arguments, although the mounting evidence for the social complexity of revolutionary conflicts is beginning to become impressive.

There have been efforts to connect socialism with the revolution more directly, principally by claiming the parentage of modern socialism for certain figures and movements of the revolutionary decade. None, however, were of particular influence or size. During the period of the terror, the active state interference in the economy to regulate prices and wages grew out of the exigencies of war. By and large, the members of the Convention ideally preferred a policy closer to laissez faire. The democratic radicalism of the Parisian crowds of the 1790's later proved susceptible to socialist appeals; at the time, however, most of the revolutionary populace supported the institution of private property. For progenitors of socialism, one is forced to turn to marginal and rather bizarre individuals who proposed to remedy the situation of the poor by expropriating the wealth of the rich. The only one of them to whom any nineteenth-century socialists traced lineage was a man named Babeuf, who rejected his Christian names (François-Noël) in favor of the more suitably classical one of Gracchus. Babeuf's aim was simple: he would create a truly egalitarian society in which there was no private property and all goods were equally shared. Such visions were a trifle expansive, even for so indulgent a regime as the Directory, which put Babeuf and several of his followers to the guillotine in 1797.

Although the French Revolution was the incubator of modern radical politics, its relationship to socialism is dubious. In the search for socialism's ancestors, one can point with more confidence to two Frenchmen who regarded the revolution with hostility, for it had handled them both roughly. The first of these, Claude-Henri de Rouvroy, Comte de Saint-Simon, had welcomed the coming of the revolution and even renounced his noble title because of it. But he came to grief during the terror, landed in prison, and narrowly escaped execution. Thereafter, he made a fortune, then lost it; the early years of the nineteenth century found him an impecunious pamphleteer, the author of various sweeping proposals for a unified federation of European states and for a new religion to replace Christianity.

But Saint-Simon was more than a slightly dotty aristocrat down on his luck. Though incapable of lengthily sustained analysis, his mind bristled with insights on the direction of social change. Saint-Simon correctly foresaw that the industrial society of the future would depend upon the vitality of its producers—by which he meant technicians and scientists as well as laborers—and not upon that of its titled aristocrats. He pleaded for an efficient, rationally organized society, one which did not pit its productive forces against one another in wasteful competition but which promoted the cooperation—or, to use his word, the "association"—of those forces. For Saint-Simon, the key to a healthy modern economy was credit—loaned capital—which would finance promising business ventures. Credit was to be centralized in a state bank and dispensed by financiers, the chief decision makers in his system.

It may be hard to see much in these scattered suggestions arising from the thought of Saint-Simon to resemble socialism as the twentieth century thinks of it. But the traces are there: the notion that the economy could be harnessed to the welfare of the whole society rather than released to create private profits, the critique of capitalism's competitive ethic, the call for nationalization of capital. Further confusion has arisen from the fact that socialism is customarily seen as a persuasion of the political left, while Saint-Simon's schemes smack of authoritarianism, with little room in his efficient society for democratic politics. The confusion is understandable. It was not until the 1830's that the people who were just beginning to use the word "socialism" showed much interest in political questions. Prior to that time, proto-socialists remained largely indifferent to politics in general and even suspicious of democracy in particular. Indeed, the term "socialist" originally meant nothing more than a person interested in "the social question," the problem of mass poverty.

Charles Fourier, like Saint-Simon, had little reason to think well of the revolution. As a young businessman in Lyon, he took sides with the movement in that city which opposed the dominance of radical Paris in 1793 and had his inventory destroyed for his trouble. Thereafter, he was forced to eke out a living as a salesman, using his spare time to contemplate an alternative to the capitalist system he had come to despise so warmly. Although Fourier's writings ranged over a vast array of subjects, commentators have tended to fix upon his more colorful predictions (as, for example, that the aurora borealis would turn the oceans into lemonade). But certain of his critical commentaries upon capitalism were acute and certain of his proposals—such as that concerning the liberation of women from a status scarcely superior to that of breeder-slaves—were far ahead of their time.

Perhaps Fourier's best-known contribution was a plan for social reorganization. He envisioned the construction of small, self-sufficient communities (known as "phalanxes") designed to meet the full scope of human needs—not merely economic needs, but cultural and sensual ones as well. Fourier calculated life in the phalanx (each of which would include exactly 1,620 persons) down to the last detail; every minute, at work or play, was prescribed in advance, in a fashion which could only offend the sensibilities of liberals and democrats. But Fourier was not interested in mere political liberty. His goal was human happiness, the harmonious integration of the human passions, a goal whose attainment could not be accomplished by either competition or caprice. Work was to be undertaken cooperatively, in teams; moreover, persons were to be assigned to tasks which—by personality and background—they were liable to find attractive and fulfilling. Although Fourier's specific brand of utopianism failed to take root in France, his effort to design ideal cooperative communities was taken up by a whole generation of social critics.*

Social Romanticism

The sort of industrial capitalist society with which socialism would ultimately do battle was being created by the grinding of British machines, and simultaneously being analyzed—and justified—by a group of British economic theorists (such as Ricardo) upon whom the early social-

* There were several attempts—all ultimately failures—to construct Fourierist phalanxes in the United States.

ists would depend heavily. Strangely, however, Britain sired but one socialist movement of note. It was led by the industrialist Robert Owen,
who began early in the nineteenth century as a pioneer in the decent
treatment of one's own workers and advanced, a generation later, to the
sponsorship of experimental cooperative communities in America. For
the first fifty years of the century, the language of socialism was French,
even though large-scale industrial capitalism made its appearance in
France only haltingly. In part, the explanation for this seeming paradox
is that Saint-Simon and Fourier gave French social thought a unique impetus, driving it in directions which Marx himself later found useful. In
part, it is that certain writers found it possible to graft socialism onto the
democratic and republican heritage of the revolution and were able to interest the French urban working classes in the result.

The focal point of French socialism was Paris, the nation's largest
urban agglomeration. Paris had grown from half a million inhabitants at
the beginning of the nineteenth century to twice that number by 1846, a
growth it was by no means equipped to absorb. Employment opportunities, housing, sanitation, and recreational facilities were wholly inadequate to this human flood. Swarms of peasants and small-town laborers
who came to Paris in search of a better life quickly found themselves
trapped in some of the more wretched slums in Europe.

Since Paris was also a cultural and intellectual capital, France's leading writers and artists were also witness to this spectacle. Especially after
1830, when the crisis became most conspicuous, most of those involved in
the French version of the romantic revolt responded with a combination
of sympathy and outrage. Touched by the sufferings of the poor, indignant with a political system which could regard the problem with indif-
ference, French romanticists broke free from the conservatism which Chateaubriand and de Maistre had bequeathed them and turned to fervent
social involvement. They read Fourier; they read Saint-Simon; and especially they read the systematizations and extensions of Saint-Simonianism
by the little knot of young men who had gathered round the master in
his later years and determined to spread the gospel after his death. The
"associationist" strain ran through virtually all the social romanticism of
these years; many writers tried their hand at imagining ideal communities.

In intellectual terms, the most important function performed by social
romanticism was that of criticism. An extensive literature detailed, and
deplored, the miserable condition of the urban poor. Theorists, extrapo-
lating from the British experience, anticipated the full-scale arrival of
capitalist industry in France and prepared a thorough critique of its ills
—its failure to provide full and fairly remunerated employment, its refusal to permit an equitable distribution of goods, its built-in proclivity

for exploitation of workers. By the 1840's, just enough of the new industry had grown up in France to give some substance to the criticism.

As French novelists poured out only technically fictionalized accounts of urban poverty (and the romanticist predilection for empirical observation served them well here), and as critics tried to imagine what a just society would look like, the working poor about whom the social romanticists were writing began to take notice. Many workers hewed to the democratic republicanism whose shock troops their forebears of the 1790's had been. But during the July Monarchy, the pressure of economic circumstances and certain reorientations in the leadership of the French left brought large numbers of the urban poor into the socialist camp. A number of radical democrats began to argue that political democracy was meaningless unless accompanied by an improvement in social conditions. "The republic without socialism," wrote Pierre Leroux, an early disciple of Saint-Simon, "is absurd." Men who had hoped that the revolution of 1830 would bring the republic now edged leftward and even began to suggest that social change should take priority over political reform. Appeals combining political and social democracy were made directly to the working-class community, apparently with some success—though not as much as supposed by conservatives, who were ready to see in every worker a revolutionary socialist panting for both the property and the blood of the bourgeoisie.

There are three important points to be made about the socialist movement in the French working classes. First, it was very far from being unified or well-organized. Rival sects abounded on the French left, competing with one another as strenuously as they opposed the monarchy. Government repression kept the various groups off-balance and many of their respective leaders behind bars; the more militant revolutionaries were obliged to operate out of underground secret societies. Next, the doctrinal content of the movement often fell short of modern conceptions of socialism. For example, the most popular slogan, coined by socialist writer Louis Blanc, was the "right to work"—by which it was meant that a worker had a right to support himself by honest labor and that if the economy failed to provide full employment he had the right to subsistence from public funds. In spite of conservative fears, social romanticism raised few voices against the institution of private property, though there was ample complaint about the distribution of property. Finally, the movement was almost exclusively confined to the large and middling cities. The countryside, where fully three-fourths of the French population still resided, had enormous social problems of its own. But social romanticists kept their attention riveted on the cities and seemed to assume—when they thought about it at all—that the great mass of peasants lay firmly in the clutch of reactionary landlords and priests.

The French Second Republic

The street fighting which broke out in Paris on February 22, 1848, had its immediate origins in political questions such as suffrage reform and freedom of assembly. (See Chapter 4.) But once Louis-Philippe had been put to flight and the republic proclaimed, it immediately became clear how violently social concerns bubbled beneath the surface. The new Provisional Government included Louis Blanc and one militant worker from the secret societies, but its majority was composed of more moderate— and antisocialist—republicans. From the very beginning, the Parisian crowds which had made the revolution clamored for action—the guarantee of the "right to work," appropriate welfare measures for the poor, the replacement of monarchist civil servants with unemployed (and often unskilled) laborers, the creation of a Ministry of Progress to deal with social problems, a symbolic substitution of the revolutionary red flag for the traditional tricolor. While the government tried to resist and deflect such demands, radical democratic and socialist leaders attempted to give organizational coherence to their movement by grouping their respective followers into political clubs (of which some 200 quickly sprouted). The club movement became the focus both of working-class agitation and of moderate and conservative apprehension.

Besides opposing socialism on principle, the majority in the Provisional Government feared that Parisian club activism—which took the occasional form of massive street demonstrations—would set off a serious reaction in the countryside. After all, the infant regime had begun by establishing universal adult male suffrage, which inflated the number of eligible voters from about 240,000 to over nine million, most of them peasants. If, indeed, most peasants were under the influence of conservative local elites, and if those elites could paint the republic as the tool of socialist madmen intent upon collectivizing even the tiniest peasant plot, then democracy might well backfire into the face of the democrats. Nobody seems to have asked what would have happened had republicans, moderate and socialist alike, tried to make their creeds relevant to the rural masses. In the April 1848 campaign for elections to the National Constituent Assembly, the republicans concentrated on the cities, with their relatively small vote, and left the countryside to its own devices. With no challenge being raised to conservative propaganda, rural voters thus elected an assembly heavily populated with conservative monarchists. Socialists and sympathetic radicals, for their part, filled only about seventy of the 900 seats.

The April election touched off a vicious, inexorable spiral of conflict over the next two months. The radical left felt somehow cheated by the election, and in mid-May a large club demonstration even invaded the assembly's hall in an abortive putsch which found the established authorities back in control by nightfall. The assembly's conservative majority, reasoning that a showdown was unavoidable, began to dismantle the welfare structure which the Provisional Government—under pressure from the crowds—had built to put unemployed workers on a dole. The clubs took this policy to mean that they could expect not the least sympathy for social reform from the assembly, and late in June Parisian workers put up barricades once more.

In the four so-called June Days which followed, socialism became identified (in the middle-class mind, at least) with bloody civil war in much the same way that the terror had linked republicanism to the guillotine a half-century earlier. However, the June Days were not a socialist revolt so much as a defensive eruption meant to preserve what many workers saw as the first part of a social reform program. But the insurgents were linked with the left-wing club and working-class movements in which so many various socialist currents swirled about. We now know that class lines were not sharply drawn in this awful struggle. Government forces, which may have lost as many as 1000 men, included some workers in various militia units; the ultimately unsuccessful insurgents, who probably lost at least 2000, were joined by a number of middle-class radicals. But contemporaries on both sides of the barricades regarded such scholarly qualifications as meaningless; for them, the June Days were class war, pure and simple.

The Second Republic remained firmly in the hands of the June victors—first, the moderate republicans and, later, the conservative monarchists (whose internal divisions between partisans of the Bourbon and Orléans lines kept them from attempting a restoration). With fears of renewed insurrection running high, the situation was ripe for a strongman who could administer the repression. The man who offered himself had, at least, the right name for the job: he was Louis-Napoleon Bonaparte, nephew, and now political heir, of the former Emperor. Elected president of the republic by a landslide vote in December 1848, he embarked upon a devious course which brought him, three years later, to a coup d'état which destroyed the regime and established a new empire.

In the meanwhile, French socialism continued to show signs of life. Socialists and radical democrats allied in elections to a new legislature in 1849 and more than doubled their representation from the previous year. The coup d'état of 1851 spelled their eclipse for twenty years, however. In the interim, socialism began to be reshaped by a man who had closely followed—and was deeply indebted to—events and ideas in France and Britain, but who brought to them a German philosophical perspective.

Karl Marx

Born in 1818 of a middle-class family in the Prussian Rhineland, Karl Marx pursued an academic career which took him in 1836 to the University of Berlin as a philosophy student. The dominant intellectual influence in Berlin was that of Georg Wilhelm Friedrich Hegel, who had taught at the University prior to his death in 1831. Hegel had imparted a special intellectual vocabulary and mode of analysis to a whole generation of philosophy students. Though his exposition was often cumbersome and abstruse, his appeal was nonetheless powerful and his impact almost incalculable.

Hegel's philosophy shares many of the dispositions of romanticism. It is thoroughly historical, insistent that the understanding of the present (and the future) depends upon unraveling the mysteries of the past; it emphasizes the importance of man's spiritual life; and it shows a preference for organic wholes. But very far from subordinating intellect to emotions, Hegel placed reason at the very center of his vast, complex, and all-embracing system. History, *true* history, was the history of mind, or at least of its rational faculties. Hegel argued that history was the process of self-realization by the Spirit, or World-Spirit (by which he meant something like the collective human mind—past, present, and future). As Spirit came to realize or "know" itself, it would be completely free, unfettered by falsehood, superstition, or error. Thus the end toward which history was working—and there had to be a goal, Hegel convinced his disciples, or else history was absurd—was absolute knowledge, mind's total conquest of the world.

On the face of it, there may seem to be little in Hegelianism to support even a moderately liberal political outlook, much less the revolutionary philosophy which Marx came to formulate. Indeed, though a youthful admirer of the early stages of the French Revolution, Hegel in later years was marked by an increasing retreat into conservative Lutheranism and a tendency to see the authoritarian Prussian state as the contemporary embodiment of the World-Spirit. But Hegel had also contended, in one of his characteristically cryptic utterances, "What is real is rational; what is rational, real." Students of conservative political leanings naturally took the first part of this remark to mean that the status quo was rationality itself. Those with more liberal sentiments concentrated on the second part, which they took as an invitation to make reality rational—a task which was possible precisely because mind was destined to become free and therefore capable of knowing what was rational and how it could be achieved. It was this latter group, the so-called Left Hegelians, that Marx fell in with during his Berlin student days.

While thoroughly absorbing Hegelian thought as he worked toward a doctorate in philosophy, Marx read a great deal else besides. He worked through the British economic theorists, and also found that his budding radicalism led him to the French socialists, with whose diverse writings he became even more familiar in 1843 when his political views forced him into exile in Paris. It was there that he met Friedrich Engels, two years his junior, the son of a well-to-do textile manufacturer. Engels would become Marx's lifelong companion, collaborator, intellectual executor, and the second half of one of history's more famous hyphenizations.

Karl Marx's career as a theorist and aspiring practitioner of social revolution began in the 1840's and stretched over four decades until his death in 1883. The mature statements of his philosophy naturally belong to the years after 1850, when his exile permanently located him in London; his research in the British Museum and his observation of British industrial capitalism helped him develop far more sophisticated views on economic and social structure. In important respects, however, the middle-aged Marx was refining and elaborating insights which he had hit upon in the 1840's. In recent years, scholars have found it increasingly fruitful to wend their way backwards from such imposing tomes as *Capital* (the first volume of which appeared in 1867) to Marx's earliest work.

The Foundations of Marxism

It is impossible to reconcile orthodox Hegelianism with political activism —as George Lichtheim, a modern authority on Marxism, has pointed out—because Hegel offered only a way to *see* the world and not a way to do anything about what one saw. Marx grasped the problem when he wrote, in the mid-1840's: "Philosophers have only *interpreted* the world, in different ways; the point, however, is to change it." Marx broke with Hegelianism over a variety of issues, none more important than that of history's essence. For Hegel, thought was the central and defining human activity; for Marx, ideas were merely another "product" of human producers, and had no meaningful existence independent of the material circumstances of production. In other words, ideas were a direct reflection of the material conditions in which they were generated. It was to those conditions, insisted Marx and Engels, that philosophy must turn.

In place of Hegel's man as thinker, Marx put man as laborer, in the broadest sense: man laboring to survive, to extract from nature the things which sustain life. Here, he claimed, was the essential and defining human activity. It was for this reason—the rejection of spiritual entities such as the World-Spirit and the concentration on the material realities of human life—that Marxian philosophy is called "materialistic." Man's struggle to conquer nature, or, more precisely, his place in the complex of social relations which arose from that struggle, determined most of what he thought.

Although man was a laboring being, not all men worked; historically, a few men had lived off the labor of others. Men who owned property—whether land or tools for transforming raw nature into useful commodities—formed social groups distinct from those who worked the property for them. Thus, there were masters and slaves, lords and serfs, bourgeois capitalists and proletarians. For Marx, the crucial determinant of social behavior was one's relationship to what he called the "means of production," by which he meant principally capital, tools, and/or land. That relationship defined one's material interest, and therefore one's "ideology." Social class therefore became the foundation of the Marxian system.

But Marx retained an important part of Hegelianism by setting social classes in an historical context. He noted that the nature of classes changed as man developed more sophisticated ways to master nature. Most recently, he argued, a capitalist bourgeoisie had begun to replace a landed aristocracy as the principal owner-employer class in the transition from an agrarian economy to industrial capitaliam. Marx saw the motor of history precisely in the relationship between social classes and in the conflict of their interests. The struggle of one class to displace another was the cause of progress, of which the French Revolution was a perfect example; the notion that history moved forward by the conflict of opposites Marx also drew from Hegel. Finally, Marx remained Hegelian enough to insist that historical progress had a goal, a single end toward which inexorable laws of development were moving it: that goal was the classless society.

Private property in the sense of ownership of the means of production entailed manifest injustice in Marx's eyes. He followed the British economists in assuming that value was a factor of labor, that raw nature was valueless until a man made it into a finished product. Yet the people who performed that vital function rarely received the full value of the product after it had been marketed. The employer, by virtue of his ownership of the means of production, kept most of that value for himself in the form of profit, after having paid his employees a wage which would barely allow them to subsist and having met other overhead costs. Moreover, the act of labor itself involved putting something of one's own personality, one's self, into the thing made. When the employer sold the product and kept the better part of the price it fetched, he was, in Marx's word, "alienating" the worker from his own personality. It was thus that the concept of alienation entered modern industrial psychology.

The only way to end this state of affairs was to abolish private property in the means of production, which would be "socialized"—owned by society at large. With everyone sharing the same relationship to the means of production, social classes would consequently cease to exist. One would naturally not expect the present owners, the bourgeoisie, to be particularly enthusiastic about this proposal, but the matter was out of their hands. The historical process, which was to say economic developments and class conflict, ensured the ultimate advent of the classless society: the inevitable course of capitalist industry would prepare it; the industrial proletariat would create it.

In the competitive capitalist economy, Marx projected, the drive for economic survival would force individual owners to seek to dominate their own particular market by means of monopolies and even international cartels. Ownership would progressively concentrate to the point where real competition was illusory and the means of production lay in relatively few hands. Prices would then soar and wages fall as the condition of those who had only their labor to sell deteriorated even further. Economic crises would be more debilitating than ever before, since the economic structure was so centralized. It was in this sense that capitalism carried within it the "seeds of its own destruction." In the midst of one of these gigantic crises, the proletariat—itself having been enlarged and concentrated by the whole process—would rise in revolt and destroy the whole capitalist system. It would not, however, destroy modern industry, which Marx regarded as the most efficient means at hand for taming nature. In a transitional period called "the dictatorship of the proletariat," private property in the means of production—industry, but also land and capital—would be systematically socialized. Once the process had been completed, and Marx was always vague on how long it would take, that dictatorship would come to an end. Indeed, the state itself would "wither away"; for political institutions were nothing more than devices for the oppression of one class by another, and social classes would have been replaced by a community of free and equal producers.

This would all come to pass, Marx was convinced, and resistance to it was futile. But the revolutionary might still nudge it along slightly, first by establishing a firm grasp of social and historical reality (that is to say, accepting Marxian theory), and second by spreading the word among the proletariat. For the proletariat would have to understand fully where its interests lay and the significance of its historical role—it would have to develop true "class consciousness"—before it could begin to act. It would have to realize that its interests would never coincide with those of the bourgeoisie,* that the hope of upward social mobility into the bourgeoi-

---

* At least not once bourgeois society had itself been created. But Marx was also certain that the historical process had to go through its appointed stages and that the

vas illusory, that exploitation and alienation would only cease with
ιe demise of capitalism.

It was this emphasis upon the role of the proletariat which Marx felt
set him off from most other social revolutionaries of the period. Marx
and Engels called themselves "communists." Their *Communist Manifesto*
(1848) not only announced the doctrines sketched out here, but attempted to define the distinction between them and other "mere" socialists. Besides the distinguishing facts that Marx preached the class struggle
(as opposed to the harmonizing message of "association") and that he
claimed that his theory rested upon a "scientific" analysis of society (as
opposed to the "utopianism" of other critics), Marxian communism was
first of all a *class* movement dedicated to the revolutionary triumph of
the proletariat. Fundamentally, the distinction between socialism and
communism at this point was not so much programmatic as tactical:
Marx and Engels hoped to stake out a claim on working-class support
and stigmatize socialism as insufficiently radical. As Engels later wrote,
with debatable accuracy: "Thus socialism was, in 1847, a middle-class
movement, communism a working-class movement. Socialism was . . . 'respectable'; communism was the very opposite." Nevertheless, authorities
of most European governments failed to grasp this distinction and
hounded both groups with equal verve.

For a man who wanted to change the world, Marx may seem to have
spent a rather great deal of time interpreting it.* He would have answered the charge by saying that his philosophy obliterated the distinction between thought and act: Marxian analysis, once properly compre-
hended, would inevitably prompt action—in no small part because it
purported to lay bare the unavoidable direction of history. As it turned
out, while Marxian communism did not exactly take the world by storm,
it did establish itself as the reigning ideology of social revolution. In
1848, Marx and Engels were but two rather obscure scribblers whose
Communist Manifesto occasioned scarcely a ripple; belying Engels' later
claims, bourgeois society regarded other threats as more serious. By the
time of Marx's death in 1883, however, Marxism was bidding to be the
orthodoxy of socialism (the distinction between socialism and communism having blurred in the meanwhile). By 1914, the bid had been successfully made.

---

proletarian revolution demanded the full development of mature capitalist industry as
a precondition. In cases where the bourgeoisie had not yet triumphed over "feudal
agrarian" society—as in Germany in 1848—Marx urged the working classes to support
the bourgeois liberals rather than work independently for their own aims.

* Marx also did work extensively to establish revolutionary organizations, of which
the International Workingmen's Association (founded in 1864) was the most important. Clearly, though, it is his work as a thinker which deserves attention in the present context.

Where did the appeal of Marxian thought lie? In part, the answer is that Marx, while undeniably an original thinker in many respects, was also a skilled synthesizer. He pulled together diverse strains of German philosophy, French socialism, and British economic thought—seemingly keeping the best and discarding the untenable. In part, his work was intellectually satisfying. It was a total world vision which ultimately came to encompass history, social structure, economics, and politics; and it was a compelling vision. The course of industrial capitalism has thus far failed to bear out Marx's predictions, and industrial laborers have demonstrated a distinct tendency to prefer present material improvements to the development of a revolutionary class consciousness. Yet these are the perspectives of the mid-twentieth century. Late in the nineteenth, Marx seemed to provide the most accurate description of what was happening and the most convincing explanation of why it was happening. Moreover, the quality of Marx's rivals on the left was none too high. No theorist emerged to challenge Marxian analysis effectively. Those who tried during Marx's lifetime were blown out of the water by the potent battery of polemical artillery he commanded. (Technical works like *Capital* might stupefy all but the devout specialist, but Marx was also a master of the lucid and devastating rejoinder.) Within a short time of Marx's death, his intellectual heirs had the field of socialism largely to themselves, though it proved difficult to keep certain glossators on the sacred texts from straying into heresy.

With respect to the success of Marxism, it should also be noted that if the European working classes had a lesson to learn from 1848, it was the need for self-reliance. When the issue had been political reform, workers and middle-class liberals stood shoulder to shoulder. When talk turned to meaningful social change, however, workers in Paris, Berlin, and Vienna suddenly found themselves alone behind the barricades. Even in Britain, where the working-class agitation of 1848 went no further than an April demonstration on behalf of truly democratic political reforms, the demonstrators met a solid front of resistance from middle-class industrialists and noble landlords alike. If the urban poor expected the world to change to their advantage, they would have to change it themselves— which was exactly the argument of Marxian communism.

But the Marxist capture of the working-class movement and the other comforts of orthodoxy lay in the future. After a peripheral, journalistic involvement in the German upheavals of 1848, the counterrevolution forced Marx out of Prussia once more and into what proved to be permanent exile in London. There he spent the last three and a half decades of his life working out the perceptions of the 1840's, and occasionally venturing into political organization. While he patiently built up the intellectual authority of his theory and skirmished with the skeptical, events were preparing a landmark in socialist history which bore no stamp of his influence.

The Paris Commune

The revolutions of 1848 were the last great left-wing eruption of the nineteenth century—save one. In 1871, the brief but spectacular episode of the Paris Commune added the finishing touches to the reputation which socialism had been building among the propertied classes since the June Days.

A year after the coup d'état of December 1851, Louis-Napoleon Bonaparte reestablished the empire in France and took the title Napoleon III. By an adroit combination of repression, concession, and diversion which conservatives everywhere were beginning to employ, the emperor was able to keep the radical and socialist movements at bay and rule in a more or less authoritarian manner. Even so, his regime never really rooted itself in the larger cities, and many inhabitants of the capital continued to harbor republican sentiments.

In 1870, France went to war against Prussia and a coalition of lesser German states. (See Chapter 6.) When the Prussians crushed a major French force and even captured the emperor himself at Sedan, northeast of Paris, the Second Empire came to an abrupt conclusion. Republicans seized the machinery of government from shocked and demoralized Bonapartists and proclaimed France's third republic in eighty years. The sensible thing at this juncture, in early September 1870, would have been to conclude a peace with the Prussians and set about the business of organizing the Third Republic on sound foundations. But the republicans were also fervent nationalists, anxious to reverse Sedan and drive the Germans off French soil. Moreover, they reasoned that a humiliating peace treaty would saddle the republic with the symbolic responsibility for losing a war it had not started. Although the military situation bordered on the hopeless, France's new leaders placed their trust in one of the unassailable legends of their movement: "the people," who had risen en masse to repel the Teutonic invader in 1793 and who would do so again.

The Prussian military juggernaut swiftly encircled Paris in mid-September and dispatched forces to the interior to mop up on tenacious resistance there. The capital and its million and a half inhabitants meanwhile settled down to the ordeal of a brutalizing siege, which would end only in late January 1871. Cut off from provincial supplies, lacking an efficient system of rationing, Parisians suffered extreme hunger and cold in an atmosphere of rising social tensions. Wild rumors of bourgeois feasts ran through working-class quarters, where both starvation and patriotic determination to hold on ran high. When the armistice finally came, followed by a legislative election which produced (as in 1848) a monarchist majority in the new National Assembly, radicalism and wounded national pride ran together to form a volatile mixture.

The assembly then accepted humiliating peace terms from the Prussians (including the loss of the French provinces of Alsace and Lorraine). It rejected Paris as a capital and sat instead in Versailles. It even went so far as to repeal the moratorium on rents and bank notes which had prevailed during the siege, when economic life had come to a halt, even though the postsiege recovery was halting and tentative. Plainly, the assembly feared Parisian radicalism and was determined to reduce this republican stronghold to impotence. When in mid-March the assembly tried to disarm the capital of the artillery it had been using during the siege, citizen militia drove regular troops from the city and a second siege of Paris ensued.

The Parisian insurgents who organized a new municipal government —called the Commune, after the name the city government had taken in the First Republic—were a rather motley collection of leftists. They included a variety of radical democrats, socialists, and only a handful of persons associated—and remotely at that—with Marx.* The principal groups making up the Commune, however, were Proudhonist and Blanquist. The Proudhonists inspired the Commune with such programmatic content as it had (which was little); the Blanquists, with much of its energy.

Pierre-Joseph Proudhon was a self-educated printer who, in the 1840's, had made a certain name for himself in social romanticist circles with the striking, if not very logical, proposition that "property is theft." Proudhon's proposals for social change called for a decentralized system of producers' cooperatives. The cooperatives would own property, not the state, since Proudhon felt that the nationalization of the means of production made the state far too strong (views which brought him into bitter conflict with Marx). Rather, Proudhon sought a radical reduction of state power and envisaged a society organized around the cooperatives, which would join togehter in a series of voluntary associations. Though Proudhon had died in 1864, he was probably the single most influential writer among French workers during the Second Empire. Auguste Blanqui, a second influence on the Commune, had plenty of opportunity for philosophical contemplation—he spent the better part of his adult life in prison for political offenses—but did little of it. He was the quintessential revolutionary activist, always plotting revolutionary coups which

* A few were members of the International Workingmen's Association, which Marx had helped organize in 1864 in hopes of uniting, and converting, proletarian movements from all over Europe. It seems unlikely that many of the French members were, as of 1871, Marxists in the doctrinal sense.

would deliver power to the underclass. Indeed, he may have been responsible for the phrase "dictatorship of the proletariat" which Marx used. Although present in Paris during the siege, the government had him jailed just prior to the proclamation of the Commune.

There may not appear to be much semantic distance between "communist" and "communard," which is what the Commune's supporters called themselves. But the communards were too divided to have any coherent program, too embattled to spend much time trying to formulate one. The Commune's call for a national reorganization into a collection of free and virtually autonomous communes has the scent of Proudhonianism in it, but it probably did not represent majority opinion and was mostly expressive of Parisian desires for independence from what they regarded as a reactionary assembly. Far from ruling Paris during its two-month career as a dictatorship of the proletariat, the communards scarcely attempted any social reforms and even took certain measures to protect bourgeois property from violation. There was simply no time for theories or reform; the Commune was too busy preparing its defenses against what it knew was the inevitable assault from the assembly.

The monarchist legislators in Versailles had reluctantly maintained the republican form of government but placed at its head the ex-Orléanist Adolphe Thiers, a former minister of Louis-Philippe's. Thiers was in the midst of a transition from royalism to conservative republicanism, but he was as resolutely committed to rooting out the communards as the most die-hard Legitimist. After a period of regrouping, in which Paris was again isolated for some two months, Thiers ordered regular army forces to attack the capital. The worst civil war in modern French history raged for a week, with the communards giving ground grudgingly and determined to see Paris go down with them. They incinerated the old royal palace and the city hall as they retreated across the city and were only barely prevented from putting other famous buildings—such as Notre Dame cathedral—to the torch. The communards lost perhaps 4000 men in the actual battle for Paris, as compared to 1000 in the regular army. But the carnage did not stop with the triumph of Thiers' troops. Special military tribunals—which is to say drumhead courts— conducted summary trials and executions of persons suspected of aiding the communards. Another 15,000 Parisians of all ages and both sexes were eliminated in these purges (and in the next few months, perhaps 13,000 more were deported to tropical island prison camps).

Respectable European society from St. Petersburg to London stood horrified at the "excesses" of the communards, who had seemed to demonstrate for once and all that socialism must issue forth in anarchy and civil war. Interestingly enough, Marx took a position not too distant. In a famous pamphlet of 1871, he described the Commune as the first battle in the proletarian revolution and the communards as martyrs to the communist cause. Both sides ignored the fact that the Commune had actually *done* little which could be described as "socialist," that its support had cut across class lines and included many middle-class radicals, that patriotism had played as large a role as class conflict. This was one of those cases in which myth overpowered reality (and Marx, for one, probably realized that he was fostering a myth, one which he hoped would galvanize workers everywhere). The notion that the Commune represented unvarnished class war was accepted by all elements of European society for at least two generations.

For Marx, the Commune was a beginning, "the glorious harbinger of a new society" (though the experience of life under communard rule was so vague that it was hard to say what that society would look like). Marx did not live long enough to see how wrong he was. The Commune announced not a beginning, but an end. It pulled the curtain on an era of classical revolutionary action, with its barricades and pitched battles in the streets, and gave way to an epoch of strikes and electoral struggles, of working-class organization and labor bargaining. European radicals discovered that they were no longer facing decrepit reactionaries like Charles X, no longer dueling with regimes unskilled in the not unrelated arts of repression and concession. The established order, which was changing under the impact of industrialization, was also learning how to defend itself better than before. Socialism would thus have to change accordingly.

Fortunately for Marx, the historical orientation of his thought helped him, and his later disciples, adjust for this. It was the height of folly, he had repeatedly argued, to attempt "premature" revolution, to force the pace of history, to snatch at power before the course of economic development had rendered the fruit ripe for the picking. By pondering this wisdom, Marxists of the later nineteenth century were able to subordinate their master's enthusiasm for the Paris Commune and proceed more patiently.

6 / *Conservatism and Concession*

The revolutions of 1848 did not remake European society, but they did force the old order to overhaul itself. Counterrevolution had been generally successful by 1850, but its most intelligent partisans understood that repression was no better than a holding action against immense pressures for change. Whereas the status quo had defended itself prior to 1848 by throttling its critics, postrevolutionary European governments resorted to more flexible and imaginative means of self-defense—in large part because 1848 had shown mere repression to be inadequate. While one hand of power remained clenched in a mailed fist, the other began to borrow selected elements from the liberal-nationalist, the democratic, and even the socialist programs. To put it another way, conservatives and moderates sought ways to realize certain of the programs of 1848 without making fundamental changes in the social system or in the distribution of political power. Their hope was that concession and co-option would avert revolutionary cataclysm.

Certain social and political changes anticipated in earlier chapters contributed to the success of these efforts. The spread of industrialization was creating an undeniably ascendant bourgeoisie which the old landed magnates could no longer ignore and with whom they finally agreed to share a degree of power. This partial realignment was also promoted by the growth of a socialist left, which tended to drive politically liberal propertied elements to the right.

By the early 1870's, Italy and Germany were both unified nations. Every major European state west of Russia had a constitution which established some version of parliamentary government. The French and German parliaments were elected by universal adult male suffrage, and France was of course a republic. The Austrians no longer ruled the Habsburg Empire alone. Here and there, some governments even engaged in a few cautious experiments in social reform. In short, much of what the revolutions of 1848 had vainly sought was realized by the fear of revolution.

The Unification of Italy

Of the three principal approaches to Italian unification, 1848 had plainly foreclosed that of papal leadership, leaving the field to the Piedmontese monarchists and to the Mazzinian republicans. (See Chapter 4.) After 1852, Piedmontese policy was decided largely by Count Camillo Benso di Cavour, an aristocrat and large landowner who became premier in 1852. The label "conservative" does not fit Cavour as snugly as it does many other national leaders of this period. Indeed, he had the reputation of being a liberal. Cavour had long championed constitutional government, was an unabashed admirer of British parliamentary institutions, and took a personal hand in sponsoring economic modernization in agriculture and industry. He was also a Piedmontese nationalist who hoped to see his government play some larger role in an at least partially unified Italy; his advocacy of reform and modernization was designed to prepare Piedmont-Sardinia for Italian leadership as much as it proceeded from purely principled commitment to liberal ideas. It is here that Cavour emerges as a conservative of sorts—not so much by virtue of his own ideas alone, but by comparison of them with the policies of his rivals. Besides, as he once remarked, moderate reform tended to strengthen rather than weaken authority, and a clever politician could do more with a parliament than without one (since representative government gave a greater degree of legitimacy to official policy). He remained a staunch foe of democracy, and was haunted by the fear that the republicans would somehow take the initiative in unification before he could do so.

In addition to removing the papal alternative, 1848 had clarified the Italian question in another important respect. It was plain that Piedmont-Sardinia lacked the resources to eject Austria from northern Italy, that a powerful ally was essential. What was less plain was who would be that ally. The British were sentimentally inclined toward Italian unity, but were not about to become involved in a continental war which did not directly affect their interests. The other likely candidate, France, was protecting the temporal sovereignty of the papacy with a garrison in Rome, after having defeated Mazzini and Garibaldi in 1849. It seemed unlikely that the French would look favorably upon any attempts to alter the status quo. On the other hand, Napoleon II, emperor of France since 1852, had developed a renewed interest in the cause of Italian nationalism. In the early 1830's, with all members of the Bonaparte family exiled

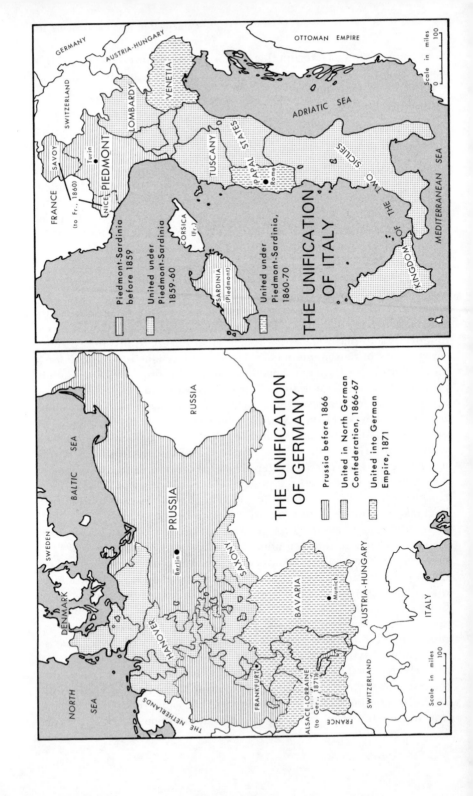

THE UNIFICATION OF ITALY

Piedmont-Sardinia before 1859

United under Piedmont-Sardinia 1859-60

United under Piedmont-Sardinia, 1860-70

Scale in miles
0   100

THE UNIFICATION OF GERMANY

Prussia before 1866

United in North German Confederation, 1866-67

United into German Empire, 1871

Scale in miles
0   100

from France, the youthful Louis-Napoleon had resided in northern Italy and become involved in the incipient unificationist movement. Once elected president of the Second Republic, though, he was obliged to yield to pressure from conservative Catholic supporters and order the Roman intervention. The fact that many Italians thereafter held him to be an enemy of their independence was brought home to him in January 1858, when an Italian nationalist tried unsuccessfully to assassinate him and the empress Eugénie.

Napoleon had always claimed to harbor a vague sympathy for subject nationalities, and the abortive assassination stirred his conscience sufficiently to give Cavour an opportunity. In July 1858, Cavour and the emperor met in secret at the French resort of Plombières. Napoleon agreed to assist in the expulsion of Austria and to a scheme for Italian unification which would reduce, but not destroy, papal temporal sovereignty. There was to be an Italian confederation, under the pope's presidency, of four kingdoms: a large one in the north, which amounted to a greatly expanded Piedmont; a smaller north-central one; a somewhat reduced papal domain in and around Rome; and the Kingdom of Naples and Sicily in the south. In return for their military generosity, the French would receive the Piedmontese territories of Nice and Savoy, which bordered on southeastern France. But the crucial provision of this agreement, formalized in a secret treaty in December 1858, was that the war had to begin in such a way that Austria would seem wholly at fault and Napoleon III blameless in the eyes of the French Catholics.

Cavour was entirely equal to the task of provoking Austria into a declaration of war. Fertile in the manufacture of incidents, he maneuvered the Habsburg government into issuing an ultimatum to Piedmont-Sardinia, which he gleefully rejected. The Austrians thereupon invaded Piedmont in April 1859, only to find themselves at war with France as well. Italian nationalists in the independent principalities of the north and center took the war as the occasion for risings against their sovereigns preparatory to unification—a development which suggested to Napoleon that it might be difficult to contain events within the framework envisaged at Plombières. Although the French won a major victory at Solferino in June, the emperor was acutely conscious of mounting antiwar protest from his Catholic subjects. Therefore, with the Austrians still holding fast to Venetia, and without consulting his Piedmontese ally, Napoleon concluded an armistice with the Habsburgs, even though his failure to fulfill his complete treaty obligations deprived him of the right to receive Nice and Savoy.

In spite of the fact that French negotiations with Austria called for the cession of Lombardy to Piedmont-Sardinia, Cavour felt betrayed. When his king, Victor Emmanuel, reasoned that there was nothing for it but to accept the terms of the major powers, Cavour resigned in disgust. But the situation still provided room for a resourceful politician to extract further advantages, as Cavour soon realized; in January 1860, considerably calmed, he returned to the premiership. His first order of business was to deal with the insurrections of north-central Italy, where the insurgents were pleading to be joined to the enlarged Piedmontese state. Although Napoleon III had originally favored restoring the banished princes of these states, Cavour dangled the bait of Nice and Savoy once more. The emperor could not resist; and in March the duchies of Modena, Parma, Tuscany, and the Romagna became part of Piedmont.

Cavour's second task was to deal with one of the more bizarre episodes of Italian history. In May 1861, Giuseppe Garibaldi, the seasoned revolutionary of 1849 and irrepressible Italian nationalist, commanded an armed force of 1,000 volunteers—the so-called Redshirts—in an assault upon Sicily. The expedition had Cavour's secret approval, though it is unclear what he expected from it—at best, perhaps, inspiration for a rising of unificationists in the south and the ultimate flanking of the Papal States by a union of Piedmont and the Kingdom of Naples and Sicily. Garibaldi, though a republican, had vowed loyalty to Piedmont as the only realistic hope for Italian unification. Yet Garibaldi also seems to have had more ambitious plans: he would conquer Sicily and then sweep up the peninsula, overwhelming both the Papal States and the Austrian stronghold in Venetia, thus presenting Cavour with a fully united Italy.

Even under the harsh and humorless gaze of modern scholarship, the expedition of Garibaldi's Thousand has a storybook flavor to it. Heroism, good luck, and decrepit enemies all combined to give Garibaldi success after astonishing success. By the end of May, he had taken Palermo, the capital of Sicily. Three months later, he surged across the Straits of Messina and in early September he entered Naples in triumph. By this time, it was clear to Cavour that his formidable emissary had no intention of confining his heroic exploits to the south. A Garibaldian march on Rome, with its French contingent protecting the pope, was bound to bring Piedmont into conflict with Napoleon III. Determined to stop Garibaldi, Cavour grabbed at some nationalist disturbances in the papal territories as a pretext for intervention—on the grounds of "restoring order." Driving south to cut off Garibaldi, Piedmontese troops conquered most of the Papal States on the way, though steering well clear of Rome itself. But French interference was averted, and in March 1861 the Kingdom of Italy, with Victor Emmanuel on its throne, was proclaimed.*

---

* Complete unification was achieved within a decade. Italy received Venetia from Austria after the Austro-Prussian war of 1866. (See below.) During the Franco-Prussian war of 1870–71, the French brought home their Roman garrison, whereupon Italian troops took the city and reduced papal sovereignty to the confines of the Vatican City.

The new Italian state was organized under a version of the Piedmontese constitution: parliamentary elections were the affair of the propertied, of landholders and urban middle classes. Although the population numbered better than 25 million, barely a half million persons had the vote. (An electoral reform of 1881 extended the franchise to another 1.5 million, but still retained a property qualification.) The rather more urban and industrial north was overrepresented, and held the whip hand over the more backward south. Politics operated within a rather narrow spectrum, and the parliamentary left differed from the right in no very significant ways save in its anticlericalism. Republicanism went into rather general eclipse, perhaps because nothing fails like failure. Cavour had beaten democratic republicanism to the draw. Although he had aspired to something like the expansion of Piedmont, he achieved something closer to the Mazzinian dream to the unification of all Italy under a single government—though of course it was a monarchical government, moderate and respectable, run by people of "sound" and "reliable" views. Perhaps Cavour's way was the only way, for its time; it is hard to imagine that Napoleon III would have given aid to republican nationalism. In any case, we cannot say what Cavour thought of the state he did so much to create. He died less than three months after its birth, at the age of fifty-one.

Bismarck and German Unification

Otto von Bismarck was born of a Prussian Junker family in 1815. An outspoken opponent of the revolution of 1848, he feared that German national unification would spell the demise of Prussia—which would be immersed in a larger state—and therefore of its ruling class. But whereas many of his peers were content to see Prussia and Austria dominate central Europe in a conservative partnership, Bismarck was an ardent *Prussian* nationalist. Serving in the 1850's as his government's chief delegate to the Diet of the revivified German Confederation, he could not abide the thought of Prussia serving as a mere extension of Habsburg policy. While cooperation with Austria was something like an article of faith for his superiors in Berlin, Bismarck began to conclude that mastery in German-speaking Europe was a prize worth seeking and conflict with Austria a price worth paying for it.

Bismarck's thinking owed little to the liberal nationalism of 1848. Again, he was a Prussian, rather than a German, nationalist; he was thinking less of German unification than of Prussian expansion under cover of the unificationist banner. It was a distinction which traditionalists in Berlin had difficulty making; unification was a liberal program, and by the early 1860's liberalism was challenging the very basis of Hohenzollern power. Prussian kings had long regarded the army as their personal instrument. In December 1859, King William I (who had succeeded his brother Frederick William IV) and his military advisers determined upon a thoroughgoing army reform. However, liberals and democrats in the Prussian parliament, whose numbers had grown substantially despite an electoral law rigged to favor the very wealthy, attempted to block the necessary credits for reform in hopes of establishing legislative control over the army. The king was totally committed to reform, lest the Prussian army find itself obsolescent. However, though he harbored no sympathy for parliamentary government, he felt himself honor-bound to obey the constitution while still loath to sacrifice royal control of the military.

The bitter constitutional stalemate dragged on into 1862, with William I on the point of abdicating rather than either compromising with parliament or overriding it illegally. As a last resort, he was persuaded to give Bismarck (then Prussian ambassador to France) a chance to break the deadlock. Summoned back to Berlin to head a new cabinet, Bismarck was able to convince the king that parliament could be ignored. There was, he argued, a "gap" or "hole" in the constitution on such matters of executive-legislative conflict. Without clear-cut constitutional guidelines, the government was within its rights to proceed as it saw best— undertaking army reform and collecting taxes as though parliament had voted the credits.

Outraged Prussian liberals could scarcely have guessed that, within but four years, many of them would vote for a bill retroactively sanctioning these unconstitutional expenditures. But Bismarck's foreign policy, geared to establish Prussian supremacy in central Europe, achieved in those years what the liberal nationalists had failed to accomplish in 1848–49—a major step toward the unification of Germany. Prussian supremacy, however, required the expulsion of Austria from German affairs, and that in its turn required the conversion of many Prussian traditionalists, who continued to regard Austro-Prussian cooperation as the cornerstone of resistance to liberalism. Bismarck's opportunity presented itself when the monumentally complicated Schleswig-Holstein question surfaced once more.

As in 1848, the Danish monarchy was preparing to annex these tiny duchies of dubious international status.* When the Danes refused to heed protests from the Confederation's Diet, Prussia and Austria went to war with Denmark in February 1864. The military issue was quickly decided, of course, but it was not until the late summer of 1865 that dip-

---

* The duchies were joined in personal union to the king of Denmark, but not to his kingdom; Holstein was a member of the German Confederation, while Schleswig was not.

lomatic negotiations resolved the duchies' status: Prussia assumed the administration of Schleswig, Austria of Holstein. While Bismarck can hardly be accused of engineering the war—any Prussian statesman would have responded similarly to the provocative Danish behavior—he does seem to have been primarily responsible for the peace settlement. Austria was not involved in the administration of territory far from its own borders and adjacent to Prussia. Tensions were bound to arise between the two powers—tensions which would nettle Prussian traditionalists likely to regard the neighboring duchies as, if anything, rightfully Prussian.

Bismarck was apparently confident enough in the eventual deterioration of Austro-Prussian relations and in the support that he would then receive from traditional conservatives that he began diplomatic preparations for war. Having already solidified his friendship with Russia, which had fallen out with Austria over foreign policy questions in the eastern Mediterranean, he won from Napoleon III a secret promise of neutrality in the event of a central European war. In the spring of 1866, he turned to Italy, where unification had been largely achieved in 1861, save that Austria still held the province of Venetia. In return for military support from Italy in any Austro-Prussian war, support which would tie down Austrian troops on the Italian frontier, Bismarck promised that a Prussian victory would be followed by the cession of Venetia to Italy. He sought further to broaden his political backing in the German Confederation by calling for a sweeping reform, including election of the Diet by a democratic franchise—a shrewd means of neutralizing anti-Prussian sentiment on the left.

War finally came over the pretext of Schleswig-Holstein, with Bismarck complaining that Austria had violated certain terms of the 1865 settlement and sending Prussian troops into Holstein. Although most of the middling German states feared absorption by Prussia and therefore sided with the Habsburgs, the reformed Prussian army proved more than a match for the coalition. On July 3, 1866, within less than a month of the outbreak of hostilities, the Prussians brought their superior command organization and modernized firepower to bear in a telling battle at Königgrätz. To the astonishment of Europe, the Prussian army had abruptly reversed the balance of power in central Europe.

The German Confederation therefore came to an end, to be replaced the next year by the North German Confederation, which encompassed all the states north of the Main River. The member states retained their domestic autonomy, but their military forces were commanded by the federal president—King William I of Prussia. A federal diet included a lower house elected by universal manhood suffrage, but members of the upper house were appointed by the respective governments, which were not equally represented—Prussia holding seventeen of the forty-three seats and influencing enough of the others to control the majority. The chief government minister of Prussia, Bismarck, acted for the federal president in the Diet, and was responsible to him rather than to the majority in the lower house.* In other words, behind the parliamentary and democratic foliage lay Prussian power, with few real constitutional checks upon it.

Bismarck's policy and the victory at Königgrätz left Prussian liberalism in utter disarray. The arch-enemy of parliamentary government had suddenly appropriated the liberal nationalist program to the authoritarian monarchy and very nearly realized the national dream of 1848. A large liberal faction decided not to argue with success and voted to legitimize government military expenditures since 1862. The assumption was widespread that total unification could not be far off.

Bismarck was in no very great hurry to take that final step. Prussia had to have time to digest the other north German states—like itself, predominantly Protestant and agrarian—before it was prepared to assimilate the largely Catholic and rapidly industrializing independent states of the south. Besides, Napoleon III was visibly dismayed at the sudden appearance of a large German state on his eastern border. He was also angered and embarrassed by Bismarck, who had helped obtain French neutrality in the war of 1866 by hinting—not promising, but hinting—at territorial compensation for France along the Rhine in the event of a Prussian victory. When, after the war, Bismarck denied any such commitment and refused all compensation, Napoleon was left empty-handed and looking rather foolish. The emperor would surely intervene forcefully in the event of total unification. Indeed, Bismarck capitalized upon the ominous anti-German grumblings emitting from Paris and concluded military alliances with the southern states. Relations between France and the North German Confederation worsened detectably.

There is no doubt that Bismarck was willing to go to war with France in order to achieve complete Prussian mastery of Germany. Some question remains, however, whether the war he got was the one he wanted. In early 1870, the Prussian chancellor began to toy with a project for the diplomatic humiliation of Napoleon III, whose regime was already troubled by domestic concern over foreign policy setbacks (not the least of which was the uncontested birth of the North German Confederation). The throne of Spain had been rendered vacant by the most recent in a series of revolutions there, and Bismarck put forward the claims of a younger, Catholic branch of the house of Hohenzollern. Operating through secret channels, he hoped to gain acceptance of the Hohenzol-

---

* In the liberal scheme of things, the prime minister would be appointed by the monarch but responsible (or accountable) to the majority in parliament, which could bring down the cabinet with a vote of no confidence.

lern candidacy and then present France publicly with the fait accompli of a Hohenzollern prince on yet another of its borders. Word of the negotiations leaked out in early July 1870, however, and the French government sent up a shriek of protest at this flanking maneuver. French public opinion, whipped into a froth by nearly two decades of official hypernationalism, demanded satisfaction—by trial of arms, if necessary. Bismarck was caught off-guard; the candidacy had to be withdrawn, a blow to both Prussian national pride and Bismarck's personal prestige.

The French determined to press forward, however, and their ambassador insisted of William I that he renounce Hohenzollern claims upon the Spanish throne for all future generations. The king, taking the waters at the spa of Ems, rejected this pointless demand. Bismarck now saw the opportunity to reverse the German setback, though it might involve war. That same day, he edited William's statement of refusal before its release in order to make it unusually terse and abrupt. His prediction that the so-called Ems Dispatch, thus doctored, would be "a red flag before the Gallic bull" was correct. Indignant, France used the dispatch as the pretext for war (although the government may have already decided that war would be necessary to salvage imperial honor).

Even after the whirlwind Prussian triumph over Austria, the French were supremely confident of victory. But the North German Confederation and its south German allies leaned heavily upon superior Prussian weaponry and organization to gain the decisive victory at Sedan on September 1, 1870. The elimination of resistance took several months longer, during which time Bismarck negotiated with the southern states on terms for their entry into a unified German state. On January 18, 1871, King William I was proclaimed Kaiser (that is, Emperor) William I of Germany in a ceremony held at the Palace of Versailles, seat of the old French monarchy. The new state over which he ruled fused the northern confederation and the southern states into the most powerful nation on the European continent.

Bismarckian Germany

The new German Empire was modeled on the confederation of 1867. It was a federal government, whose twenty-five member states retained a degree of separate identity and of control over their internal affairs. Most major questions, however, were settled in the parliament, or Reichstag, elected by universal manhood suffrage. Bismarck had long since discarded such crude tactics as the "gap" theory of the constitution. Germany counted a population of over 40 million persons, less than half of them Prussian. The addition of the southern states brought in a large Catholic, urban, liberal, and sometimes even radical bloc too large and unstable to be ruled by naked repression. Bismarck, now chancellor of

Germany, hoped that the rural vote would return a conservative majority to the Reichstag and that he could therefore preserve power for Prussian Junkerdom, the house of Hohenzollern, and of course himself.

The power of Protestant Prussia was one of the first major issues in the new Reich, for Catholics were anxious for a more meaningful federalism in which the individual states exercised a greater degree of autonomy. In response, Bismarck seized upon the Roman Catholic Church's declaration of papal infallibility in July 1870 to launch a vigorous campaign against Catholics, which his underlings styled a *Kulturkampf,* or "cultural struggle." Legislation discriminatory to Catholics was confined largely to Prussia, although Bismarck did ram a law through the Reichstag requiring civil marriage. He dissolved various religious orders in Prussia and jailed all the Catholic bishops in Prussia who had not fled into exile. But he also excited solid Catholic opposition which grouped into a major new political group, the Center party, and which doubtless was encouraged by the papacy's instructions that Germans treat the *Kulturkampf* legislation as null and void. The struggle raged on bitterly, if intermittently, until 1878, when—troubled by the growing strength of the Center—Bismarck began to reconsider. By that time, he had decided to make Austria—Catholic Austria—the key partner of an alliance system designed to hold the French at bay. Moreover, Bismarck had determined upon a policy of higher tariffs, a move which could only alienate the free-trade northern liberals who had backed the *Kulturkampf.* To compensate for the loss of their votes in the Reichstag, he began to cultivate the Catholic Center party. In return for promises not to enforce the anti-Catholic laws, the Center supported Bismarck's tariff measures. It was a typically flexible and pragmatic maneuver on Bismarck's part, demonstrating that conservatism had learned how to play the parliamentary game.

The first decade of German unity also witnessed a sizeable growth in the socialist movement, fed by rapid industrialization and urbanization. There were a variety of socialist sects in preunification Germany, the most important of which was led by Ferdinand Lassalle (whose father was a well-to-do merchant). Lassalle's socialism was of a modest sort, envisioning only a network of producers' cooperatives funded by the state and nothing so sweeping as a classless and stateless society. Marx considered him a bourgeois reformer at best and was furious when the German socialists merged into a single party in 1875 on a more or less Lassallean program. (Lassalle himself had died in 1864.) As it happened, Lassallean socialism had reached the peak of its influence and gave way in the next decade or so to Marxism. The German Social Democratic party went on to become the largest Marxist party in Europe.

Prior to the late 1870's, Bismarck had paid relatively little attention to socialism. But 1878 was a Reichstag election year, and the chancellor needed an issue with which to mobilize conservatives. Events gave him the issue: in May and June, there were two assassination attempts on Emperor William I—the second a very near miss—by left-wing radicals. Neither of the men was a socialist, but Bismarck organized the election campaign as though they were, fulminating about the dangerous revolutionaries who were on the verge of destroying respectable society. The conservative groups rode this red scare to substantial electoral gains (mostly at the expense of the liberals, whose reduced numbers left them in no position to block the new tariff policy). The new Reichstag thereupon passed a law outlawing the Social Democratic party, which was forced to operate underground for the next twelve years.

Characteristically, however, Bismarck refused to rely upon pure repression. In 1883, he authored the first of three major social measures meant to take the reform issue away from the socialists and win their working-class constituency over to the state. First came a sickness insurance bill, followed (in 1884 and 1889, respectively) by accident and retirement insurance legislation. Such programs were virtually unthinkable prior to 1848, when authority regarded concession to the left as equivalent to surrender. For Bismarck, they were a means of reinforcing the conservative order, though before succumbing to the temptation of seeing Bismarck as some kind of crypto-socialist, one would do well to remember that he also engineered the prohibition of the Social Democratic party.

For all the fact that the Emperor of Germany retained substantial powers under the constitution of 1871, and for all the trappings of parliamentary government, Bismarck was the country's real ruler. He knew how to manipulate and exploit parliament, how to turn electoral politics to his own advantage. He was a master at *using* events and at serving up sweet nectar and bitter draughts on the same tray. He shamelessly bullied the aging Emperor William (who was already seventy-five in 1871)— alternately screaming, weeping, and threatening to resign in order to get his way with his sovereign. He was tough, ruthless, and plainly did not shrink from spending other persons' lives to achieve his political goals.

But although Bismarck plunged unflinchingly into three wars between 1864 and 1870 in the pursuit of Prussian national interest (as he saw it), he was no mindless war-monger. From 1871 until his fall from power in 1890, Germany was at peace—though Bismarck was not above whipping up a war scare with France in 1887 in order to get Reichstag support for new military appropriations. It was not that Bismarck had been suddenly stricken with a bout of pacifism, but rather that war had ceased to be in Germany's interest. The Austro-Prussian and Franco-Prussian wars had created a new structure for European international politics. Prior to 1871, France had been the major continental power, and Napoleon III had been a restless, ambitious ruler, ready to support such disruptive ideas as Italian unification and to provide moral support for subject nationalities elsewhere (such as the Poles). The battle of Sedan replaced France with the new Germany as the dominant continental power; and Germany—having achieved unification and military superiority over all challengers—was now interested in preserving an agreeable status quo. As far as Bismarck could see, there was nothing else that Germany needed. A conservative foreign policy therefore recommended itself.

The hinge upon which that policy moved was yet another example of the new conservatism's flexibility. Since, obviously, the continental power which had suffered most from German unification was France, the problem was to keep France from reversing the verdict of 1870–71 and winning back the territories of Alsace and Lorraine. To build an anti-French partnership, Bismarck turned to another power which German unification had wounded—Austria. Immediately after the completion of German unification, Bismarck set about repairing relations between Berlin and Vienna, guarding against the prospect of any Austrian alliance—with France, for example—which might be directed against Germany. By 1879, he was able to conclude a firm military alliance between the two nations, an agreement which remained in force for almost forty years.

Bismarck also worked tirelessly to maintain the friendship of Russia —no easy task, since the Russians and Bismarck's principal ally, the Austrians, were in conflict over their respective territorial ambitions in the Balkans. Although unable to realize the sort of firm alliance which bound Austria to Germany, Bismarck was still able to ensure that the nightmare of a Franco-Russian alliance, flanking Germany to the east and west remained just that—a nightmare, and not a reality. After bringing Italy into the Austro-German alliance in 1882, and with Great Britain still resolved to stay out of continental politics, Bismarck had achieved the diplomatic isolation of France.

From a purely technical point of view, Bismarck's accomplishments in his thirty-eight years as chancellor of Prussia and then Germany were dazzling. With phenomenal political skill, he had engineered a reversal in the European balance of power and created a powerful modern state where none had existed before, all the while keeping the class and the dynasty he represented in a commanding position. He defanged German liberalism, neutralized Catholic opposition, and kept the socialists on the defensive. Although the Germany of 1890 was no longer rural and agrarian, but rather industrializing and urbanizing at the fastest rate in Europe, the Junker aristocracy remained in firm control of the crucial institutions of the army and the bureaucracy.

Over the next quarter-century, there were signs that the Bismarckian synthesis was beginning to come undone, something for which Bismarck's successors—including Emperor William II, who ascended the throne in 1888 at the age of twenty-nine—have traditionally taken the blame. It is sometimes argued that Bismarck, somehow rendered immortal, would never have allowed Russia to drift out of the German orbit and into alliance with France in the 1890's, and would never have allowed Germany to enter the war of 1914 (which destroyed the empire he created). In fact, a strong opposing case can be made that many of Germany's later tribulations were Bismarck's personal, if unwitting, bequest. For one thing, it was Germany's ties to Austria that dragged it into World War I, ties which Bismarck considered absolutely essential. (See Chapter 11.) For another, it was simply impossible to keep hold of Russia and Austria at the same time: their rivalry in the Balkans necessitated choosing between them. Moreover, neither the German socialists nor the discontent in which their movement was rooted would go away. When prohibition of the Social Democratic party was lifted in 1890, its ranks swelled rapidly. By 1914, it was the largest single party in Germany. Bismarck himself seemed to realize that there was little future for him with either democracy or repression. Just before his dismissal in 1890, he was contemplating the abrogation of universal suffrage.

Bismarck's conservatism was imaginative and innovative, but it was still conservatism. Although the chancellor had learned to live with parliamentary institutions and even exploit them to his own ends, he never learned to respect them. In his regime, the democratic franchise was a device to be manipulated, the legislature a tool to be used—and sometimes an obstacle to be sidestepped. He failed, or rather he refused, to make constitutional and parliamentary government a reality, refused to give Germany a meaningful experience in representative government, for the absence of which the Germans paid heavily in future generations. *He* was the government, and it was over precisely this issue that William II, who aspired to rule and not merely reign, forced Bismarck to resign in 1890. Bismarckian Germany was a new state, but the essential inspiration of its structure was remarkably akin to that of authoritarian Prussia prior to 1848. For all the ground that it gave, the old order was still holding on tenaciously.

Austria and France

The unification of Italy and Germany were the most important instances in which the liberal and radical aims of 1848 were realized by moderates and conservatives and in which the old order preserved much of itself by appropriating features of the new. But there were other variations on the theme, two of which were prompted by confrontations with unifying Germany.

The nationalities question had emerged in 1848 as the central dilemma of Habsburg politics. Austrian Germans felt that a policy of leniency toward the Empire's Slav and Magyar peoples would only encourage their separatist tendencies. But a policy of strict Germanization—with no concession to ethnic autonomy—ran the risk of so alienating the non-German population (which numbered better than three-fourths of the whole) that a reenactment of 1848 seemed likely. It was this latter policy which Chancellor Prince Felix zu Schwarzenberg and his successors selected. Perhaps Germanization would have proved more durable had the government remained otherwise stronger. But its fiscal position was precarious and in no way improved by the Italian war of 1859. Moreover, the Magyars, who had been humiliated in 1849, proved remarkably resilient, agitating continuously for autonomous status and even making credible threats of revolt during the war.

By 1860, the Austrians had reluctantly resolved to reorganize the Empire, at least in part. The government agreed to the establishment of provincial assemblies which would in turn send delegates to an imperial Diet (of rather narrow powers). The Magyars scoffed at this pallid gesture and at further Austrian concessions. In frustration, Viennese officialdom even returned briefly to Germanization, an avenue which had already been demonstrated to lead nowhere. Finally, in 1865, the crown reopened talks with the Magyars, only to have its bargaining position undercut the next year by the battle of Königgrätz (in which, interestingly enough, the Magyars staunchly backed the Austrians). Shaken by a defeat which he feared the subject Slavs might try to exploit, Emperor Francis Joseph now determined upon a settlement with Hungary.

The compromise of 1867 produced a peculiar political form—the so-called dual monarchy. The Empire was now defined as including two separate entities, Hungary (to be ruled by the Magyars) and Austria (to be ruled by the Germans). Each area had extensive domestic autonomy and its own parliament; matters of common interest—foreign policy, tariffs, and so forth—were handled by representatives from each parliament who met each year. In short, the Habsburgs sacrificed centralization for survival. But 1867 was more than a compromise; it marked the formation of a partnership for the domination of the central European Slavs. The two non-Slavic groups now joined to rule the Slavic majority, which went unrecognized in the new constitutional arrangements. The creation of Austria-Hungary marked a liberalization insofar as Habsburg absolutism was concerned. But from the point of view of Slavic nationalism, the Austro-Hungarian agreement simply meant a more efficient form of repression.

The Franco-Prussian war of 1870–71 had helped bring down Napoleon III's Second Empire, itself a sort of model of flexible conservatism. Napoleon left no doubt that his first priority was order (as opposed to liberty or equality or social justice), and his government was unmistakably authoritarian for the most part. But he was also adept at the game of piecemeal concession and accommodation with the left. He did establish a two-house legislature, and though it was at first powerless, the Emperor played out responsibility to it cautiously over the years. As a young man, Napoleon had also dabbled with early socialism and considered himself a sort of crypto-Saint-Simonian. In power, he initiated or encouraged a variety of economic reforms designed to modernize French industry, increase its production and national prosperity, and thus blunt social antagonisms. He retained universal suffrage (while also manipulating elections) and even went so far as to legalize strikes in hopes of defusing working-class discontent.

Like the Magyars, the French republicans owed Bismarck a debt of gratitude. But while French republicans proclaimed the new regime in the backwash of Sedan, two monarchists—Adolphe Thiers and the Comte de Chambord—actually did more to give it roots. The legislative election of February 1871 was held in an atmosphere of national demoralization and disarray. In these circumstances, and in the absence of any accepted national leadership, the predominantly peasant electorate turned to familiar local leaders, men of substance and standing in the rural community. The National Assembly was therefore heavily populated with large landowners, frequently of aristocratic lineage and monarchist proclivities. They promptly selected as Chief of the Executive Power (a title which was later changed to President of the Republic) Adolphe Thiers, one of the chief critics of the Second Empire and a leading Orléanist for four decades.

There is no question that the assembly, once it had annihilated the communards, had the votes for the restoration of the monarchy. What it did not have was agreement on which royal house to restore. The monarchist majority was about equally divided between Legitimists (that is, partisans of the Bourbon line) and Orléanists. As a result, the wounds of 1830 opened up again. The Bourbon pretender, who was already calling himself Henry V, was the Comte de Chambord, grandson of Charles X. Chambord was a rigid Catholic and political conservative; he had spent his entire adult life in exile, mostly in Austria and Switzerland, and had little sense of the realities of French politics. He assumed that the populace wanted a return to the days of his grandfather and insisted, for example, that his own rule be accompanied by rejection of the tricolor and the adoption of the white flag of the Bourbons as the national standard. Such follies alarmed the Orléanists, who pictured Chambord as an unreconstructed absolutist quite out of sympathy with their own preference for parliamentary and constitutional monarchy.

While the monarchists quarreled bitterly, the republicans were gaining ground in legislative by-elections held to fill seats left vacant by death, resignation, and multiple elections. (There being no residence requirement for election, several well-known candidates—such as Thiers—were elected by more than one constituency.) Republican spokesmen—most notably the young lawyer Leon Gambetta—labored to dissociate their cause from the excesses of the Commune and to identify the monarchists as partisans of despotism and theocracy. It was clear that the February 1871 vote, held in such abnormal conditions, had not accurately reflected the popular mood, and that the republican experience of 1848 had—for all its turmoil—worked something of a conversion in the French countryside and small towns. In these circumstances, Thiers began to doubt the wisdom of a restoration.

Like many conservatives of the post-1848 era, Thiers was more interested in substance than in forms. When he announced that the republic was "the government which divides us least," he was placing the need for order before his philosophical preference for monarchy. Restoration would keep the republicans in a state of agitation and threaten not only the throne but perhaps the social order itself. Moreover, France remained obliged to pay Germany a sizeable war indemnity and would have to submit to German occupation until the bill had been settled. For France to meet this challenge and to take its place once more as a major European power, national unity was absolutely indispensable. A conservative republic—and Thiers was convinced that the republic could ke kept conservative—would pacify the republicans and still preserve the interests of property and traditional authority. Thiers threw his own considerable personal prestige behind the republic, a prestige much heightened by the dispatch with which he organized payment of the indemnity and cleared French soil of foreign troops. His treatment of the Commune had shown that the republic meant to tolerate no antics on the radical left. In May 1873, the monarchist majority in the assembly finally determined to be done with this apostate. But by the time he was forced from office, Thiers had done much to legitimize the republicans and to make the republic itself respectable.

The Comte de Chambord did nearly as much to aid his enemies. The monarchists had worked out a compromise to heal their breach: Chambord was childless, and it was agreed that his successor would be the Orléanist claimant, the Comte de Paris. The assembly's majority was therefore confident that a restoration was within reach and appointed a royalist army officer, Marshal MacMahon, to the presidency while they worked out the details. Chambord, however, refused to yield on such questions as the white flag. His supporters realized that if they let him have his way, they would have an open republican revolt on their hands. Instead, they simply waited, hoping that Chambord would at least have the decency to expire in some haste and thus clear the way for the more flexible Comte de Paris. But Chambord lived until 1883, by which time the voters had delivered the legislature firmly into republican hands. With Chambord and Thiers, the old conservatism and the new combined to give France its third republic, one which lasted until another military defeat at German hands brought it down in 1940.

The Third Republic was not a regime from which conservatives had much to fear. Universal suffrage, and the fact that France was urbanizing and industrializing at a sluggish rate, kept the two-house legislature created by the constitution of 1875 in the control of the countryside and the small towns. For all the fervent devotion to the republic there, fierce regional economic conflicts and a persistent spirit of individualism generated several versions of republicanism rather than one to go with Legitism, Orléanism, and even a small but dogged Bonapartist group. The republicans were even more divided than the monarchists and suffered from the added (and self-imposed) handicap that they rejected the idea of strong, unifying leadership. They had had their fill of strongmen with Louis-Napoleon, and they feared that people bidding for republican leadership—as Gambetta appeared to be doing in the late 1870's—had designs on rather too extensive powers. Most of the republicans preferred genuine parliamentary rule, and the constitution accorded sharply limited responsibilities to the president. President MacMahon only reinforced those concerns when, in 1877, he dismissed the republican premier and dissolved the republican-dominated assembly. The republicans held their majority in the subsequent election and forced MacMahon to resign in early 1879.

Thereafter, presidents of the Third Republic served mainly ornamental functions. Cabinets tended to be filled with moderate, satisfied republicans who did not intend to disturb the status quo. The system of multiple parties meant government by coalition, which necessitated compromise rather than bold action. Politics tended to focus on ideological disputes, such as the question of state versus church control of education, rather than on conflicts of material interest. A socialist movement was beginning to make noises, but it too was divided into several warring factions. In sum, the Third Republic hardly fulfilled the dreams of those who had gone to the barricades in June 1848. It was not so much the regime which divided Frenchmen least, as it was a negative compromise reached by a deeply divided France.

Great Britain and Russia

No social group in Europe coped better with the challenge of change than the British aristocracy. The Great Reform Bill of 1832 and the tariff repeal of 1846 had loosened but by no means broken its grip on power. By mid-century, Britain was the most industrialized, and rapidly industrializing, nation on earth, and its political institutions the most liberal outside of the United States; but it was also largely governed by the same elites which had dominated eighteenth-century politics. Middle-class politicians were taking a more prominent role in government, but the strategic positions were still occupied by titled landholders.

Whereas Bismarck, for instance, viewed parliamentary institutions as a distasteful but expedient means of co-opting critics, the British elite took a more positive view, having historically regarded parliamentary government as the alternative to royal absolutism. Still, British Conservatives were inclined to give way grudgingly. Their resistance to reform in 1832 had been massive, if vain, and their refusal to bend before democratic agitation was not only successful, but mobilized support from the industrial bourgeoisie. Even in the 1860's, the Conservative party saw no compelling reason why it should go beyond 1832; and it took the efforts of an outsider—Benjamin Disraeli, middle-class and Jewish—to convince Conservatives otherwise.

Disraeli was a novelist, and the son of an author, who entered Parliament in 1837 at the age of thirty-three. At first he gave few signs of political suppleness. He held firm to protectionism and was instrumental in leading the backbench revolt which overthrew his own party leader, Sir Robert Peel, in 1846. But he continued to rise steadily in the party, thanks in large part to his oratorical talents, until by the late 1850's he was the Conservative leader in the House of Commons.

Like most Conservatives, Disraeli viewed a mounting campaign for further extension of the franchise with deep concern, but he became convinced that resistance was pointless. Rather, he hoped to steal some of the new electorate from the Liberal party and identify the Conservatives with reform. When his party, under the Earl of Derby, formed a government in 1866, Disraeli simply picked up a rather lukewarm Liberal program for electoral reform, expanded it substantially, placed the Conservative label on it, and guided it through the House of Commons—much to the consternation of Conservative landed interests whose cause Disraeli insisted he was serving. The Second Reform Bill of 1867 made some changes in representation, in view of continued urbanization, and doubled the electorate to nearly two million voters (out of a population in excess of 30 million).

The newly enfranchised voters showed little gratitude; and although Disraeli had formed his own government early in 1868, the elections that November swept the Conservatives from office. For more than five years, Britain was ruled by one of the most formidable liberals of the century, William Gladstone. The son of a merchant and cast in the mold of unswerving Christian moralism, Gladstone guided Britain through an unprecedented experience of broad-gauged reform. His cabinet sponsored improvements in public education, the judicial system, and the system of civil service appointments. It overhauled the army, among other things ending the purchase of commissions. It initiated the secret ballot in legislative elections. It abolished religious barriers to college degrees. Such bursts of reform naturally irritate nearly as many persons as they please, and the election of 1874 turned the Liberals out of office. Disraeli promised a reduction in the pace of reform, a pause in which the country could take stock of things, but he did not repudiate reform altogether. Even though Disraeli's chief tactic was to divert attention from domestic questions with an aggressive imperial policy, his government also enacted important legislation on public sanitation and housing conditions. In the late 1860's and 1870's, therefore, both of Britain's political parties committed themselves to reform, and the Conservatives in particular learned to swallow principles in order to keep the taste of power.

In strong contrast to Britain, the most reactionary government in Europe at mid-century was easily that of Russia. Czar Nicholas I ruled his huge empire from 1825 to 1855 by sheer repression, with a huge bureaucracy dedicated to domestic spying, and infiltration and exposure of underground reformist groups, and censorship. Although radical ideas from the west began to find their way eastward, 1848 occasioned not a ripple in this rigorous autocracy. But some conservatives were beginning to fear that there was no holding the lid on, that without a safety valve an explosion was inevitable, and that Russia could not avoid some recognition that the nineteenth century was well under way. Change from the top is frequently precipitated only by crisis, which came in Russia's case with military defeat at the hands of Britain and France in the Crimean War of 1854–56. Nicholas' death in the midst of war gave enlightened conservatives their chance, for his successor, Alexander II, was amenable to reform.

The reform era opened in 1861 with the abolition of serfdom, which even the Russian nobility had come to regard as an anachronism. Serfs, bound for life to work a piece of land they did not own, were now granted personal freedom. In addition, they were made landowners: the government purchased land from the aristocracy and redistributed it to the peasantry in small plots (the size determined by the size of the family). Peasants then had nearly fifty years to pay the government for the land. The scheme scarcely ended the staggering poverty of Russia's rural poor; the land allotments were tiny, and the nobility kept the choicest acreage for itself. But it was a promising start.

By 1864, the reformist impulse had reached to government, and an important decree established local councils (known as *zemstvos*) representing all classes and empowered to levy taxes for such needs as roads and schools. In the same year, a new court system rationalized a hopelessly antiquated legal structure. In 1870, municipal government passed into the hands of new administrative bodies elected by property owners.

Czarist absolutism remained untouched, however, and the whole machinery of repression remained intact. Indeed, by the 1870's, there was more than enough radical activity to keep it busy. New secret societies sought to spread their revolutionary message to the peasantry and to intimidate authority with terrorist attacks upon some of its representatives. Such patent lack of gratitude for officially sponsored reform gave conservatives pause, yet by 1881 they were apparently ready to proceed again. Alexander, who had come through two assassination attempts the year before, approved a plan for a sort of proto-parliament: *zemstvo* representatives would be permitted to consult with government officials on proposed legislation. On the same day, however, the revolutionary terrorists struck again, and successfully. The czar's successor, Alexander III, considered reform a sign of weakness, an encouragement to subversion, and led a return to strenuously autocratic rule. His government refused to take the first step toward parliamentarism and, if anything, cracked down even harder on all forms of deviation—political dissent, religious variations from Orthodox Christianity, the nationalist pulsations among subject peoples like the Poles, the Lithuanians, and so forth. The decade of reform faded into memory, and Russia reassumed its status as Europe's most reactionary state.

7 / *Man over Nature*

The uneven development of parliamentary institutions in continental Europe was accompanied by the equally uneven spread of modern industry. Northwestern and north-central Europe did participate in what was generally regarded at the time as "progress." Elsewhere, man's age-old struggle to conquer nature was conducted largely by the same means and with the same implements as in the eighteenth century. Where advances did take place, they did so in an atmosphere of growing confidence, and even exhilaration, that both material progress and the knowledge which made it possible were boundless.

The Development of Industry

In the last half of the nineteenth century, European industrial capitalism appeared to be following precisely the course which Karl Marx had said it must. It was spreading inexorably, thoroughly transforming the economies of Germany and Belgium, making impressive advances in France and northern Italy, and becoming a major force in the Austrian half of the Austro-Hungarian empire. Only southern and eastern Europe remained in the preindustrial age, though government stimulation was producing some impressive growth in the handful of large Russian cities where modern industry had sprouted up. Moreover, capitalist industry was concentrating and consolidating, just as Marx had predicted. Geographically, it tended to locate not merely in cities, but in regions of any given nation which offered such advantages as proximity to raw materials and to major transportation routes. But it was also concentrating in fewer and fewer hands. Competition had by no means eliminated small producers from the marketplace. But as the twentieth century came bustling into sight, the trend was distinctly toward larger firms, toward efforts at monopolistic domination of a market, and toward international cartels. Finally, Marx seemed justified in his faith that growing, concentrating industry would be racked by increasingly severe crises. In 1857, again in 1866, and again in 1873, financial panics touched off major industrial depressions. Although Europe pulled out of each of these slumps, and although the subsequent crises of the 1880's and early 1890's were less grave, every decade of the closing century brought with it economic convulsion.

What the Marxists failed to see was that these upheavals were not the suicidal spasms of mature capitalism, but rather the symptoms of immaturity. With growth proceeding at an unprecedented, indeed unthought of, pace, little consideration was given to security. Financiers were frantically establishing credit structures for industrial investment but disregarding curbs on speculation. In the absence of international monetary cooperation and controls, financial panics were unavoidable; the failure of one overextended bank inevitably threatened others in other countries. Capitalist economists admitted that the boom-and-clump pattern might very well be in the nature of things, but pointed out also that recovery had followed each instance of faltering. Their arguments were given added weight after the crisis of the early 1890's, when recovery and growth were unmistakably vigorous.

While the Marxists hovered about, waiting for industrial capitalism to fulfill their direst predictions, the machines of continental industry were whirring away and even threatening to drown out the British. In the critical area of textiles, the continent modernized rapidly in the last half of the century, and by the late 1880's German garments were making alarming inroads into the British domestic market itself. Metallurgical industry followed suit, fueled by the discovery of huge coal and iron ore fields in northeastern France and adjacent sectors of western Germany. The railroad began knitting together national markets. Power-driven machinery left no doubt that it would displace manual power in the production of most goods. And all the while, the burgeoning financial community, with an assist from government legislation, was creating investment banks which would both underwrite and profit from industrial growth.

The statistical expressions of continental industrialization are, like most of the numbers in economic history, at the same time impressive, in dispute, and forgettable. Any version of them is likely to occasion sputterings from specialists, and perhaps rightly so. Yet specialists will also agree that Europe *did* move into the modern industrial age in this period, however much their bar graphs may fail to correlate. The important point is not that the major continental nations closed the gap between themselves and Britain—on this there is little debate—but that they were substantially aided in so doing because Britain had enjoyed a head start.

To reiterate an observation made in Chapter 2, the British industrial revolution proceeded without benefit of a model. By mid-century, however, Britain itself constituted such a model for other nations. The continent could (which is not to say that it did in every case) avoid British mistakes, dead-ends, and false starts. Moreover, continental Europe did not need to grope through the primitive stages of industrialization in the drive to emulate the mature, or maturing, British economy. Rather it could simply *copy* Britain at the contemporary level of British development.

There is never an easy way to industrialize, but it is still less difficult when one knows where one is going. A group of scientists in the 1970's who wished to land a man on the moon would not be condemned to begin with the rocketry of the 1920's and gradually work their way toward the technology which achieved a moon landing in 1969. They would attempt to replicate the American technology of the 1970's. In just the same manner, the continental nations best equipped to industrialize in the nineteenth century were able to overleap, or at least to collapse, some of the earlier phases of British industrial development; to avoid the expense of replacing obsolete machinery with that devised by the latest inventions; and to move toward industrial modernity with remarkable speed.

Growth was also facilitated by the destruction of certain residual practices of the preindustrial age. Where craft-guild restrictions on competition persisted, they were abolished. Laws against usury were hardly effective by the second half of the nineteenth century, but their reversal in those decades at least helped to clear the way for modernized credit structures. Legal obstacles to streamlined business organization began to fall, and the limited liability joint-stock corporation became virtually synonymous with modern capitalism. At the same time, technical and scientific education came into their own, as European educators and governments began to admit that a man who could quote Latin poetry might be of little use when it came to developing a sophisticated method of refining steel.

The intricate play of demand and supply also promoted industrial expansion. The growth of population opened up new markets. The discovery of new sources of fuel—coalfields in northwestern Europe, electricity, and petroleum—made increased output possible. When, toward the end of the century, European nations began to acquire colonial possessions in Africa and Asia, these areas provided both a certain demand (as a market) and supply (as a source of raw materials). As the national and international market grew, improved communications and transport became essential. Europe shrank itself and the world through the development of steamships, telegraphy, telephonic communications, and the internal combustion engine. All the while, the volume of European industrial production and trade did not merely rise, it soared.

The progress of industrialization was of course uneven on the continent. Russia, the largest European nation, remained an agricultural and handicraft economy until the very end of the nineteenth century, and even then factory production was largely confined to a few large cities. On the other hand, Belgium, one of the smallest nations, was also the most thoroughly industrialized. Northern Italy plunged headlong into the industrial era, while south of Rome a society which had altered little for centuries held back. Austria modernized its economy in substantial part, while Hungary (outside of Budapest) remained a land of huge agricultural estates. The major industrial powers were France and Germany.

In the first half of the nineteenth century, the production of French textiles made notable gains, but did so largely (if not exclusively) within the framework of domestic industry. Steam-powered machinery located in large factories was of marginal importance until the period of the Second Empire, when Napoleon III—perhaps impressed by what he saw during several years of exile in Britain—energetically encouraged the modernization of French manufacturing. The emperor gave official sanction to new industry, promoted railroad building, and worked to make credit resources more accessible. He also exposed French industry to what he felt (as most French businessmen did not) was the healthy effect of competition with the British by concluding a free-trade treaty in 1860. Still, it is possible to exaggerate Napoleon's contribution to the French transition into the industrial age. It can be argued that the Second Empire was merely there at the right time, that it only reaped the benefits of preparatory work done during the July Monarchy. It is indeed possible to see France in the 1840's as a nation poised on the threshold of industrial takeoff, ready to synthesize capital, resources, and know-how into an industrial revolution, only to have the disruptions of 1848 depress the economy, deflate business confidence, and postpone change until order could be restored. In any event, Napoleon III did restore order, at some cost to political liberty, and at least presided sympathetically over France's economic modernization.

That process did not take place overnight. For one thing, France remained primarily an agricultural nation; urban population did not outweigh rural population until the 1930's. For another, the free-trade treaty may have helped weed out backward and inefficient enterprises by forcing them to compete with the British. But French industrialists were still rattled by the sight of British goods swamping their own markets. Without protected markets guaranteeing a high profit return, French industry was reluctant to risk competitive expansion, and the boom of the 1850's tapered off markedly in the 1860's. More important, French investors found they could expect a better return in certain foreign ventures —Russian factories, for instance, or railroad building in a number of European countries. As a result, while the industrial sector steadily expanded throughout the second half of the nineteenth century (helped in the 1890's by the reintroduction of high tariffs), it failed to grow at anything like the rate of Germany's.

Even before unification, certain individual German states were demonstrating impressive industrial potential; Bismarck did not so much create an industrial colossus as he welded together its various components. The Germans had several advantages: a large population, abundant natural resources and wealth, and domestic stability, not to mention the example of Britain. By the early 1870's, Germany had already outstripped France in textile, metallurgical, and coal production; by the end of the century, German industry had still not yet caught the British in every sector, but the trend in that direction was plain. By 1900, Great Britain had not lost industrial leadership in Europe, but was losing it.

Although Germany's resources were surely enviable, the evidence that they exceeded Britain's is not convincing. The British were as wealthy and as well supplied (in most crucial respects) as the Germans; the British colonial empire provided markets and materials which no European nation could match. Britain suffered in its struggle with Germany for industrial supremacy not so much from inferiority as from superiority. Again, German industry possessed the incalculable advantage of the British model, and it was a financial as well as a technological advantage. German business could, for example, purchase the most up-to-date machinery at relatively little expense, since it did not have to scrap a huge industrial plant inherited from a previous generation—which is precisely what the British had to do in such a case. As a result, innovation in production proved easier, because cheaper, in Germany. Furthermore, success apparently fostered a certain confidence in the tried and true. British industrialists showed a relative lack of interest in the untested methods which their German counterparts employed to great advantage. British investors seemed wary of risking capital in new, if potentially rewarding, enterprises of the sort which did not go begging in Germany. The British tended to rely on industry itself to produce technological advance, much as it had in the 1770's and 1780's. The Germans established a system of technical education designed to produce a corps of skilled engineers which was publicly funded and second to none in Europe. State support was also critical when it came to the establishment of sophisticated financial institutions and to processing legislation which allowed German businessmen to reduce competition by creating massive cartels.

Technology and Science

Economic historians have hotly debated whether primacy in continental industrialization ought to be awarded to the role of technology, supply, demand, social structural considerations, or some other factor. Most contemporaries, for their part, were convinced that technology was responsible for the remarkable transformation of nature into useful commodities for increasing man's control over his environment. Machines which could produce items by the hundreds in the same time that mere humans could produce the same items by the dozens were the wonder of Europe. Educated persons were confident that superior technology was at the base of their superior economies, and that modern science was in its turn the source of technology.

The relationship of theoretical, laboratory science to technology is complex and problematical. It is commonly held that technology is the practical application of science, a means of turning abstract theory into something workable and useful. On the other hand, we know that technology is often its own source, that machinists and engineers sometimes make improvements in blissful ignorance of relevant scientific theory. After all, it was not until a half century *after* the invention of the steam engine that physicists came up with an adequate theoretical account of the principles upon which it operated. But it was something like an article of faith for enlightened Europeans in the last half of the nineteenth century that the progress of society was closely linked to the progress of science. In a fashion which would have warmed the hearts of most *philosophes,* it was firmly believed that the growth of man's knowledge about the world increased his control over it.

"Scientism" is an unattractive word, but it describes this faith reasonably well. Modern industry appeared to result from the application of scientific principles; modern business enterprises similarly demanded rational organization and scientific exactitude. One could hardly argue with progress, and thus the scientistic mentality—born in the eighteenth century—came of age in the nineteenth.

In Charles Dickens' novel *Hard Times* (1854), Thomas Gradgrind, a retired wholesale hardware merchant—described as "A man of realities. A man of facts and calculations"—tells the local schoolmaster:

> Now, what I want is Facts. Teach these boys and girls nothing but Facts. Facts alone are wanted in life. Plant nothing else, and root out everything else. You can only form the minds of reasoning animals upon Facts: nothing else will ever be of any service to them. This is the principle on which I bring up my own children, and this is the principle on which I bring up these children. Stick to Facts, sir!

Gradgrind was plainly no scientist, but he is a splendid example of the scientistic mind. He proceeds to tell the schoolchildren:

You are to be in all things regulated and governed by fact. We hope to have, before long, a board of fact, composed of commissioners of fact, who will force the people to be a people of fact, and of nothing but fact. You must discard the word Fancy altogether.

Gradgrind would have disliked using a fictional character to illustrate an historical argument (though Dickens was surely creating what he was confident his audience would regard as a recognizable type). But one need not be limited to fiction to grasp the status of science. Marx claimed that his version of socialism was superior to those of his competitors (whom he labeled "utopians") because it was "scientific." The Frenchman Auguste Comte determined to create a "science of society." The Englishman Herbert Spencer tried to apply the newest biological theories to social analysis, and his compatriot Henry Thomas Buckle wrote a purportedly scientific *History of Civilization in England* (1857–61). Biblical criticism, which had been incorporating techniques of rational analysis since the seventeenth century, become self-consciously "scientific" in the nineteenth. David Strauss published a *Life of Jesus* (1835) in Germany which treated Christianity in purely nonmetaphysical terms, and Ernest Renan's *Life of Jesus* (1863) offered French readers a "scientific" explanation for the miracles related in the Gospels. Scientism, in short, was a disposition which took the word "scientific" to be equivalent to "truth."

The scientistic mentality rested on more than impressive industrial technology. Science itself had been making important advances in the nineteenth century. Investigation into what was then taken to be the irreducible unit of inorganic matter—the atom—spurred chemists to group chemical elements according to atomic weight. Such work led to the systematic identification of elements and the progressive discovery of new ones—which is to say that science was learning to name and to categorize all nature. A German biologist named Theodor Schwann convincingly demonstrated in the late 1830's that the cell was the organic counterpart of the atom, the basic and irreducible unit of living tissue. His findings opened the way to important discoveries with respect to bacterial disease and immunology. Michael Faraday's electromagnetic research in the 1820's and 1830's in England helped lead modern physics into the study of a new source of energy. In the following decade, Hermann von Helmholtz mathematically formulated a law which held that energy took several forms (electricity, magnetism, heat) and that there was a constant, unchanging fund of it in the world, though it might be converted from one form to another. The law of the "conservation of energy" combined with that of the "conservation of matter"—formulated in the late eighteenth century and asserting that matter might change forms but was ultimately indestructible—as the cornerstones of the nineteenth-century vision of nature. The very fact that such fundamental laws could be formulated, revealing nature's most profound workings, only reinforced the scientistic faith. Nature seemed to be grudgingly revealing its most intimate secrets to science. Each new discovery seemed to promise that the mysteries of life would soon be mysteries no more.

Much of nineteenth-century science was the affair of scholarly journals and learned societies. As the various disciplines became more specialized and more mathematical, it was difficult even for interested intellectuals to engage in experiments which were at all up to date (as Goethe and Voltaire had done in earlier generations). Science became increasingly the province of a specially trained caste, and the general public was ever more dependent upon popularizers (a fact which failed to discourage faith in the truth revealing powers of science). One important case, however, ran counter to the prevailing tendency. The publication of Charles Darwin's *On the Origin of Species* in 1859 deeply engaged the public interest and provoked a major furor over the findings of modern science. On no occasion since has a scientist provoked such direct popular reaction.

Darwin and Darwinism

Charles Darwin was one of those men who happened along at just the right time. His was not a brilliantly innovative mind, capable of dazzling insight or inspired intuition. Darwin's strengths lay rather in diligence and synthesis, the ability to pull together great masses of disparate evidence into a coherent whole. This is not to belittle his contribution, but merely to define it: *both* original discovery and synthesis are integral to scientific progress.

Darwin's name is closely associated with the theory of biological evolution. In fact, evolutionary notions had been circulating among scientists for nearly a century prior to the appearance of *On the Origin of Species*. Eighteenth-century biologists and botanists involved in classifying the various versions of fauna and flora had noticed several structural similarities between certain separate forms. The implication was of course that the more complex variations might have evolved from the simpler forms, though no one was prepared to say how. Geologists of the early nineteenth century accumulated impressive data suggesting that the earth itself was the product of gradual development. By mid-century, there was abundant evidence at hand waiting to be synthesized into a theory of evolution. Indeed, Darwin was moved to publish his own conclusions when he learned in 1858 that an English scientist working in the far east named Alfred Wallace was rapidly approaching a theory similar to his own.

What had hitherto discouraged a full-blown statement of biological evolution was not an absence of empirical evidence but rather the testimony from an admittedly nonscholarly publication: the Bible. The first chapter of the first book of the Old Testament described a creation in which all organic and inorganic matter were divinely confected in six days. In strict Christian biology, everything on earth—and the earth itself—was created "in the beginning" and had not altered since. The works of God are immutable, ran the argument; he who would say nay contradicts scripture. The solvent of rationalism had of course been eating away at literal interpretation of the Bible for some time, but in 1859 numerous and respected defenders of the Genesis version were still about. They took Darwin's work as not merely a defiance of biblical teachings but as an effort to make of man something other than a creature cast in the image of God.

On the Origin of Species presented voluminous evidence in support of the theory that species evolve rather than having all been created at once. It was the range of materials upon which Darwin drew which helped clinch his argument for the scientific community, already prepared to believe in evolution if a convincing synthesis of data could be made. There was stiff resistance, laced with liberal doses of misinterpretation, among religious fundamentalists; and a lively public controversy ensued. The anti-Darwinians shrieked that Darwin saw man as nothing more than a descendant of the apes, and the penny press in England was filled with satirical cartoons—such as one of a creature with the head of Charles Darwin and the body of a monkey. The Darwinians pointed out that *On the Origin of Species* only claimed that men and the primates had a common ancestor and insisted that the conclusions of dispassionate science, however disconcerting, were preferable to myth and ignorance.

This aspect of Darwinism was entertaining, and sold newspapers, but in the long run was of marginal importance. Christians were ultimately able to square their belief in a divine creation with acceptance of Darwin's arguments, treating Genesis as a metaphor rather than a literal description; and evolution gradually assumed a certain respectability. A far more profound influence emerged from Darwin's theory of "natural selection," which was elaborated into a sweeping social philosophy.

Besides proving that species evolved, Darwin would also have liked to explain *how* they evolved, by what means new species were created. This he could not accomplish, since he lacked an adequate theory of heredity, and even flirted with the disreputable notion of the inheritance of acquired characteristics.* Short of accounting for the appearance of new species, Darwin had to content himself with explaining the persistence of

---

* It was not until the end of the century that geneticists discovered mutation, the process whereby parents can transmit characteristics to their progeny which they themselves lack.

old ones and thus the great diversity of animal and vegetable life. The Darwinian vision of nature, appropriate to an age of advancing industrialization, bore little resemblance to that of early romanticism. Nature was not a sylvan dell, but an arena in which all living things combated for survival, devouring one another in the process. In this Malthusian world, survival went to those best suited for the struggle, those best able to adapt to the challenges posed by other combatants. According to Darwin, nature "selects" for survival the species which adapt most successfully, and they proliferate while others do not. All sorts of adaptations were involved in this theory of natural selection—protective coloration, the ability to exist on certain sorts of nutrition, the capacity to withstand intemperate climates, and so forth. Yet the tendency of many lay readers was to conclude that success went to the "strong," a tendency perhaps encouraged by Darwin's reference to the "survival of the fittest" and his emphasis on "struggle." The weak rarely won struggles.

It did not take long for social philosophers to grasp the implications of natural selection. Indeed, some had been thinking along parallel lines well before 1859. Most of the tenets of what came to be known as Social Darwinism were already at hand in the doctrines of laissez faire; however, *On the Origin of Species* cloaked them in the mantle of science. The Social Darwinists argued that human society was no less a part of nature than an anthill or a bird's nest, and was therefore governed by the same scientific laws. The fit would survive, the unfit would not—though no question of exploitation was here involved; this was merely the way of nature, as irreversible as the tides. The possessing classes had adapted; they were the strong, the successful competitors in modern society. Those who contended that the successful had been harsh with the weak whom they had trampled in the struggle, should keep in mind that nature's ways *were* harsh, that survival itself was at stake. Moreover, there were no fairy godmothers in nature to rescue the unfit from extinction, no referees to make certain the rules were being observed—since there were no rules. How foolish, how "unnatural" it was, therefore, to allow intervention in the struggles of human society and run the risk of upsetting its delicate balance.

Obviously, Social Darwinism was tailor-made for European society in the late nineteenth century, a "scientific" updated version of laissez faire to be flung at bleeding hearts and do-gooders. It is interesting to note that Darwin's ideas, which bore certain general resemblances to those of Marx—both thought-systems were basically historical, both rather mechanistic and deterministic, both centered on the process of conflict—were appropriated to justify the very status quo which Marx was determined to destroy. Nor was Social Darwinism exclusively a tool for the justification of industrial capitalist society. It clearly fitted neatly also into the more superheated versions of nationalism and provided "scientific" ammunition for racists and imperialists as well. It comes as no particular surprise to discover Adolf Hitler spouting Social Darwinist doctrine in the 1920's. (See Chapter 13.) Charles Darwin did not create this ethos, but he unwittingly encouraged it and gave it scientific credentials. Yet he also provided a response to it more telling than any moralist's: evolution itself. The wealthy and powerful at any given time see their position of dominance as the result of "natural" processes, the inevitable outcome of their fitness. They forget that change—just as much as struggle—is the way of nature. Had the dinosaur possessed a reflective brain, he would doubtless have scoffed at the notion that something the size of homo sapiens would rule the earth. Unlike Marx's classless, stateless society, Darwinian evolution has no "end." Social Darwinists failed to understand that the dinosaurs of one era are the museum pieces of another.

Scientism and Its Critics

Scientism is the name we give to the growing faith in the efficacy of science, the confidence that science was the key to intellectual and material progress. One problem in dealing with scientism, however, is that it was never codified into a formal philosophy. The French thinker Auguste Comte worked out a systematic program in the 1840's which he called "positivism" ("positive" in the sense that it would be free of superstition, metaphysics, myth) which was clearly scientistic. Utilitarianism, which was most important in England under the inspiration of Jeremy Bentham and, in the mid-nineteenth century, John Stuart Mill, valued usefulness above all other criteria. But such schools or movements of thought cannot envelop the entire scientistic mentality, which was a set of popularly shared assumptions (at least in the minds of much of the educated middle classes) rather than a carefully worked out philosophy.*

The mentality at issue here was thoroughly materialistic: it admitted no reality beyond matter, no reality which could not be apprehended by the human senses. Religion it regarded as at best an intellectual error and at worst a conspiracy hatched by reactionary obscurantists. Human beings, in the scientistic vision, were complex bundles of chemical and electrical energy which also possessed the rational faculty to understand how the whole process worked. Man and his world could be infinitely improved by exercising that faculty, for humans were capable of appreciating what was in their best interest and then pursuing it. One had only to make that interest clear, to expose men to the proper stimuli in order to

---

* Although "scientism" is a good label, "secularism" or "materialism" would probably do just as well.

receive the desired response. That which was "bad" in the world was the result of the wrong stimuli. "Virtue and vice," wrote the French positivist literary critic Hippolyte Taine in 1863, "are products, like sulphuric acid and sugar."

Scientism, like Social Darwinism, was plainly the reflection of an industrial age. While insisting upon the existence of free, rational choice, it was ultimately mechanistic. Men were machines which could be operated "correctly" simply by pressing the correct buttons. Just as engineers could improve machines by refining them according to the most up-to-date scientific principles, social engineers could "improve" human behavior by following the same principles. Again, Taine gives a concise summation of this positivist position: "In our view, nothing exists but facts and laws." Once these were all known, human society would function as smoothly as the best modern cotton looms.

Although in part a recrudescence of Enlightenment empiricism, the scientistic persuasion was somewhat bloodless and humorless when compared to its eighteenth-century progenitor. It lacked the tragic dimension so fully present in Voltaire and Diderot, who would have regarded its boundless confidence with suspicion. At bottom, the *philosophes* shared nearly as much with romanticism as with scientism. And, although nineteenth-century materialists were eager to stamp out romanticism in all its forms, the romanticists had done their work too well. The insistence that there was "more than one layer of experience" proved difficult to uproot from the public consciousness. Religion refused to evaporate; human beings stubbornly persisted in behaving irrationally; quite unlike good machines; and certain writers tried to explain why this was so.

Fyodor Dostoevsky, the Russian novelist, answered this materialistic secularism with classical Christian arguments. Dostoevsky could not conceive of man apart from original sin, which expressed itself in perverse and frequently destructive impulses to commit evil acts, even when they ran contrary to man's rationally calculated interests. In *Notes from the Underground* (1863), Dostoevsky's narrator railed at the positivists:

> . . . even if man were only a piano key, even if this were proved to him by science and mathematics, even then he would not become reasonable, but would purposely do something perverse, simply out of ingratitude, simply to have his own way. And if he cannot, he will devise destruction and chaos, he will devise all manner of suffering, and then he will have his own way.

Friedrich Nietzsche, a German philosopher, was a fervent anti-Christian; but he too saw man as propelled by deep inner urges and drives, some of which—such as masochism—made no sense in scientistic terms.

At the same time, creative artists began to rebel against the influence of scientism in art. For Auguste Comte, "The principle function of art is to construct types on the basis furnished by Science." Writers and painters who felt that romanticism was falsifying reality sought to give art a "realistic" flavor. Still others found realism too patently fabricated and attempted a completely accurate reproduction of nature (a movement much stimulated by the development of photography). "I don't worry much about beauty or perfection," wrote the French novelist Emile Zola in 1866. His interest, instead, was "truth." Yet art's traditional relationship to something called "beauty"—a category Gradgrind would have had difficulty defining—proved hard to sever. Aesthetes described the drabness of naturalism, which they correctly diagnosed as a symptom of industrial society, and began to proclaim that art served no social function. Rather, it existed for its own sake, and was its own justification. "What is beautiful," asserted the French novelist Gustave Flaubert in 1880, "is moral, that is all there is to it."

Critiques of scientism steadily gathered momentum, but it was not until the early twentieth century that they widely shook confidence in the "facts and laws" of which Taine wrote. (See Chapter 12.) Even when cracks in the synthesis began to be revealed by science itself, the educated public paid little attention. For just at the time that certain scientists began to raise questions about the scientistic version of reality, science was becoming almost incomprehensible to laymen—even those with an amateur interest in the subject. To grasp new developments increasingly demanded an expertise in mathematics which was confined to a relative handful of professionals. As a result, the old synthesis tended to persist in the lay mind after experts had begun to doubt it.

Moreover, the conspicuous progress of industrial technology and material growth persuaded most persons that man's conquest of nature was proceeding apace—perhaps even a little ahead of schedule. Western and central Europeans born in the second half of the nineteenth century had usually been taught that technological progress was a reflection of scientific progress, that there was little that science did not know and nothing it could not know. As man increased his mastery over his environment, there seemed no good reason to think otherwise.

8 / *Industrial Society and Culture*

One thing may be said with confidence of Europeans at the end of the nineteenth century: there were more of them than ever before. Estimates vary wildly, of course, and for some countries (such as the Balkan states) there is no reliable census data for the period. Population growth in the second half of the century was perhaps one percent, so that there were probably half again as many Europeans in 1900 as in 1850. From place to place, of course, the growth rate differed drastically, as the following table of major states illustrates:

State	1850	1900
Great Britain	27.3 million	41.5 million
(England and Wales)	(17.9)	(32.5)
(Scotland)	(2.9)	(4.5)
(Ireland)	(6.5)	(4.5)
Germany (1871 area)	35.4	56.4
(Prussia)	(17.0)	(37.5)
France	35.8	39.0
Italy	24.3	32.5
Belgium	4.4	6.7
Austria-Hungary	31.4	45.4
Russia (European only)	61.0	103.3

It now appears that while population was increasing, the birth rate was declining slightly. Growth was the product not so much of fertility as of longevity. Progress in medicine curtailed the traditional rate of infant mortality (so that persons desiring children were not obliged to reproduce so often) and lengthened the life span (so that many of the Europeans in the second column above were also in the first column).

It is one thing to count people. It is quite another to characterize their social and cultural experience, a task which demands that we employ more than one perspective.

Society Old and New

The most dramatic development which the census data reveal is not raw growth, but urbanization. Large cities (in excess of 100,000 residents) contained roughly 15 percent of the European population in 1900, as opposed to scarcely 2 percent a century earlier. There were no cities of one million inhabitants in 1800; by 1890, there were five. But even these aggregate figures, which include many heavily rural countries, disguise the degree to which certain nations were becoming preponderantly urban. When the new century opened, better than 80 percent of the British population lived in what were officially classified as cities, as did more than 50 percent of the German. If the total population indeed increased at an average of one percent a year in the period 1850–1900, urban population easily outstripped it. London averaged almost 2 percent annual growth; Paris more than 3 percent; Vienna more than 5 percent; Berlin nearly 8 percent.

Someone interested in the origins of contemporary European urbanization—there are presently more than fifty cities over one million population—will surely emphasize these trends. It is worth keeping in mind, however, that as of 1900, they were still only trends. Europe was urbanizing, but not yet decisively urbanized. That 15 percent residing in large cities represents a substantial increase; it still leaves 85 percent in smaller cities, towns, and in the countryside. What passed officially for a city in late nineteenth-century Britain could run as small as 3,000 inhabitants; and only half the population of England and Wales lived in agglomerations larger than 20,000 by the 1890's. With the exception of Britain and Germany, more than half the population in every major European state still drew its livelihood from agriculture. A perceptive observer in 1900 could have seen that the future lay with the cities, but he would have had to admit that they shared the present with the countryside.

Rural Europe had not yet been relegated to the status of an underpopulated backwater, but the very fact of urban growth is evidence that conditions in the countryside were unenviable. After all, the burgeoning cities were filled principally by internal migrations. When people left farm for factory, they reduced the rural labor supply and thus helped agricultual wages increase somewhat. But migration, which occurred heavily among the young, also deprived the countryside of a vital and dynamic segment of the population and did nothing to improve the level of peasant food, shelter, working conditions, or education. Increased food tariffs in the last third of the century and the growing urban market kept most peasants from starvation. The quality of their lives remained dismal, increasingly unable to compete with urban excitement and opportunity (however much an illusion they proved to be).

Historians impressed by success (and also, perhaps, by Karl Marx) have seen the nineteenth century as a "bourgeois" century, one whose shape and direction were dictated by Europe's middle classes. There is no question that the bourgeoisie played an increasingly central role in European political, social, economic, and cultural life. Unquestionably, the European middle classes were coming into possession of larger and larger shares of the national wealth in most states. Their representatives were filling more and more seats in European parliaments. Bourgeois patterns of taste were spreading and even beginning to displace the aristocratic fashions which had for so long set the pace. It was becoming relatively rare in the late nineteenth century for prosperous businessmen to cash in their holdings and retire to a country estate. At the same time, titled landholders were concluding that there was nothing objectionable about making money and were widely involved in capitalistic enterprises both agrarian and industrial.

There is no doubt that Europe was becoming embourgeoisified. But there are legitimate doubts as to how complete the middle-class triumph was by 1900. Aristocracy was giving ground, but then it still had ground to give. Outside of Britain, Germany, and Belgium, it should be recalled, agriculture remained the major economic enterprise, and no one benefited more from rising food prices and protective tariffs than large noble landowners. The advance of democracy diminished the political power of the aristocracy. Still, with the exception of France, noblemen occupied strategic positions in all the large states; and their influence remained supreme in their two traditional bastions—the foreign office and the military. When Europe went to war in 1914, it was led by officer corps very nearly as blue-blooded as those which had battled Napoleon a century earlier. The British House of Lords remained an important part of the legislative process until its definitive emasculation in 1911. All this is simply to say that, in the second half of the nineteenth century, the nobility and the middle classes shared wealth and power. Aristocratic society was gone; the aristocracy was not.

"Bourgeoisie" is, of course, the label—and not a very good one—we use to cover a broad spectrum of persons who might differ from one another as much as they differed from the nobility. Such persons ranged from a wealthy London financier to a French lawyer making do in a small provincial town, from a highly placed German civil servant to an obscure Russian school inspector, from an Italian international wine merchant to a Viennese shopkeeper in marginal circumstances. Bourgeois might be capitalists, but then the leaders of most of Europe's socialist parties were also of middle-class origins. What the middle classes shared was not values or life styles but the fact that they lived in cities and towns, did not bear a noble title, possessed some modicum of wealth (though it might be small), and did not make their living from hard manual labor.

The traditional identification of the bourgeoisie with industrial capitalism is unfortunate, not so much because it is mistaken as because it leaves the picture incomplete. To begin with, many bourgeois were capitalists but not industrialists: small shopkeepers were still an important part of the so-called lower middle classes. Though it was fashionable in some circles—aristocratic, socialist, and bohemian intellectual ones—to portray the bourgeois as avarice incarnate, in fact, many members of the middle classes fit perfectly the Marxian definition of proletarians: those who have nothing but their labor to sell. Owners of the means of production were a minority of the bourgeoisie by 1900, even if one includes all those small investors with a few stocks. As industries grew, they acquired a somewhat greater number of owners (with the spread of the joint stock company) and many more employees in lower- and middle-echelon posts. Similarly, as government continued to expand, to accept broader responsibilities and offer new services, it needed to put increasing numbers of people behind the new bureaucratic desks thus created. The demand for service personnel in business and government was massive, and gave birth to what has come to be known as the "white-collar class." These persons, and there were millions of them in late nineteenth-century Europe, pose delicate problems of social classification. They were hardly "capitalists," being bank tellers rather than bank presidents. Neither were they what socialists meant by "workers," since they were postal clerks rather than mail carriers.

The new white-collar elements, generally grouped with shopkeepers in the petite bourgeoisie, were in a precarious social position. It is true that they possessed enough education and status to mark them off from manual laborers. They set their sights upward toward a better-paying job which might also carry the right to order around a few subordinates. But they were also close enough to the margin to be concerned about losing such bourgeois identity as they commanded and sinking into the ranks of the proletariat. Their politics were highly variable. In some cases, socialist parties drew heavily on lower middle-class support. The French socialist party, for example, had a substantial following among schoolteachers and lesser civil servants. Yet many other people from the same strata were antisocialist, affirming traditional values and often supporting the stridently nationalist and conservative political movements of the early twentieth century. (See Chapter 9.)

Although it is easy enough to distinguish between the multimillionaire merchant and the humble accountant who kept his books, it is difficult to establish clear and consistent boundaries separating them both from what lay between—the unpleasantly named "middle middle classes." The latter were sometimes simply better paid employees than mere clerks, but they might also be men who owned their own businesses (though the business would have to be larger than the neighborhood corner grocery). They might be relatively responsible bureaucrats or perhaps professional men—physicians, attorneys, professors. They might not work for a living at all, supported instead by an adequate if not princely inheritance and engaged in some respectable and genteel pursuit (such as amateur scientific investigation, philanthropic work, or even, in those days, writing history). The temptation is strong to see them not as a distinct class at all but as a group of people of differing circumstances to which we have given a rather unsatisfactory collective name.

In a cold table of relevant sociological indices, there may appear to be little distance between, say, an ill-paid junior customs inspector and a skilled machinist. In the actual social life of late nineteenth-century Europe, such distinctions were manifest, often visually and aurally. The bourgeois, however petit, unfailingly signified his status by a coat and tie; a customs inspector would have had the further advantage of a uniform. On the other hand, the machinist wore a work shirt, open at the neck, besides which his hands may have been soiled by daily exposure to grease. The bourgeois would have had some education beyond simple literacy, a fact he advertised largely through his speech by aping the "correct" grammar and accent of his social betters. The worker spoke a ruder, simpler tongue, peppered with technical errors and "vulgar" slang, marked with the accent of his class. It is hard to quantify these facts, but impossible to ignore them.

The working classes performed manual labor for their livelihood and, on the whole, were less generously compensated for their work than were the bourgeoisie. But the working classes were no more a monolith than were the middle classes. Internal stratifications between skilled and unskilled labor, between traditional artisan crafts and assembly line or extremely demanding physical labor, carried on. Some stratification even became institutionalized with the coming of labor unions and their officialdom, such as shop stewards.

It is possible that a good many workers in the second half of the nineteenth century lived in conditions which, by statistical measures, were less rigorous than those of their forebearers. In most places, lower-class diet, shelter, and dress as of roughly 1900 were superior to what was the general rule for 1850. Few laborers appear to have been overcome by gratitude, however. Perhaps relative improvement—being a little less poor than one's grandparents—was small consolation when one was still poor, and when the distance between rich and poor was obviously expanding. Perhaps the new experience of marginal participation in the consumption of goods hitherto purchased by the middle classes—potted meats or Sunday clothes—generated impatience for more, and faster. Or perhaps the implorings of socialist orators finally convinced workers of the unavoidability of class struggle. In any case, the quarter-century prior to World War I was riddled with working-class agitation, crippling strikes, and a sharp rise in the fortunes of socialist political parties. (See Chapter 9.) Whatever economic history tells us about the improved purchasing power of the workers in this period, political history demonstrates profound working-class discontent.

As if the workers were not making life difficult enough for the men of power in late nineteenth-century Europe, women were becoming increasingly vocal in the denunciation of the myriad discriminations being suffered by their sex. Feminism, even though largely confined to middle-class women, was on the verge of becoming a major social and political force. The early socialists had been among the first to demand that woman be liberated from mere childbearing, house-management, and general male-pleasing. A steady flow of publications familiarized European audiences with feminist arguments; perhaps the most famous was *The Subjection of Women,* published in 1869 by the renowned English philosopher and critic John Stuart Mill. Industrial society was offering women the opportunity to leave the house and seek employment in the expanding job market, to attain economic independence and a personal identity. At first, however, most of the jobs open to women were unattractive and menial. Few middle-class women interested in constructive work wished to collect fares on trolley cars. Nursing and teaching were the two most "respectable" sorts of employment open to women. Because women were denied admission to postgraduate professional schools, female professionals were extremely rare. Middle-class women who wished to escape traditional roles thus still found it difficult to do so by the end of the century. (Working-class wives had long been forced to be workers, of course.)

The force of feminist agitation centered on less subtle matters, such as the right to vote and blatantly discriminatory statutes.* Male opposition was stubborn, though wildly illogical, unable to answer Mill's observation that a queen ruled Britain but no women sat in Parliament. French

---

* In many countries, to choose but one example, women simply had no legal standing and could not commit civil acts—such as bringing lawsuits.

leftists hinted darkly that female suffrage would bring the state under the spell of the church, since priests were widely assumed to wield unusual influence over women. Civil disobedience by the suffragettes proved an embarrassment to the male political establishment. When the militants engaged in disruptive demonstrations, authorities had to choose between enduring the inconvenience and unleashing police upon the allegedly gentle sex. Still, although some of the worst discriminatory legislation was repealed (and in most places, women could at least be legal property owners), the vote remained a male monopoly until the twentieth century.

The Quality of Life

Europeans were living longer in the second half of the nineteenth century, thanks largely to advances in medical science and improvements in health services. Although Edward Jenner had developed his vaccine against smallpox in the 1790's, vaccination was not widely practiced—much less made compulsory—for better than a half-century. When finally employed, however, it virtually eliminated the disease which had been probably the largest single killer in the previous century. By the 1870's, inoculation against disease was increasingly accepted, so that Louis Pasteur's findings with regard to virulent bacteria could be quickly absorbed and applied. By the end of the century, immunization was possible against several epidemic diseases—plague, cholera, typhoid, and diphtheria.

The conviction spread, though slowly, that cleanliness bore some relationship to health. Microbe research left little doubt, however, that germs could cause disease and infection. Physicians and the hospitals in which they worked began to pay some attention to sanitation. Conditions in private homes gradually improved with the introduction of drainage and sewage systems and of running water, which made more frequent bathing possible. Government also responded to the need for cleanliness, and legislation began to appear in the 1860's and 1870's setting (not very high) standards for water purity. A sizeable bureaucracy of sanitary inspectors sprouted up in several countries. As with most instances of material progress, these developments were most conspicuous the farther west and north one proceeded. Eastern and southern Europe accepted innovation in public and private health more slowly.

By 1900, a child born in one of the more progressive European countries was liable, if delivered in an urban hospital, to emerge into a clean room, having been coaxed into the world by a set of forceps, or perhaps even by the newly developed Caesarian operation. (If delivered at home, chances were the midwife would wash her hands and keep plenty of hot water about.) The child would soon have a stethoscope applied to its chest and have its temperature taken by a thermometer. If prematurely born or otherwise feeble, it would be popped into one of the incubators pioneered by Pasteur and perhaps put on a special diet of the new foods designed especially for babies. A corps of professional nurses kept watch over its progress, and physicians made periodic checkups. In sum, the child's chances of survival were radically increased, and as medicine continued to advance—turning, in the early twentieth century, to new drugs, better diagnostic and surgical techniques, and greater availability of health care—the life expectancy lengthened correspondingly.

On the other hand, most European children were not born in modernized hospitals in 1900. Progress was undemocratic: it favored city dwellers over peasants, Germans and Frenchmen and Englishmen over Russians and Serbs and Spaniards, and more and more it was coming to favor the rich over the poor. There was nothing particularly new about this latter discrimination, of course, but the discrepancy became more glaring as medical treatment became both more competent and more expensive. In 1850, a wealthy merchant could die—in a hospital—of the same diseases which killed a streetsweeper who could not afford hospital care. Fifty years later, however, the rich man's wealth could buy him a cure, still out of reach of the poor. Churches and other charitable organizations expended much time and money in philanthropic work, financing hospitals and sanitaria open to those unable to pay. But their efforts, commendable as they were, did little more than publicize the problem. Ultimately, government alone commanded the resources to subsidize a democratic health program (a fact most of them failed to recognize for more than a generation).

Health and longevity also fed upon a distinctly improved diet for most Europeans in the second half of the nineteenth century. Meat and green vegetables began to appear on the tables of poorer families with greater frequency, varying the traditional regimen of starches (mostly bread and potatoes). The development of refrigeration made the long-distance transportation of perishable commodities practicable. Canned foods, which began to appear in quantity toward the end of the century, also made for meals with more protein. Thanks to prosperity and technology, more people were able to afford better food more often than earlier in the century. After government began to involve itself in food inspection, people were able to eat certain foods—chiefly meat and dairy products—with growing confidence that they would not induce death. Again, however, these advances were uneven, geographically and socially. Even in England, France, and Germany, army medical authorities examining recruits after the outbreak of war in 1914 found an alarming rate of disease and deficiency attributable to substandard diet.

Industrial society made at least some gestures toward nourishing the mind as well as the body. In the traditional rural society, literacy was not a particularly essential skill. The ability to write could not help keep a peasant alive, a chore so time-consuming that there was little opportunity to explore the pleasures of reading. Literacy was therefore the property of the propertied. But industrial society was a more complex and intellectually demanding affair altogether. It gradually became accepted that workers who could not read were a liability, that some minimal degree of education was an advantage to everyone. A literate employee could perform a wider range of tasks, and the more efficiently instructed in them; besides, he made a better consumer if he was susceptible to written advertising. Scientism, with its passion for knowledge—"Facts, facts, facts"— reinforced this impulse, as did political democracy, with its emphasis on responsible citizenship, and Protestant evangelism, with the priority it placed on scripture. By the last third of the nineteenth century, free compulsory primary eduation was widely regarded as a public obligation. In urban-industrial states, illiteracy dropped off sharply as a consequence. By the end of the century, only a fraction of the population could not read and write, as compared to one-third to one-half sixty years earlier. In areas where industrialization was slow in making headway, older patterns prevailed. In Spain, for instance, nearly 70 percent of the population was illiterate as of 1900, and the figure for Russia was probably higher.

More Europeans were becoming literate, but whether they were becoming better educated in a broader sense is doubtful. Instruction for the overwhelming majority rarely went beyond the most basic skills. Few persons went on to secondary school; fewer still—in general, the children of the well-to-do—received a university degree. The cultural distance between rich and poor equaled the economic one. But if university students were of the same socioeconomic strata as at the beginning of the century, their studies were showing the impact of industrialization. The traditional curricula—classical languages, literature, history and philosophy —still dominated the great universities, in part due to characteristic academic inertia. Moreover, higher education was still regarded as a means of producing "gentlemen," of adding polish and refinement to wealth and high birth, rather than teaching occupational skills. Yet scientism made inroads here too. Science was establishing itself as a "respectable" endeavor, and social science began to attract its share of bright young men (especially in Germany and France). More and more institutions accepted the argument that a "truly educated" person would know something about science—a proposition held in high suspicion by traditionalists, who still considered intellectual cultivation to be inextricably bound up with the ability to quote something from Horace in the original Latin. But conservatives were fighting a losing battle. Society's need for engineers, economists, and technically knowledgeable bureaucrats was steadily outstripping the demand for gentlemen.

The great mass of barely literate persons were thus not trained to employ their newly acquired mental skills in the investigation of high culture. What, then, did they do with their leisure time, in an era prior to radio, television, and cinema? In the countryside, of course, leisure was a rare commodity, since agricultural labor went on from dawn to dusk. In the cities, however, where the sixty-hour work week was becoming the rule by the end of the century, people did have some leisure time, and evidence is that the poorer ones spent much of it in the consumption of alcoholic beverages. The pub, the café, the wineshop, the beer hall— these were the recreational centers for the European working classes. Alcoholism was widespread, and for all the energy of the temperance movements which sprang up in the last half of the century, it was plainly a social rather than a moral disease. The proper treatment was the opportunity for a more rewarding life, and not upright Christian ethics.

The audience for a mass culture was being created in the late nineteenth century, with its increments of literacy, purchasing power, and leisure. Only the culture itself was lacking. It would appear in the electronic twentieth century, but there were some anticipations of it in the growth of a popular press. Newspapers had originated as intellectual journals and as organs of political parties. Gradually, however, they began to function as a medium devoted to information and entertainment. It was not until the 1890's that cheaply priced newspapers full of sensationalistic stories and lurid features made their appearance in Europe. They found an avid mass readership ready and waiting for them; the penny press quickly became a staple in the European working-class diet. In addition to newspapers, spectator sports became an increasingly important diversion (though nothing like the gigantic industry of the mid-twentieth century). Contests featuring a high degree of physical brutality seemed to be the most popular among the masses, who left tennis, cricket, rowing, and golf to the well mannered and flocked to bareknuckled boxing brawls and viciously waged soccer matches. Yet cultural entrepreneurs had barely discerned the new audience and generally directed their products toward the middle and lower-middle classes.

The culture consumed by those strata was relentlessly mediocre. The European bourgeoisie's appetite for trash was apparently insatiable. A few of the people who produced for this market have, to be sure, established solid critical reputations. Dickens was a best-selling novelist; Dostoevsky's stories were often serialized in the Russian press; Richard Wagner's music dramas were immensely popular. Mostly, however, the famous artists of the time have since slipped into an oblivion they warmly merit. Still, the predominant themes of their work deserve some mention. Sentimentalism and sex (the latter usually accompanied by an uplifting moral lesson) were the stuff of which best sellers were made, an interesting commentary upon an age of scientism. Perhaps people who lived in a world of "facts" of cold, grinding machines, needed some release—and sought it in tear-jerking and titillation. Similarly, in the nonliterary arts, sensual excess was popular. Elaborate Victorian architecture, with its mishmash of classical and Gothic elements, is an excellent example of the reigning passion for ornamentation. All this could be squared with the materialistic ethos by arguing that it was merely art, neither productive nor otherwise useful, to be enjoyed but not taken very seriously (as though the two responses were incompatible).

Realism and Beyond

Artists of the second half of the nineteenth century frequently regarded romanticism as wrongheadedly as the romanticists had sometimes judged classicism. The advocates of "realism" tended to concentrate on romanticism's penchant for the fabulous and the mysterious, its attitudinizing, its preference for the "merely beautiful" as opposed to often ugly and unpleasant reality. Forgetting that the romantic movement had begun in an attempt to depict the real world in all its uniqueness and diversity, mid-century artists began to speak scornfully of "romanticizing"—that is, prettification which falsified. They insisted that art ought not to falsify, any more than science, and they proclaimed their intention to portray reality warts and all. Realists felt, moreover, that romanticists dealt too much with the grand and inspirational, ignoring the drama of the ordinary and the mediocre, and that they preached and moralized rather than allowing reality to "speak for itself." In other words, the realist's complaint about romanticism was virtually identical to the early romanticist's complaint about classicism. It is perhaps for this reason that some critics have labeled realists "disillusioned romanticists"—people who shared the values of romanticism in many respects but who saw the movement as failing to live up to those values.

The first major realist artist was Honoré de Balzac, a prolific novelist whose work in the 1830's and 1840's gives a remarkable portrait of French society. Balzac frequently researched his novels with some thoroughness and was at pains to provide accurate and extensive detail—whether of conditions in an army barracks, the furnishings of a Parisian rooming house, or regional peculiarities in peasant dress and dialect. Gustave Flaubert and Emile Zola carried on the tradition in France—Flaubert with his masterly portrait of provincial morals in *Madame Bovary* (1857), Zola with a long series of self-consciously "naturalistic" novels in the last thirty years of the century. Across the channel, Charles Dickens, William Thackeray, and Anthony Trollope mastered the realistic social novel and helped make it a popular form (even if they could not outsell semipornographic potboilers). The Russian Ivan Turgenev, who was intimately familiar with French literature, also pioneered the realist novel in his absorbing account of generational conflict between romanticism and positivism, *Fathers and Sons* (1862).

Although the novel proved to be the primary vehicle for realism, painters also participated in the rejection of romanticism, or what they took to be romanticism. Again, the lead came from France, where Gustave Courbet, Camille Corot, and Jean-François Millet resolutely refused to glamorize the world around them and attempted detached, "objective" studies of plain and homely people (often peasants and laborers). At first, their paintings met with responses from the critical establishment which ran from outrage to revulsion—their work was not "noble," edifying, uplifting. But with the advance of the scientistic world view, realism became the reigning style, especially in popular tastes; and a painter's abilities were usually measured by his skill in photographic reproduction.

The realists betrayed scientistic proclivities by their tendency to identify reality with the empirically observable. Zola, for instance, liked to think of himself as a sort of laboratory scientist, his characters as so many subjects of ironclad laws of heredity and environment. But just as scientism came under attack as too narrow, a world view incapable of accounting for certain aspects of human behavior and mistakenly describing others, so realism was also found wanting. Many artists agreed with the notion of trying to depict the "real world," but simply disagreed over the interpretation of reality. Any individual's perception of the world was "real," whether or not any other person saw the world in just that way. Dreams are real (though you would never convince Courbet to paint one), and so are colors and geometric forms and sounds. A realist painting of a human head in profile will show but one eye and one ear, although most humans have two of each; how "realistic" is the painting?

France, the birthplace of realism, led the way out. French poets challenged the realist novel with verses written in a wholly different spirit—drenched with color, sensuality, and rich, evocative symbolism. The seminal figure was Charles Baudelaire, an art and literary critic who published a book of poetry entitled *The Flowers of Evil* in 1857. In Baudelaire's poetry, to quote one of his own lines, "Fragrances, colors, and sounds echo one another," and subtle, suggestive symbols open a world beyond literal reference. At the same time, Baudelaire found much in man which is perverse, flatly contrary to the claims of positive science (not to mention upright bourgeois morality): "The unique and supreme pleasure of love lies in the certainty of doing *evil*." Baudelaire helped spawn a whole generation of poets—Stéphane Mallarmé, Paul Verlaine, and Arthur Rimbaud were the most notable—who gloried in image and sound, and counted symbolist poetry as an art superior to the realistic social novel. Mallarmé put their position succinctly when he wrote, in 1891, "To *name* an object is to suppress three-fourths of the pleasure in a poem, which consists in guessing it little by little; to *suggest* it, there is the ideal." The subjects of the symbolists were "real," but their poetry was vastly removed from realism.

In French painting, Edouard Manet rejected the style of quasi-photographic realism—a dead end, since painters could never surpass the camera in the *reproduction* of reality. Critics of the 1860's called Manet a realist; and it is true that he continued to paint "common" subjects—barmaids, ordinary bourgeois, his friends. But Manet's style, which elicited howls of derision from established critics, clearly marked him as a transitional figure from realism to something new. His primary interest was color and the changes it underwent in different light. He imaginatively explored the possibilities of color rather than painting simply easily recognizable and conventionally lighted subjects. Moreover, Manet dismissed the fiction that painting was reality in the sense that a photograph was. A painting was a *painting*—blocks and strips of colored forms spatially related to one another. His work was self-consciously "art," his own personal vision, reality *created* by Edouard Manet.

Manet's personalism and his fascination with form moved other French painters in the last third of the century to experiment along similar lines. Like Manet, they used everyday subjects—simple landscapes, buildings, street scenes, portraits of perfectly ordinary people. But they intensified his preoccupation with color and light, and their work was even more strenuously personal. Alfred Degas, Auguste Renoir, Claude Monet, Alfred Sisley, and Camille Pissaro were called "impressionists" because they painted their *impressions* of reality. Sisley's studies of a flooding river make no attempt at photographic reproduction, but concentrate on what struck him most in the scene—the shimmering reflections of sunlight on water. Monet's painting of a railroad station is largely bound up with rendering iron grillwork, light, and steam, which is what he "saw."

Impressionism marked a major departure in European art. It signified the beginnings of a movement away from representational painting; its masters were starting to abstract from reality, an important step toward the nonrepresentational art of the twentieth century. Of course, modernist painters sometimes claimed that they were only revivifying classicism, emphasizing the basic geometrical forms inherent in nature. Paul Cézanne, a French contemporary of the impressionists whose work more properly falls into the postimpressionist category, insisted that nature was composed of cylinders, spheres, and cones, and saw himself as a modern classicist. Yet modern painting had no patience for the idea of simply working within a tradition. Cézanne himself urged painters to "give the image of what we see, forgetting all that has been seen before our time."

Modern art aggressively defied tradition and convention, and not merely aesthetic ones. The artist as bohemian—flaunting orthodox fashions and customs—seems to have emerged definitively in the 1840's. Many artists who refused to adopt the pose, engaging instead in entirely accepted personal behavior, still shared the central principle of bohemianism: rejection of the bourgeoisie and its values. Artists came increasingly in the nineteenth century to identify as "bourgeois" the stolid, machine-like pursuit of material gain, to the exclusion of all other interests (including especially art). They counted such behavior as deadening and dehumanizing, liable to rob the world of beauty, and all too characteristic of industrial society. "What a horrible invention, the bourgeois, isn't he?" wrote Flaubert. "Why is he on earth, and what is he doing here, the wretch? As for me, I do not know how people uninterested in art spent their time here. Their way of living is a mystery to me." These were attitudes shared by late romantics, realists, and those who looked beyond realism toward the end of the century.

It is worth emphasizing, however, that the bourgeoisie being stigmatized was not merely equivalent to the middle classes. "By the word 'bourgeoisie,'" wrote Flaubert to the novelist George Sand in 1867, "I understand the bourgeois in work-shirt as well as the bourgeois in frock-coat. It is we, and we alone, we of literature, who are the People, or better yet, the tradition of humanity." Even those artists whose work appeared consonant with scientistic thinking recoiled at the utilitarian idea that value was a factor of usefulness. Art was not useful in the sense that electricity was; it was created and existed not to serve some practical end but—as more and more artists were coming to say—for its own sake. The bourgeoisie could never appreciate "true" art; therefore, let us ignore the bourgeoisie and create for the tiny aesthetic elite capable of understanding that art is mankind's salvation. Sentiments of this sort lay beneath the radical departures of artists of the early twentieth century. Self-consciously, modern artists asserted their individuality and advertised their superiority in work which veered farther and farther from the mainstream of popular tastes. The gap between high culture and middle-class culture had been large in the nineteenth century. Modern artists threatened to make it unbridgeable.

9 / Politics in Industrial Society

In the last decade of the nineteenth century, the political synthesis fashioned by European conservatives in the 1860's began to fray at the edges and even unravel in places. That synthesis had woven together elements of authoritarianism, liberalism, and even social reform in order to maintain the power of the traditional elites. Although there were variations on the theme, in general conservatives and moderates ruled industrializing Europe with a mixture of repression and concession, gradually absorbing liberal reformers into the ranks of the satisfied.

The problem was that growing numbers of people remained resolutely dissatisfied. The very process of industrialization was increasing the size of the working classes; although their conditions of life and work were an improvement upon those of the early industrial revolution, still they left much to be desired. Working-class consciousness was intensifying; working-class organization was spreading. The conservative synthesis had worked well enough in an age of nascent industrialization. But when large masses of poor people began to concentrate in cities and became exposed to the message of left-wing politics, it was more difficult both to apply repressive measures and to satisfy them with an occasional sop. Pressure for fundamental change was building up, and in the years prior to World War I there was visible apprehension that a general revolutionary crisis, a new 1848, was in the making.

Social Democracy

After Marx's death in 1883, his colleague Friedrich Engels labored in the cause for another dozen years—bringing out new editions of Marx's earlier work as well as writing on his own, trying to make certain that younger disciples did not stray into heresy, serving as a kind of minor patriarch to the European socialist movement. One theme upon which Engels played repeatedly was the danger of premature revolution; he emphasized that the socialists could not expect to win their struggle with capitalism in the streets—not yet, at least—since the bourgeois state monopolized massive police and military forces. Though violence would one day become unavoidable, socialists would for the present be better off by restraining themselves from any major provocations of the powerful. Engels, like Marx in his later years (his enthusiasm for the Paris Commune notwithstanding), preached the cause of social democracy.

Although Marx had begun his career by castigating radical political reformers as "mere" democrats, he later convinced himself that—for the time being, at least—socialism had to proceed along constitutionally sanctioned paths. He therefore approved of the formation of "social democratic" parties which would work within parliamentary systems—campaigning in elections, taking legislative seats, seeking power by legal means. The banner of these parties was social democracy—that is, making democracy meaningful by extending it from "mere" political questions into social relationships.

If Marx's economic analysis of capitalism was accurate, then the strategy of social democratic politics was sound. Capitalist industry was bound to proletarianize a majority of the population, and socialists had only to capture the support of that majority at the polls in order to conquer power legally. Marx and Engels insisted that political power should be the first goal of the social democrats, a goal that could be achieved once the proletariat had been brought to full consciousness of its interests. By the end of the century, moreover, facts seemed to be bearing out theory. In the nations industrializing most rapidly, social democratic parties were making correspondingly dramatic advances at the polls.

As promising as the strategy seemed to be, however, there were drawbacks. First of all, Marx had always felt that a class-conscious proletariat could only be attracted by a truly revolutionary movement, one which placed itself in absolute opposition to bourgeois-capitalist society. How revolutionary was it to accept the political framework of the bourgeois state? Socialism could, in the existing circumstances, progress toward its ends and avoid a serious blow only by hewing to legal procedures, building a large electoral following. By the same token, the acceptance of bourgeois constitutionalism could blunt the revolutionary edge of the movement and forfeit that mass following. The trick was to remain "revolutionary" and "legal" at the same time, something which could only be accomplished by consistently describing revolutionary ends and promising to realize them by legal means. The leaders not only had to keep up the enthusiasm and confidence of the followers, they had to stay "revolutionary" themselves. As the parliamentary strength of social democratic parties increased, bourgeois parties would inevitably try to co-opt them, buy them off with a ministry or two in a coalition government, subtly involve them in the management of a system they were pledged to destroy. Therefore, it was a central article of Marxist orthodoxy in the late nineteenth century that social democrats would not participate in bourgeois governments.

The second drawback was that the relationship between social democratic political parties and their working-class constituents proved delicate and complicated. The whole social democratic strategy rested upon the parties winning the support of organized labor, and in the major industrial nations there were commonly rather close ties between the labor unions and the parties. Still, they remained separate entities, with distinct origins and purposes. The parties had come into existence in order to pursue political power, to advance toward socialist revolution. Unions originated from a desire to improve the bargaining position of workers and, ultimately, their condition in life. Workers might applaud socialist slogans, but they also faced the necessity of living from day to day; therefore, their most urgent concerns were with wages, hours, working conditions, fringe benefits, and the like. Anyone interested in labor's support would have to demonstrate a similar interest.

Marxist politicians were thus faced with a harsh dilemma. Capitalist economic development was supposed to debase the worker's condition; the revolutionary's job was to explain to workers what was happening and convince them that their interests lay in socialism—to awaken their class consciousness. When bourgeoisie and proletariat had polarized, when the workers were fully conscious that their class interests could never be realized under capitalism, the revolutionary situation would appear. By ameliorating the workers' condition *within the capitalist framework*—by putting a floor under wages, for instance, or a ceiling on the work week—socialists were retarding rather than hastening the development of class consciousness. A socialist who worked for "mere" labor reforms was working to prolong the life of capitalism, not shorten it; by improving the workers' lot, he was minimizing rather than enhancing the friction between the proletariat and the bourgeoisie. On the other hand, if social democrats refused to support meliorative reforms, they ran the risk of one day glancing over their shoulders only to discover that their followers were no longer there. In general, the socialists took the more expedient course, which was also the more humane one, promoting reform while still insisting that revolution was inevitable.

A final problem built into the social democratic movement was the cost of its success. For the parties were successful, at least in attracting a large membership and electoral support. By the eve of World War I, the social democrats had the largest single party (though short of a majority) in Germany and Austria-Hungary, and the second largest in France; the British Labor party, cut from slightly different cloth, was also making impressive gains. Although the social democrats were in this respect fulfilling Marx's predictions, he would probably have been distressed to discover that these large political parties were coming to resemble major industrial corporations more than revolutionary movements. In order to communicate effectively with the party following, in order to draw to full advantage upon its backers at election time, it was essential that the movement be given organization.

The parties began to create their own bureaucracies.* There appears to be no historical record of a bureaucracy ever having perpetrated a revolution. Bureaucracies—whether of government, business, political parties, labor unions, or universities—exist to control. They represent, rather than defy, authority. The whole bureaucratic mentality is, of necessity, geared to seeing that things operate smoothly, that matters stay well in hand, that people who give orders are obeyed—hardly habits liable to promote revolution.

Revisionism

Several elements combined, then, to militate against social democracy remaining "revolutionary," at least in a sense that would have satisfied Marx. Certain social democrats even attempted to make a virtue of this apparent necessity and to revise Marx's theory on the advent of socialism. Marx seems to have felt that the social democrats would never actually take power by peaceful, parliamentary means. When power was in sight, the bourgeoisie would try to delay the inevitable by some sort of counterstroke—a coup d'état, suspension of the constitution, repression of the movement. At this point, violent revolution would occur.

Since Marx regarded the revolution as inevitable, he saw no point in moralizing about the violence bound to accompany it. Later socialists wondered whether violence might not be avoided. In part, they were moved by moral scruples, and in part by the progress, however modest, that social reform was making under the prodding of social democratic parties. In the mid-1880's, a number of British intellectuals formed the Fabian Society, dedicated to propagation of socialist ideas. The Fabians, at whose center stood Sidney and Beatrice Webb, hoped to persuade the largely middle-class audience for whom they wrote, of socialism's superiority to capitalism. They foresaw a slow, gradual, and peaceful transition

---

* As did the labor unions; in some places, the two tended to mesh.

to socialism in which people steadily came to accept as inevitable the end of private property in the means of production.

More than a decade later, the German Marxist Eduard Bernstein gave "revisionism" (that is, the revision of orthodox Marxism) an even more elaborate theoretical base. Bernstein pointed out that, for all of Marx's predictions, capitalism was manifestly not in its death throes and was in fact showing unmistakable signs of vitality. In these circumstances, socialists had better forget all talk of revolution and concentrate on achieving socialism by evolutionary means. Bernstein argued that socialism would be achieved by precisely the methods social democrats were presently employing: parliamentary and electoral politics, exerting pressure for social reform through legal channels, gradually extending the public sector of the economy at the expense of the private, winning over middle-class converts to the movement.

The revisionist controversy raged fiercely in European socialism in the early 1900's. Orthodox Marxists insisted that the revisionists were compromising the revolutionary nature of social democracy. Revisionists retorted that Marxism had to adjust itself to reality if it was to be a useful theory, that Marx's analysis of the nature of capitalism was the crux of his thought, not his predictions on its future development. The Second International—the body founded in 1889 to coordinate national social democratic parties—ruled against revisionism in 1904. But the International was only a kind of doctrinal arbiter; it could not set policy for national parties, which paid lip service to its ruling and in practice behaved in a largely revisionist fashion.

In point of fact, the social democrats had become reformers, playing the historical role of liberals—advocating slow and peaceful change so that abrupt and violent change did not take place. Few social democrats would have admitted the truth of this description, and still liked to think of themselves as in some sense "revolutionaries." Equally important, many people believed them. For all the transformations that had taken place in social democracy since the 1880's, the great majority of the European middle classes regarded socialists as "dangerous enemies of society." Class antagonisms and social tension therefore remained sharp, heightened by mounting strike activity and the ominous growth of the social democrats at the polls. Even though they may have given up all notions of revolution, social democrats clung to the orthodox Marxist rhetoric of class struggle and proletarian dictatorship which they felt sure thrilled working-class audiences. Finally, the middle classes tended to confuse socialism with the other prominent left-wing movement of the period, anarchist syndicalism.

The Anarchists

"The government of man by man (under whatever name it may be disguised) is oppression." Proudhon's judgment neatly captures anarchism's rejection of any authority which presumed to set itself above the individual. Ideally, Proudhon saw men grouped in producers' cooperatives, a nonstatist socialism which achieved justice without the suffocating machinery of government. Later anarchist theorists, most notably the Russian prince Peter Kropotkin, argued that the state was not only oppressive but simply unnecessary: man's innate social instincts naturally drove him into groups which could, given the opportunity, operate without outside interference.

Given such ideological predispositions, anarchists did not customarily participate in politics, which is after all a dimension of government. Their aim was not to make the state operate more rationally or humanely, but to destroy it. Therefore, they worked out of smallish sects —usually underground, given the hostility of the authorities—which spread the gospel to the people and engaged in terrorist activities. The most direct means of destroying the state, as they saw it, was to destroy the people who ran the state. Assassination thus became a serious occupational hazard for heads of state and prominent ministers: between 1881 and 1900, anarchists murdered a Russian czar, a French president, an Austrian empress, and an Italian king, not to mention dozens of ranking officials.

This sort of activity was far removed from the pursuits of the social democrats, yet conservatives and moderates alike tended to blur the distinction between socialism and anarchism. It is true, of course, that anarchism had always included vaguely socialist schemes regarding the production and distribution of wealth. Mikhail Bakunin, an itinerant Russian anarchist active in Europe during the middle decades of the nineteenth century, was a co-founder of the First International with Marx. Yet Marx (who also despised Proudhon) seemed to consider Bakunin both a fool and a knave and rejected the socialist streak of anarchism as fuzzy-headed, unscientific, and politically worthless. The confusion between anarchism and socialism was further compounded by certain inroads made into socialism's traditional strongholds, the labor unions. In France, Spain, Belgium, and Italy, large segments of organized labor treated politics and political parties with suspicion and distrust. Rather than pursue reform through legal means, they preferred "direct action" to achieve short-term economic gains. The strike was the most potent, and the most frequently employed, weapon in their arsenal.

These labor movements, whose ties to the local socialist parties were often tenuous, were heavily influenced by the doctrines of what was known as anarchist syndicalism (from the French word *syndicat,* "trade union"). Short-term improvements would be won by individual strikes, thought syndicalists. The ultimate goal—the destruction of the capitalist state and society—would be won by a general strike, involving *all* workers, which would cripple the economic system and deliver it over to those whose labor made it work. Society would then be reorganized in stateless form, with federated *syndicats* owning the means of production. The general strike was the key to this strategy.

Though it would appear on paper that no advanced industrial society could long sustain such a shutdown, in fact none of the several general strikes which have been called in Europe since the 1890's has had the result envisaged by syndicalists. Most governments have either been able to negotiate their way out of general strikes with economic concessions or to employ police and army to break the strike. Still, in pre-World War I Europe, the very idea of a general strike was terrifying and tended to create the impression that the working classes (whom the socialists claimed to represent) were thoroughly syndicalist and therefore partisans of anarchist terror. All things considered, anarchism caused as many problems for socialism as for bourgeois society.

The Shape of Domestic Politics

The generation prior to World War I was fraught with political tension. Social democratic parties and labor unions dramatically increased their membership and influence; anarchist shootings and bombings heightened the sense that respectable society was on the verge of all-out war with its enemies. Conservatives and liberals alike had to decide whether a policy of concession and reform was liable to deflate or to encourage the radical movements. But the patterns of tension varied enough from place to place to demand a slightly more detailed survey of European politics during these years.

France. No major European power experienced more political turmoil than France in the late nineteenth and early twentieth centuries, yet French political institutions remained in 1914 substantially what they had been in 1880. What changed were the issues of political conflict and the groups debating them. As the British scholar David Thomson so persuasively argued in his book *Democracy in France Since 1870,* the early Third Republic devoted itself largely to ideological politics, to contention over questions of principle between roughly the same groups which had done battle in the 1870's as to whether France would be a republic or a monarchy. At stake was the matter of how "republican" the republic would be, to what degree it would tolerate monarchist and clerical influence in institutions such as the army and the schools.

Social politics, expressing conflicts of material interest, were of marginal importance prior to the early twentieth century. It was not, of course, that French society was so homogeneous that such conflicts did not exist. To the contrary, they existed in abundance—between employer and employee, between pro- and antitariff groups, between industry and agriculture, between competing regions of the country. No single group, however, was strong enough to impose its will upon all the others, or even seriously threaten to do so. Accordingly, economic interest groups tended toward the defense of the status quo rather than aggrandizement. Politics naturally reflected this fragmentation. In the absence of a few large social blocs of harmonious material interests, there could hardly be a small number of large political parties. Instead, the various interest groups—economic, social, and regional—generated numerous parties to protect their interests. No party was able to command a majority, so that parliamentary politics had to operate by coalitions. For coalitions to work at all, participating parties had to mute their disagreements, thus largely removing social issues from politics. Yet coalitions remained fragile, largely because majorities were so narrow. In these circumstances, the votes of a small faction or even an individual deputy could be decisive, which meant in turn that the temptation to vote against incumbent cabinets was great. A deputy might easily find himself controlling the swing votes and being offered some attractive prize—a ministry, perhaps —to withdraw from the ruling coalition and join an aspiring one. Consequently, the republic suffered from perpetual ministerial instability: from the time the constitutional laws of 1875 went into effect until the outbreak of World War I, there were no less than 56 separate cabinets—an average of one every eight and one-half months.

Republicans not only considered the Church a stronghold of monarchist sentiment; enough of them were informed by the positivist persuasion that they were determined to keep the Church from exercising any hold upon the young. In the early 1880's, the parliament passed legislation which made primary education not only mandatory and free, but "neutral"—that is, secular, without any of the religious teachings which had hitherto been standard. Many republicans were equally suspicious of the army, whose officer corps sported a long list of aristocratic names and often openly criticized republican anticlericalism. Still, there was a certain reluctance among civilian authorities to tamper with the principal instrument of national defense until the late 1890's, when one of the most famous controversies of modern politics set state and army against one another.

In 1894, an army court martial convicted one Captain Alfred Dreyfus of selling military secrets to the Germans and sent him to Devil's Island. Although republicans had congratulated the army for its efficiency in the affair, evidence began to emerge in 1896 that Dreyfus was in fact innocent. Growing demands that the case be reopened were met with intransigence by the general staff, which deemed its honor and credibility at stake. As it became increasingly clear that the original verdict was questionable, the army insisted that it could never be an effective shield for the nation without public trust and the independence to handle its own internal affairs. Republicans championing Dreyfus' cause argued that the army sought to become nothing less than a state within a state, responsible to no higher authority and capable of flaunting the dictates of simple justice.

By 1898, the Dreyfus affair had reached a level of intensity unprecedented in a society not actually engaged in civil war. Demonstrations, street brawls, and private duels were becoming common. Army sympathizers played upon the fact that Dreyfus was Jewish, and thus somehow not "really French," incapable of patriotism; one officer even forged documents further implicating Dreyfus. The pro-Dreyfus camp, which included most of the republican left, insisted that the army was hatching a monarchist coup d'état in concert with the Church. Finally, in 1899, after a retrial had confirmed the verdict of guilty, the republican government granted Dreyfus a pardon.*

The republicans thereafter pursued their advantage on two fronts. First, they engaged in purges of the officer corps, bringing reliable republicans into most of the sensitive positions. Second, they renewed their assault upon the Church. The Catholic hierarchy had largely stood distant from the Dreyfus affair; a few lesser orders, however, such as the Assumptionist Fathers, had taken part in the antisemitic campaign, giving hostile republican journalists the opportunity to associate the Church with the anti-Dreyfus forces. Anticlerical propaganda reached new heights, and the Church's enemies in parliament aimed at the virtual destruction of Catholicism in France. Since Napoleon I's Concordat of 1801, the Church had operated as an agency of the state, with clerical salaries coming out of public funds. Anticlericals now hoped to confront the Church with financial crisis by legally separating church and state. The separation law, voted in 1905, also deprived the Church of all its property—including the parish church buildings themselves, which were handed over to newly formed "corporations" of laymen. The corporations might in turn lease the buildings to the Church for religious purposes, though obviously most of those voting for the law hoped they would not. The Church was rocked by the law, its fiscal viability seriously challenged. But religious sentiment in the populace remained strong enough that it

---

* Yet a third trial was held in 1906, which removed the equivocal implications of the pardon and totally acquitted Dreyfus of all charges.

was able to continue to use its places of worship, and ultimately the Church emerged from the financial crisis successfully.

It was characteristic of the early Third Republic that neither the Dreyfus affair nor the separation of church and state altered the distribution of property nor the relations of social classes. They were purely ideological conflicts, and their resolution served to "liquidate," in Thomson's word, the struggles of which the republic had been born. By 1905, however, all the major ideological struggles had been decided, while at the same time a new force had appeared which would alter French politics. In that year, several socialist factions which had been competing for the leadership of the working classes united into a single party. Unification took place on an orthodox social democratic program—opposed to participation in bourgeois governments and to revisionist doctrine. While in fact the differences between the several sects did not simply disappear, still socialism could now take its place as an electoral force to be reckoned with; in less than a decade, it commanded fully one-sixth of the national vote (the second largest single slice).

Industrialization had not yet proceeded in France to the point of creating a working-class bloc capable of dominating French politics. Besides, anarcho-syndicalist strains in the labor movement impeded full cooperation between the major unions and the party. Yet labor and the socialists together were a formidable enough movement to impress a profound change upon the nature of political debate. Acrimonious disputes over clerical influence in the military and the schools gave way to strikes and demands for improved working conditions and wages; discussions of the quality of military justice were replaced by cries for social justice. In this situation left republicans, who had liked to call themselves the heirs of 1793 (but whose social program had scarcely exceeded a graduated income tax), suddenly found themselves in the position of strikebreakers. Moderate republicans, men of wealth and substance, defended the established social order side by side with monarchists.

Strike activity intensified sharply after 1905, encompassing civil servants as well as workers in the private sector. In 1910, a general strike threatened to develop from a railroad strike, though it quickly collapsed. Equally menacing, however, were the left's stands on military questions. When a government of the right-center sought to enlarge the size of the army by lengthening military service from two to three years, socialists (joined by a faction of left republicans) strenuously resisted. Marx had always argued that the proletariat was international in scope, that workers in countries with hostile governments were in fact brothers, the victims of exploitation by international capitalism. French socialists, most notably the great scholar and orator Jean Jaurès, opposed army expansion;

preached a pacific foreign policy; and threatened that the working classes would refuse to follow its bourgeois government into war. Such talk only further exacerbated political polarization and helped excite the nationalist right, which was able to maneuver one of its own, Raymond Poincaré, into the French presidency in 1913. As of that year, deep and perhaps irreparable fissures appeared to most observers to run through French society.

Germany. Although Kaiser William II, who took the throne in 1888 at the age of 29, could not abide Bismarck's insistence upon running the government himself, still he tried to follow the paths Bismarck had marked out. It is true that William opposed the law which outlawed the socialist party and used his influence to defeat its renewal in 1890. (Two months later, he forced Bismarck from the chancellorship.) But he hoped that by legalizing the party and by following in the tradition established by Bismarck's social legislation, he could woo the working classes away from socialism and into the fold of a benevolent paternalism. He and his chief ministers over the next two decades were comparatively generous in sponsoring or supporting a variety of welfare measures which extended and consolidated Bismarck's social insurance programs.

From one perspective, it may be argued that the German social democrats ignored these blandishments. They remained a separate, opposition party after their reinstatement in 1890. Far from seeing their support drained off, the party grew with remarkable speed, until by 1912 it was the largest single parliamentary group. Still, the progress of social reform, though hardly breathtaking, may well have taken the starch out of the movement's more militant wing. When it could be demonstrated that meaningful change was indeed taking place, Bernstein's revisionist position became more attractive. Although the party officially condemned gradualism, it practiced parliamentary reformism rather than revolutionary tactics. At the same time, as the party grew it began to manifest the classic symptoms of bureaucratization. Anyone who still, as of 1914, thought of the German socialists as revolutionaries was simply a knee-jerk reactionary.

But if the German social democrats were not bomb-throwers, the society for which they were working was vastly different from the sort Bismarck had been trying to preserve. The changes they envisaged far outran the handouts they had received from the Kaiser, who was not contemplating socialization of the means of production. Thus from one standpoint, they were indeed "dangerous enemies of society"—at any rate of society as the landed magnates and big business thought of it. Moreover, at least one wing of the social democratic party was making ominously pacifistic noises similar to those emitting from the French left.

Yet German socialism remained fundamentally patriotic, as the events of 1914 revealed, besides which doctrinal dogmatism tended to dilute pacifistic tendencies. For example, the socialists voted against a 1913 bill which would expand the army substantially. The bill passed, but still needed to be financed. The government then sweetened the appropriations measure by promising to pay for army expansion with a special tax levy which would fall mainly upon the richer classes. The social democrats voted *for* this bill, thereby facilitating enactment of the army measure they had so vigorously opposed.

The rapid rise of social democracy was not so much a cause as a characteristic of the deterioration of the Bismarckian synthesis. Bismarck had sought to ensure the preponderance of the Junker class within a democratic political framework. The scheme was workable only so long as it was rooted in economic reality—only so long, that is, as large agricultural estates constituted the principal form of wealth. By the 1890's, however, German industry had progressed to the point where its importance rivaled landed wealth. Government itself recognized that fact when it negotiated a series of trade treaties with central and eastern European states which lowered import duties on foreign food. The main point of these treaties, which undercut German agricultural producers, was to induce the other states to lower their own tariffs so as to admit German industrial commodities. This admission that manufacturing had replaced agriculture as the critical sector of the German economy both shocked landowners and mobilized them into action. Agrarian interest groups, representing large and small producers alike, pressured government for a reinstatement of food tariffs. They finally won in 1902, when the cabinet reversed itself largely because it needed the agrarian bloc's votes on another question. In short, it was not merely social radicalism which created stresses within the old system; economic development was disturbing the balance of forces which had prevailed in the mid-nineteenth century and even momentarily estranged Junkerdom from the government which had been designed to rule in its interests.

It is difficult to say how long Bismarckian conservatism could have held the upper hand had not war and domestic collapse intervened. The conflict between industry and agriculture boded ill for the Junkers. Yet the tendency of many moderates and liberals to view the socialists as revolutionary madmen drove them into a natural ideological alliance with the old conservatives. On the other hand, social democracy was not a purely working-class movement. It appealed to certain middle and lower-middle class radicals as well and might, given the time, have developed into an even more broadly based movement capable of attaining an electoral majority. As it turned out, the war thrust power once more into the hands of the army, and the peace saddled social democrats with an unhappy image which they were unable to erase.

Great Britain. After a generation of inactivity, the British labor movement was revitalized in the 1880's. Trade unions were rapidly increasing their membership, and socialist political organizations began to sprout up. In 1884, the Marxist H.M. Hyndman founded a Social Democratic Federation. But Marxist politics somehow lacked the appeal they had on the continent, and the social democratic movement failed to strike very deep roots. The future lay rather with a rather mild version of revisionism, the sort preached by the Fabian Society—socialist, to be sure, but resolutely nonrevolutionary. It was this approach which informed the Independent Labor Party, established in 1893.

British labor, like its counterparts across the channel, harbored deep suspicions about the efficacy of parliamentary politics. Although one of the Labor party's chief founders, the socialist James Keir Hardie, won election to the House of Commons in 1892, there had been no original intention to turn the party into a mass electoral machine. Besides, the labor movement was by no means sufficiently unified to undertake such a task. Social democrats were inclined to go their own way, and the trade unions—themselves grievously divided—at first provided the party with negligible support. Finally, the socialists could hardly claim to be the only group committed to serious social reform. Although the Conservatives had largely disavowed reformism after Disraeli's death, Gladstone and his heirs in the Liberal party continued to press for social legislation, thus cutting into Labor's natural constituency. By the early 1900's, labor leaders decided that the movement's interests could only be protected and the cause of socialism advanced by attempting to overcome these obstacles and building a major parliamentary party. It was not until after World War I, however, that the Labor party became a serious force in British politics.

Social reform, as promoted by the Liberals, was still a central issue in Britain in the prewar decades; cutting across it, however, and dividing Liberals from one another as much as from Conservatives was the question of Ireland. Although Irish Catholics had been allowed to sit in parliament since 1829, the growing nationalist movement voiced demands ranging from that of a semiautonomous status under the British crown to complete independence. In the meantime, nationalist terrorists kept Ireland in a constant state of upheaval. Conservatives supported continued "union" of Ireland and Britain, though they were occasionally moved to make a few economic concessions (such as land reform). Gladstone determined upon a more conciliatory line, and in 1886 sponsored a Home Rule bill which would have created an Irish parliament with substantial domestic powers, though ultimately under British sovereignty. It was still too much for the Conservatives and for a faction from Gladstone's own party—the Liberal Unionists—who combined to defeat the bill. The

Conservatives thereafter assumed power and ruled for nearly seventeen of the next nineteen years.

When the Liberals mustered a solid majority again, in 1905, they offered a program combining social welfare and Irish Home Rule. The welfare measures—principally, workmen's compensation which made employers liable in case of workers' accidents and old-age pensions—proved expensive. The Liberals could find no way to fund them save by restructuring the tax system to the disadvantage of the wealthy classes (who scarcely paid their fair share under existing arrangements). This so-called People's Budget, sponsored by Chancellor of the Exchequer David Lloyd George, squeaked through the House of Commons. But the House of Lords, an arch-conservative stronghold, rejected the proposal in 1909. Since members of the House of Lords were of course not elected, but sat by virtue of their possession of noble titles, electoral politics were of little use in combating them. Liberal leader Herbert Asquith therefore resorted to drastic action—constitutional change which would emasculate the Lords by giving them no right of veto over money bills and only a suspensive veto over all others. The upper house resisted bitterly, and only capitulated in 1911 when Asquith threatened to have the crown appoint enough Liberals to the peerage to ensure passage of the bill.

The Liberals quickly followed up this landmark victory with another foray into social reform, a national health and unemployment insurance law. Even so, they were unable to nail down the working-class vote for themselves. Indeed, 1911 saw an abrupt renewal of major strikes. Workers complained of lagging wages, and the government responded with a minimum wage law in early 1912. But agitation continued, most spectacularly among the coal miners who produced the country's principal form of fuel; a million and a half miners went out on strike later that year. The Liberals had gone to their ideological limits—farther than Gladstone had ever envisaged, light years beyond the liberalism of the 1830's —and still could not sap the vigor of the independent working-class movement, which a decade later would replace the Liberals with Labor as the second major party.

The Irish question proved equally troublesome under the Liberal government. A Home Rule bill introduced in 1912 had the particularly odious feature, in Unionist eyes, of leaving Ulster—Protestant northern Ireland—to the mercies of the Catholic majority to the south. Unionist opposition at home turned riotous, frequently disturbing the public peace; in Ulster itself, Protestants organized, armed, and threatened violent resistance to the bill. The Liberals had the votes in the Commons, however, and no longer had to worry about more than a delaying action from the Lords. Britain was at this time perhaps running its more serious risk of civil war since the mid-seventeenth century, but for the moment it was averted by the intrusion of another form of violence. When Home Rule became law on September 18, 1914, Britain had been at war for more than a month, and a proviso hastily attached to the legislation suspended its application until war's end. Subjects of the British crown thus ceased preparing to kill one another and set about killing Germans.

Russia. Wherever there were cities of any consequence in nineteenth-century Europe, there was liable to be trade unionism, social democratic parties, perhaps even anarchist syndicalism. Socialists built a sizable parliamentary contingent in Austria and were plainly on the rise in Italy. Northern Italy and northern Spain were also the seats of syndicalist activity, repeated strikes around the beginning of the century, and spasmodic bursts of terrorism. Social democratic parties were organized in both Denmark and Sweden. Limitations of space demand, however, that we focus on the country where the growth of a socialist left had the most profound consequences.

Russia's relapse into political repression after the era of the great reforms was accompanied by a remarkably intense experience of industrialization. Government initiative was decisive here: beginning in the 1880's, the state sponsored extensive railway construction and the building of large factories, all financed by foreign capital (much of it French). Statistically, of course, Russian industry could hardly compare with that of Germany, Britain, or even France; agriculture remained far and away the most important form of production. Yet the new industry was also centered almost exclusively in the cities of St. Petersburg and Moscow. The sudden demand for labor brought swarms of peasants in from the countryside, where conditions remained miserable in spite of emancipation and famine was a threat that occasionally materialized, as in the early 1890's. The abrupt transition to factory discipline and urban slums touched relatively few people, but it touched them intensely. Moreover, they were concentrated, sharing experiences, so that the creation of a common consciousness could take place rather quickly.

Most radical political movements were geared not to this small though potentially explosive constituency, but to the peasant masses. Underground sects preached socialism of one sort or another to the rural poor and also engaged in terrorist acts (such as the assassination of Czar Alexander II). The twentieth-century heirs of this so-called populist movement were the middle-class intellectuals and students who were the spine of the Socialist Revolutionary party, organized in 1901. The only avowedly Marxist group, interested first of all in the urban working classes, was the Social Democratic party. Formed in 1898, the party had originally planned to follow the route of western social democracy—the building of a mass party which would take power at the polls (when and if Russia ever instituted an electoral and parliamentary system). Within five years, however, the party split badly when one of its chief theoreticians posed a new conception of what a socialist party in Russia ought to be.

Vladimir Ilich Ulyanov, known better by his *nom de guerre* of Lenin, was born in 1870, the son of a petty civil servant. His older brother became involved in radical student politics, and was executed in 1887 for his trouble. Vladimir himself began investigating Marxism during his university days of the late 1880's and was shortly converted to the revolutionary cause. Engaged in various propagandistic activities which landed him in Siberia and then forced him into exile, he had no major impact upon Russian Marxist politics until 1902, when he published *What Is to Be Done?* Two concerns informed this important work: first, that revisionism was draining the Marxist movement of its revolutionary energies and visions; and second, that the working classes themselves were having the same effect, turning revolutionary parties into mouthpieces for mere trade unionism. Despairing that the workers would ever crystallize their class consciousness, and thus seize the revolutionary initiative when the time was right, Lenin argued that the party had to replace the proletariat as the "vanguard" of revolution. It would not, however, be a party on the orthodox model, working for power by legal, parliamentary means. Instead, it would be a small, tightly organized, and highly disciplined body of professional revolutionaries which would lead the workers into battle.

There was not massive enthusiasm for Lenin's position among Russian social democrats, but by slick parliamentary maneuvering at the party congress of 1903, held in London, his plan received approval from a majority of the delegates.* It was an illusory victory, however. Lenin soon discovered that he commanded only a tiny group of followers; such progress as the social democrats counted in recruiting support among Russian workers was made by his opponents. In truth, neither faction was of particular importance in Russian politics prior to World War I.

The principal opposition party in czarist Russia was not socialist at all, but liberal and middle class, anxious for the establishment of constitutional and parliamentary government. Their chance came when Russia and Japan went to war in 1904 over conflicting territorial ambitions in northeastern Asia. The economic rigors of war stirred the urban poor, while liberal spokesmen called for political reform. Amidst strikes and growing unrest, violence broke out in early 1905 when troops fired upon working-class demonstrators in St. Petersburg, killing some 70 persons. Disorders continued through the year, spreading to several provincial cities and even to a few army and navy units. Czar Nicholas II offered a few

---

* Thus the name "Bolsheviks," standing for "majority"; the minority faction was known as the Mensheviks.

flimsy concessions, which were answered in October with a massive, though largely spontaneous, general strike. Since the army was either mired down in the Japanese war or in revolt, the government had no means of breaking the strike and was finally forced to give in. Nicholas promulgated the October Manifesto, which promised a constitution and a legislature (the Duma) with significant powers to be elected by a generous franchise.

The liberals, who now grouped into the Constitutional Democratic (or, for short, Cadet) party, were inclined to think that the revolution of 1905 spelled the end of czarist autocracy. Once order had been restored and the war brought to an end, however, the government felt sufficiently confident to renege on some of its October promises. A series of "fundamental laws," issued just prior to the Duma's first meeting in 1906, confirmed that all sovereignty rested in the czar; Nicholas retained control over the executive branch, the right to legislate by decree during Duma recesses, and certain financial prerogatives which ruled out any hope of real power for the legislature. When the Cadets and other reformers continued to behave as though they took the 1905 manifesto seriously, the government enacted a new electoral law which was rigged to overrepresent the wealthy.

Such developments were bound not merely to frustrate liberals, but also to polarize political conditions and play into the hands of revolutionaries. For czarist autocracy was far from immune to disorder, as 1905 so vividly demonstrated. A longer, more costly, more agonizing war would once again expose the regime to even more dangerous revolutionary challenges.

10 / *World Powers in Conflict*

Between 1871 and 1914, no two major European states went to war with one another. Even so, this was scarcely an era of peace. The Balkan states were in a continual uproar and the several wars between them threatened to involve the larger powers. Although a network of alliances appeared to establish a stalemate in Europe, it did not prevent saber rattling. There were war scares between Britain and France, between France and Germany, between Russia and Austria-Hungary. Moreover, the opportunities for conflict were multiplied when the powers sought to expand their domain outside of Europe, an expansion which was itself a partial outgrowth of European rivalries. Britain, France, Germany, and Russia each engaged in overseas military actions which ranged from minor sorties against African or Asian resistance to their intervention, to major colonial wars. Thus, to look ahead slightly, World War I was not an aberration, a summer storm which suddenly burst with little warning. Rather, it was an acceleration of tendencies and tensions long present.

Post-Bismarckian Diplomacy

For Bismarck, it was not enough to have defeated France in 1871. German security thereafter depended upon keeping France weak. Germany would remain formally allied to Austria-Hungary and Italy and maintain close ties with Russia as well. (See Chapter 6.) Great Britain would follow its traditional policy of staying out of continental politics and attending to its overseas possessions. France would remain isolated and therefore be unlikely to undertake a war of revenge. There were variations on the theme: in the mid-1880's, Bismarck toyed briefly with the notion of closer relations with France as an alternative to isolation. But the idea of keeping the French from concluding a partnership with some other European power remained constant.

Bismarck developed this policy with consummate skill. However, as long as he insisted that a strong alliance with the Habsburgs was the key to German strength, the policy was doomed to failure. Russia and Austria-Hungary had both committed themselves to expanding their influence in southeastern Europe, where the decline of centuries-old Ottoman authority and the growth of Slavic nationalism had created a volatile situation. The Austrians were anxious to bring the Balkan states under their economic sway and to silence nationalist hotheads there who were urging Slavs in the Dual Monarchy to revolt against the Habsburgs. The Russians, in their turn, posed as the champions of Slav independence and hoped that somehow, in the process, they could realize the ancient dream of a Mediterranean seaport—to be wrested, perhaps, from the grip of a faltering Ottoman Empire. In the final analysis, Germany would have to choose between them, casting one adrift.

Bismarck's successors accepted these realities, and shortly after Kaiser William II forced the Chancellor from office, they chose Austria. Strategically, the massive central European bloc formed by the Hohenzollern and Habsburg territories seemed the soundest choice; an Austro-German alliance seemed culturally "natural." Besides, some policy makers in the German foreign office discounted the likelihood of a Franco-Russian alliance. On ideological grounds alone, they argued, the czarist autocracy would reject the idea of cooperation with a republican democracy.

What such arguments overlooked was that the czar had already put aside scruple and welcomed substantial amounts of democratic money. For years, French investors had supplied the principal capital for Russia's crash program of industrialization. Once the Germans declined to continue Bismarck's juggling act and threw their support firmly behind Austria-Hungary (though still hoping to remain on amicable terms with Russia), the French swiftly converted a financial relationship into a military alliance. By 1893, the respective governments agreed that should Germany attack either one, the other would come to its support.

At the time, statesmen saw neither the Franco-Russian alliance nor the Triple Alliance (of Germany, Austria-Hungary, and Italy) as vehicles for aggression. Rather, they were instruments of defense, deterrents to aggression by potential enemies. Russia did not link up with France in order to endorse a French war of revenge against Germany. Instead, it was thought that the German government—now flanked east and west—would think twice before backing up Austria should Austria and Russia come to blows in the Balkans. Similarly, the French did not seek a Russian alliance in order to facilitate a war against Germany (much less to promote Russian interests in the Balkans). The alliance was meant to provide security should the Germans ever contemplate another war against France. And, of course, Germany's alliances with Austria-Hungary and Italy had been concluded in hopes of discouraging France from trying to reverse the results of 1871. In other words, statesmen at first saw these arrangements as a reversion from Bismarck's approach—in which one powerful state virtually dominated continental politics—to a balance of power, each side deterred from attacking the other by the strength of the opponent.

Ultimately, of course, this apparent balance of power failed to deter Europe from war. One critical factor in this failure was the conflict generated by overseas imperialism. European industrialization in the second half of the nineteenth century brought a brisk competition in international trade; the scramble for markets became a concern in all the major countries. Even before 1900, not merely merchants but statesmen as well, in both Britain and Germany—the greatest industrial powers—were talking in terms of a race for world trade supremacy. Thus, although great-power confrontations in Europe itself were rare, overseas friction mounted.

The sudden burst of European imperialism which began in the 1880's had a variety of consequences, some of which are still being experienced. For present purposes, it may be noted that imperialism broadened the field of European politics to include the whole globe and had a direct impact on European political alignments and alliances. Clearly, some grasp of this complex phenomenon is vital for an understanding of European international politics.

A New Imperialism?

While industry and democracy were transforming Europe in the three decades before World War I, Europe was also transforming the world. A world map of, say, 1880 reveals but a few European flags scattered around the globe at strategic trading outposts. The only major overseas areas under direct European rule were the British colonies in India and South Africa and the French colony of Algeria.* Britain, France, and Portugal each had a number of toeholds along the African coastline; France had established itself in southern Indo-China, and the British had held Hong Kong since 1842.

A world map of 1914 presents a radically different picture. The entire continent of Africa—excepting only Liberia and Abyssinia—had been partitioned among the European powers. Southeast Asia was completely under British and French domination, while the Dutch, British, Ger-

---

* Britain had granted what amounted to self-government to Australia in 1850 and to Canada in 1867.

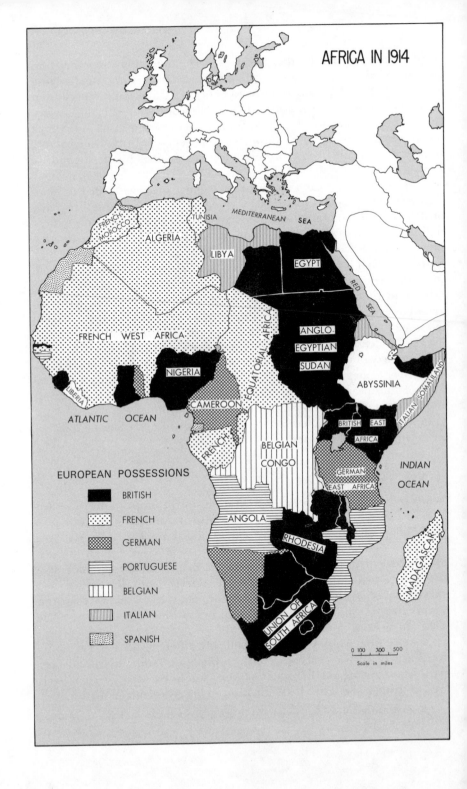

AFRICA IN 1914

MEDITERRANEAN SEA

FRENCH MOROCCO
TUNISIA
ALGERIA
LIBYA
EGYPT

RED SEA

FRENCH WEST AFRICA

ANGLO-EGYPTIAN SUDAN

NIGERIA

LIBERIA

ATLANTIC OCEAN

CAMEROON

FRENCH EQUATORIAL AFRICA

ABYSSINIA

ITALIAN SOMALILAND

BRITISH EAST AFRICA

FRENCH

BELGIAN CONGO

GERMAN EAST AFRICA

INDIAN OCEAN

EUROPEAN POSSESSIONS

BRITISH

FRENCH

GERMAN

PORTUGUESE

BELGIAN

ITALIAN

SPANISH

ANGOLA

RHODESIA

MADAGASCAR

UNION OF SOUTH AFRICA

0 100   300   500
Scale in miles

mans, and Americans were firmly ensconced in the principal neighboring island groups. The sprawling empire of China was only nominally independent; the European powers and Japan controlled most of its port cities and had divided much of the hinterland into their respective "spheres of influence." In sum, the white man had very nearly conquered the non-white world in order to put it to his own use.

Impressed by this sudden burst of expansionist energy, historians not long after coined the concept of a "new" imperialism, a new phase of foreign ventures by the European powers. For while European imperialism was hardly unprecedented, ran the argument, overseas acquisitions had been at best a minor theme in modern politics after the middle of the eighteenth century. Since that time, social and political developments at home had absorbed European energies, and the European presence abroad had if anything receded—witness the British withdrawal from North America. The events of the late nineteenth century therefore represented a new departure in Europe's relations with the world.

Upon closer inspection, late nineteenth-century imperialism seems less a departure from what had gone before than an intensification and partial modification of early practices. Europe's maritime powers were very far from being inactive in the search for new markets abroad prior to the 1880's. With the British naturally in the vanguard, they traded extensively with the new Latin American republics, probed about for likely entrances into the vast market of China, began to explore the possibilities of gain in mysterious Africa. As Ottoman authority began to erode throughout the Mediterranean world, Europeans were quick to move in and seize economic advantage. In general, however, these enterprises were undertaken by private traders (though often with the encouragement and from time to time with the subsidy of the government). Although officials were always happy to see their own merchants dominating a given overseas market, formal political annexation was another matter. For planting the flag was an expensive business; it meant military and administrative costs for overcoming and keeping in check the native population. Most political leaders therefore preferred the "informal imperialism" of economic domination.

From time to time, it was necessary to go farther. When the Chinese resisted British designs upon their lucrative opium trade, the British resorted to war in 1839, from which their prize was Hong Kong, thereafter a crown colony and the center for British far-eastern trade. Even earlier, the French had found it necessary to conquer and colonize Algeria. Where possible, however, Europeans sought to minimize their political commitments while enlarging their economic presence. Thus, as of the 1880's, there was nothing new about the fact of European interests in the Mediterranean, in Africa, and in Asia. What changed was the rate at which they were pursued and the mode of European involvement. As long as an economic presence went unchallenged, there was no sound reason to take on the burden of formal empire. But challenges to that presence forced the development of new policies. The example of Egypt is particularly instructive.

Egypt had originally been a possession of the Ottoman Empire. The empire had been in a state of advancing decay since the early nineteenth century, however, increasingly unable to keep its subject states under control. In 1841, the Egyptians wrested free and achieved an autonomous status under the nominal rule of the Ottoman sultan. Almost at once, the new Egyptian rulers (or Khedives) began to modernize their country—developing railways, installing roads, canals, and telegraph systems, improving the harbors, expanding the educational system. Such projects were of course massively expensive, but they were both encouraged and financed by European investors, whose generous loans to the Egyptian government were accompanied by walloping interest rates. British bankers were the first to exploit this rich investment field, but they were quickly followed by the French.

By the 1870's, however, the reigning Khedive had dug himself so deeply into debt that rumors of government bankruptcy were in the air. The British and the French therefore established a joint commission which gave them sweeping powers over Egyptian finances. In order to meet the government's obligation to European creditors, the Anglo-French condominium forced sharp retrenchment and severe exactions upon the population. These policies, and the inroads upon Egyptian sovereignty which made them possible, swiftly ran head-on into a burgeoning nationalist movement which demanded expulsion of the westerners. The Khedive was powerless to eject the Europeans, and therefore equally powerless to deflect the nationalists. The anti-western movement quickly spread to the army, and there were riots in the major cities which cost dozens of European lives.

By 1882, it was plain that the nationalist movement would overwhelm the Khedive and the Europeans unless decisive action was taken. Interestingly enough, no French or British statesman was anxious to take it. Overseas adventures were in bad odor in both governments. The French ministry, under Jules Ferry, was under sharp attack for moving into Tunisia (adjacent to Algeria) to combat conditions remarkably similar to those in Egypt. French parliamentarians generally considered colonial possessions a drain on national energies and resources. In Britain, Gladstone's government opposed imperial expansion on principle, and had indeed been working to disentangle itself from involvements in southern Africa. Still, a nationalist victory in Egypt would do more than imperil British investors there. It would deliver into the hands of avowed anti-

Europeans the Suez Canal, opened in 1869 and thereafter the principal route to India, the cornerstone of the British empire.

With marked reluctance, the British and French decided upon a show of force in Egypt which they hoped would intimidate the nationalists into acquiescence and stabilize the Khedive. At the last moment, however, the French backed out, fearing domestic political consequences; and a British squadron proceeded to bombard the city of Alexandria. Such extreme action only further excited the nationalists, and the British had no choice but to engage in still more extensive counterinsurrectionary tactics. By September 1882, they had taken Cairo and broken the nationalist resistance. Events had swept them much farther along than they had planned; in order to subdue the nationalists, they were forced to conquer and occupy virtually the entire country.

Although the British saw themselves as the victims of circumstance, the French view was rather different. It was generally held in Paris that the British had deceived their former partners as to their intentions and finessed the French out of Egypt so as to have it for themselves. Politicians who, a few months before, had disdained to exercise themselves over the Egyptian question now complained roundly about "national humiliation." They insisted that France's north African holdings demanded a French voice in Egyptian affairs. For the next fifteen years, French policy in Africa was mainly directed toward restoring the *status quo ante* 1882 in Egypt.

Direct action was unthinkable, however: the French were not about to invade Egypt in order to evict the British. France therefore sought to exert pressure elsewhere. All along the west African coast, from the mouth of the Congo River north to Liberia, French and British traders were engaged in commerce with the natives. Most of these enterprises were modest and their scope hardly extended beyond the beaches. When French traders had asked (before Egypt) for government support and protection so that they might expand their operations inland, they had been coldly rebuffed. Developments in Egypt swiftly reversed policy. The French decided to lay claim to large inland areas, not because they valued those areas or the trade they might hold, but rather in hopes of threatening the British coastal outposts. When the British complained, as they must, the French would offer to pull back in return for the restoration of dual control in Egypt.

But the British found unilateral control, which they had not at first sought, too convenient to give up so easily. They did complain about French advances in west Africa. However, they sought to protect their minor interests there not by compromising their major interests in Egypt but by expanding their own holdings into the western interior. At the same time, the French found themselves involved in precisely the same sort of situation which had confronted the British in Egypt. France's inland thrusts quickly stirred up African resistance, largely in the form of Islamic hostility to the Christian invaders. The French had to fight for what the government had originally regarded as a diplomatic bargaining tool. Instead of merely asserting a claim to territory and planting a few troops and bureaucrats there, they were forced to conquer it. Once land had been bought with blood, no government was about to relinquish it. Thus did France build its massive west African empire, stretching all the way north to the Algerian border.

Two conclusions may be drawn from the case of Egypt and the chain reaction which its conquest set off. In the first place, the Europeans did not suddenly swoop down on Africa from out of nowhere. By 1882, their interests there had been long standing, if smaller than they were soon to be. Had the British not held and so highly valued India, their action in Egypt would have been almost inconceivable. In these terms, the "new" imperialism looks rather like a means of protecting "old" imperial holdings, though it also involved numerous unforeseen consequences. In the second place, however, and quite abruptly, both Britain and France took on huge territorial responsibilities wholly in defiance of established policy. Instead of relying largely on economic domination, Britain and France were now hoisting the flag as well—and, joined by Germany, they began to do so in Asia as well as in Africa. It is the extent to which imperialism became formal at the end of the nineteenth century that was the novelty.

Imperialism, Capitalism, and Nationalism

Industrialization and imperialism were two of the most prominent phenomena at the beginning of the twentieth century and some observers argued that there was a close connection between them. In 1902, the British economist and political journalist J.A. Hobson published his enormously influential *Imperialism: A Study*. Hobson, a Liberal of the left, argued that European industrial capitalism was producing wealth faster than it could in turn be absorbed. Because of domestic "underconsumption," it was no longer profitable for capitalists to invest their substantial returns in the home market. Yet this abundance of surplus wealth insistently sought outlets, for which it turned to areas hitherto unpenetrated by European capital—principally, Africa and Asia. In order to protect investments there, however, the capitalists needed the cooperation of their own governments. Political imperialism, according to Hobson, was only a shield for an aggressive economic version of imperialism, which subdued native populations and secured foreign lands for European capital. "It is not too much to say," he wrote, "that the modern foreign policy of Great Britain is primarily a struggle for profitable markets of investment."

Hobson was careful to identify investors—financiers and bankers—as the principal villains. Though manufacturers and merchants followed along, their profit from imperial ventures was small by comparison to the investors'—for that of the former was eaten up by a variety of hidden costs such as increased taxation prompted by the government's conquest and administration of colonies. There were a few groups besides investors which profited from what Hobson called "pushful policy": armaments manufacturers, the shipping trade, the military, the colonial civil service, to name several. By and large, however, imperialism was socially unprofitable, lining a few pockets and advancing a few careers at the expense of the great majority.

Lenin, in his pamphlet *Imperialism: The Highest Stage of Capitalism* (1916), cast Hobson's arguments in Marxist categories. Marx had theorized that capitalism's intrinsic logic would lead it out of its earlier, competitive stage into one in which gigantic monopolies controlled huge markets. Lenin claimed that this "highest" (and final) stage had now been reached. Further investment in monopolized markets would only increase production and thus lower both prices and profits. In order to maintain acceptable profits, capitalism had to seek out untilled fields. However, the competition of firms from different countries for foreign markets would bring them into political, and finally military, conflict. The result would be a world conflagration—which had in fact begun in 1914. Capitalism would destroy itself in the process and socialism emerge from its ruins, as Marx had predicted.

Over the years, scholars have subjected Hobson's and Lenin's approach to some telling analysis. It would now appear that, as of the nineteenth century, no European nation was in the situation where surplus capital desperately sought outlets. Or, to put the matter in another way, such investment capital as was available had no difficulty in finding markets without resorting to Africa and Asia. The British, during these years, were investing far more heavily in Latin America and the United States than in their own colonies; the French were sinking money into Russian factories and railways. Many European traders on the coast of Africa were pleading for government support precisely because private capital had shown so little interest in them. Furthermore, few serious historians have contended that World War I was at bottom a clash of monster monopolies in search of markets. Similarly, whatever else the war destroyed, it did not dispatch capitalism (a fact which has not dimmed enthusiasm for the validity of Lenin's theory in certain quarters).

One can acknowledge the truth of these criticisms without conceding that Hobson and Lenin were utterly misguided, for it is difficult to give even the most cursory glance at the history of modern imperialism without beginning to suspect that acquisitive motives were somehow involved. Although it seems plain that the British did not go into Egypt in 1882 because their banks were bursting at the seams with surplus capital, the British were protecting interests in both Egypt and India which were manifestly economic in nature. Somewhat later, the British acquired Burma—not so much for the trading and investment opportunities it offered as to buffer their Indian holdings from the threat of French westward expansion from Indo-China. There were also some cases in which the pursuit (as opposed to the protection) of profit was the primary goal: the British conquest of the Boer republics in South Africa, the spread of European spheres of influence in China.

By the 1880's, industrial capitalism in Germany, Britain, and France was in a vigorous, expansive state. Competition for markets was keen, the ambitions of traders ran high. It would have been remarkable had businessmen in these countries *not* seen Africa and Asia as, variously, a huge untapped reservoir of consumers, labor, or raw materials. It was natural for them to wish to exploit these markets and just as natural for them to press those wishes upon their governments. But what of the governments themselves, the men who made the political decisions? How did they respond to these pressures? Why did they engage in overseas expansion?

Political leaders in the major states had long since arrived at the conclusion that power assumed several shapes. It could be population, territory, military might, but it was also industrial strength and mercantile wealth. To ignore these realities was to compromise great power status. In an age when nationalistic feelings ran increasingly high, it was both unacceptable to consider anything less than great-power status and imperative to enhance it. In part, this thinking was political, a response to public opinion (or what was perceived to be public opinion); but it was also sometimes an attempt to manipulate public opinion by waving the flag and mouthing slogans about national honor. In part, it was ideological, in that many conservatives and moderate liberals alike were unbending nationalists who believed in the great power mystique. In any event, when one of the major states made a significant territorial annexation, the others had to ask themselves if they could risk *not* expanding their own dominion. The logic of this sort of competition is plain, and it leads directly to a definition of national stature in global terms: to be a great power was to be a world power.*

The nationalism of the late nineteenth and early twentieth centuries

---

* This sort of thinking is relevant first of all to the overseas imperialism being discussed here. However, it applies just as well to the basically imperialist policies of Austria-Hungary in the Balkans and of Russia in the Balkans and in Asia, even though in those instances no oceans were crossed.

was neither exclusively political nor exclusively economic. Again, when it came to national power, statesmen of the period would have failed to comprehend the academic distinction between these categories. Moreover, the nationalism which motivated imperial conquest was dialectical: the general policy of attempting to enlarge the national interest was carried out in direct response to corresponding attempts by other states. The British and French annexations in Egypt and in west Africa were followed by German forays in east Africa, which in their turn spurred the British to activity in the east. Similarly, each European intervention (whatever its specific motivation) inspired indigenous resistance; once that had been put down at the cost of some lives, the Europeans were not about to leave.

Much the same was true in the Orient, where European trade had been increasingly brisk in the nineteenth century but which—because of its distance from the west—had never seemed a suitable locale for formal domain. Prior to the mid-1890's, France alone of the powers which had become involved in Africa showed any interest in far-eastern territory. (As early as 1862, the French had begun the gradual conquest of Indo-China, establishing a protectorate in 1883.) By 1900, however, the vast empire of China and most of its neighboring dependencies were only nominally independent, having been carved up into "spheres of influence" by half a dozen nations.

China's precipitous collapse was in no small part occasioned by the rapid renovation of Japanese society in the second half of the nineteenth century. Prior to the 1850's, the Japanese had maintained a hostile and exclusionist attitude toward westerners, although scattered trading contacts with Dutch and Americans steadily multiplied. The conservative effort to resist the penetration of western influences finally buckled in 1854, when the American Commodore M.C. Perry negotiated a treaty opening two Japanese ports. Similar treaties with Britain, Russia, and the Netherlands followed quickly. With the Americans expanding their economic influence westward across the Pacific and the Russians pursuing territorial ambitions southeastward from Siberia, Japan faced a future of total subservience to modernizing western nations.

In response to these challenges, Japanese leaders determined to overhaul their government and society along the lines of the occidental powers. Beginning in the late 1860's, the feudal system and ramshackle government were replaced by a centralized bureaucracy built on western models. Japan embarked upon an experiment in swift, forced industrialization, the better to compete with the industrial nations which were gradually encroaching upon the northeastern Pacific. At the same time, it was decided that Japan would meet western advance by itself expanding —principally eastward to the Chinese mainland.

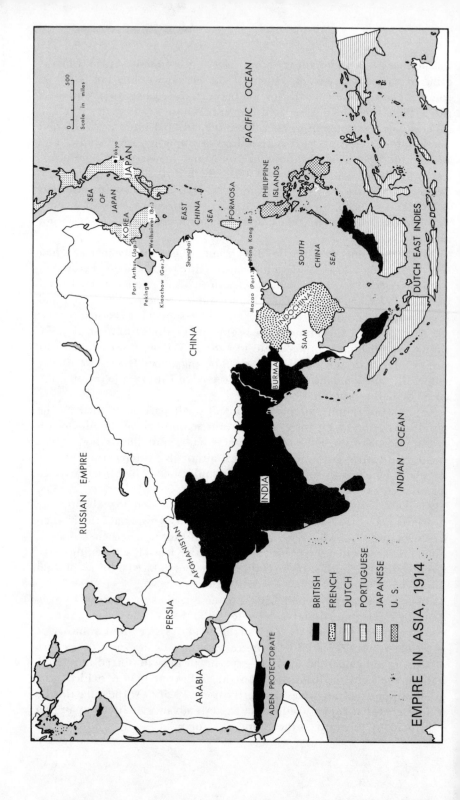

EMPIRE IN ASIA, 1914

BRITISH
FRENCH
DUTCH
PORTUGUESE
JAPANESE
U. S.

RUSSIAN EMPIRE

PERSIA

ARABIA

AFGHANISTAN

ADEN PROTECTORATE

INDIA

BURMA

CHINA

SIAM

INDOCHINA

Peking

Port Arthur (Jap.)

Kiaochow (Ger.)

Weihaiwei (Br.)

Shanghai

KOREA

JAPAN

Tokyo

SEA
OF
JAPAN

EAST
CHINA
SEA

FORMOSA

Macao (Port.)

Hong Kong (Br.)

PHILIPPINE
ISLANDS

SOUTH
CHINA
SEA

DUTCH EAST INDIES

PACIFIC OCEAN

INDIAN OCEAN

Scale in miles

0   500

China was in no position to fend off Japanese advances. By the late nineteenth century, the government scarcely governed, and large sections of the country were ruled by rapacious warlords who did not bother to pay tribute to the government. Commercial treaties with western traders limited Chinese import tariffs to five percent, though inflation naturally rendered these revenues even smaller. Therefore, when the Japanese sought to detach the semiautonomous state of Korea, China suddenly found itself in a war which it had no hope of winning. The impressively modernized Japanese army and navy overwhelmed Chinese forces during the war of 1894–95. The ensuing treaty granted Japan what amounted to a protectorate over Korea and ownership of the neighboring Liaotung peninsula, the Pescadores islands, and Formosa, along with a huge indemnity the Chinese could ill afford to pay.

The Sino-Japanese war left China in total disarray and exhaustion. Collapse was plainly imminent. If any one power picked up most of the pieces, it would be in a position to threaten the interests (however modest) of the others. It clearly behooved any power which wished to retain what it had to expand its holdings—a logic which, when applied between 1895 and 1900, spelled the end of Chinese independence. The Germans occupied Kiaochow Bay, and received the exclusive right to industrial development of nearby Shantung province. The Russians extracted similar concessions for the area around Port Arthur; the French, for Kwangchow Bay. The British succeeded in opening up Chinese inland waterways to their trading vessels, and developed a sphere of influence throughout the whole Yangtse River valley. A move by any power led to countermoves by all the rest. In the meantime, large loans from the European powers kept the empire propped up—and, of course, deeply obligated to the creditors. When nationalist sentiment welled up into violent resistance in 1900—in the so-called Boxer Rebellion—the Europeans further asserted their right to be in China by suppressing the uprising and extracting a large indemnity from the government.

In addition to the impulses for personal gain and national power which motivated imperialism, there was an important cultural dimension to imperialism. Almost uniformly, Europeans regarded Asians and Africans as morally and intellectually inferior to themselves—"Half devil and half child," the British poet Rudyard Kipling called them. Such creatures needed the firm hand of white, Christian civilization to survive in a modernizing, industrializing world. Whether an imperial power sought strategic advantage over a rival, national glory, or a trading concession, its agents generally justified their behavior as part of a great "civilizing mission."

The racist premises which underlay such verbiage are indeed ugly. But that does not mean that the words were always spoken in hypocrisy.

There were genuinely altruistic motives in the call for the acquisition of colonies, and it would have been difficult for Europeans of the 1890's even to communicate with anticolonialists of the mid-twentieth century. In the late nineteenth century it seemed perfectly obvious that European civilization was vastly superior to those civilizations to be found in Africa and Asia. What possible arguments could therefore be raised against extending the benefits of European civilization to the "barbarians"? What possible ill effects could arise from introducing to them the advantages of material progress and sound government? It never occurred to pro-imperialists that Africans and Asians might desire such benefits *and* political independence as well, nor that paternalistic rule would inevitably involve exploitation.

No imperial power was more resolutely committed to carrying its culture abroad than France. The original French approach to colonial rule was expressed in the doctrine of "assimilation"—that is, the native population would be turned into proper civilized Frenchmen. When Senegalese and Vietnamese and the rest spoke and thought like Frenchmen and practiced the Christian faith (or at least hewed to western moral codes), then they would be ready for greater political responsibilities, such as representation in the French parliament and a degree of domestic political autonomy. But the price they would have to pay was the destruction of their indigenous culture. The British took a somewhat similar position in India, where they determined to smash the caste system and eliminate what they regarded as superstitions rooted in Hinduism. Their efforts were greeted in 1857 with a gigantic Indian rebellion against the assaults upon traditional customs and institutions; order was not restored until 1859. Thereafter, and elsewhere in the British empire, the British tended to be more circumspect, reforming with a certain sensitivity toward established ways.

British policy was that all colonies could anticipate independence and self-government once they had developed the capability for it. In fact, in both British and French colonies, the "civilizing mission" was relatively superficial. A thin, elite layer of the population was exposed to European education and was then absorbed into the colonial administration. A program of Europeanization and "improvement" which reached large masses of the population would have been impossibly expensive, difficult to implement, not to mention politically unprecedented. The sooner one prepared colonials for self-government, the sooner colonies became independent—no longer available for economic exploitation, strategic military bases, and so forth. Many Europeans may have *wanted* to do more for their new charges. But the social, economic, and educational condition of most African and Asian colonies at the time of their liberation, in the 1950's and 1960's, lagged behind Western standards. Most of these former colonies are still struggling to realize the reforms which Europeans had confidently promised them in the 1890's.

Rather than creating modern, progressive, Europeanized societies around the globe, the age of imperialism created something with which its successors are still grappling (and none too successfully): African and Asian nationalism. The abrupt intrusion of foreign, white administrators, soldiers, traders, and missionaries aroused local populations, forcing them to redefine and assert their identities and their goals. The sight of Europeans siphoning off the precious resources of one's country, glutting the local market with their cheaply made industrial goods, and employing native labor at rock-bottom wages provoked a powerful reaction. Political domination, economic exploitation, and racist administration by white, capitalist nations of nonwhite, poor ones made the charge that imperialism was a form of capitalism credible. When nationalists from so-called Third World nations snarl at westerners as "imperialist dogs," the charge may sound like nothing more than rancid political rhetoric. Yet the imperial experience is at the root of both the nationalism and the radicalism which have swept nonwhite peoples since World War II. From China to Cuba to Egypt, bitter memories of the foreign presence—not so very distant—remain.

Imperialism and European Politics

While European rivalries were reflected in and intensified by imperial conflicts, those conflicts in turn helped reshape European political alignments. Once Britain had broken with France over Egypt and once France had subsequently allied with Russia on the continent, the British found themselves in an awkward situation. Their chief antagonist in Africa (France) was now the ally of their chief antagonist in south Asia (Russia). Russia's steady expansion southeastward from the Caucasus, toward Persia and Afghanistan, appeared to pose a direct challenge to the British position in India. Although the British government had no intention of entering into binding continental alliances, still it seemed likely that Egypt and India would force Britain into a closer relationship with Germany—the enemy of Britain's enemies. For a time, an Anglo-German partnership seemed, if not exactly a probability, then at least a subject for serious consideration in London. In 1890, for example, the two nations reached a formal settlement over a number of colonial questions which had been at issue between them.

Any such partnership, however, would have had to carry one overriding condition to be acceptable to the British. Empire was the major source of British strength; naval power was the guarantee of empire, the shield of trade routes and of the merchant fleet which brought home the imports (and particularly foodstuffs) upon which Britain was utterly dependent. Any challenge to British naval superiority was interpreted as a mortal threat, such that in 1889 Britain defined its policy as a "two-power standard"—that is, the navy would always be maintained at a level greater than that of the next two largest navies in the world combined. It was exactly this formula which the Germans refused to countenance.

The idea of such an inferior status deeply rankled in Germany, where aspirations for far-flung empire were as strong as in Britain and France. At the urgings of Naval Minister Alfred von Tirpitz, the German government finally determined in the late 1890's to repudiate the two-power standard and launch a naval building program which would make Germany a major sea power. With a large and modern fleet, the Germans might intimidate Britain into important colonial concessions and hope to play a dominant role in world politics. Predictably, the British responded with resentment and fear, rushing into a naval expansion and modernization program of their own. By the early years of the twentieth century, the two nations were locked in a gigantically expensive and politically explosive naval race.

German colonial and naval ambitions only further increased the British sense of isolation, especially when overseas conflicts arose with other powers. In 1882, Britain had been forced to take Egypt in order to protect Suez. But the question which no one then thought to ask was: what will have to be taken in order to protect Egypt? Ultimately, the answer came from the south. The Sudan, conquered by the Egyptians a generation earlier, had been in open revolt since 1881; two years later, the Sudanese turned against the new masters of Egypt. Their nationalist movement was inseparable from a religious revival which preached the purification of Islam by the rejection of all infidels. A nationalist and religious fanatic known as the Mahdi led Sudanese armies which routed Egyptian and then British armies, and by 1885 had evicted foreigners from the land.

At first, the British were more concerned to consolidate their position in Egypt than to invest lives and money in the reconquest of what was mostly worthless desert. Through that desert, however, flowed the Nile, the key to Egypt's agricultural economy. In the early 1890's, French hydraulic engineers announced that the Nile could be dammed up in the Sudan, literally choking off Egypt. At the same time, France was moving steadily eastward from its holdings in Senegal and the Congo. In 1896, a small, secret transcontinental mission under Captain Jean-Baptiste Marchand set out from west Africa with the purpose of capturing a French outpost on the upper Nile. In the same year, the British determined to begin the reconquest of the Sudan, and a large military force under General Herbert Kitchener began to work its way up the Nile valley.

HISTORICAL PICTURES SERVICE, CHICAGO

On August 2, 1914, an anonymous photographer inadvertently snapped one of the most astounding pictures of the century. The crowd is gathered in a public square in Munich to cheer the announcement that Germany is about to go to war; among the celebrants (see circle and enlargement) is Adolf Hitler, at the time only an obscure immigrant from his native Austria, another face in the crowd. Needless to say, such enthusiasm tended to wilt under the rigors of trench warfare, here depicted in a stretch of the British front during the Battle of the Somme.

HISTORICAL PICTURES SERVICE, CHICAGO

THE METROPOLITAN MUSEUM OF ART, BEQUEST OF MRS. H. O. HAVEMEYER, 1929. THE H. O. HAVEMEYER COLLECTION

STAATSGALERIE, STUTTGART

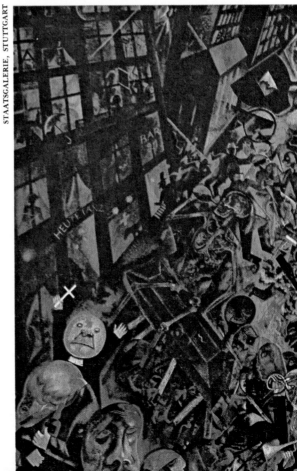

Paul Cézanne represented both a transition out of Impressionism and an answer to it. His several studies of Mont Sainte-Victoire, made toward the end of the nineteenth century, demonstrate his attempt to move from a personal interpretation of reality to one reduced to geometrical forms —"the cylinder, the sphere, and the cone." Right, George Grosz was a German painter and graphic artist who fused cubist perspectives with Expressionism. In his "Funeral Procession" (1917), the horrors of World War I and its attendant social turmoil find their way onto the canvas as a projection of the artist's psychological obsessions.

Cézanne's abstractions from reality remained partial. The paintings of Vasily Kandinsky, a Russian who emigrated to Germany before World War I, were an uncompromising attempt to reduce art to shape and color. Like his work "Black Lines, No. 189" (1913), Kandinsky's efforts denied that art had a representational function and returned, in the classicist tradition, to pure form.

HE SOLOMON R. GUGGENHEIM
MUSEUM COLLECTION

Picasso was the most
ıs, most commercially suc-
l, and most versatile
ieth-century painter. He
imented with, and popular-
ıumerous styles; but per-
his most fruitful and influ-
phase came before World
I, when he explored the
ilities of Cubism. The
ts acknowledged their debt
ssicism by returning to
trical forms—consider
o's "The Accordionist"
—but they also anticipated
nd toward personalism by
ng to admit that reality
be regarded from any
angle. For the Cubists, the
world—all 360°—was to be
enced at once.

THE SOLOMON R. GUGGENHEIM
MUSEUM COLLECTION

GERMAN INFORMATION CENTER

The Bauhaus school of architecture, founded in Germany in 1919 and disbanded by the Nazis in 1933, emphasized functionalism in art—"the marriage of art and engineering." One of the Bauhaus's leading lights was Mies van der Rohe, whose Stuttgart apartment house is shown here.

HISTORICAL PICTURES SERVICE, CHICAGO

There were people who found Sigmund Freud's psychological theories neither exciting nor shocking, but simply funny. This English cartoon, with the legend "Go on about Mummy," poked fun at the idea of the Oedipus complex. Note that the couch had not yet become synonymous with psycho-analysis.

MUSEUM OF MODERN ART/FILM STILLS ARCHIVE

By 1934, Hitler had emerged from the German crowd to command it. Here, in a still from the Nazi propaganda film "The Triumph of the Will," Hitler (flanked by two colleagues) marches through the regimented masses—a striking visual statement of the Nazi ideal.

SOVFOTO

oseph Stalin, in one of the haracteristically genial but unistakably authoritarian poses mployed by official Soviet ainters. He is addressing one of e party congresses which was in ct rendered impotent by his wn dictatorship.

These two visions of the fascist Leader hint at some of the differences between their respective regimes and political styles. Mussolini in 1930 is all posturing and bombast, very nearly a caricature of himself, and difficult to take seriously— a mistake made by some Italian liberals in the 1920's. There is no such problem with Hitler, shown here in 1935. The Fuehrer is altogether cooler, more menacing, deadlier. At the extreme right is Nazi Minister of Propaganda Joseph Goebbels.

SOVFOTO

...he American 'Peace Pipe' "—a Soviet ...toon of the early 1950's on American ...ervention (through the United Na-...ns) in the Korean War. The Ameri-..., diplomat offers the pipe and an ...e branch; the soldier offers death ...d prisoner-of-war camps, as indicated ...the labels on the bomb and axe.

THE CHICAGO TRIBUNE

...American version of decolonization ...1962 tries for paternalistic tolerance ...t smacks of racism. The underlying ...ggestion is strongly that we cannot ...pect small black children to drive ...ge high-powered cars responsibly. ...te also that independence is *granted* ...the white benefactor.

JANUS FILMS

Once postwar economic reconstruction had been accomplished, affluence posed its own problems. The classic study of the bored, alienated, and essentially empty well-to-do classes came in Michelangelo Antonioni's film "L'Avventura" (1960), whose characters have lost all capacity for human feeling. An equally fascinating cultural phenomenon has been the steady Americanization of Europe, taken by some as a sign of healthy diversification. Others wonder whether the opening of a McDonald's hamburger stand in Paris, the capital of *haute cuisine,* points to a day when the Eiffel Tower will be overshadowed by the golden arches.

MONKMEYER PRESS PHOTO SERVICE

Marchand's scraggly little band, exhausted from a harrowing journey which had taken nearly two and one-half years, reached Fashoda on the Nile in July 1898. Two months later, Kitchener arrived, at the head of a large and victorious army. The issue at Fashoda was never in doubt; the question was whether Paris would back down before the demands from London that France renounce all claims on the Nile. Angry noises emanated from both capitals, and there was talk of war. France, however, was in the midst of the infinitely disruptive Dreyfus affair and finally ordered Marchand to leave Fashoda in November. Early in 1899, the French government made its formal renunciation of claims in the Nile valley, in return for which Britain recognized French rights to vast reaches of the Sahara desert south of Algeria and Tunisia.

At the time, the Fashoda crisis appeared to be but the most dramatic episode in Anglo-French rivalry in Africa. In perspective, it is clear that the French withdrawal marked the end of that rivalry. The British had finally secured Egypt, and nothing short of a major European war was going to dislodge them. Once that fact had been recognized, as it swiftly was in Paris once the Dreyfus affair had been resolved, colonial antagonism between France and Britain had no further point. Egypt had been at the root of the conflict, and now the Egyptian question was closed. France recognized how much more convenient it would be to return to the cooperative spirit of pre-1882 days; Britain regarded French friendship as a welcome alternative to diplomatic isolation. Therefore, in 1904, the respective governments negotiated a resolution to virtually all their outstanding colonial quarrels. This so-called entente between Britain and France was nothing like a formal alliance; it simply smoothed out long-standing differences from Siam to the New Hebrides. But it meant that the French and British were talking again and opened the way for future agreements.

Three years after the conclusion of the entente, Britain reached a similar agreement with Russia—hastened, no doubt, by yet another step-up in German naval building. The British were of course anxious to eliminate imperial friction wherever possible so as to concentrate on the growing German menace. The Russian government, in its turn, had been deeply shaken by the military defeat it had suffered in 1905 at the hands of Japan (contending with the Russians in Manchuria and Korea). In the midst of the war, revolt had broken out within Russia itself, forcing the czar to grant a constitution and establish at least the semblance of parliamentary government. By 1907, the Russians were therefore ready to give up dreams of an even larger south Asian empire. In return for a substantial sphere of influence in northern Persia, they recognized British rights in the Persian Gulf and renounced all designs on Afghanistan. The Anglo-Russian entente, like its counterpart of 1904, was not an alliance; it was a handshake on overseas questions, meant to have little direct reference to continental affairs. But its conclusion meant that the only nation with which the British had not come to an understanding on imperial questions was Germany.

Though not formally a part of the Franco-Russian alliance, the British were increasingly finding that their national interest ran in flat contradiction to German official policy. When the Germans and the French became embroiled over various questions, the British found themselves offering stronger and stronger support to the French. In 1905, Germany raised vague but ominous challenges to the French sphere of influence in Morocco; startled by this display of German aggressiveness, British officials began the first of a long series of secret Anglo-French military discussions. When the Germans repeated this performance in 1911, they again succeeded in binding the entente even tighter. Even so, by 1914 few people in Germany believed that, should it come to war between France and Germany, the British would intervene. There was little appreciation in the German government of how frightened the British were about the growth of German power and ambition, and to what lengths the British would go to stem its further expansion.

Part Three
THE
TWENTIETH
CENTURY

No matter what happens in the next quarter-century, it seems likely that the twentieth century will in the future be viewed as the century of violence. Though industrialization continues to work its widespread changes, the twentieth century has thus far been given its shape by massive upheavals in which industrial technology has been employed to kill human beings. In the process, European power in the world has sharply diminished.

The following chapters attempt to show how European revolutions and wars have become worldwide in scope and how Europeans have responded to these events and to the changes in their global status. Chapter 11 deals with World War I and the Russian revolutions of 1917. Chapter 12 sketches some of the intellectual and cultural changes of the post-positivist era. Communism and fascism are the focus of Chapter 13, which compares them and charts the history of their conflict in the period from 1919 to 1939. Chapter 14 takes up World War II, and Chapter 15 studies the aftermath of Cold War and decolonization. Chapter 16, the concluding chapter, discusses principally the development of social and economic policy in the postwar world.

11 / *War and Revolution*

No event in modern history has spawned a larger literature of controversy than World War I. Sixty years after its outbreak, the origins and causes of the war are still hotly debated. This abiding interest is wholly justified by the fact that World War I is also the most consequential event of twentieth-century history. It destroyed millions of lives, brought down regimes, served as midwife to the Russian revolutions of 1917, reordered the map of Europe, seriously altered the world economy, and brought a permanent change in the global balance of power. The war and the efforts to settle it with a lasting peace led directly to another world war just twenty years later.

The Sources of Conflict

German imperial and naval ambitions during the early twentieth century assumed an increasingly large role in British politics. The German naval program was itself a sufficient case for alarm in London as long as British policy makers were determined to adhere to the two-power standard. But there was mounting evidence as well that the Germans entertained serious and concrete plans for expanding their political and economic influence beyond their already existing imperial outposts in Africa and Asia. In 1911, for example, the Germans dispatched a gunboat to Morocco, ostensibly to protect German nationals from various depredations in that French sphere of influence, but actually to extort a concession in the form of a slice of the French Congo (which the Germans ultimately received). Throughout this period, moreover, the German presence in the Mediterranean was becoming more conspicuous. German capital was funding a projected railroad which would have stretched from Berlin to

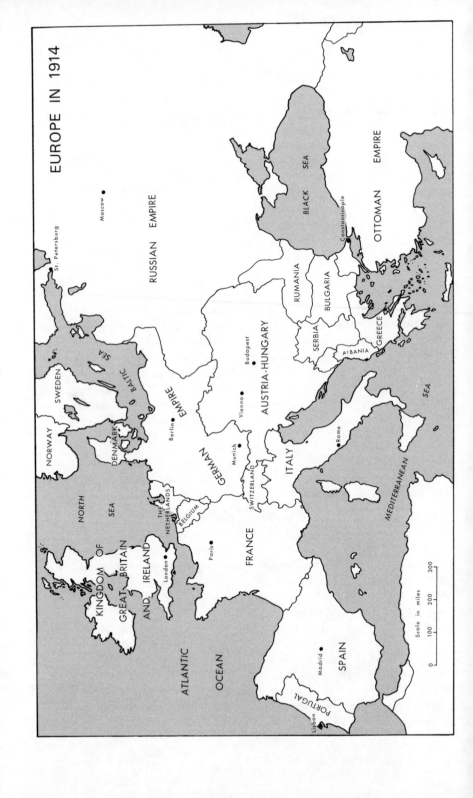

EUROPE IN 1914

Bagdad and thus given Germany a considerable stake in middle-eastern trade. These activities also occasioned profound concern in Russia, since it now appeared that the Germans were prepared to compete with the Russians for influence in the eastern Mediterranean.

It was plain in Britain that German policy was becoming inimical to British imperial interests. It was less plain what ought to be done about it, beyond continuing to build naval vessels at a rate which would maintain the two-power standard. How, in particular, would the British respond if the Germans chose to move against them indirectly, attacking France and/or Russia and thus threatening a return to British isolation? British involvement in a Franco-German war in which Britain was not attacked nor British interests clearly and directly involved might be difficult to justify to the British public. Yet a small number of highly placed British officials had come to the conclusion that such involvement was absolutely imperative in the event of such a war. They were convinced that Britain could not afford to stand idly by while Germany eliminated France and thus broadened its own power on the continent. Yet these officials were still uncertain of public reaction and while they were prepared to make some reasonably extensive assurances to their French counterparts about British intervention in a Franco-German war, intervention was not announced publicly as British policy.

As a result, and also because of traditional British policy regarding noninvolvement in continental affairs, German authorities were certain that the British would sit out any continental war. Equally significant, they were certain that such a war was becoming increasingly likely *and* increasingly advisable. For two decades, Germany had lived with the uncomfortable reality of the Franco-Russian alliance flanking its western and eastern borders. Although that alliance had originally been intended as a defensive mechanism, high German political and military leaders tended to see it as part of a policy of "encirclement," and thus potentially offensive in character. This thinking intensified sharply in 1913 when the French parliament voted a series of military reforms which would have both enlarged and modernized the French army; similar reforms were under way in Russia. Military spokesmen argued privately that while German power now remained supreme on the continent, the completion of these reforms in a few years would shift the balance of power in favor of the Franco-Russian alliance. In other words, the "encirclement" mentality strongly implied that war was inevitable at some stage, and the analysis of the Franco-Russian military reforms implied that if war was unavoidable, it was in Germany's best interests that it come sooner rather than later. The longer war was put off, the greater the advantage for the enemy. It is a short step from this sort of thinking to an argument for a preventive war, a preemptive strike which would simply advance the inevitable to a time more satisfactory for Germany. Clearly, German leaders in 1913–14 faced the prospect of a continental war unflinchingly, not as a horror to be avoided at all costs but as an opportunity to sustain and even enhance Germany's great power status.

One important feature of that status was Austria-Hungary, allied to Germany since 1879. For the Germans to play a major role in continental (and even world) affairs, its principal ally had to be of believably great power stature itself. To weaken Austria-Hungary was to weaken Germany. Therefore, German policy makers took a keen interest in Habsburg policy in the Balkans.

The Habsburg Empire was a multinational state ruled by Austrians and Hungarians but with a population which was in its majority Slavic. The steady growth of Slavic nationalism within the Empire during the nineteenth century was accompanied by encouragement from the independent Slavic states of the Balkans, and especially Serbia. At the same time, the authority of the Ottoman Empire gradually receded from the Balkan Peninsula, which it had once ruled, leaving this region open for competition between the neighboring great powers, Russia and Austria-Hungary. It was plainly in the interest of the Habsburg Empire to silence the Slavic nationalists to its south in order to keep control of its own Slavs. Correspondingly, the Balkans represented the logical field for the expansion of Habsburg economic power. Russia, seeking greater influence to the south and ultimately a Mediterranean port, took up the cause of its brother Slavic states in the Balkans and posed as their defender against Austro-Hungarian expansion.

In 1878, as part of the breakup of the Ottoman Empire in the Balkans, the Austrians occupied the former Ottoman provinces of Bosnia and Herzegovina—provinces which the independent state of Serbia considered rightfully its own. Exactly thirty years later, in a complicated diplomatic finesse, the Habsburgs formally annexed the provinces, to the consternation of the Serbs and their Russian benefactors. There was talk of war, which eventually subsided (although Serb and Russian dissatisfaction did not). Serbian nationalists agitated ever more energetically for the transfer of Bosnia and Herzegovina to Serbia and for a revolt of the Habsburg Slavs. The Russian government, in order to maintain its credibility among Balkan Slavs after the 1908 fiasco, continually assured the Serbs of its support.

These were the concrete issues from which war arose in 1914—deep British apprehensions about German naval and imperial aims, German fears of encirclement and projections of future military advantage on the continent, Austro-Serbian and Austro-Russian rivalry in the unstable and explosive Balkans. Even so, it is debatable whether or not war would have come at all without the prevailing attitudes of statesmen, generals, and the public at large toward war itself.

European military leaders in the early twentieth century thought almost exclusively in offensive terms. The plans that they had formulated in the event of war focused on attack, on the swift engagement of the enemy in a major battle in which the outcome would quickly be decided. The models which generals studied were the Austro-Prussian war of 1866, in which the Prussians won the decisive battle of Königgrätz three weeks after war had been declared, and the Franco-Prussian war, which the Prussians won to all intents and purposes after scarcely six weeks of fighting. In other words, it was widely assumed that war, should it come, would be short—a matter of weeks at most. Military and civilian leaders alike were agreed upon this point; they argued—with an astounding lack of logic—that since no state's political or economic system could bear the strains of a long, drawn-out war, then no such war would be fought.

The men who would direct war thus gave the men who would fight it no particular cause for alarm. Should war come, it would all be over very quickly. But European public opinion was not merely sanguine about the prospect of war; in some quarters, there was positive enthusiasm. Opportunities for heroism and individual glory in industrial society were rare. How could a man test his worth over an accounts ledger? What poet could sing of production quotas met? Many people romanticized the excitement and danger of war and, when it came, considered it a wholly welcome release from the unglamorous routine of modern life. Rupert Brooke, a young British poet, likened the men going off to battle to "swimmers into cleanness leaping . . . ." Pacifist sentiment was weak and muted. Although internationalism remained the official policy of the social democratic parties, whose leaders insisted that proletarian brotherhood extended across national frontiers, strong patriotic feeling ran through the working-class rank and file. Since most people regarded war as, at worst, a potential inconvenience, and at best a splendid opportunity, it is perhaps not surprising that war came.

The Summer Crisis

On June 28, 1914, Archduke Franz Ferdinand, heir to the Habsburg throne, and his wife paid a state visit to Sarajevo, the capital of Bosnia. They were assassinated there by members of a terrorist secret society of Serbian nationalist fanatics. Although Austrian officials immediately began to contemplate reprisals for this provocative act, they were divided on the nature of their response. Moreover, behind tiny Serbia stood the power of Russia; before proceeding with any actions which might embroil them with the Russians, the Austrians naturally turned to their own ally, Germany.

The Austrians received at first no uniform counsel. German foreign office spokesmen advised only political action against Serbia; the military preferred war, and they were supported by Kaiser William II, who told the Austrians that it was "now or never." With these assurances, the Austrians prepared an ultimatum for the Serbian government so humiliating that it seemed unlikely the Serbs would accept. But the Austrians also moved along at a leisurely pace. The French president and prime minister were in Russia on a state visit; since Austrian action against Serbia would probably involve Russia, the Austrians had no desire to have Russian and French leaders together—the easier to communicate and coordinate their plans—when they sprang their ultimatum. When the French finally left St. Petersburg, the Austrians presented their demands in Belgrade, on July 23.

The ultimatum called, among other things, for the Serbian government to cease all anti-Austrian propaganda; to fire officials designated by the Austrians; and to allow the Habsburg government to join in the search (on Serbian soil) for the assassins. Its acceptance would have entailed a serious compromise of Serbian sovereignty. The Austrians gave forty-eight hours for its consideration and insisted upon total acceptance; rejection of any of the ten points would be treated as rejection of all. Since it would have been unthinkable for the Serbs to wage war alone against Austria-Hungary, they had no choice but to accede unless they could count on Russian support. The Russian government, though far from wildly anxious for war, felt that its credibility in the Balkans depended upon a show of strength for its ally. Fortified with Russian backing the Serbs formulated an unusually conciliatory response to the ultimatum—accepting most of its points, calling for some clarifications, and rejecting only one demand. Since the Serbs knew full well the conditions of the ultimatum, they cannot have been surprised when the Austrians immediately severed diplomatic relations; but at least Serbia won a significant propaganda advantage in European opinion.

One person impressed with Serbian behavior was the Kaiser himself. William II felt that the Serbian response represented a great boost to Habsburg prestige, and he urged that it be used as the basis for immediate negotiations. But he learned of it three days after its issuance (having been vacationing aboard his yacht) and by that time his sudden attack of moderation was too late. The same day, Austria-Hungary—repeatedly prodded by the German military and by the chancellor, Bethmann-Hollweg—declared war on Serbia. The next day, July 29, Austrian troops began the bombardment of Belgrade—just across the Danube from Habsburg territory. At this point, the Russians felt they could wait no longer, and the government ordered general mobilization—calling up reserve units, putting troops on a footing of immediate readiness, and transporting them to strategic locations along the German and Austro-Hungarian borders.

The fact to be kept most prominently in mind here is that decisive German authorities—Bethmann-Hollweg, the general staff of the army, and now the foreign office as well—were not merely accepting the approaching prospect of war with equanimity, they were trying to ensure that it would occur. For that reason, they had been pushing Austria toward war with Serbia even faster than most Austrian officials were ready to move. Moreover, on July 31, the Germans dispatched their own ultimatum to the Russians: desist in mobilization against *both* Germany and Austria-Hungary. In other words, the Germans were demanding that Russia leave Serbia to the mercies of the Austrians or face a war with Germany as the alternative. Although the Kaiser still preferred negotiation, his military chieftains overruled him, arguing that Germany could not risk Russian mobilization against its borders without a response in kind.

It hardly seemed likely that the French would stand aside and watch the Austro-German forces demolish the Russians, a fact as clearly appreciated in Berlin as in Paris. When the Germans somewhat perfunctorily inquired as to what French policy would be, they received the replay, "France will be guided by her own interests." Hours later, the Germans declared war upon Russia, and on August 3 upon France. It came as a much greater surprise to Bethmann-Hollweg when Britain made clear that it would not remain neutral in the case of a Franco-German war. The chancellor had completely failed to grasp the extent of alarm in Britain over German expansiveness and presumed that a promise that Germany would annex no French territory in Europe would mollify the British, keeping the war a continental affair. On July 29, Lord Edward Grey, the British foreign minister, flatly rejected such an offer. As Grey told Parliament a few days later, "if we are engaged in war, we shall suffer but little more than we shall suffer if we stand aside." The Germans now discovered that the continental war they had sought to create ever since the assassination of Franz Ferdinand was a world war, with British sea power and capacity for blockade a very important element in it.

War of Attrition

Even though German leaders were startled at the British entry into the war, they did not at first imagine that it would alter the shape of hostilities. Like nearly everyone else, they assumed that this exhilarating adventure would be intense, but brief; troops in every country departed for battle in the full expectation that they would be home by Christmas. The Germans anticipated that they would gain victory in France within six weeks.

The German strategic response to the difficulties of a two-front war had been formulated by General Alfred von Schlieffen, chief of the general staff until his death in 1905. The Schlieffen Plan, which the Germans put into effect in August 1914, called for a holding action in the east, conducted by a relatively small force. The Germans would give ground before the Russian attack, concentrating their forces in the west for an assault upon France. But Schlieffen refused to hurl his troops upon the strong fortifications along the Franco-German border. Instead, he would go into France through Belgium and move on Paris from the west. (Belgium, after it won independence in 1831, had been declared neutral by international treaty.) Somewhere in the vicinity of the French capital, a decisive battle would be fought. Once the Germans had won it, they could besiege Paris with a token force and transfer the bulk of the army to the eastern front to deal with the Russians.

The Schlieffen Plan was full of flaws. It asked for too much speed, it stretched supply lines too thin, and most fatally it left field commanders with the unwelcome choice of either separating their armies so that the French could drive a wedge between them, or stay closer together and thereby present an unguarded flank to the French. The commanders chose the second alternative in 1914; the French seized the opportunity, and slowed down the German rush. Shortly thereafter, on September 5, the antagonists joined in the region of the Marne River, little more than twenty-five miles from Paris; and the Germans had what they hoped was their decisive battle. But they were unable to break the French lines. The French raced reinforcements from the capital to the front, using every possible conveyance (including most Parisian taxicabs). By the 12th, it was clear the French had held, and the Germans withdrew somewhat to the north.

Although the Battle of the Marne had nearly shredded French lines, subsequent German probes failed to reveal a likely spot for a breakthrough. By early October, each side began to establish defensive positions while regrouping in anticipation of a new offensive. Since neither side wished to have its flank turned, each side began to extend its front —all the way to the Channel in the northwest and to the Swiss border in the southeast, a huge diagonal extending more than 300 miles. The troops dug in, and quickly built a relatively sophisticated network of trenches.

Attacking these fronts was no simple matter of breaking through a front-line trench; for behind them were fall-back trenches from which to wage further resistance, trench systems for reserves, artillery and communications trenches, and highly fortified trenches for a last stand—all ranging back several miles from the first trench. The trench system proved an effective obstacle to massive offensive breakthroughs, especially when coupled with use of the machine gun. When properly spaced along a line, machine guns could command a field of fire against onrushing infantry. Even if the attacker gained the first ribbon of trenches, his forces were usually badly mauled, in poor condition to attempt a run at the second or third trench, and often unable to stand fast against a counterattack.

In spite of these facts, the French and British commanders clung tenaciously to the strategy of offensive warfare. Certain that a breakthrough was possible, anxious to restore a "war of movement," the generals confidently mounted enormous offensives which senselessly battered the enemy line and gained little ground but lost unprecedented numbers of men. In the spring of 1915, the French pounded away at German positions. Following lengthy artillery barrages—designed to "soften up" the enemy, but in fact only alerting him that an attack was coming and sending him scurrying into impregnable underground bunkers until the barrage lifted —thousands of French infantrymen poured across no-man's-land toward the German lines. Between February and May, the French suffered about 110,000 casualties—with no appreciable change in the front. A major French offensive in May and June 1915 gained no more than three miles, at a cost of 400,000 men. In the Battle of the Somme River the following year, the British and French attackers lost 420,000 and 200,000 men respectively, while the German defenders lost perhaps 450,000—mostly in counterattacks—without altering the front significantly.

Before the allied generals actually realized it, they had become involved in a war the point of which was not to win a single, decisive battle nor even to capture strategic territory, but rather to kill more of the enemy's soldiers than he killed of yours. In other words, although offensive warfare remained the rule, it gradually was redesigned to achieve a different effect: to wear the enemy down over a long period of time by inflicting upon him an unbearable rate of casualties. The British and the French were swept into a strategy of attrition largely by circumstances; the new German commander, Erich von Falkenhayn, who succeeded von Moltke late in 1914, chose it more deliberately. In early 1916, he decided to attack the French fortress of Verdun, which was of no particular value of itself but which the French had long touted as their one "impregnable" position. Falkenhayn correctly reasoned that French prestige would demand total commitment to the defense of Verdun, and his purpose in attacking it was simply, in his own words, "to bleed France white." By July, when the Germans began to draw back from Verdun, they had indeed killed or wounded some 315,000 Frenchmen; but in the process they had lost 280,000 of their own men.

The war was, of course, by no means confined to the western front. In the east, the Germans had begun by falling back before the Russian advance, as the Schlieffen Plan dictated, while they awaited reinforcements once victory in France had been achieved. However, a gap suddenly discovered in the Russian lines allowed the Germans to encircle one large detachment of enemy forces and win a major victory at Tannenberg at the end of August 1914. Though losses on both sides were substantial in the following years, the general pattern was one of steady German advance into western Russia. A new theater of operations opened in the Mediterranean late in 1914 when the Ottoman Empire, traditional enemy of Russia and secretly allied to Germany since August, joined the war on the German side. The Turks soon found themselves embroiled in campaigns against the Russians in the Caucasus, and against the British in Mesopotamia and Arabia. In 1915, the British even attempted an invasion of Turkey itself, at Gallipoli, only to be turned back later in the year. German colonial possessions in Africa also came under British assault, while in Asia Japan declared war on Germany late in August 1914 and joined with the British in actions against German holdings on the Chinese mainland. The Italians, despite their membership in the Triple Alliance, had declared neutrality upon the outbreak of hostilities—motivated in part by a desire to sell their army to the highest bidder. French and British diplomacy, which offered Italy several territorial concessions at the expense of Austria-Hungary, proved most persuasive. Italy entered the war on the side of the entente in May 1915 and opened a new front for the Austrians to contend with.

For all these far-flung activities, contemporaries generally regarded the western front as the most important one, the area where the war would ultimately be decided. The western allies still hoped to wear the Germans down there. The Germans, for their part, hoped for victory in the east, so that they could transfer troops engaged against the Russians to the west (the exact opposite of what Schlieffen had envisaged). Maximum effort in the west became particularly important after the United States joined the war on the allied side in April 1917.* Although it was to be some months before the Americans could make a vital contribution to the Anglo-French effort, the Germans were anxious to strike a telling blow while they still faced only two antagonists in the west.

The Bolshevik Revolution of November 1917 gave the Germans their chance. Lenin, at the head of the new Bolshevik government, was deter-

---

* American sentiment since 1914 had been decidedly on the side of the western democracies, to whom the United States sold massive amounts of war matériel. When the Germans began engaging in unrestricted submarine warfare against American convoys to Europe in 1917, and when word of vague but menacing German machinations in Mexico surfaced at the same time, the United States declared war on Germany.

mined to consolidate the revolution at all costs—even large expanses of Russian territory. In December 1917, he concluded an armistice with Germany (followed by a formal peace early in 1918) which released German troops for combat in the west. The spring offensive, under General Erich von Ludendorff, breached the allied front at several points; certain German units advanced to within thirty-seven miles of Paris. In July and early August, the French and the Americans held off a critical attack— once more, at the Marne. Immediately, all three western powers launched a counterattack; Ludendorff's troops, exhausted by the long offensive, began to give ground with alarming speed. In the meantime, Austria-Hungary was collapsing under the impact of Italian and French forces and of internal Slavic nationalist revolts. Without an ally, and without any means of reversing the tide of war in the west, Germany concluded an armistice—though not a single enemy soldier had as yet set foot on German soil.

The Home Front

The fact that World War I turned out to be very different from what had been so widely anticipated necessitated profound domestic adjustments. None of the nations had stockpiled material for a long war of attrition; none of the economies were geared for extended wartime production. In September 1914, at the conclusion of the first Battle of the Marne, the French discovered that they had only enough artillery shells for a few weeks more of war. All the powers had to institute crash programs in munitions production. When the head of the British army pronounced that four machine guns per battalion was a sufficient number, David Lloyd George, the Minister of War, insisted that nothing less than 64 per battalion would do—and turned out to be correct. Yet large-scale wartime production for a conflict which would last years and be waged on several continents could hardly take place randomly, in the best traditions of laissez faire. Centralized planning became unavoidable; government agencies, however reluctantly, were forced to organize production and set quotas, to interfere in private business to an unprecedented degree, and even to create private businesses which existed largely on government contracts. It was a development experienced by every major power—most strenuously, perhaps, in Germany, but in France and Britain as well.

Political centralization accompanied economic centralization. Whatever a nation's political institutions—democratic or authoritarian, parliamentary or executive—it tends to vest decision-making power in wartime in a very few persons. World War I was no exception. In some places, to be sure, this amounted to no change at all: Russia's parliament, the

Duma, created after the 1905 revolution, had never had important powers to begin with, so that wartime government was simply a continuation of czarist autocracy. In Germany, the executive power had long outweighed the legislative, although increasingly the pressures of war placed the initiative in the hands of military rather than civilian authorities. From 1916 onward, General Ludendorff and his superior, Field Marshal Paul von Hindenburg, functioned as virtual dictators, far more powerful than the chancellor, the Reichstag, or even the Kaiser himself. Although the French and the British tried to maintain regular parliamentary processes, war placed a premium upon swift and decisive decisions. Increasingly, power devolved upon a handful of cabinet ministers. In December 1916, David Lloyd George formed a special war cabinet which ruled without serious parliamentary restraint. In November 1917, Georges Clemenceau was made premier of France, with sweeping powers to combat defeatism and organize total victory.

Wartime exigencies meant that government was bound to become more pervasive than usual. Once it became clear that the war was not going to end speedily, the state had both to mobilize the population for a long and costly war and to hold defeatist and pacifist elements in check. Repressive efforts were occasionally necessary, as when British pacifists resisted the enactment of compulsory military service in 1916, or when mutinies spread in the French army during 1917. Even more important, however, were the extensive programs for molding domestic opinion—positively, by vigorous propaganda programs ("the murderous Hun," etc.), and negatively, by the control of information. Every state practiced censorship (though British authorities were able to a considerable degree to rely upon the "self-censorship" of the press), but none more rigorously than Germany.

The German public knew only what the government—which meant, increasingly, the military—wanted it to know about the war; frequently, that involved pure fabrication. With more and more of the economy being devoted to the war effort, German citizens began to experience severe deprivation; by 1917 this was becoming difficult to square with the repeated reports of glorious German victories. The defeat of Russia, however, and the absence of any authoritative news to the contrary gave the official version of the war continued credibility. When Ludendorff's 1918 offensive collapsed and the army went into full retreat, word at last began to seep into Germany, and an immense wave of disillusionment engulfed the country. Naval mutinies, strikes, and protest demonstrations erupted throughout the first week of November. With the army still in France, systematic repression at home was impossible. To make matters worse, American President Woodrow Wilson, speaking for the western allies, had shown himself disinclined to negotiate a peace with the imperial government, on the ground that it did not truly represent the German people. In these desperate circumstances, Kaiser William II abdicated on November 9; the same day, the Social Democrats proclaimed the German Republic.

The Habsburg Monarchy, in spite of tight governmental controls over the population, collapsed just as abruptly. As the war effort strained the monarchy and stretched its resources thin, Slav nationalism seized upon the opportunity to receive legitimizing recognition from the enemies of Austria-Hungary. Czech and Polish units served with the Italian, Russian, and French armies; by 1918 the several subject nationalities of the Dual Monarchy had established national councils claiming to be formal governments. By early September, Italy, France, Britain, and the United States had all recognized the independence of Czechoslovakia, which amounted to endorsing the dissolution of the Habsburg state. Other Slavic groups immediately began announcing their own independence; and by the time the Austrians concluded an armistice on November 3, the old Empire existed in name only. Within weeks, separate states of Austria, Hungary, and Yugoslavia had been proclaimed, their establishment being later formalized by the several peace treaties which concluded the war.

The Peace

When the statesmen of the victorious powers gathered at Versailles early in 1919 to draft formal peace treaties, the problems which faced them were, by the most conservative estimate, formidable. All of them were anxious to find means to prevent the recurrence of war. Yet they had also just emerged from the most destructive conflict in human history— resulting in as many as thirteen million military and civilian dead, and incalculable damage to property. A strong desire for vengeance ran through the populations of the conquering nations, and of course the peacemakers were all politicians accountable to the electorate. Finally, the international situation was full of uncertain new elements: the creation of new, small, weak states in central Europe; the sudden emergence of the United States as a major force in European politics; and the ominous presence of the world's first communist government looming on the western horizon.

Of all the victorious leaders, Clemenceau was the most fiercely committed to a punitive and vengeful peace. It was not enough for him that the Germans would pay for the awesome damage wreaked in France, where the western war had been almost exclusively fought. He sought to guarantee against a future renaissance of German power and aggressiveness by depriving Germany of all its military and much of its industrial might. Lloyd George's position was more complex. Ever since becoming prime minister in 1916, he had promised a hard peace on the Germans; in a parliamentary election of 1918, he took a similarly tough line; and at the Paris talks he consequently represented an electorate which had just demanded the most severe terms. On the other hand, many of his objectives had been achieved before the peace treaty was completed: the virtual destruction of the German navy and merchant marine, the redistribution of the German colonies (many of them to the British). Lloyd George could therefore afford to indulge his more moderate instincts and urge that Clemenceau take a less harsh stance.

Woodrow Wilson arrived in Paris as the proponent of a just and even-handed peace, and in the subsequent negotiations he frequently blocked some of the sterner anti-German proposals of his counterparts. But Wilson was also concerned with a durable peace, to which end he developed the idea of a League of Nations—a forum in which international conflicts could be settled by negotiation and arbitration and which would confront potential aggressors with the armed might of most of the world. He insisted from the beginning that the covenant of the League be written into the treaty itself, thus ensuring the League's eventual establishment. By concentrating so heavily upon this issue, Wilson neglected numerous other issues in which Clemenceau and, to a lesser degree, Lloyd George were able to have their way. Moreover, the French and British leaders were extremely dubious about the concept of collective security, which seemed to impinge upon the tradition of national sovereignty and to force their nations into the unwelcome role of policemen for the world. Basically, they used Wilson's deep commitment to the establishment of the League as a means of extracting other concessions from him —concessions which strengthened their own respective national positions vis-à-vis Germany.

In retrospect, of course, it is clear that Germany hardly bore sole responsibility for the war. But the treaty of Versailles, which formally concluded peace between the allies and Germany alone and which was signed in June 1919, specifically designated Germany as uniquely responsible for the outbreak of hostilities. Once guilt had been thus allocated, then clearly anything was justified. German territories were ceded to France (the regions annexed by Bismarck in 1871), Belgium, and to the newly created states of Poland and Czechoslovakia; German overseas colonies passed to Britain and France. The Franco-German border along the Rhineland was to be demilitarized on the German side; Germany was to have no military aircraft, no submarines, only six warships, and a token army of 100,000 men. Finally, the Germans were to pay reparations for the civilian damages of the war, although a figure was not mentioned in the treaty; when the bill was set at $33 billion in 1921, it became clear that the allies had in mind nothing less than debilitating the German economy.

The Germans themselves had nothing to say about all this: they were not allowed to take part in the negotiations and were given forty-eight hours to sign the final version under threat of the resumption of hostilities. In short, the treaty was precisely what its German critics called it—a *Diktat,* or dictated treaty. Whether or not the treaty was unworkably severe remains a matter of some debate. There can be little doubt, however, that it prejudiced the chances for Germans to build a viable republican democracy. The allies were imposing the treaty not upon the authoritarian and military elements who had ruled Germany in 1914, but upon the liberal and social democratic groups who picked up the pieces after the collapse of November 1918. These groups, which had enough domestic problems as it was, now bore the added stigma of having signed the treaty—though with Germany now in inner turmoil and being occupied by western troops, there was little else they could have done. A preposterous but nonetheless powerful myth emanating from right-wing circles claimed that the end of the war and the fall of the monarchy were nothing less than a "stab in the back"; that is, left-wing elements had somehow conspired with the allies to sell out the army and the nation in return for power. Though there was no shred of truth to this slander, still it seemed to offer a convincing explanation to a traumatized nation of the sudden reversal of German military fortunes in the last months of the war.

Also prominent on the agenda at Paris was the definition and legitimization of the new nations which sprang into existence in late 1918: Poland, Czechoslovakia, Yugoslavia, Austria, and Hungary. The latter two were of course treated as vanquished powers, and large cessions of territories were made to their new Slavic neighbors. However, territory alone, even with defensible frontiers, does not make a viable nation. It has since been argued that the dismantling of the Habsburg Empire was a foolish act, taken in the heat of wartime passion, and that a more reasoned view would have seen that none of these successors to the Empire was economically strong enough to become a going conern. (Clemenceau himself wanted to keep the Empire intact in order to ensure political stability in south central Europe.) By maintaining the Empire, or some version of it, runs this thesis, the peacemakers could have given stability and security to this troubled corner of Europe from which issued so many of the ensuing generation's problems.

It is an attractive case, but its main difficulty is that the Habsburg Empire was not dismantled at the Paris peace conference. The Empire came undone under the pressures of military defeat and nationalism, the latter much encouraged by Wilson and his promise of self-determination

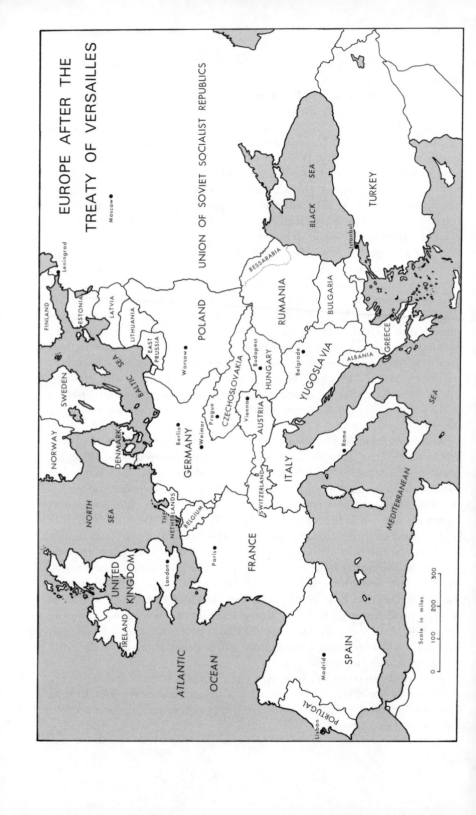

EUROPE AFTER THE
TREATY OF VERSAILLES

for all nationalities. That promise both foreclosed the future of the Empire and proved impossible to effect: Austrians, Magyars, and the several strains of Slavs simply did not live in neat, homogeneous little blocs. In any event, the peacemakers for the most part only certified a dissolution which had already taken place by the time they set to work.

As unsettling as anything in early 1919 was the specter of communist revolution which appeared to be materializing in central Europe. In January, revolutionary socialists had attempted to take Berlin; a communist government had briefly captured control of Munich. In March, Hungarian communists seized Budapest and held it for nearly five months. Labor unrest was boiling over everywhere, and sympathy for the Russian Bolsheviks seemed to be running high. The leaders of the new Russian government were both encouraging such activity and predicting that revolution would swiftly sweep westward across the continent. Although Bolshevism was not formally on the peacemakers' agenda, it was very much in their minds.

The Russian Revolutions

World War I found Russia with the largest army of the major belligerents, but also with the one most poorly led and equipped. As the smaller German force pushed eastward, the Russians suffered a string of serious defeats and a high rate of casualties. The Duma looked on with increasing alarm, but was powerless to affect events. Critical decisions were being made exclusively by a small circle around Czar Nicholas II—including principally his wife, the Czarina Alexandra, and a Russian Orthodox monk of dubious reputation, Gregory Rasputin, widely thought to have extensive powers over the Empress. Rasputin's influence may well have been overrated, but what is important is that contemporaries clearly *thought* that he manipulated Alexandra at will.

Late in 1915, Nicholas dismissed his military commander-in-chief and went to the front to assume personal control of the war effort. But the Russian situation continued to deteriorate, and the economic condition of the country was desperate. When Alexandra, who was German, appointed Baron Stürmer (of German descent) to head the government, rumors of treason began to crop up as the only possible explanation for the debacle. A broad coalition in the Duma, encompassing liberals and conservatives alike who feared for the safety of the state itself, began to press for change. In December 1916, a group of aristocratic conspirators assassinated Rasputin without actually attempting to seize power. Alexandra went into something like a state of shock at Rasputin's death, so that at this crucial juncture a power vacuum existed at the center of the government. The Duma did not act to fill it, however; the revolutionary initiative ultimately had to come from the populace.

On March 8, 1917, a spontaneous wave of strikes and rioting erupted in Petrograd (the new name bestowed at the beginning of the war upon St. Petersburg, which had a Germanic flavor to it). The workers were joined by the troops garrisoned there, mostly raw peasant recruits who had heard that they were to be sent to the front. The violence was more protest than positive action, but the government quickly demonstrated that it was powerless to restore order. The Duma therefore formed from its ranks a Provisional Government representing nearly all shades of opinion (including the Socialist Revolutionaries, in the person of Alexander Kerensky). Upon the government's request, Nicholas II abdicated in favor of his brother, Michael. But Michael sensed that the monarchy had come to the end of its tether, and in his turn refused to assume the throne. By March 16, Russia was a republic.

The Provisional Government began its eight-month tenure with a flurry of proclamations describing the great new era of political and social reform into which Russia was about to enter. Mostly, however, these remained promises, left for fulfillment to the election of a constituent assembly; in fact, the government's position was that the revolution would have to await the successful conclusion of the war. Although the war had seriously exacerbated social misery and strained the archaic governmental machine past the breaking point, the government refused to withdraw from the conflict, in spite of its demonstrated unpopularity among the people. In part, the decision arose from a desire to avoid identifying the Provisional Government with defeat and the cession of territory to a victorious Germany. In part, it was motivated by expansive ambitions (once Turkey joined the German side, the western allies had promised Constantinople to the Russians as a further enticement for staying in the war). In any event, it was a decision which opened the door to Lenin and the Bolsheviks.

Lenin spent the first three years languishing in his Zurich exile. When German agents offered him assistance in returning to Russia in 1917, he leaped at the opportunity. The Germans were ready to do anything which would intensify Russia's domestic turmoil. Lenin, a known opponent of Russia's participation in what he called a "bourgeois capitalist war," might help stir defeatist sentiment. (The Germans were clearly not expecting Lenin to be as successful as he ultimately was and were not thinking either in terms of financing a revolution; they were merely fishing in troubled waters.) Lenin received German money and transportation across Germany to Sweden, whence he made his way to Petrograd. Upon his arrival, on April 16, he called for immediate withdrawal from the war. At the same time, he urged peasants to seize control of the land and industrial workers to take over the factories—radical social reform without waiting for a constituent assembly. Finally, he demanded that the Provisional Government transfer "all power to the Soviets."

The Soviets (or "councils") of workers and soldiers had first sprung up during the revolution of 1905 as spontaneously organized bodies which would speak for, and lead, the new urban masses. Their reappearance in March 1917 bespoke at least a trace of that class consciousness for which the Russian Social Democrats had been searching so earnestly. The Petrograd Soviet, the most important of the similar groups which came together in the very largest cities, distrusted the middle-class and aristocratic Provisional Government and proclaimed itself an independent and sovereign authority. Lenin saw in the Soviets a potential power base, a link to mass support; and he quickly identified himself as a partisan of the claims of these bodies.

It was, of course, an article of the Marxist faith that a proletarian revolution would not and could not take place until industrial capitalism and bourgeois society had fully matured. No one could delude himself that the Russia of 1917 had more than just begun that experience. Most of the little knot of Bolsheviks regarded March 1917 as a welcome prologue to the final presocialist phase of social development, but they assumed that *the* revolution was still distant. Lenin stunned them by arguing privately that the Bolsheviks ought to prepare immediately to take power. His theoretical justification was something he called "permanent revolution": in certain circumstances, the bourgeois-democratic revolution might deepen and lead directly to a proletarian uprising. In fact, though he may have felt the need to swathe his policy in theoretical terms, Lenin's astoundingly sensitive political instincts told him that the Provisional Government had no anchor in the Russian masses, that its pro-war policy would ruin it, that popular sentiment detested the war and wanted immediate social change. Although his colleagues on the Central Committee of the Bolshevik party were highly skeptical, Lenin's energetic arguments finally won them over.

The Provisional Government encountered serious difficulty in dealing with the Petrograd Soviet, which was heavily populated with Socialist Revolutionaries. Power in the government thus began to gravitate toward its one SR member, Kerensky. Kerensky, however, remained firmly committed to the war, and thus in sharp conflict with the Bolsheviks. Some popular disorders in Petrograd during July 1917 were widely construed as an abortive Bolshevik coup; Kerensky used the occasion to crack down on the party, arresting several of its leaders and nearly capturing Lenin (who made for Finland). Within another two months, however, Kerensky found that he had to turn to the radical left for backing, when a counterrevolutionary and czarist threat began to develop in certain sections of the army. The party was allowed to function once again (though Lenin was forced to remain in Finland). However, lower-echelon administrators were pessimistic about morale, and membership figures were falling off. Yet when Lenin, in disguise, returned to Petrograd for a secret meeting of the Central Committee, he insisted that plans be laid for an immediate revolution. Bolshevik arguments about the war and immediate revolutionary action at home had begun to score in the Petrograd Soviet, which was steadily drifting away from Kerensky; discontent was visibly mounting in the country. For these reasons, Lenin argued, revolution was possible; the time was ripe.

On the night of November 6–7, 1917, teams of Bolshevik revolutionaries—mostly workers and servicemen—captured the principal government offices in Petrograd and Moscow. Resistance was light and scattered; the take over was accomplished with a minimum of bloodshed. The coup had been timed to coincide with the meeting, on November 7, of representatives from Soviets of all the major cities. This Congress of Soviets, from which the SR's and Mensheviks quickly departed, approved the fait accompli which confronted them.

Socialist revolution in Russia began with a series of sweeping decrees —the nationalization of all land, the nationalization of all banks (with private accounts therein becoming state property), the repudiation of the national debt, the confiscation of church property. But the most pressing problems which Lenin faced during the early years of his power were civil war and foreign intervention. Regardless of the response to the November revolution in Petrograd and Moscow, the Bolsheviks still did not command anything remotely approaching a majority in the nation. Elections to the constituent assembly, prepared prior to November but held three weeks after the coup, produced a majority for the SR's. (When the assembly finally met, in January 1918, Bolshevik troops unceremoniously dispersed it.) Mixed motives prompted resistance from place to place— sometimes political opposition to the Bolsheviks, sometimes cultural opposition from ethnic strains which had long resented Great Russian domination and now saw their opportunity to break away. Thus, the Bolsheviks were soon embroiled in not one but several civil wars— against monarchists, SR's, and even Mensheviks; but also against separatist movements in the Ukraine, Georgia, and Armenia.

At the same time, Lenin quickly fulfilled his promise to withdraw from the war—now made all the more urgent lest the war wreck his government the way it had Kerensky's. An armistice was concluded on December 5. Realizing Lenin's predicament, the Germans made gargantuan demands of territory, and Lenin had no choice but to give in: at stake, he was convinced, was the success of his fragile and threatened revolution. But the peace treaty, signed in March 1918 at Brest-Litovsk, now placed Russia at odds with its western allies. In the summer of 1918, French and British troops landed in extreme northern Russia, at Murmansk and Archangel, on the pretext of keeping supplies they had sent to their ally from falling to the Germans. In fact, the idea was to intimidate the Bolsheviks with a show of force. When it became clear that Lenin was not going to be swayed, foreign intervention became more overtly directed toward displacing the Bolsheviks with a government which would reopen hostilities with Germany and take the pressure off the western front. But when the war in the west ended in November 1918, foreign troops not only stayed on Russian soil, their activities increased. American units joined the British and French in the north, and there were a number of clashes with Bolshevik contingents. The French also sent troops to support the Ukrainians, and the allies sent both military advisers and money to various counterrevolutionary groups.

The bewildering diversity of the anti-Bolshevik forces made it difficult for them to forge a cohesive movement. While the counterrevolutionary and secessionist groups waxed and waned, Lenin turned over responsibility for building an effective military force to one of his chief lieutenants, Leon Trotsky, a former Menshevik who had thrown in his lot with Lenin and been influential in bringing the Petrograd Soviet over to the Bolshevik side. Trotsky, an intellectual and facile theoretician, showed great skill in organizing and directing the Red Army. By early 1921, the motley counterrevolutionary coalition—known as the White Army—had been defeated and scattered, the secessionist forces overwhelmed, the western territories annexed by Germany reconquered after the German evacuation late in 1918. Facing its first challenge, Bolshevism had won an impressive victory.

The western powers realized by mid-1919 that it would take a massive effort to uproot the Bolsheviks; and although the French were apparently willing to make the commitment, the British and the Americans were not. Allied policy therefore turned from counterrevolution to containment. Russia had succumbed to social revolution, but the disease would not spread. The great powers supported liberal democracy in the new states along Russia's western border—Poland, Czechoslovakia, Rumania —in the hopes of building a buffer zone between communism and the major noncommunist states. The large cessions of territory from Germany and Hungary to these new states were intended to increase their viability. Meanwhile, strenuous repressive action was taken against the left throughout Europe.

In July 1914, Europe had confidently prepared for the adventure of six or perhaps eight weeks of war. Five years later, it emerged— exhausted, confused, much of it in wreckage both material and psychological, three of its proudest crowns shattered, its map drastically redrawn, its political stability threatened by the appearance of a new radical force, its economy and public finances in chaos, and increasingly dependent upon a new colossus across the Atlantic. In America, a new President elected in 1920 spoke soothingly of a "return to normalcy." In Europe, there could be no such return, since so much that had been "normal" had simply disappeared. As stated at the beginning of this book, it is rare that historical watersheds are compressed into a few years—rare, but not unheard of.

12 / *The Modern Imagination: Beyond Scientism and Realism*

Scientism was nothing if not optimistic. The world, if not yet fully known, was still fully knowable. It operated according to strict rational laws which science was in the process of discovering. Human beings did not always behave rationally, but they were capable of doing so, once they were properly educated. Just as engineers continually refined the operation of machines so that they worked more and more efficiently, the scientistic mentality anticipated the corresponding refinement of human society.

World War I surely helped demolish that cheerful vision. Yet it is clear that it had been eroding for a long time prior to Sarajevo. Physicists, psychologists, philosophers, and artists had been chipping away at it for years; soldiers and politicians only hastened its demise. The reaction to scientism—and to its aesthetic counterparts, realism and naturalism— did as much to shape the modern imagination as four and one-half years of senseless carnage. Experimental departures in the arts, which sometimes seemed to be almost self-enclosed, were thus part of a broader movement which included a frontal challenge to traditional physics and psychology. In other words, the distance from E-mc² to dadaism and atonal music is not so great as it might appear.

Indeterminate Nature

The comfortable certainties of nineteenth-century physics rested upon the twin foundations of a profound faith in science and a mechanistic conception of nature. The parts of a machine fit together in a certain way; once one determined the nature and function of all the parts, one could tell what the machine—when switched on—would do. And so it was with nature: find out what all the "parts" (particles of matter) did, what laws they obeyed, and you could predict the way nature would operate.

The machine of nature was made up of matter and energy, the latter motivating the former and both governed by immutable laws which science had revealed. Matter itself was composed of atoms, which differed in weight according to which of the 90-odd chemical elements they belonged. Any crack in these foundation stones was bound to cause trembling throughout the structure, and the first faults began to open up as early as the 1870's. Electrical experiments in that decade revealed the existence of minute particles (that is, matter) which emitted both light and heat (that is, energy). In 1895, a German physicist named Wilhelm Roentgen found that the rays thus generated could penetrate matter; still dubious about their nature, however, he named them X-rays. J.J. Thomson, a British scientist, demonstrated in 1897 that the rays were indeed matter, but of a smaller size than any atom. Thomson's "electrons" were negative electrical particles whose existence implied a positive particle—the "proton," discovered a few days later. In short, there was a subatomic level of matter, a level at which the neat distinction between matter and energy failed to hold. Between 1898 and 1902, Marie and Pierre Curie further disturbed the old synthesis by showing that the particles composing certain elements—radium, for example—spontaneously generated energy and also disintegrated, a fact which the law of the conservation of matter could not accommodate.

In 1901, a German theoretical physicist named Max Planck offered yet another critique of the mechanistic outlook. Whereas it was generally believed that energy was transmitted in steady "waves," Planck's work in heat radiation led him to hypothesize that energy was produced discontinuously, in discrete units or "quanta." Although it was several years before Planck's ideas gained general acceptance, his quantum theory administered the coup de grace to the idea of a regular and predictable machine. Planck also lent further support to those who were blurring the distinction between energy and matter, demonstrating that energy was composed of particles of matter.

For the generation of Europeans brought up in the tradition of scientism and positivism, these developments were profoundly disturbing (once they had been translated into simple language). Nineteenth-century physics had been shown to be fallible, its conclusions in part mistaken. Inevitably, questions arose about scientific methodology. If the scientist was indeed a dispassionate empirical observer, inductively proceeding toward general laws, how was it that "truth" had failed to result? What were scientific laws, and were they really laws at all if they could be so precipitously overturned?

When respected men of science and sympathetic philosophers began to suggest that scientific laws were not the embodiment of absolute truth, positivism obviously faced serious challenges. Ernst Mach and Hans Vaihinger were German philosophers working in the late nineteenth and early twentieth centuries. Along with their French contemporary, the renowned mathematician Henri Poincaré, they argued persuasively that what purported to be laws or comprehensive generalizations in science were really only convenient formulations—"fictions," Vaihinger called them—which illuminated reality and helped guide further research. A scientific law was only the best way of explaining the facts as we now know them, an orientation toward nature which would help us ask questions the answers to which would produce new "laws" of roughly the same status.*

These developments were not confined to "hard" science. At the same time, Auguste Comte's plan for a positive science of society was undergoing similar revision. Marx's claim to have constructed a "scientific" socialism began to meet with considerable skepticism—in part because western capitalism was failing to bear out his predictions, and in part because the increasing mathematical sophistication of economists made it possible for them to savage Marx's sometimes primitive analyses. Emile Durkheim, a French sociologist, insisted, "Socialism is not a science, a sociology in miniature: it is a cry of pain." Social scientists and historians, who in the second half of the nineteenth century had hoped their disciplines would increasingly approximate the laboratory sciences, began to change as the image of their model itself changed. Max Weber, a German sociologist, pioneered the development of the "ideal type," sociology's version of science's convenient fiction. The ideal type was also a conceptual fiction, abstracted from but nowhere fully existing in reality, yet designed to highlight reality. In a study of modern capitalism, Weber concocted such a fiction, which he called "the Protestant Ethic": no one person or group of persons seems to have shared that ethic at any one time, but Weber used his construct to measure the degree to which it was approximated in reality and to identify critical variables.

The idea that human events, past or present, could be studied in the same empirical fashion that one dissected a foetal pig also came under attack. In Germany and Italy, and later in France and England, social scientists began to plead for a method more appropriate to the subject matter. It was maintained that since every human act is the result of thought, in some form or another, it was that thought which the observer had to penetrate. This he could not do by employing the empirical tools

---

* It is worth emphasizing that all three of these men retained their faith in the efficacy of science, and saw themselves not as debunking but as rescuing science from the misleading and excessive claims of positivism (a tradition in which all of them were reared).

of the scientist. Rather, he had to engage in a sympathetic reenactment of the thought processes under study, he had to "get inside" the minds of his subjects by a process which the Germans called *Verstehen*—usually translated into English as "intuition." Although such arguments doubtless set Comte whirling in his grave, they gained mounting currency in the first years of the new century.

In 1905, a young German employed as a clerk in the Swiss patent offices continued the assault on positivist physics. Albert Einstein's special theory of relativity, which he elaborated into a general theory in 1916, is complex, mathematically abstract, and difficult to paraphrase in ordinary language. Concepts such as "curved space," a four-dimensional world, and a "space-time continuum" are not easily rendered by analogy. Yet in spite of the rarefied level of abstraction upon which Einstein was working, his central idea has penetrated lay thought to a remarkable degree. For Einstein, the nature of phenomena was dependent upon the observer of them. As a result, the idea of a single objective reality simply disappeared, and with it the positivist version of both nature and science.

The nineteenth-century synthesis disintegrated with startling rapidity, especially when a series of experiments in 1919 verified a number of Einstein's important hypotheses. Yet postwar science did not really construct a comparable synthesis to take its place. The world of quantum mechanics and relativity was not one in which particles whirred about according to ironclad laws, but one in which physical events occurred in a discontinuous and more or less random fashion—at best conforming to certain statistical probabilities. Since there was no objective reality, comprehensive objective knowledge of it was impossible. Although individual scientists offered approaches to a new synthesis, the agreeable consensus which had reigned throughout much of the nineteenth century had evaporated.

Levels of the Mind

Late nineteenth-century critics of scientism pointed out that however much man *ought* to behave according to some rational calculus, he stubbornly refused to do so. The human personality unmistakably contained irrational dimensions—variously characterized as "appetite," "passions," "drives," original sin, and so forth. The best-known proponent of these views in the early 1900's was Henri Bergson, an immensely popular philosopher whose lectures and writings gained him a large audience.

Bergson combined antiscientism with a celebration of the nonratiocinating elements of the mind—instinct, intuition, what like-minded Germans called *Verstehen*. His philosophy was not analytical, but metaphorical: he wrote of the "stream of consciousness," of the creative life force (*élan vital*), the thrust of experience, without ever saying very precisely what he meant by these things. His neo-romantic exaltation of feeling as the authentic human activity, his taste for the mysterious and the mystical (which ultimately led him into Roman Catholicism) were not so much philosophy as antipositivist propaganda. Bergson's writings reached a large audience. But he did not so much persuade readers to accept a coherent and consistent set of principles as he played upon their (legitimate) dissatisfaction with a cold and desiccated positivism. Bergsonism was fashionable, but it was more than that, too. The swiftness with which it captured a large middle-class following suggests that, even among the well-to-do, the appeal of scientism had reached its limits.

Bergson did not so much explore the nonrational strata of the mind as he proved, by his popularity, that many persons believed such strata existed, were important, and were being ignored. The more systematic and scientific exploration of the recesses of the mind overlooked by positivism was conducted not by Bergson, but by Sigmund Freud, an Austrian physician brought up in the positivist tradition who used its tools to destroy it.

Freud, born in 1856, became interested early in his medical practice in the treatment of nervous disorders such as amnesia and various forms of hysteria. In the 1880's, he participated in a number of clinical experiments which employed hypnosis to probe the roots of these disorders. He soon became convinced that most neurosis related to some traumatic experience which patients were unable to identify in a "normal" state of consciousness. Instead, they had repressed it into some layer of the mind "beneath" the conscious mind which Freud called the "sub-conscious" or "unconscious." He thereafter devoted most of his therapeutic efforts and his research to unlocking the secrets of the unconscious—by hypnosis, free association, the analysis of verbal slips (which indicated unconscious associations), and especially dream analysis. Dreams, Freud concluded, contained a vast fund of complex symbols through which a person psychically lived out experiences and desires he could not admit or face in his conscious life. Freud spent the better part of the 1890's deciphering these symbols and preparing what he ever after considered his most important contribution, *The Interpretation of Dreams* (published in 1899).

Freud, like Nietzsche before him, but with far more impressive empirical data, argued that the unconscious harbored a large number of urges and drives—most of them, said Freud, sexual—which the conscious mind had repressed there out of guilt. The guilt had been prompted largely by cultural restraints and taboos (a subject upon which Freud considered himself an authority, since he had grown up in a middle-class Jewish family of rather strict regimen). Typically, a person experienced sexual urges which his culture regarded as immoral and therefore punished; guilt prompted him to force those urges from his conscious into his un-

conscious mind. But the guilt frequently persisted, since the urges continued to exist in the unconscious (as in dreams), though the conscious
mind might not be able to recognize the cause of guilt.

One common, almost pervasive instance of this pattern was the so-
called Oedipus complex. It is worth pointing out, with respect to this
much misunderstood question, that Freud did *not* argue that a young
male-child simply loves his mother and hates his father. Rather, he begins by loving both parents, but then discovers that the father is a rival
for the affections of his mother. At this point, the child experiences an
ambivalent emotional response which is far more difficult to handle than
pure hatred: he both continues to love *and* begins to hate his father. The
latter impulse leads him to wish his father's death, but *that* in turn runs
up against powerful cultural taboos. As a result, he guiltily represses both
his hatred for his father and his lustful feelings for his mother into his
unconscious mind. Yet the guilt may linger on—fed by the unconscious
recognition that he has nurtured thoughts of incest and parricide—and
express itself in mental disorders of varying seriousness.

Freud's therapeutic response to these disorders was strategically simple, though tactically difficult. The patient would have to delve into his
own unconscious (usually by describing dreams), thus providing the psychoanalyst with a code to be cracked. When the analyst discovered the
difficulty, he would simply reveal it to the patient. Conscious recognition
of that which had been repressed, Freud often demonstrated, banished all
the symptoms of neurosis. In brief, the cure reversed the process of repression which had brought on the illness.

Yet such an approach also suggested a form of *preventive* treatment. If
guilt and repression caused neurosis (and sometimes extreme mental im-
balance, or psychosis), then could not such illnesses be avoided by minimizing taboos and therefore repression? More specifically, might not a
person anticipate a healthier emotional life if he gave freer rein to his
sexual drives? As a practicing psychoanalyst counseling private patients,
Freud sometimes gave a qualified "yes" to these questions. Yet he could
never bring himself to suggest greater sexual freedom as a matter of gen-
eralized social policy. Although his name has become inextricably linked
in the popular mind with the recognition of powerful sexual drives,
Freud himself regarded the unleashing of such drives darkly. His personal (as opposed to professional) views on sex were straitened, even to
the point of prudishness. Even more important, he feared that sexual desire was potentially destructive.

Early in the twentieth century, while continuing with his purely psy-
choanalytical work, Freud also began to explore the social implications of
his findings. In 1913, he published *Totem and Taboo,* a curious work labeled fantasy by his critics, metaphor by his defenders, and fact by Freud

himself, somewhat stubbornly. The book attempts to locate the historical origins of the Oedipus complex in a "primal tribe" of humans ruled by a polygamous patriarch. The sons of the tribal father, said Freud, lusted after their respective mothers, a desire they could only fulfill by eliminating their common father. Ultimately, they murder and devour him, and proceed to satiate their sexual appetites. They are then overwhelmed by guilt, and in consequence establish a taboo against incest. Needless to say, Freud's story is not accompanied by documentary evidence; *Totem and Taboo* is neither history nor anthropology, but social philosophy. The incest taboo represents man's first law, and Freud was positive that laws alone made civilized life possible: without them, the "primal crime" —not to mention countless others—would be incessantly repeated.

As Freud elaborated some years later in *Civilization and its Discontents* (1930), the enforcement of such taboos or laws was not always accomplished by government authorities—police, courts, and so forth. Rather, the system also functioned psychologically. Cultural taboos generated guilt and repression, which in turn kept sexual aggression and other antisocial behavior in check. In other words, civilized social life as we know it is made possible by—is inseparable from—repression. Since guilt and repression are the sources of mental disorder, the lot of civilized man is not a happy one. In one particularly gloomy passage, Freud writes:

> If civilization is an inevitable course of development from the group of the family to the group of humanity as a whole, then an intensification of the sense of guilt . . . will be inextricably bound up with it, until perhaps the sense of guilt may swell to a magnitude that individuals can hardly support.

To remove repression was to risk returning to the uncertain anarchy of the "primal state."

What Freud found, then, was not the rational machine of the positivist model. But neither was the Freudian unconscious a reservoir of child-like, innocent instincts, as the romantics had claimed, or of creative Bergsonian life forces. Freud insisted "that the primitive, savage, and evil impulses of mankind have not vanished in any individual, but continue their existence, although in a repressed state . . . and that they wait for opportunities to display their activity."

The early resistance to Freudianism was fairly vigorous. The Oedipus complex, critical to the whole system, was broadly rejected on the ground that childhood sexuality was physiologically impossible prior to puberty (not to mention offensive to regnant moral sensibilities), whereas Freud had insisted that Oedipal feelings arose in very young children. Positivist psychologists objected that too much of Freud's theory was conjectural, depending upon interpretation rather than measurable data. Ironically, Freud was himself a product of the positivist tradition; and though he occasionally played the role of therapist and social philosopher, he thought of himself first of all as a scientist.

Freud's relationship to positivism can perhaps best be seen in his scheme of the human mental structure. Freud divided the mind into three parts (in a manner not dissimilar to the theories of Plato and Aristotle): ego, id, and superego. The ego, the "I," was the rational element, what Freud called the "reality principle," which governed common decisions, perceptions, or evaluations; it was the principal operative element of the mind. The id, or "it," was appetite broadly conceived—a purely desiring repository of urges (many of them sexual) which Freud called the "pleasure principle." It was no uncommon matter to find that the id might overpower the ego, that desire might drive a person into behavior which flaunted the rational dictates of the ego. At this point, the superego—conscience, or guilt—came into play; its function was to keep the id in check, to ensure that the mind operated according to the reality principle. Positivists complained that this scheme was wholly unempirical, that Freud could not point to any concrete part of the human nervous system and say into which of the three categories it fell. In fact, Freud's theory, whatever else is to be said of it, is a model of positivist mechanistic psychology, with neatly interlocking and rationally explicable parts.

Even Freud's social pessimism had a scientistic counterweight: psychoanalysis could not change human nature, but it claimed it could treat neurosis successfully; and psychoanalysis, Freud pointed out, was itself a science. In other words, if critical reason can create psychoanalysis, then perhaps reason can begin to solve the problems which psychoanalysis has defined.

> The voice of the intellect [wrote Freud] is a soft one, but it does not rest until it has gained a hearing. Ultimately, after endlessly repeated rebuffs, it succeeds. This is one of the few points in which one may be optimistic about the future of mankind, but in itself, it signifies not a little. And one can make it a starting-point for yet other hopes. The primacy of the intellect certainly lies in the far, far, but still probably not infinite, distance.

Freudianism was neither an all-conquering nor a coherent movement. Its reception varied widely—spotty in central Europe and France, enthusiastic in England and in the United States. Although a number of brilliant young students came to Vienna in the early twentieth century to sit at the master's feet, they did not always go out to propagate the true gospel and sometimes even wandered into apostasy. Erik Erikson, who ultimately found his way to America, made a number of major qualifications and came increasingly to focus on the importance of "identity crisis." Wilhelm Reich attempted to fuse Freud with the teachings of his own political muse, Marx. At the same time, Reich preached that "true" liberation was impossible without full sexual liberation. Perhaps most disappointing to Freud was Carl G. Jung, a Swiss whom Freud had expected to carry on the cause after his own demise. But Jung turned instead to his own theories, in particular to the study of a universal shared repository of human experience which he called the "collective unconscious"; and his semireligious ruminations angered Freud, an atheist.

Yet a surprising amount of Freudianism entered the popular consciousness, in however mangled a form. The notion that childhood years are the formative ones, the idea of sublimation (channeling sexual energy into nonsexual directions), the conviction that mental slips convey meaningful data—all are Freudian insights, not to mention that most of the meaning that we find in words like "repression," "libido," and "death wish" was put there by Freud. Even more important, Freud, along with his disciples (faithful and otherwise) and his most severe critics, awakened what has proved to be an abiding interest in the inner workings of the human psyche. Nonrational and irrational impulses have come to be taken for granted, both by those who count them as a legitimate and valuable component of human nature and those who fear those impulses and are determined to keep them in check.

Neither Freud nor Einstein could, by the most prodigious stretch of the imagination, be called "irrationalist." Each had worked out his theory by the most painstaking processes of rational intellection. Yet each had also, in his way, undermined mechanistic positivist rationalism. The world they separately described—on the one hand, uncertain, indeterminate, subjectively perceived, and on the other, full of guilt-ridden beings fired by destructive sexual urges which could only be kept in check by repression—seemed to be in a separate galaxy from that described by nineteenth-century science.

A Personal Reality

The arts in the first three decades of the twentieth century, like physics and psychology, demonstrated deep dissatisfaction with the scientistic world view and its principal stylistic progeny, realism and naturalism. This discontent was hardly new. Since the 1860's, people like Dostoevsky and Manet had protested on moral, psychological, and aesthetic grounds against positivism and realism. Nor did the twentieth century witness a total revolution in artistic themes and styles. Such traditional genres as the realistic social novel met with both commercial and critical success, as witness John Galsworthy's *The Forsyte Saga* (published between 1906 and 1921) and Roger Martin du Gard's *Les Thibaults* (1922–40). Yet the new century did bring restless and persistent experimentation in all the arts (not to mention the creation of a new one, the cinema). While sometimes purely aesthetic imperatives governed these experiments, still both substance and treatment generally betrayed a self-conscious attempt to explore a reality beyond that of positivism.

It is impossible to describe briefly the numerous directions taken by early twentieth-century art or even to provide labels which will adequately cover all the different experiments. For there was no unity in this explosion of energy. The very desire to be different—which took on a value of its own—frustrates neat historical categorization. It does seem to be true, however, that many artists in all media—the written word, the plastic arts, the performing arts—strove to recast reality in more personal terms. In this venture, they were perhaps the heirs of the French impressionist painters, though they made even more radical departures from accepted norms. The concept of a more personal, even more "subjective," art by no means adequately characterizes the work of all the individuals and movements and "schools" which flourished in this period. Yet it was probably as widely shared a feature of the modern imagination as there was. Moreover, it serves to root art in the broader intellectual culture—one in which notions of objective reality and a single truth were fast fading. Personal, psychological reality moved into the vacuum left by the crumbling certainties of positivist science.

One convenient starting point for the examination of modern art is in French painting. The development of photography had rendered mere accurate representation obsolete. With Manet, the canvas became a reality in itself, upon which the artist confected his own personal impressions. Yet impressionism was only a beginning. Paul Cézanne, who had begun as an impressionist, soon became dissatisfied with the style. As E.H. Gombrich has put it, "Impressionist pictures tended to be brilliant but messy. Cézanne abhorred messiness." He longed for a return to the formal clarity of classicism but without its rigid conventions and binding rules. Cézanne sought a conceptual formulation of nature, but it had to be the nature *he* saw. He was not interested in reproduction, but rather with the problems of shape and color which personally interested him. He insisted that he was extracting essential, geometrical forms from nature, reducing it to its richest and most harmonious color schemes. At its best, this personal vision conveyed an imposing sense of stability and aesthetic integration (as in several paintings of Mont Sainte-Victoire done in the 1880's and 1890's).

Cézanne's advice that painters see in nature "the cylinder, the sphere, and the cone" quickly issued forth into a geometrically oriented style of the early twentieth century, cubism. But the cubists added an almost Einsteinian gloss to this dictum by refusing to view space as an absolute dimension. For example, the cubists tried to "see" a human face from all possible angles at once, depicting frontal and profile views side by side (or overlapping) on the canvas. By reducing nature to even more austere essentials than Cézanne had attempted, and by frequently working in collages whose heterogeneous materials were meant to evoke a reality as personally conceived, the cubists plainly prepared the way for "pure," nonrepresentational abstraction. The first great abstract painter was Wasily Kandinsky, a Russian, whose work in the years just prior to World War I dealt solely with line and color, making no effort to impart "meaning" or to represent (even by suggestive personal symbols) the world as ordinarily viewed.

The other postimpressionist painters of the late nineteenth century moved in influential ways toward the expression of reality as internally perceived. Vincent van Gogh, the Dutch painter who did most of his work in France, began increasingly to view the world through his own special mental lens (one which showed signs of severe distortion in the late 1880's). Van Gogh gave up painting nature for turning nature into a reflection of his own emotional turmoil. Paul Gauguin, van Gogh's sometime friend, left Europe for Tahiti at the end of the 1880's in search of a more vital art, unencumbered by superficial sophistication and accepted standards. His later work pulsates with lush, exotic colors, with mauve horses and green flames.

Artists in the tradition of Cézanne broke up nature into geometric shards, ultimately keeping the shards and discarding nature. Those who took their lead from van Gogh and Gauguin turned nature into a reflection or projection of their psychological states. Since "inner" reality was primary, the "outer" world took on its shape, or expressed it—and thus the term "expressionism." In painting, expressionism took several courses, sometimes representational, sometimes abstract, but uniformly so personal that the audience had to come to it on the artist's own terms. The physical world was no longer a constant, but clay to be molded in the individual mind. The German theater and, in the postwar years, German films were instrumental in popularizing a version of expressionism. In the famous film *The Cabinet of Dr. Caligari* (1919), distorted sets and severe lighting which cast deep, ominous shadows created an atmosphere which chillingly reflected the madness of the narrator.

The effort to give primacy to the personal psychological experience was widespread. Franz Kafka's novels, which were not published until after his death in 1924 (at forty-one), sketched out a frightening and irrational world full of oppressive and unpredictable authority in all forms. Marcel Proust's multivolumed *Remembrance of Things Past* was a meticulous examination of the novelist's memory, of psychological motivation and the nature of time. The characters of Italian dramatist Luigi Pirandello abandoned the "real" world for one of psychic illusion; in the films of German director Fritz Lang, the "real" world was full of potent and evil psychic compulsions. The partisans of surrealism, which thrived in France in the years after the war, argued that a "higher truth" existed "beyond" the banalities of observed reality. It could be reached, however, only by a Freudian process of free association, the linkage of symbols drawn from mere reality (as well as psychic reality) into some new order. The paintings of Salvador Dali and Marc Chagall are among the best known works of this exhilarating movement, for they convey something of the dreamlike quality which surrealism counted as "true" reality.*

Obviously, the idea that modern artists were consumed by the quest to find and express a personal reality has both limitations and numerous exceptions. The concept has been employed here largely as an organizing device, in an attempt to show that the apparently anarchic art of the early twentieth century did indeed share certain things in common. Many movements and individual figures, however, steadfastly resist categorization. Dadaism, for example, was a brief but furiously energetic upheaval, beginning in 1916. Its participants preached no particular aesthetic principles, but instead sought primarily to ridicule and shock. Dada (itself simply a nonsense term) was patently a child of the war, absurdist, nihilistic, proclaiming that "dada signifies nothing," but convinced that nonsensical art—such as Marcel Duchamp's marble urinal entitled "Fountain"—made more sense than the world produced by rational logic. Immediately after the war, Walter Gropius organized a group of German architects and designers into the Bauhaus, a sort of artists' collective which also fits into no neat historical pigeonhole. The Bauhaus rejected the impersonality of much prewar architecture in favor of organic relationships, and its principal concern was to harmonize the form of buildings, and the objects which filled them, with their function. James Joyce, the Irish novelist, explored the "stream of consciousness," the ceaseless flow of conscious thought, in his masterpiece *Ulysses* (1922). But Joyce's psychological concerns were in fact secondary to his commitment to explore the full riches of the English language. The German dramatist Bertolt Brecht was deeply influenced by expressionist theater, but he was less concerned with portraying tortured psychological states than in confronting his audience with hard political and social truths. Although the modern imagination *tended* to stress personal reality, realism

---

* Surrealism was also hilariously satirized by two of its leading exponents, Dali and filmmaker Luis Bunuel. Their film *Un chien andalou* (*An Andalusian Dog*), released in 1929, was a pastiche of utterly unrelated scenes and symbols: a man is on his hands and knees, pursuing a woman across a room, and pulling a grand piano with a rope over his shoulder; on top of the piano are two dead donkeys; holding back the piano from the rear are two Catholic priests. Film critics certain that Dali and Bunuel were being serious have been trying to unravel their (nonexistent) symbolic structure ever since.

was hardly dead: no writer of fiction was more influential in this period than the German, Thomas Mann.

Just as with science, these developments in the arts took place for a steadily shrinking audience. As artistic expression became, in general, more personal, it became perforce more hermetic, less accessible to broad popular tastes. Not that high culture had ever been the property of the masses, or even of the broad range of educated bourgeois; but the early twentieth century witnessed an acceleration in the divorce between art and society. Serious artists were increasingly involved in working out what were essentially private problems (however much they may have been shared by the populace at large), and frequently did so in a language impenetrable by the popular mind, or in a style deliberately intended to violate established conventions and to shock respectable audiences. A symphony by Stravinsky, a painting by Picasso, a novel by Joyce —in retrospect, such were the cultural landmarks of the period. To most contemporaries, however, they made about as much sense, were as immediately relevant, as one of Einstein's abstract mathematical formulas.

13 / *The Politics of Extremism*

If it is legitimate to move from science to art in following the course of the modern mind, it is tempting also to move from art to politics. Fascism, a creature of the 1920's, seemed both to play upon and unleash all the demonic forces in the European psyche. (Hitler, for what it is worth, was an avid fan of expressionist films.) By the same token, the Soviet Union could be taken as a model of the scientistic world view—from its ordered society and government and its rational calculations for economic modernization all the way down to its officially promoted artistic style, "socialist realism." Whatever the usefulness of such comparisons, it is clear that the twentieth century's forms of political extremism were as new and startling in the European experience as the most avant-garde poem or Dadaist prank. They proved far more costly in terms of human suffering, however.

The Bolshevik Revolution added an ominous new dimension to European politics in the postwar world. Before 1914, the social democratic parties had appeared to pose a serious enough threat to the status quo supported by moderates and conservatives. For all their Marxist rhetoric, however, these parties had effectively separated themselves from revolutionary anarchist syndicalism and were working within the established constitutional frameworks of their respective countries. Moreover, they had demonstrated their patriotism by supporting the war effort (with but a few exceptions toward the end of the war). The Bolshevik Revolution signaled a new era of left-wing militancy. Sympathizers in western and central Europe broke off from the fundamentally reformist social democrats and proclaimed themselves "communists," bent on social revolution. The political and economic instability of the postwar years seemed to give the communists precisely the opportunity they sought, not to mention that an established government appeared to give them aid and encouragement.

In these circumstances, it is not surprising that the 1920's also gave rise to explicitly anticommunist movements on the extreme right. Although the groups generally brought under the collective rubric of "fascism" had their origins in a variety of discontents, they flourished most in those climates where the radical left also prospered. Liberal democracy, already shaken by the rigors of war, found itself thereafter in a dangerous political squeeze.

The Soviet Union

In utter defiance of Marxian theory, the Bolshevik Revolution had been triumphant in a society still overwhelmingly agricultural, with the inroads of modern industrial capitalism confined to a few urban enclaves. Once the civil war had been won, the Bolsheviks dedicated their energies to modernizing the Russian economy—first, because the transition to a classless, stateless society was deemed impossible without a sophisticated industrial economy which would rescue the Russian masses from need; and second, because the Soviet Union could never hope to hold its own in an advanced industrial world if it remained a backward agrarian society. The imperative to modernization was posed so unmistakably to the Soviet leaders that Lenin was even willing to violate socialist doctrine and employ a quasi-capitalist system of profit incentives (the so-called New Economic Policy of 1921) in both industry and agriculture to shake the economy out of its postwar stagnation.

Far-reaching industrial modernization at a rapid pace does not take place randomly. The process demands planned growth, with centralized direction and control. Following in the footsteps of the government-stimulated industrialization of the czars, the Bolsheviks undertook the first *organized* large-scale industrial revolution of modern times. Once the economy had found its bearings again under the relative leniency of the New Economic Policy, central government authorities began to overhaul the industrial plant, laying a new foundation of heavy industries, modernizing the power plant, and setting new production quotas. The first Five Year Plan, begun in 1928, quickly brought dramatic advances in such basic sectors as the output of oil, steel, and hydroelectric power; progress under a second Five Year Plan, in the mid-1930's, was almost equally impressive.

Such great transformations do not occur, of course, without an accompanying impact upon political and social structure. In the first place, the governmental apparatus achieved a degree of centralization which would have amazed even the most zealous advocates of czarist autocracy. This development was not exactly surprising. The prerevolutionary Bolshevik party, following Lenin's model, had been highly centralized, with sole decision-making power vested in its Central Committee.* The exigencies of civil war had kept authority in the hands of a very few Bolsheviks. The very concept of a dictatorship of the proletariat—the phase in which the Bolsheviks saw the revolution after November 1917—strongly implied centralized rule. But the task of modernization decisively reinforced these already strong tendencies. A large bureaucracy was necessary not merely to govern the state and consolidate the Bolsheviks' position, but also to manage the economy and bring it into the twentieth century.

Forced industrialization meant forced urbanization, and the growth of cities meant that a steady food supply from the countryside would have to be assured. But the Russian peasantry was reluctant to produce for the urban market when nothing substantial was forthcoming in return: the Five Year Plans, after all, concentrated on heavy industry—metallurgy, machinery, and the like—and produced little in the way of consumer goods. In order to guarantee food for the industrial workers and to control agricultural production, the bureaucracy therefore instigated in the late 1920's a massive program of agrarian collectivization. All land and the means to work it (both animal and mechanical) were nationalized; agricultural produce therefore became state property. Whereas peasants had been accustomed to keeping what they needed of a harvest and selling the surplus, the practice was now reversed. To ensure an acceptable level of production, produce up to a certain point went to the state; anything that was left went to the peasants. Predictably, resistance to collectivization was substantial, especially among those relatively well-to-do peasants (or *Kulaks*) who had the most to lose. But official ruthlessness knew no limits. Collectives which refused to produce up to their quota simply went hungry; other recalcitrants were forcefully liquidated. It has been estimated that, whether by starvation or official violence, as many as ten million peasants died in the period of collectivization; the *Kulak* class, stigmatized by the Bolsheviks as a sort of rural bourgeoisie, was almost thoroughly eliminated.

Industrialization and collectivization were carried out under the rule of Joseph Stalin, who succeeded Lenin as head of the party. Prior to the revolution, Stalin had been a relatively minor Bolshevik whose principal gift was an undeniable administrative talent. Lenin had turned to him after November 1917, giving Stalin the principal responsibility for staffing the new bureaucracy. (The state administration was to grow directly out of the Bolshevik party bureaucracy, with the party maintaining con-

---

* According to the dictates of "democratic centralism," free discussion did reign in the Central Committee, although total unity was expected once a decision had been reached.

trol at all the crucial points.) Stalin proceeded to place a number of his own men at strategic locations within the hierarchy, people who were therefore obligated first of all to him for their position. When Lenin was physically incapacitated by a stroke at the end of 1922, Stalin began to insinuate himself into the vacuum, a task facilitated by his connections in the party and state apparatus. By the time Lenin perceived what was happening, it was too late. After Lenin's death in 1924, Stalin found it relatively easy to outmaneuver (and ultimately exile) his chief rival, Leon Trotsky, and to assume leadership of both the party and the state.

In the early 1930's Stalin further solidified his position by modifying mere bureaucratic power into personal power. While promoting a personal cult through state propaganda, he also began to root out officials high and low who showed the slightest sign of personal independence. Most of the old Bolsheviks who harbored any residual sympathy for Lenin or Trotsky were physically eliminated, usually after recantations in trials before kangaroo courts. With great cunning, utter lack of scruple, and not a little paranoia, Stalin systematically terrorized high state officials and obscure citizens alike. The loss of life involved is a matter of speculation, but some guesses run into the millions. By the end of the 1930's, the purges had rendered the dictator's position unassailable.

The human cost of Stalinism remained largely a matter of rumor outside the Soviet Union, occasioning a few defections among non-Russian communists. In general, however, the atrocities associated with collectivization were not widely known, and the purge trials at least appeared to proceed in an atmosphere of legality. Far more troublesome for Europeans was the existence of the Communist International, or Comintern, established in 1919 as a successor to the Social Democrats' Second Workers International. The earlier organization had been a relatively loose one, handing down rulings on broad doctrinal and tactical questions but allowing national social democratic parties a considerable degree of autonomy. Lenin insisted that the Comintern be more rigorously structured, with policy set in Moscow and member parties from other nations swearing strict obedience to it. Many social democrats refused to adhere, and even those westerners who applauded the Bolshevik Revolution chafed under the Russian harness. As a result, European communist parties frequently underwent internal purges, engineered from Russia, until a more pliable leadership had been created. Thereafter, European communism could boast of precious little independent action, and became—through the Comintern—basically an instrument of Soviet foreign policy.

This very fact put noncommunists, from social democrats to extreme conservatives, even more on the defensive. Communist parties could no longer be viewed as distasteful indigenous movements. Instead, they were agents of a foreign power. Moreover, the idea of an international communist organization seemed to suggest that the Soviet Union was assiduously preparing the expansion of its own revolution—and of course it was true that Lenin had encouraged proletarian revolt throughout Europe immediately after the Bolshevik seizure of power. (Indeed, Lenin had even supposed that the Bolsheviks would have serious difficulty holding power in Russia unless socialist revolt removed the prospect of invasion by more powerful capitalist nations.) Thus it was that the capitalist governments cracked down on postwar labor unrest and left-wing agitation with unusual force.

As it turned out, the pressures of Russian internal politics took precedence over the fomenting of international revolution. Modernization absorbed Soviet energies, and in the 1930's Stalin was too busy fortifying his personal authority to be engaged in foreign adventures. Stalin had even explicitly rejected the Leninist idea of expanding communism, arguing that the home base had first of all to be protected and calling for "socialism in one country." European communist parties were thus kept on a short leash. Until the rise of fascism in the mid-1930's, they were directed to forego revolutionary action in favor of securing their control on the political left in their own countries (which translated largely into attacking social democrats and competing with them for working-class support). Yet the image of the early 1920's died hard. Noncommunists remained at best suspicious of both the Soviet Union and its western extensions, constantly anticipating a new revolutionary upheaval.

Fascism

"Fascist" is a difficult historical term made the more elusive by perverse overuse; the recent tendency of Americans to apply it to any person in a position of authority renders definition that much harder. Authoritarian but still nonfascist regimes are often labeled fascist, so that the word is in danger of spreading to all species of conservatism. Moreover, fascism lacks a theory, a coherent statement of its nature, goals, and historical uniqueness; most of what passes for fascist philosophy is at best unreadable claptrap. Perhaps the safest way to proceed is by fairly stringent criteria, calling "fascist" only those movements and parties which called themselves by that name (or some variant, such as national socialist).

Thus limited, fascism in its several incarnations in postwar Europe does have several characteristics in common. To begin with, fascism was a mass movement, or at least aspired to become a mass movement. Though frequently elitist in principle, fascists thought in terms not of the tiny Leninist vanguard but of being swept into power by the mass of the population. Second, although fascist parties played the role of the elite within their movements, above the party stood the leader, a single man whose will was supreme. Other party functionaries largely served and celebrated the leader rather than truly cooperating with him. Fascism's success from place to place depended in no small part upon the mystique which its various leaders were able to generate.

Numerous themes ran through fascist ideology—racism, anticapitalism, antiliberalism—mostly negative ideas which served as the focus for inchoate protest. One of the few positive strains was nationalism, the preachment of the nation's superior traditions and culture, the pursuit of national gain, and the advancement of national pride and honor. The institutions which best served such ends were of course the state, ideally centralized under leader and party, and the military, which might both protect and enlarge the national territory. The penchant of fascists for military and pseudomilitary uniforms and display was no whim.

Fascism was also ardently anticommunist, and where it achieved success, it was frequently as a counterweight to incipient Bolshevism, real or imagined. Although several fascist movements dabbled from time to time in versions of socialism, playing upon economic discontent with a foundering capitalist system, they still spoke of "national socialism"—socialism to strengthen the nation rather than the proletariat—and they flatly rejected Marxist internationalism. In any case, traditional conservatives, who generally considered the fascists nothing better than political thugs, often chose to work with them in order to combat the radical left. The fascist reputation for anticommunism even earned them a measure of respectability among liberal democrats, some of whom argued in the early 1930's that Hitler had at least the virtue of buffering western Europe from the Soviet Union.

In spite of this fact, many commentators have argued that fascism and communism had much in common—that space in the political world was curved just as in Einstein's universe, so that extreme right and extreme left would in fact meet. During the 1950's in particular, at the height of the Cold War, it was fashionable for American intellectuals to describe fascism and communism as simply two versions of something called "totalitarianism," ideologies which sought to achieve total state power over their citizens. (The point, of course, was to persuade people that the Soviet enemy was nothing more than a reincarnation of the Nazi enemy just defeated.) The comparison is sustained largely by such similarities as the fascist mystique of leadership and the Stalinist personality cult, the extent of state centralization and power in Soviet Russia and Nazi Germany, the crucial role of the party elite (staffing all sensitive positions in both regimes), and the fact that both movements repudiated parliamentary democracy.

Although this view of the extremes from the moderate center is tempting, the mirror-image thesis will not sustain close analysis. On paper, fascism and communism bear certain resemblances. But in practice, critical differences immediately emerge. Soviet communism was undeniably revolutionary: for better or worse, the Bolsheviks engineered huge transformations in the Russian society, economy, and government. The two principal fascist governments, Italy and Germany, were responsible for relatively little profound change, most of it related to gearing up for total war. The socialism in national socialism turned out to be a sham, a piece of ideological window dressing which Hitler discarded even before he assumed power in 1933. In every fascist movement there were some who had been attracted by the vague social revolutionary rhetoric. In general, however, people frightened of communism turned to the fascists in order to resist social revolution, not in order to effect it. By the same token, European communists rarely thought of themselves as Stalinists, and saw themselves as struggling *against* one-man rule. Whether or not the Comintern under Stalin was a revolutionary movement remains debatable; but most noncommunists *thought* it was. The appeal of fascism was in substantial part as a *counterrevolutionary* movement.

There may have been one important sense in which fascism and communism were meaningfully comparable. Both seemed to thrive in the same sorts of environment—economic discontent, political disorder, sweeping public alienation with the policies of traditional conservatism or liberalism. It is true that the communists drew their support principally from the working classes, but there is also evidence of white-collar and even occasional peasant backing. Fascism was more of a lower-middle-class movement, attracting precisely those strata which feared a loss of their fragile status in the event of working-class revolution. Yet both some workers and more substantial middle-class elements also appear in the fascist ranks. In other words, political extremism of both varieties was not a clear-cut reflection of class struggle. Rather, fascism and communism alike appealed to widespread dissatisfactions and represented radical protest against existing conditions.

Although there has been a discernible tendency to label any historical figure of authoritarian proclivities—Julius Caesar, Innocent III, Napoleon Bonaparte—a fascist (or cryptofascist, or protofascist), still fascism was a movement with highly specific and localized historical boundaries. With the exception of a few marginal recrudescences in post-1945 Europe, it was largely confined to the period between the two world wars and owed its unique character to conditions prevailing in those decades. Fascism was manifestly a product of the political, socioeconomic, and psychological dislocation occasioned by World War I.

The war had touched off massive upheaval, especially in Germany and Italy, and the apparent threat of revolution from the left created a need and desire for an equally potent counterrevolutionary movement. Moreover, the war bred the nucleus of fascist parties: many soldiers found reintegration into civilian society difficult (particularly in view of the postwar economic crisis), regarded "mere" civilians as cowardly slackers, and yearned for the adventure which peace denied them. Such feeling was particularly intense among German war veterans, most of whom believed that left-wing traitors had conspired to sell out the army in 1918. These men were easily recruited into fascist goon squads, employed to terrorize social democratic and communist political rallies, break into left-wing newspaper offices, and engage in hypernationalist demonstrations. These new paramilitary organizations supplied a uniform (Black Shirts in Italy, Brown Shirts in Germany), camaraderie, and an outlet for the violent instincts legitimized by the war.

Fascism also owed much to the staggering economic depression (itself closely related to World War I) which engulfed Europe in the early 1930's. The causes of the depression are a matter of major controversy, but it does seem likely that the war played an important role in its origins. Most governments had financed the war through inflation rather than taxation, also depending heavily upon liberal infusions of American capital. All the European currencies suffered when wartime controls upon them were removed in 1919. Besides wreaking havoc with currencies, the war also virtually suspended European international trade for more than four years, and the combatants thus emerged in 1919 significantly poorer in terms of national wealth. Postwar tariff barriers slowed the reestablishment of trade and therefore of industrial growth.

When international commerce finally regained prewar levels in the mid-1920's, it rested on an elaborate but fundamentally unstable credit base heavily dependent on foreign (and especially American) investments. In order to preserve the German economy from total collapse under the pressure of reparations, various international commissions arranged for Germany to pay its bills to British and France out of American loans.* While the agreements helped stabilize the German economy and contributed to the brief but hopeful period of European prosperity between approximately 1924 and 1929, they also created an unhealthy reliance of overextended European industries upon American capital and economic strength. When the American stock market collapsed in October 1929, it knocked the crutch out from beneath Europe. Within a year, the depression reached Europe in the form of thousands of bank and business fail-

---

* The British and French governments had also contracted sizable debts in America during the war which were being called in during the 1920's. The most ready source of cash at hand was German reparations payments, so that a peculiar cash flow resulted—from America to Germany, from Germany to France and Britain, and thence back across the Atlantic.

ures, drastic cutbacks in industrial production, and unemployment of gargantuan proportions. In the midst of this chaos, fascism prospered.

Finally, fascism is almost unthinkable prior to 1914 because of its heavy reliance upon the technology of modern mass politics. The radio allowed politicians to reach masses of people hitherto inaccessible to a single voice. The airplane made possible whirlwind political tours and saturation campaigning. To a somewhat lesser but still important degree, the film proved a powerful new propaganda medium. Traditional conservatives, who feared and distrusted the masses, never really learned how to manipulate the new communications instruments effectively. Fascists recognized their potential value and mastered them. Without them, movements so heavily dependent upon communicating a leader's charisma might never have become significant political forces.

Mussolini and Fascist Italy

The first fascist movement, indeed the one from which the term derived,* developed in Italy. The halting Italian war effort had produced no epic victories in which the nation could take pride. At the peace table in Versailles, Italian negotiators came away without the extensive territorial prizes they had expected. Wounded nationalism coupled with a murderous postwar inflation which in turn provoked widespread labor violence and the fear of working-class revolt. The moderate liberal parliamentary government was unable to maintain public order. Into this mounting crisis stepped Benito Mussolini, leader of the new Fascist party.

In retrospect, it is difficult to believe that Mussolini was in fact the head of a major European state. His ludicrous posturings and frequently ineffectual statesmanship make him seem more like a fugitive from some comic opera about a Ruritanian dictator. During the 1920's and 1930's, however, Mussolini was not only taken seriously, he gained the respect of political leaders throughout the western world for having brought order to tumultuous Italy.

Mussolini, born in 1883 into a family of modest means, drifted into leftist politics in his youth and was an important figure in the Italian Socialist party before he reached thirty. Professing a confused ideology composed of socialism and anarchism, he repudiated liberal parliamentary democracy—in favor of what it was not clear. Internationalism and anti-war feeling ran higher in the Italian Socialist party than in any of its European counterparts, and the party applauded the government's declaration of neutrality when war came in 1914. In a startling about-face, however, Mussolini campaigned for Italian intervention and was rejected from the Socialist party in November 1914. The new strain of national-

---

* Ultimately from the Latin *fasces,* an axe bound in rods which was associated with positions of high authority.

ism in his writings was accentuated after the war (in which he fought and was wounded); and by 1918 the newspaper he edited was accepting covert subsidies from big business, preaching colonial expansion, and by 1919 insisting that Italy receive its territorial due as one of the victors. At the same time, Mussolini began to organize ragtag bands of army veterans into paramilitary groups which did battle with assorted strikers and radicals. These fascist Black Shirts, as they were called after their uniform, were an important factor in the mounting public violence, though at the same time Mussolini was excoriating the government for its inability to keep order. By 1922, the fascist ranks had swelled to the point where they could create a fairly constant uproar. In a move which smacked distinctly of blackmail, Mussolini demanded that the king name him to form a new government. The implication was of course that royal refusal would only lead to the perpetuation of fascist-inspired brawls, riots, and political violence. In October, the fascists staged a massive March on Rome from all over the nation, presumably to take over the capital forcibly. In order to avoid further violence and perhaps even civil war, the king buckled and named Mussolini prime minister.

Few persons could have said what the new government stood for beyond nationalism and militant anticommunism. The fascists had nothing remotely approaching a parliamentary majority, and the extent of their support in the nation at large was simply unknown. In these circumstances, Mussolini had to proceed toward the consolidation of his personal power with some discretion, playing the parliamentary game he despised while maneuvering to destroy the whole constitutional system. He did move energetically against strikers and other disorderly behavior. Reestablishment of the public peace was widely popular (except among those pacified), and in legislative elections of 1924 the fascists commanded a majority. Now, by perfectly legal means, Mussolini could dismantle the institutions of liberal democracy and have his deputies legislate a dictatorship. All political parties save the fascists were prohibited, and power was formally concentrated into the hands of the executive. Although the monarchy remained as an ornament, and the Catholic Church was granted virtual autonomy (as long as it kept free of politics), the structure of the Italian state was thoroughly transformed.

The structure of Italian society, however, was left largely intact. In the 1930's, there were some feeble gestures toward "corporatism"—the organization of various sectors of the economy into corporate bodies which included both employers and employees. In principle, the state was to coordinate the corporations and guide the economy toward higher and more efficient production than had been attained under the system of random competition. In practice, corporatism remained largely a paper concept, erratically applied.

Although the fascist regime resorted to repression without visible qualms, it does seem to have generated authentic public support. Mussolini's relentless sloganeering about a new Roman Empire and his forays into overseas expansion boosted patriotic pride. The restoration of public order, the extinction of the (presumed) threat of red revolution, and the partial stabilization of the economy were popular. Yet Italian fascism never systematically pursued any aim of great magnitude other than fortifying Mussolini's own power and popularity. As a result, the regime was unable to strike deep roots. People were doubtless grateful when the government got the trains to run on time, but it took more than that to create durable loyalty to the government and its institutions. Instead, fascism in Italy seemed to be thought of as an amusing adventure, but one which—in crisis—could be abandoned as swiftly as it had been undertaken.

In the 1920's, however, *Il Duce* (The Leader) was thought of as a forceful and dynamic executive, a man who by will and political wisdom had found an attractive solution to postwar upheaval. Ambitious nationalists across Europe sought to bring similar movements to their own countries, to unify their fractious and despairing populations, to restore the vitality which the war ought to have enhanced but had somehow sapped—in short, to make their nations great. Fascist boomlets erupted in a number of states, were undermined briefly by the prosperity of the mid-1920's, and reemerged with a vengeance during the depression.

Hitler and Nazi Germany

The Weimar Republic, so named for the provincial German town in which its constitution had been written, began in singularly inauspicious circumstances. The sudden collapse of the monarchy, in the backwash of the astonishing news of allied victory, had propelled the social democrats into the vacuum of power. Bolshevik admirers supposed their hour had struck, seized power in Munich, and tried the same in Berlin. The more moderate social democrats felt that violent revolution could only be averted with the aid of the army—the principal prop of authoritarian government against which the social democrats had struggled for a generation. Army officials agreed to cooperate in the suppression of the radical left, but only at the price that the army would maintain its integrity in the new regime. The new republican Germany therefore began its career by granting virtual independence to an institution hostile to the very idea of democracy. Fifteen years later, the army would show its gratitude by joining the conspiracy to overthrow the republic.

Although they eliminated the threat from the left, the social democrats earned no thanks from the right. Monarchist sympathies remained particularly strong, and there was no huge enthusiasm for authentic parliamentary democracy (as opposed to the fundamentally sham version fabricated by Bismarck). Even more important, the "stab in the back" myth gained widespread credence, and the new republican leaders had to bear the obloquy of having signed the humiliating Treaty of Versailles. The nation began to bubble with right-wing plots and antirepublican conspiracies; simultaneously, postwar inflation set in, threatening to wipe out the savings of the middle classes and plunge Germany into social chaos. None of the coups which issued forth from the extremist groups succeeded, but at least one has special historical significance.

The National Socialist German Workers' party, founded in Munich just after the war, began as a coffeehouse political party, with half a dozen self-styled political theorists sitting about trading prescriptions for the maladies of the world. Since Munich had actually experienced a left-wing coup in the postwar months, numerous right-wing groups began to crop up, of which the Nazis were but one. Their own remedy for Germany's tribulations was a mixture of nationalism and socialism— rejecting both Bolshevik internationalism and capitalist liberalism. The formula had a certain following among army veterans in the area, who were later organized in open emulation of the Italian fascists into the brown-shirted SA (*Sturmabteilung*, or Storm Troopers). The SA gave the party its muscle, but its real vitality came from an early convert who soon maneuvered himself into a position of absolute leadership, Adolf Hitler.

Hitler was Austrian born, the son of a customs official and himself an aspiring artist. When he failed to gain admission to the Viennese Academy of Fine Arts, he supported himself by hand-painting postcards, existing on the fringes of society and developing an acute interest in politics. He watched with interest the growth of mass-based parties of both left and right in Vienna and was impressed by the propaganda techniques by which political leaders manipulated large crowds. It was in this period that Hitler also picked up his anti-Semitism: the Jews made a convenient scapegoat for all social grievances, especially since central Europe had nurtured a long tradition of anti-Semitism. But the spine of Hitler's politics was nationalism. Since his school days, he had been a fanatical Great German nationalist who believed that Austria and Germany must unite into a single colossus which would dominate Europe's "inferior" peoples (Jews, of course, but also Slavs). Hitler happened to be in Munich in the summer of 1914, when the war broke out. He immediately volunteered for service in the German army and served for three years as a runner, constantly exposed to fire.

As of 1923, there was no particular reason to suspect that the National Socialist party would rise to greater distinction than any of the other obscure right-wing factions. Indeed, the abortive Nazi coup in Munich in later November of that year—in which Hitler and the SA tried to provoke a rising which would sweep over the city and ultimately the whole nation—was a pathetic little affair which the authorities had little trouble squashing. Hitler was arrested, and though he received a mere token prison sentence from a sympathetic court, it seemed safe to conclude that Germany had heard the last of this odd little man with the demonic eyes and the Charlie Chaplin mustache.

Ill-educated, a narrow man who neither read nor traveled, intellectually inflexible, but possessed of great cunning and political insight, Hitler nevertheless was able to rescue the Nazis from oblivion. While in prison, he wrote a vaguely autobiographical and strongly programmatic book, *Mein Kampf* (*My Struggle*), which elaborated in none too coherent a fashion the principles of National Socialism. Its principal message was German nationalism—rejection of the Versailles settlement and of the flabby bourgeois democracy which rendered Germany a second-rate power, in favor of a powerful state which would expand its boundaries to afford the superior race of Germans new "living space." Historians continue to debate whether *Mein Kampf* was a serious program which Hitler tried faithfully to implement in later years or whether it was mere propaganda designed to draw attention to his movement. In either case, however, it brought Hitler a national audience and gave his party something of an identity in the public mind.

Once released from prison, Hitler set about the task of organizing the party on a national basis and achieving ever greater personal recognition by a constant schedule of speeches. His oratorical talents were considerable; his shrewd appeals to injured national pride and his emotional evocations of past German greatness were effective in publicizing his movement. At the same time, Hitler vowed that the Nazis would not again seek power by a coup d'état. They would confine themselves to constitutionally sanctioned political action, running candidates for election to the Reichstag and seeking a parliamentary majority. (Such commitments to legal processes did not of course rule out employing the SA to disrupt left-wing political rallies and thrash social democratic and communist politicians.) But Hitler was at least frank about his ends. "The Constitution prescribes only the arena of the struggle," he said in 1930; "it does not specify the goal. We shall enter the legitimate organizations and in this way make our party the decisive factor. Once we possess the constitutional rights to do so, we shall, of course, cast the state in the mold that we consider to be the right one." Or, as the Nazi propaganda chief Joseph Goebbels put it, "As the wolf breaks into the sheepfold, so we come."

However, the Nazis failed to become a "decisive factor" in German politics until toward the end of the 1920's, when economic difficulties shook an already precarious republic. The depression put millions of

Germans out of work and reexcited middle-class fears of a communist uprising. In these conditions of extreme crisis, protest began translating into a
vote for the Nazis. Their showing in the legislative elections of 1928 had
been negligible—just over 800,000 votes, good for but twelve seats. The
1930 elections, held amidst the gathering momentum of the depression,
catapulted their popular support to 6.5 million votes and 107 Reichstag
seats. By 1932, the Nazis more than doubled their popular vote and with
their 230 deputies were the largest single party in Germany (though still
falling short of a majority). In all probability, there was a strong negative
streak in these votes, a protest *against* the existing system made by endorsing one of its most extreme opponents. This suggestion seems to be
borne out by the fact that the communists, at the other extreme, were
gaining ground in the same elections (though somewhat less rapidly).

One of the favorite targets of Hitler's savage contempt was parliamentary government, which he characterized as weak, indecisive, organized
according to the nation's divisions rather than trying to unify them. In
fact, by 1932, parliamentary government scarcely existed any longer. A
series of right-center coalitions had found themselves unable to put together any durable government and increasingly had to resort to ruling
by decree (as provided for in "emergency" situations by the constitution).
Even so, the authorities were unable either to extricate Germany from
the depression (a task being accomplished nowhere in 1932) or to preserve order in the streets. Political violence, especially involving the Nazis
and the left, had become chronic, a fact of which Hitler made much while
also contributing heavily to it.

Even in such desperate circumstances, however, it is unlikely that the
Nazis would have come to power by winning a parliamentary majority. A
second legislative election of 1932 reversed the trend of the preceding
two years: the Nazis lost fully two million votes, although the communists continued to advance at the polls. The election touched off deep despair in the party leadership. The campaign had been expensive; critical
funds which had come from wealthy anticommunist industrialists (whose
support had moved Hitler to soft-pedal the socialism of National Socialism) were in danger of drying up. Without money, the party could not
pay the nearly 400,000 Storm Troopers, whose stipend was all that stood
between most of them and unemployment. Even more alarmed by the results of the election than the Nazis, however, were the nonfascist conservatives, the men who represented the ruling elites of Imperial Germany
—large agrarian interests, big business, the army—and who had maintained a strategic location under the republic. The communist showing
in the most recent election startled these traditional conservatives, but
they had no mass counterweight of their own. In brief, they decided to
turn to Hitler—but only to "use" him, to bring him into government, to

utilize his own mass following as a means of crushing the radical left. Once he had served their purpose, he would be discarded.

At the end of January 1933, the conservative advisers to President of the Republic Paul von Hindenburg—a monarchist and Germany's greatest military hero—convinced him to name Hitler as chancellor, with the power to form a new cabinet. The move would have the advantages of associating the Nazis with the responsibilities of government (and therefore presumably ending their disruptive antics in the street) and bringing to power an anticommunist movement backed by twelve million votes.

It can scarcely be overemphasized that Germany received a Nazi government because of a political deal, and not because a majority of Germans voted for it. Hitler very swiftly proved how naive his conservative benefactors had been by vastly extending his power to the point where they were his tools, rather than the opposite. In February 1933, Hitler used the burning of the Reichstag building by a demented Dutch communist to ram emergency measures through the legislature on the pretext that a general left-wing rising was imminent. Armed with enlarged executive powers, Hitler called another election for March. Even under these favorable conditions, however, the Nazis failed to gain a popular majority, capturing only 44 percent of the vote.

Hitler continued to play upon the crisis atmosphere, and the new Reichstag therefore passed the critical Enabling Act, which transferred all legislative functions to the executive branch. Thereafter, Hitler simply ruled by decree—abolishing all political parties but his own, outlawing labor unions, installing Nazis in many sensitive positions, assuming the presidency upon Hindenburg's death in 1934, extracting an oath of loyalty to his person from the army, bringing the judicial and educational systems directly under state (and Nazi party) control. And, as Hitler constantly emphasized, the whole process—euphemistically called *Gleichschaltung,* or "coordination" of the state—was entirely "legal," since the Enabling Act had been passed by a duly elected legislature.

On paper, the Nazi state was a perfectly centralized structure, with all power flowing through a graduated hierarchy with Hitler at its summit. In practice, Germany was a bureaucrat's nightmare. Lines of command were confused; jurisdictions overlapped; authority in the middle echelons was uncertain. Hitler was extremely jealous of his power, and he liked to keep his subordinates dependent upon him; amidst bureaucratic confusion, only his own authority remained certain, his own decisions final. His state operated, therefore, not by means of administrative efficiency. Its real motive force was the *Fuehrerprinzip,* or Leader Principle; the position of the Fuehrer, and of his party, was in turn sustained by force. Nazi Germany was simply a police state in which coercion produced obedience, and dissent, whether real or potential, met with terror. Long before the ghastly death camps of the war years, the Nazis erected concentration camps into which were flung communists, labor leaders, and liberal intellectuals whose incarceration was meant not only to punish their own behavior but to serve as a deterrent to dissenters on the outside. Arbitrary imprisonments, confiscations of property, and even political murder all became tools of government.

Needless to say, the conservative elites watched the process of *Gleichschaltung* with mounting dismay, but found themselves incapable of halting Hitler as he gathered into his own hands all the reins of state power. The only institution with the wherewithal to resist, the army, was seduced by Hitler's plans for rearmament, which restored the army to its rightful place in the nation and the nation to its rightful place in Europe. Ironically, however, rearmament proved the undoing of the old monarchist officer corps, once the private preserve of the Prussian aristocracy, but whose ranks were now flooded with thousands of new men. The officers were no longer a closed corporation, bound together by cohesive class ties and ideology; diluted by rearmament, the army proved much more malleable in Hitler's hands. Moreover, Hitler held the old elites at bay by refusing to tamper in any significant way with major social and economic institutions. While crushing labor unions and eliminating left-wing political movements, he raised no challenge to large industrial, financial, and agrarian interests. Indeed, rearmament provided a tonic to the depressed economy in the form of contracts for business and jobs for workers.

The only serious domestic challenge to Hitler came finally from the same conservatives who had put him in power. But it was too little, too late—an abortive assassination plot and coup in July 1944. By that time, the conservative conspirators were a tiny isolated group. They had brought in Hitler to eliminate the left, and then were astounded to discover that his success in this task also deprived them of any allies.

Left Versus Right

The rigors of the depression and the examples of Mussolini and Hitler did much to promote fascist and cryptofascist movements outside Italy and Germany. Mixing nationalist, racist, and anticommunist appeals, fascism became a force to contend with in the Balkan states, Austria, Spain, and France. Street violence between the partisans of left and right, accompanied by the rhetoric of Armageddon, was almost commonplace. At the same time, German rearmament raised disturbing questions as to whether fascism might not carry its war against both liberal democracy and communism into the international arena. The prospect worried Stalin in particular, who was in the midst of the purges and in no domestic position to wage a major war against Europe's most powerful industrial nation.

From these circumstances arose the Popular Front, an attempt to create a broad antifascist coalition running from communists through anticommunist democrats. Strangely, the initiative came from the communists, who had taken the line for the previous fifteen years that their principal enemies were not fascists but the social democrats—the moderate, nonrevolutionary socialists whom European communists persisted in calling "social fascists." Hitler's rise to power necessitated a drastic reshuffling of priorities, however. Rather than compete with the social democrats for exclusive leadership of the working classes, the communists would now have to seek allies in what was shaping up as a life-and-death battle with fascism. Therefore, in 1935, the Comintern endorsed the formation of Popular Fronts of all antifascist groups and promised that communists would work within them.

The Popular Front concept was basically defensive. Yet some anticommunists on the left could not help suspecting that it contained some trap, some devious plan for Bolshevik revolution. In France, for example, it took the continued growth of domestic fascism—which was in fact far less formidable than it appeared at the time—coupled with an increasingly aggressive German foreign policy to break down the suspicions of noncommunist left-wing parties. The concept was also thoroughly misunderstood among French moderates and conservatives, who saw the cooperation of leftist parties not as a device for the defense of the republic but as a prologue to revolution. In the spring of 1936, these fears were exacerbated by the aftermath of a legislative election in which the Popular Front captured a majority and proceeded to form a government under socialist leader Léon Blum (a moderate and anticommunist). Exhilarated with their victory at the polls, and in anticipation of the wave of social reform they trusted would follow, French laborers spontaneously began a series of sit-down strikes, physically taking over their factories and locking out employers until certain wage demands had been met. Blum and the Popular Front had no part in the strike and moved quickly to negotiate a settlement. But the new government never overcame suspicions that it was merely fronting for the communists, suspicions which even began to infect the liberal-democratic wing of the Front. Within a year, the government fell.

The Spanish Popular Front also began as a defensive improvisation, but it soon took a more aggressive line than the French. Politics in the new Spanish republic—the monarchy had disappeared only in 1931—were badly polarized between the military, the clergy, and large landholding elements on the right, and radical democrats, socialists, anarchosyndicalists, and a handful of communists on the left. The Popular

Front's electoral victory of early 1936 was followed by a series of far-reaching social reforms affecting the church and by attempts to bring the army firmly under civilian control. The right responded with a counter-revolutionary civil war, led by General Francisco Franco, an authoritarian conservative who courted the support of the Spanish fascists but never became their tool.

It soon looked as though the Spanish Civil War would be the first battle in the international struggle between radical right and radical left. Mussolini dispatched a large contingent of "volunteers" to support Franco, and Hitler contributed a number of air and tank units. The British government stood by indifferently. The French Popular Front government would have liked to help the Spanish republicans, but Blum feared that intervention would further energize French fascists, precipitate civil war in his own country, and perhaps even risk a general European war. Finally, in 1937, Stalin stepped in, providing the Spanish Popular Front with war matériel and advisers both technical and political. Soviet intervention was relatively limited. No ground troops were involved, and Stalin had enjoined his political commissars to avoid any behavior which would excite anxieties about a communist takeover (something which would not have done Stalin much good in any case). As a result, Russian aid was too insignificant to be militarily decisive, but just visible enough to scare moderates. Radicals sympathetic to the Spanish Popular Front were disgusted with what they took to be nothing more than a face-saving gesture on Stalin's part.

By early 1939, Franco's forces had overwhelmed the republicans, and European observers looked about anxiously for the next confrontation between right and left. To the astonishment of nearly everyone, it did not occur—at least for some two years. Fascism and Bolshevism, presumably the bitterest of enemies, postponed their struggle, and the radical right unleashed its energies upon the bastions of liberal democracy.

14 / *The End of the European Era*

The Europe created in the mid-nineteenth century had been dominated by the major nation-states of the center and the west, which in turn dominated much of the world. That Europe, already badly mauled by World War I, was utterly destroyed in the conflict of 1939–45. When World War II engaged the Soviet Union and the United States, the European heartland became one theater of operations among several. With war's end, it turned into one battleground among several in the developing Cold War. Great power and middling state alike found that they had lost world stature; lost the ability to control events; and had become politically, economically, and militarily dependent upon one of the two superpowers which had emerged with such astonishing rapidity.

The Origins of War

Hitler's foreign policy ambitions were no secret; he had outlined them with utter candor in *Mein Kampf*, published in 1925. His general principles were simple: the "superior" Aryans (that is, Germans) would dominate the racially "inferior" Slavs. Although implicit in Hitler's grandiose schemes was German preponderance on the continent, his specific ideas were for eastward expansion—absorbing Slavic eastern Europe and turning Russia into what he called "Germany's India." The Germans' need for *Lebensraum,* or "living space," and German national honor—besmirched by the Versailles treaty—demanded nothing less.

An aggressive foreign policy naturally entailed sweeping rearmament, which Hitler undertook in open defiance of the Versailles treaty shortly after assuming power. While rearmament naturally gratified the old military leaders, they were less sanguine about risking war until the army had attained at least its pre-Versailles strength—a task they assumed would take nearly a decade to complete. Although the western allies had ignored German rearmament, the generals were convinced that any further violations of the treaty would bring prompt retaliation. When Hitler proposed to remilitarize the German Rhineland—where Germany bordered France and in which the peacemakers had forbidden weapons of war—the military establishment resisted. But the Fuehrer prevailed, and with impunity. In March 1936, when the German army began openly wheeling arms into the Rhineland, the French government was caught in one of its chronic ministerial crises and thus lacked decisive leadership. Moreover, unilateral French action was unthinkable, and the British government rejected the idea of allied resistance to remilitarization. Hitler's gamble was successful, his self-confidence immensely bolstered, and his inclination to listen to military counsel was correspondingly diminished.

In the present generation, the Anglo-French failure to resist Hitler's expansionist tendencies and the so-called policy of appeasement have come in for extensive criticism. It is generally held that had the western allies stood firm and refused to tolerate either defiance of the Versailles treaty or aggression, world war might have been averted. Whatever the merits of such arguments—and they are as much a part of Cold War politics as of historical analysis—they overlook the political mood of France and Britain in the 1930's. The experience of World War I and its incredible carnage was still immediate; war was not a prospect to be taken lightly. The left in both countries was torn between strong antifascism and its traditional pacifist sentiments. The right tended to view Hitler, at least in his early years, as a bulwark of social order and as western Europe's shield against a Bolshevik onslaught. In Britain especially, the view had spread that the Versailles treaty had not in fact been a just and sound settlement, that the Germans had arguable territorial claims to the east, and that conflict could be averted by admitting that a mistake had been made in 1919.

In these circumstances, Hitler was able substantially to enlarge the boundaries of the Reich with relative ease. In March 1938, he pulled off a bloodless *Anschluss,* or annexation, of Austria, thus fulfilling the Great German nationalism of his youth and uniting the country of his birth with his adopted nation. Later in the same year, he raised demands upon Czechoslovakia. Prodded by the Nazis, a large German population in the Czech Sudetenland—a conspicuous nub of territory which bordered on Germany—demanded unification with the Reich. Cession of this province, which had been a part of pre-Versailles Germany, would leave the Czechs with an indefensible border and thus virtually invited Nazi invasion. However, Neville Chamberlain, the British prime minister, seemed certain that this would be the last of Hitler's demands. In a September summit conference at Munich involving Chamberlain, Hitler, Mussolini, and Edouard Daladier, the French premier, German annexation of the Sudetenland was arranged. Subsequently, the very name Munich has become synonymous in most quarters with international cowardice; but in 1938, there was general relief in the west that war had been avoided.

It soon became clear, however, that the Sudetenland did not satiate Hitler. In March 1939, he marched unopposed into western Czechoslovakia, occupying Bohemia and placing Slovakia under a German protectorate. It was now clear to all that war was virtually inevitable. When Hitler began later in the year to press claims upon Poland—which was formally allied with both France and Britain—the issue over which war would come was equally clear. People now became convinced that the vision expressed in *Mein Kampf* had been serious; the western allies resolved that further concession was both pointless and dangerous.

The uncertain factor in the equation was the Soviet Union. War with Germany was somewhat more conscionable if Hitler could be flanked east and west, and the allies therefore explored the possibility of a close military relationship with the Russians. But Stalin was deeply suspicious, fearing a trick by which the Nazis would be unleashed against the Bolsheviks while the French and British stood idly by, watching their enemies destroy one another. Indeed, the Munich arrangements looked to him uncomfortably like a western mandate for Hitler's eastern ambitions. Besides, Stalin was not at all prepared for major war against anyone, and badly needed time. Therefore, the simplest way out was to protect himself against war with Germany, which he did to the utter astonishment of the world in August 1939. The two bitter ideological enemies, Bolshevik and fascist, signed a mutual nonaggression treaty which protected Hitler's eastern flank and bought time for Stalin (who never doubted that war with Hitler would someday come). Within a week, Hitler escalated his demands upon the Poles into an ultimatum which he neither expected nor wanted them to accept. On September 1, 1939, German forces invaded Poland and, within a few days, the French and British declared war on Germany.

The European War

Few persons expected that French and British forces would be of much help to the Poles, who were overrun by the Germans in three weeks. The major war would be in the west; strangely, however, it failed to materialize. Hitler's plans to strike through the Low Countries into France were foiled by bad weather and an early winter. World War II entered 1940 with few shots being fired.

When the fighting resumed that spring, the German army over-whelmed France with astonishing ease; the German invasion began in the second week of May, and six weeks later the French signed an armi-stice. Many observers at the time and historians since have concluded that such a thorough rout cannot be explained solely in military terms. They usually point to the fact that, shortly after the armistice, the par-liament of the Third Republic voted that seventy-year-old regime out of existence and handed power over to an authoritarian government under the leadership of Marshal Philippe Pétain, an octogenarian who had come to prominence during World War I. The implication is that the fall of France was not a failure of French arms but a political collapse, an institutional crisis in which lack of faith in the republican regime nur-tured bad policy and a defeatist morale.

It is true that the Third Republic continued to be plagued by minis-terial instability, unimpressive leadership, and deep social divisions in the post-1918 years. Yet it is difficult to see how these considerations came into play, at least directly, in 1940. World War I had demonstrated the apparent superiority of a well-constructed defense, and French military authorities assumed that the next war would be like the last one in most important particulars. Therefore, they built across northeastern France the Maginot Line—a network of heavily fortified emplacements con-nected by underground railways which could rush troops from place to place.

Had a 1914-style infantry hurled itself against the Maginot Line, it would doubtless have been turned back. But most French army leaders ignored the fact that some important technological developments had rendered this sophisticated trench system obsolete. The Germans had cre-ated a highly mobile infantry spearheaded by armored vehicles and sup-ported from the air—dive bombers proved far more effective in softening up defensive positions than mere artillery barrages. The army could both move quickly and concentrate its superior firepower on the enemy. More-over, this *Blitzkrieg* warfare struck at a point where the French had not expected attack, where their troops were stretched far too thinly. Finally, although France also had a large tank corps, it was used less effectively than the Germans'—for defensive rather than offensive purposes. In brief, the fall of France is a chapter in military history.

The French defeat, which had proceeded by a successful German sweep through the Netherlands and Belgium, left Britain alone against Hitler's juggernaut. Once again, the English Channel proved to be Brit-ain's greatest national resource. Before the Germans could hope to mount an attack across the Channel, they would have to achieve air superiority in order to protect their troops. Hermann Goering, one of Hitler's chief aides since the 1920's and now head of the German air force, predicted rapid annihilation of the British Royal Air Force. But the RAF, though outnumbered, proved equal to the task, and inflicted heavy losses on the Germans. When Goering could no longer afford to send fighters over Britain, he switched to bombers—aimed primarily at London and designed to crush civilian morale. Although the destruction was awesome, the British held; besides, bombing did nothing to achieve German air superiority. By mid-September 1940, Hitler momentarily admitted his defeat and canceled plans for the invasion.

The Battle of Britain was the first major air battle in history, a new experience for both the men who fought it and the civilian population upon whom it rained death. The sudden development of air warfare meant that a whole new dimension had been added to war. Ground superiority could not be gained without mastery of the air. Noncombatants were now brought into the war as never before, and with the later development of strategic bombing it was possible to strike at the enemy's industrial plant. As a result, soldiers and technicians began to devote massive attention to air technology and such supportive devices as radar. The jet plane, the guided missile, and the rocketry which later led to space flight were all direct outgrowths of the Battle of Britain.

Besides marking a new era in the history of war, the Battle of Britain also created a living political legend. In May 1940, Winston Churchill became prime minister at the age of 66. Churchill's political career stretched back four decades; although a man of profoundly conservative instincts, he had the reputation of being something of a maverick, and while he had attained high office—First Lord of the Admiralty during World War I—the highest had eluded him. After a relative political eclipse in the early 1930's, Churchill regained prominence as a vociferous opponent of appeasement (though he was also on record with some flattering remarks made about Herr Hitler's stable and orderly regime). Churchill warned repeatedly that war with Nazi Germany was inevitable, and urged the government to prepare accordingly. Brought into the government in September 1939 largely as a gesture, he was at its head the next spring.

After the fall of France and with Hitler massing his invasion forces along the Channel coast, there was one commodity which the British needed nearly as much as airplanes—confidence. Churchill was vital in helping to supply it, largely through frequent radio addresses. His somewhat baroque oratorical cadenzas, delivered in a rich and vibrating lower register, struck just the right tone. His message was simple: not merely resistance, but victory, against whatever odds, at whatever cost. On June 17, the day that the French sued for peace on the continent, Churchill took to the air and told British listeners:

> the news from France is very bad, and I grieve for the gallant French people who have fallen into this terrible misfortune. Nothing will alter our feelings

towards them or our faith that the genius of France will rise again. What has happened in France makes no difference to our actions and purpose. We have become the sole champions now in arms to defend the world cause. We shall do our best to be worthy of this high honour. We shall defend our island home, and with the British Empire we shall fight on unconquerable until the curse of Hitler is lifted from the brows of mankind. We are sure that in the end all will come right.

Churchill's leadership was as important a part in the Battle of Britain as the heroism of RAF pilots.

Hitler was convinced, and Churchill fully agreed, that British power was thoroughly bound up with the empire. Although he had not conquered Britain, Hitler had at least bottled up its forces. Now he would turn to the empire itself, in concert with an expansive new Asian ally. The Tripartite Pact of September 1940—between Germany, Italy, and Japan—parceled out the British empire among these so-called Axis powers. Although Hitler claimed that he intended to broaden this global alliance to include the Soviet Union, to which he would offer India, Stalin was inclined to see the pact as a flanking movement which surrounded him east and west. These suspicions were reinforced by the combined Italian-German offensive in the Balkans, which the Russians regarded as their own sphere of influence, and ultimately justified when Hitler suddenly postponed destruction of the British empire to turn his attention to Russia.

As it turned out, Stalin had not been suspicious enough of his Nazi ally. While the Germans began to mass forces along the Russian border, the Soviet dictator simply refused to believe that attack was imminent. When it came, in June 1941, Russian defenses were wholly inadequate. By mid-August, the Germans had won several major battles and ripped large units of the Red Army to shreds.

Hitler's Russian campaign was no mere strategical flourish. It was an ideological invasion, intended to implement the vision sketched out in *Mein Kampf.* The rich Ukraine would be entirely cleared out and repopulated with German settlers. Elsewhere, the Bolshevik leadership—commissars, intelligentsia, and the like—would be exterminated and replaced by an "Aryan" elite. "The Slavs are born slaves," remarked Hitler in September 1941, "who feel the need of a master." When the civilian population showed any signs of resistance to the German invasion, Hitler ordered them murdered—on the grounds that the killing of "inferior" peoples was nothing less than patriotic.

The World War

In 1941, what had begun as largely European conflict spread quickly over most of the globe. In Africa, the Italians were engaged in a clumsy attempt to wrest Egypt and the Suez Canal from Britain. In Asia, the Japanese were steadily gobbling up China and threatening British outposts there. Hitler, confident that he could demolish Russia without assistance, urged the Japanese on, and in December 1941 they struck at the other major Pacific power, the United States.

The winter of 1941–42 was unquestionably a decisive turning point in the war. The Japanese attack on Pearl Harbor was followed immediately by Hitler's extraordinarily stupid declaration of war on the United States. The Axis had now fulfilled Churchill's most fervent hope—bringing the world's greatest industrial power into the struggle on the British side.* In a far-flung world war, air and sea power would likely tip the balance; and the American capacity to produce planes, ships, and other material in abundance seemed limitless. Moreover, American entry coincided with the first sputterings of the German campaign in Russia. Although the Germans had inflicted gigantic losses on the Soviets and occupied vast expanses of territory, they had failed to capture any of the three major cities—Leningrad, Moscow, or Stalingrad. As the brutal Russian winter descended, the German armies were forced to dig in and endure severe hardships—among which was a vigorous counteroffensive by reserves gathered in eastern Russia.

In perspective, it is clear that the next three and a half years saw a steady decline in German military fortunes. As of early 1942, however, Hitler saw things differently: the war was all but won, and while the Fuehrer himself continued to expend most of his energies in directing the Russian campaign, his subordinates set about restructuring conquered Europe according to the dictates of Nazi ideology. The first task was racial "purification"—that is, the elimination of "inferior" strains, meaning principally the Jews. While the Nazis were content merely to dominate Slavic peoples, they could not bear the presence of Jews. As Hitler told luncheon guests in late January 1942:

> The Jew must clear out of Europe. Otherwise no understanding will be possible between Europeans. It's the Jew who prevents everything. When I think about it, I realize that I'm extraordinarily humane. At the time of the rule of the Popes, the Jews were mistreated in Rome. Until 1830, eight Jews mounted on donkeys were led once a year through the streets of Rome. For my part, I restrict myself to telling them they must go away. If they break their pipes on the journey, I can't do anything about it. But if they refuse to go voluntarily, I see no other solution but extermination. Why should I look at a Jew through other eyes than if he were a Russian prisoner-of-war? In the p.o.w.

---

* The American government was not exactly dragged in kicking and screaming. For a year and a half, President Franklin D. Roosevelt had been convinced that confrontation with fascism was unavoidable. In spite of official neutrality and the strong streak of isolationism that ran through American opinion, Roosevelt had committed massive aid to Britain and, after mid-1941, the Soviet Union.

camps, many are dying. It's not my fault. I didn't want either the war or the p.o.w. camps. Why did the Jew provoke this war? *

At this time, plans were being developed in the Berlin suburb of Wannsee to implement "the final solution to the Jewish question." Forced emigration had proved impracticable; extermination was the only choice. But the extermination of millions of people could hardly be undertaken by random murders; even the roving squads of SS men who were shooting hundreds of Jews at a time in Poland and western Russia were too inefficient. The "final solution" envisaged a more systematic operation. Execution centers had to be established; Jews across Europe had to be identified and transported to the death camps—in short, a massive bureaucratic problem presented itself. The Nazis proved worthy of the challenge, constructing a gigantic bureaucracy of death which may have encompassed as many as 80,000 persons—administrators, transport officials, camp commandants and guards, and so forth. Labor was divided; no single person was responsible for the whole program. Thus extermination could be carried out in an impersonal, anonymous, businesslike manner.

The "final solution" was a fiendish conception, and we would feel better if we could find authentic fiends at its heart. In fact, it was carried out by "normal" people—people doing their jobs, taking orders, running the whole institution rather the way in which one would run a large railway or tourist agency. The business of this particular institution, however, was genocide. By various means—mostly gas, which proved the most efficient—it removed perhaps six million persons from the face of the earth.†

When the Nazis were not deliberately annihilating their racial "inferiors," they were exposing them to conditions which spelled near-certain death. As the Russian front began to devour more and more Germans of fighting age, the German economy became increasingly dependent upon slave labor from conquered nations. Millions of Europeans were literally worked to death.

Since the military effort consumed the bulk of German energies, the Nazis had little chance to remake Europe in their own image (though one can guess at what the New Order might have looked like). In the Balkans and western Europe, they preferred to avoid massive occupation and rule indirectly—in cooperation with local collaborators—thus freeing German occupation troops for active duty elsewhere. Collabora-

---

* *Hitler's Secret Conversations*, trans. N. Cameron and R.H. Stevens (New York, 1953).

† Countless Slavs were also systematically exterminated, along with such other "inferior" groups as the Gypsies—who were nearly decimated in central and eastern Europe by perhaps 100,000 murders.

tionist regimes were usually ramshackle affairs headed by leading figures of the indigenous right wing and numbering many opportunists who thought that German victory was inevitable. Yet they could never wholly escape the image of puppets, and thus it was hard for them to mobilize the support of their populations.

Perhaps the best-known collaborationist government was that of France, which set up shop in the sleepy little resort town of Vichy after the armistice and the German occupation of the northern half of the country. The Vichy regime, under Marshal Pétain, was no mere effort to hold things together until the war was resolved one way or the other. The Vichyites were all sworn enemies of the republic, which they held responsible for France's humiliation in 1940, although their individual ideologies ranged from fascism to a sort of wistful monarchism. Domestically, they sought to revitalize the nation with tough new authoritarian institutions which would decisively transform French character where flabby parliamentarianism had failed. And with the prospect of German victory appearing imminent, they sought also to capitalize upon it—endearing themselves to their German conquerors in hopes that France could play some major role in Nazi Europe. Collaboration was thus not so much forced upon Vichy by the Germans as it was actively chosen by some of the French as the most attractive alternative. Therefore, the new government tried in every way to make the German task in France easier, assuming police and administrative functions which released German personnel for responsibilities in other areas. The argument that Vichy was a shield which buffered Frenchmen from the harsher treatment at the hands of the Germans themselves was concocted only after the liberation of France and the overthrow of the regime.

Few persons after 1945 admitted that they had collaborated enthusiastically, almost everyone claiming to have been a part of the resistance. In fact, while it is impossible to estimate the size of the various resistance movements, active participants in them remained relatively few—far fewer certainly than those who tacitly accepted collaborationist regimes. Resistance was everywhere diversified in membership, running from conservatives through communists, and bound together not so much organizationally as ideologically by patriotism and anti-German feeling. In most places—France, Italy, and the Balkans—the communists were the chief element in the resistance. The period from August 1939 to June 1941 had been an agonizing one for European communists. For years, they had been in the front rank of antifascists. Then, the Nazi-Soviet nonaggression treaty placed them in a compromising position. On orders from Moscow not to take an anti-German position, they found themselves in the role of virtual traitors in their homelands. Stalin was so intent upon keeping Hitler's friendship that he even went so far as to turn over those German communists who sought political asylum in Russia. But Hitler's attack upon the Soviet Union liberated the European communists and gave them the chance to play a more agreeable role.

The communists were well suited to working in the resistance by more than their antifascist ideology. Their organization and discipline, the fact that they were accustomed to political persecution, made the transition to underground operations relatively easy. They were a cohesive group, about the only one to be found in the varied ranks of the resistance. Although there was frequently considerable reluctance on the part of other resisters to working with them, the communists generally submerged their revolutionary politics and presented themselves as patriots. Even so, friction remained, and surfaced abruptly whenever the common Nazi enemy was beaten back.

It was difficult for the resistance to make a major military contribution, to fight classical pitched battles of great significance. (The exception was Yugoslavia, where the partisan forces drove out the German army almost without assistance.) Still, the scattered acts of sabotage were highly annoying to the Nazis, if not debilitating. Even more important, the bravery and dedication of the resistance fighters were an inspiration to many of their own people. When the war had ended, and formerly occupied Europe tried to put itself together again, the one bright spot of the wartime nightmare was in the spirit of the resistance—tough, committed, idealistic.

The End

Two decisive battles in 1942 dealt crippling blows to the Axis powers and threw them henceforth on the defensive. The United States regained mastery of the Pacific Ocean in June 1942 when it overpowered the Japanese fleet in a huge naval battle off Midway Island. Toward the end of the year, the German drive to capture Stalingrad stalled, and then was reversed by a sharp Russian counterattack. Hitler refused to countenance retreat, and by January 1943 the Red Army had enveloped a large German force, which had no choice but to surrender. Hitler vowed that the Reich would redouble its war effort and now began the use of slave labor on a gigantic scale. But it was the end for the Germans in Russia, and Stalin's forces pushed them slowly, but inexorably, westward.

In the meantime, a German force had to be sent into north Africa to rescue the Italians after their abortive attempt to invade Egypt from Libya. The German tank units, under General Erwin Rommel, posed a serious threat to the British position, but they were finally beaten at El Alamein in October 1942. Shortly thereafter, they were surrounded by the landing of Anglo-American forces further west in north Africa. In the spring of 1943, the Italians and Germans—nearly 250,000 of them—were forced to surrender.

The western allies now had a Mediterranean base from which to threaten Europe itself, and in July 1943 they moved on Italy. The Italian army could not hold back the tide, and German forces were rushed in. In the chaos, Mussolini was overthrown by Italian dissidents, though Hitler later restored him to titular power over the part of northern Italy which the Axis still held. The Italian campaign went badly for the allies, in part because of their own tactical mistakes. But it was never intended to be the major second front which Stalin had been demanding that Churchill and Roosevelt open, thus taking some pressure off the Russians. That front was opened only in June 1944, when an enormous Anglo-American force landed in Normandy and began to sweep the Nazis out of Europe.

Although the German army was able to prolong the war for another year, the brutal crush of the pincers from west and east could not be broken. Shortly after the Normandy invasion, a number of German officers recognized that the end was near and plotted to assassinate Hitler in hopes of making peace on satisfactory terms. But the assassination, attempted in July 1944, misfired. Hitler was only wounded, and enough loyalists were left to move with dispatch against the conspirators, who were thoroughly liquidated. Resistance went on, with each fresh defeat eliciting from Hitler cries that the German people were betraying him.

The end came in May 1945, when the Red Army fought its way into Berlin. Hitler committed suicide, and his appointed successor swiftly sued for peace. The war in the Pacific dragged on, even though the Japanese had been on the defensive since Midway. Rather than contemplate a costly invasion of the Japanese islands themselves, however, the United States chose to end the war swiftly, and in early August it dropped atomic bombs on the cities of Hiroshima and Nagasaki. These hideously destructive new weapons of war caused about 115,000 casualties, most of them civilian.* Japan swiftly gave in.

A generation earlier, the slaughter of World War I had seemed unbearable. By 1945, the figure of perhaps 13 million dead during that conflict seemed paltry. World War II took about 55 million lives. Fully half of them wore no uniforms, bore no arms.

East Versus West

As the Soviet armies pushed the German forces westward, political considerations preoccupied Stalin nearly as much as military problems.

---

* Even so, the atomic bombs were less costly than the use of conventional bombs upon the German city of Dresden, attacked in February 1945: as many as 135,000 persons perished in this attack.

Without doubt, he looked beyond the defeat of Germany to the shape of postwar Europe, in which victorious Russia—in spite of the ferocious beating it had absorbed—would play a major role. In particular, he anticipated the extension of Soviet influence into the small eastern European nations which had either been conquered by Hitler or had been dragooned into fighting on the Nazi side. The Red Army with commissars in its train arrived in eastern Europe and the Balkans as both conqueror and liberator, confiscating material, assisting in the purge of fascist and collaborationist elements, and encouraging local communists as postwar governments began to take shape.

With German troops retreating from Russia, the Balkans, and France, the leaders of the allied coalition were able to give increasing attention to the matter of postwar politics. In October 1944, Churchill and Stalin met in Moscow and sketched out a plan for their respective nations' influence in eastern Europe. Their informal agreement would leave Rumania, Bulgaria, and Hungary largely under Soviet sway; would leave Greece in the western orbit; and would leave Yugoslavia in a sort of twilight zone. Four months later, President Roosevelt joined his European allies in a secret conference at Yalta, in southern Russia. The meeting was brief and not wholly conclusive. Roosevelt was banking heavily on the projected institution of the United Nations to handle future international problems, and thus was momentarily inclined to recognize Soviet preponderance in eastern Europe. Stalin in turn endorsed a Declaration on Liberated Europe which promised that political reconstruction in formerly Nazi-occupied states would proceed by democratic means.

In all probability, Stalin supposed that the Declaration had been devised as nothing more than a cynical cover for political expansion, a facade of democracy behind which the great powers would operate in their respective spheres of influence according to their own interests. After all, the British and the Americans were behaving in precisely that way in Italy and Greece, where liberation from the Nazis went hand in hand with the repression of communist elements. At Yalta, moreover, Churchill and Roosevelt had in effect agreed to turn over a large chunk of eastern Poland to the Soviet Union. The Poles, who were not consulted about this arrangement, were to be compensated in the west at German expense. Stalin could thus understandably assume that he had received an implicit recognition of the fait accompli that his armies were in control of eastern Europe. He seemed surprised a few months later, after having manipulated communist governments into power in Rumania and Bulgaria, when his allies accused him of violating the Declaration on Liberated Europe (which of course the Polish settlement had already done).

Stalin's position was brutally simple: the Slavic nations of eastern and southeastern Europe were a Soviet sphere of influence, established by right of conquest and legitimized by the Russian need for a buffer against future German attack. If he were to follow the Yalta Declaration, a combination of local nationalism and democratic sentiments would certainly compromise his position in the area. While Churchill was willing to let Rumania, Bulgaria, and Hungary fall into the Soviet orbit, he became increasingly concerned about Stalin's designs on Poland, Yugoslavia, and Germany itself. Increasingly, he began to think in terms of the defeat of Germany being followed by a struggle for continental hegemony between the Anglo-American coalition and Russia. In this struggle, Germany would be strategically decisive, and Churchill therefore urged that the western forces move quickly to capture Berlin and establish a line in central Europe against the Russian advance.

Harry Truman, who had acceded to the American presidency upon Roosevelt's death in April 1945, still hoped to settle problems in Europe by negotiation rather than armed confrontation. Rather than challenge the Russians over Berlin, he supported the commander of the western armies, General Dwight D. Eisenhower, who preferred to mop up Nazi forces in southern Germany. Still, Truman and several of his most influential advisors were suspicious about Soviet motives and were at pains to demonstrate that the United States would tolerate no untoward Russian behavior. Therefore, after Berlin had fallen to the Red Army and Hitler's successor had sued for peace on May 8, Truman abruptly terminated the four-year-old program of Lend Lease aid to the Soviet Union on May 9.

In July, Truman, Stalin, and Clement Atlee, the new British prime minister, met for peace talks in the Berlin suburb of Potsdam.* The Polish settlement sketched out at Yalta was completed, though not formally endorsed by the western powers. Otherwise, the conference accomplished relatively little beyond establishing a reparations bill which the Germans would pay the Russians. Atlee and Truman were both new in their respective offices, unwilling to negotiate for high stakes or make long-term commitments. The United States and the Soviet Union were still formally allies, the Russians having belatedly joined the war on Japan. But mutual suspicions ran high, and the ground for confrontation was being staked out in Germany itself. The month before the conference, Soviet, British, American, and French forces had moved into prearranged occupation zones in Germany. The rights and jurisdictions of the conquering powers were bound to prove a source of friction. Within two years, Germany, the keystone of central Europe, became the focus of a new sort of war.

The mounting conflict between east and west was not confined to in-

---

* Churchill had represented Britain at the beginning of the conference, in the midst of an election campaign at home. In a startling turn of events, his Conservative party was beaten at the polls by the Labor party, thus bringing Atlee to power.

ternational politics; it was mirrored also in the domestic politics of the liberation and immediate postwar years. The most important groups involved here were the various resistance movements and especially the communist nuclei within them. In every country in occupied Europe, the resistance emerged from the war with considerable prestige for its undaunted heroism. As the Nazi tide had begun to ebb in 1944–45, resistance leaders—like the leaders of the great powers—began to think in terms of postwar reconstruction. From place to place, their governing councils declared themselves provisional governments or otherwise prepared for some share in political power. What complicated matters, as far as the western allies were concerned, was the presence in these bodies of strong communist representation.

In the Slavic states of the east and south, these circumstances proved generally convenient for Stalin. Building on such local communist foundations as existed—cajoling, manipulating, and threatening where necessary—he was able to bring pro-Soviet groups to power in Rumania, Bulgaria, and Albania, and to ease the way for their later triumph in Poland and Hungary.* In Yugoslavia, the resistance movement had been dominated by communists under the leadership of Marshal Tito, who took power in November 1945. But Tito turned out to be an implacable Yugoslav nationalist as well, uninterested in seeing his country become a Soviet satrap. Relations between the two countries steadily deteriorated. Still, Stalin had been able to use the presence or proximity of his armies and the prestige built up by communists in the resistance to establish a vast sphere of Soviet influence. By 1946, Churchill could speak—in a famous address delivered in the unlikely location of Fulton, Missouri—of a communist and anticommunist Europe divided by an "iron curtain."

Stalin's transformation of most east European and Balkan nations into mere Soviet satellites was a ruthless act of political expansionism, undertaken solely according to the dictates of what he conceived to be Russian national interest. Simply put, he used Soviet power to replace independents and potential enemies with those who would obey orders from Moscow. What Stalin had trouble understanding was why this behavior provoked so much hostility in the west, since his former allies there seemed to be doing precisely the same sort of thing.

In Italy, Anglo-American military authorities tried to ignore the Italian resistance council (with its large communist contingent). Instead, having cleared the fascists out, they attempted to create their own puppet government while conspicuously failing to aid communist partisans who were fighting the retreating Germans in the north. (As a result, the Germans decimated the helpless resistance groups there.) In Greece, the anti-

---

* Czechoslovakia proved less tractable and would necessitate a communist coup in 1948. (See Chapter 15.)

communist policy of the liberating armies was equally pronounced, and Stalin stood by his October 1944 agreement with Churchill as British forces repressed communist legions in the Greek resistance movement.

Thus the transition from hot war to cold was nearly imperceptible, although the two conflicts were of course vastly different. In the Cold War, there was hardly any illusion that the European states, of east or west, were anything like equal partners with the superpowers. Although Europe would continue to be the site of important events in the postwar era, it would be some time before Europeans precipitated them.

15 / Europe in the Postwar World

World War II facilitated the creation of a new structure for international politics. In the tense atmosphere of Cold War confrontation between the two military superpowers, the United States and the Soviet Union, no European nation could hope to play more than a subordinate role. Although the Cold War was frequently waged on European soil, the principal combatants were Russians or Americans. Increasingly, the political decisions made in London or Paris or Prague were dictated by interests in or pressures from Washington and Moscow. Europe's influence was further diminished by the convergence of the Cold War with the powerful currents of the colonial independence movements in Africa and Asia. Decolonization sometimes escalated to the level of international crisis when local nationalist movements took on a Marxist coloration, so that once again Europeans experienced intervention from one or both of the superpowers. The post-1945 generation was thus one of increasing frustration in which Europeans tried to adjust to a world they no longer mastered.

The Cold War in Europe

Most Americans are familiar with one version of how the Cold War began. Marxist ideology, so runs this version, was bent on nothing less than the total eradication of capitalism and the communist conquest of the entire world. Thus Stalin's ambitions were indistinguishable from Hitler's, just as Soviet totalitarianism was scarcely distinguishable from the Nazi variety. The only obstacle between Stalin and democracy was the power of the United States, which reluctantly but decisively answered the call from free peoples everywhere. The Americans had at least

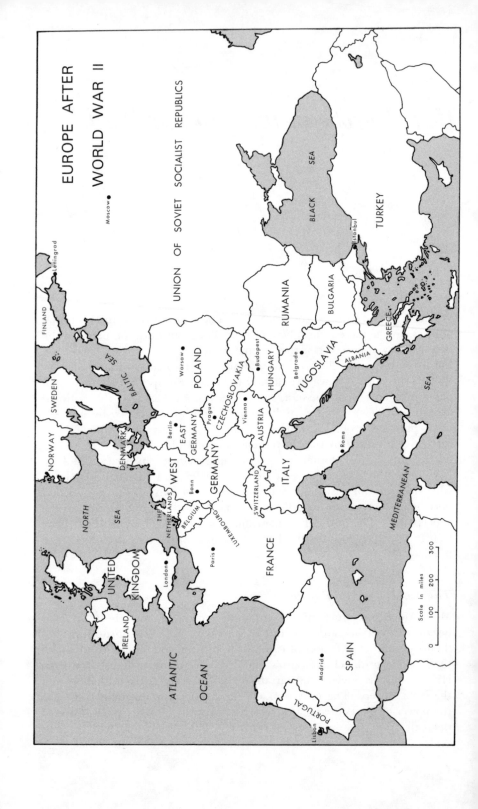

EUROPE AFTER
WORLD WAR II

UNION OF SOVIET SOCIALIST REPUBLICS

Moscow

Leningrad

FINLAND

NORWAY

SWEDEN

BALTIC SEA

DENMARK

POLAND

Warsaw

Berlin

EAST GERMANY

WEST GERMANY

Prague

CZECHOSLOVAKIA

Bonn

THE NETHERLANDS

BELGIUM

LUXEMBOURG

FRANCE

Paris

SWITZERLAND

AUSTRIA

Vienna

Budapest

HUNGARY

RUMANIA

YUGOSLAVIA

Belgrade

ITALY

Rome

ALBANIA

BULGARIA

GREECE

BLACK SEA

Istanbul

TURKEY

MEDITERRANEAN

SEA

SPAIN

Madrid

PORTUGAL

Lisbon

UNITED KINGDOM

London

IRELAND

ATLANTIC

OCEAN

NORTH SEA

Scale in miles

0   100   200   300

learned the lesson of the 1930's: totalitarian aggression would have to be met with firmness; there would be no more Munichs. Therefore, when the Soviets engaged in subversion—in Greece, in western Europe, in Korea—the Americans intervened in one form or another. American statesmen increasingly came to define their role in such phrases as "leadership of the free world."

It often comes as a shock to Americans accustomed to this version that there is another one. Americans have long looked upon communists in general and Russian communists in particular as their enemy, and one does not customarily adopt the viewpoint or perspective of the enemy. But when one views the origins of the Cold War from the Soviet perspective, a rather different view emerges. The Anglo-American treatment of the Italian and Greek communist partisans and President Truman's abrupt cancellation of Lend Lease aid to Russia immediately upon the cessation of hostilities in Europe were hardly gestures of friendship. The Americans were indignant at the extension of Soviet influence through eastern Europe, but were impervious to references concerning the Monroe Doctrine and United States influence in Latin America. Truman was not above meddling in the politics of independent states, as when he pressured the French and Italian governments to evict the communist members of their respective coalition cabinets early in 1947.

From the Soviet perspective, American policy in 1947 became increasingly provocative and threatening. The Greek communists had regrouped and were waging a troublesome insurrection. They were receiving aid from the communist governments in neighboring Yugoslavia, Bulgaria, and Albania, but not—it now appears—from the Soviet Union. Although Greece had been deemed to fall within the British sphere of influence, the new British government was in severe financial straits. Forced to make military cutbacks, it had to announce that it could no longer take responsibility for the defense of Greek democracy. (The Greek government was in fact a right-wing military dictatorship.) At this point, Truman intervened, proclaiming that the United States would not only provide massive injections of aid for Greece, but would also "help free peoples to maintain their institutions and their national integrity against aggressive movements that seek to impose on them totalitarian regimes." Greece being rather closer to the borders of the Soviet Union than to those of the United States, to whose security the Greek communists did not seem to pose an immediate threat, it is no wonder that Soviet observers might view the Truman Doctrine as potentially offensive rather than defensive.

Much the same interpretation appeared to fit the European Recovery Plan, better known as the Marshall Plan (for the American Secretary of State who announced it in the spring of 1947). Postwar economic reconstruction was proceeding sluggishly in Europe, and was further impeded by a savage winter in 1946–47. Fuel shortages led directly to an energy crisis which threatened to cut industrial production. In response, Secretary George C. Marshall offered to place American resources at the disposal of precarious European economies, and shortly thereafter Congress appropriated $17 billion for both grants and loans. Marshall's original conception of the program was generous: aid would be available to all who applied, regardless of a government's political makeup. Stalin, who seems in any event to have been given to bouts of paranoia, regarded the Marshall Plan with suspicion—especially since it came just weeks after the enunciation of the Truman Doctrine. Convinced that it was a form of economic imperialism, he scotched plans in Poland and Czechoslovakia to apply for aid. In the meantime, American policy was beginning to justify his suspicions. Since Stalin was unwilling to accept aid for his satellites, American policy makers determined to confine the Marshall Plan to "safe" western European democracies and justified the program to Congress on the grounds that it would further defend these nations against communist encroachment.

In the face of what he deemed to be pressure, Stalin moved to the offensive himself. In the autumn of 1947, he inspired the reestablishment of the old Communist International, under the name of the Cominform, in order to unify and coordinate the activities of Europe's communist parties. In November, the new mood of militancy surfaced in France, where the communist-dominated labor unions attempted a general strike which it was widely supposed was only the prelude to insurrection. The government ultimately subdued the strikers, but few persons supposed that the communists were about to lapse into inactivity. In February 1948, these fears were justified when a communist coup d'état toppled the democratic government of Czechoslovakia and installed a puppet regime. Thereafter, every vague flex of communist agitation inspired apprehension of what came to be known as a *coup de Prague.*

The next battlefield appeared to be Italy, where an alliance of communists and socialists prepared for spring legislative elections. It was widely assumed that their victory would bring the Stalinization of Italy, and democratic nations counted it a major victory when the left coalition failed to poll even one-third of the vote. Later in 1948, general strikes in both Italy and France aborted. Suddenly, attention switched to Germany, where Russian provocation demanded the physical presence of the Americans.

At war's end in 1945, Germany had been divided into four occupation zones, administered respectively by the Soviet Union, the United States, Great Britain, and France. The city of Berlin was similarly divided, although it lay far within the Soviet zone itself. The occupying powers, who became embroiled in a variety of jurisdictional squabbles, soon discovered themselves at odds over the future of Germany—the length of occupation, the shape of the German government, and so forth. When the Soviets found that their own vision was plainly not shared by the western allies, and after disputes between the Russians and the municipal government of Berlin, they resorted to intimidation, choking off all ground access from the western zones to Berlin itself in June 1948. Air traffic was not controlled, however, and the British and Americans immediately began a massive airlift. Over the next eleven months, nearly 200,000 flights brought the Berliners their food and fuel. In May 1949, Stalin finally acknowledged the pointlessness of the blockade, and it was lifted.

American power and determination had thus won a substantial victory, and there were signs that the communist offensive was stalling. The Greek insurgents were on the run, and by autumn 1949 the established government had restored order. In Yugoslavia, Tito showed little taste for mere satellite status and tried to stake out neutral ground between the two camps in the Cold War; by early 1949, it was plain he was not taking orders from Moscow. The Americans were swift to follow up these advantages by constructing a massive military alliance on the European continent. The North Atlantic Treaty Organization, first established in the spring of 1949, ultimately embraced fifteen states as distant as Canada and Turkey, as discrepant in power as Iceland and the United States. Though all members contributed troops and material, NATO was unmistakably an American creature. The United States carried the major financial burden and an American was the organization's supreme commander.

Again, the question of perspective is critical. For most Americans, NATO was simply a line of defense, an instrument for blunting any Soviet attack upon the west. For the Soviets, NATO was an ominous warning: after all, these troops stood on European soil, and no Atlantic ocean separated them from the Russian borders.* It should not therefore have been surprising when Stalin's successors (after his death in March 1953) treated the east European satellites which buffered Russia from NATO troops with brutal possessiveness.

Stalin's demise touched off more than mere jockeying for position in the upper levels of the Soviet administration. His last years had been accompanied by a variety of shakeups and purges which seemed an overture to the reintroduction of the domestic terror of the 1930's. (See Chapter 13.) When the dictator finally expired, a struggle between old-line

* Soviet leaders may well have wondered what the American reaction would be should Russians have located weapons of war in such close proximity to the United States. In 1962, they got an answer, when President John F. Kennedy flirted with nuclear war after Soviet missiles were discovered in Cuba.

Stalinists and opponents of terrorism ensued. The partisans of a certain relaxation of police-state rule emerged victorious; principal among them was the new Communist party chairman, Nikita Khrushchev. By February 1956, Khrushchev was sufficiently secure to launch a rather remarkable anti-Stalinist movement at the Twentieth Annual Party Congress in Moscow. He flayed Stalin for having created a cult of personality and vaguely promised a certain loosening up of the dictatorial government.

Khrushchev's program of de-Stalinization rapidly generated expectations far beyond the scope of his own plans. That summer, a strike in Posnan, Poland, suddenly escalated into a broad and angry protest against the rigidity of government control. In response, the ruling elites purged themselves of their most notoriously Stalinist elements and brought to power a man known as much for his Polish nationalism as for his communist principles, Wladislaw Gomulka. Polish loyalty to the Soviet Union was a cornerstone of Russian policy, and Gomulka probably averted Russian intervention only by reaffirming that loyalty. In October 1956, reformist simmerings in Hungary boiled over, and there took on an even more explicitly anti-Soviet flavor. Demonstrations turned quickly into riots, and a number of officials closely identified with the repressive regime were assaulted and killed. A group of liberal communists, under Imre Nagy, took power and immediately asserted Hungary's independence from the Soviet Union, whereupon Khrushchev responded with what amounted to armed invasion. Soviet tanks cruised into Budapest and ultimately put down the riots and evicted the liberal-nationalist government. Nagy was shot, many of his associates imprisoned, and a pliable puppet installed in his place. Khrushchev's intervention, widely interpreted at the time as a reflection of communism's inflexible insistence upon ideological uniformity, was actually more in the nature of traditional great-power diplomacy. The east European satellites were a crucial part of the Russian defense system; indeed, they were militarily allied to the Soviet Union in the Warsaw Pact, an eastern counterpart to NATO. Khrushchev, like Stalin before him, was convinced that Russian national interests and security demanded that these east European buffers be firmly under Soviet influence. His concern was for foreign policy loyalty, not ideological purity.

The European Cold War was not a simple confrontation which happened all at once. Rather, it was a dialectical process, full of distorted perceptions and falsely interpreted intentions, with each side responding to the other rather than setting out on a predetermined policy. For present purposes, it is important to point out that the Europeans (excluding, of course, the Russians) played a relatively minor role in it. The European members of NATO and of the Warsaw Pact each had their cold warriors, to be sure; but initiative, influence, and final authority resided in Moscow and Washington.

Ultimately, this situation became intolerable. A certain tour guide in Copenhagen during the early 1960's always made it a point to take foreign tourists past the American and Soviet embassies, which were on the same city block, and to point out that between the two buildings lay a cemetery. European leaders during the 1960's became increasingly concerned to establish some degree of foreign policy independence, though usually without completely forsaking the support of American arms. The most vigorous champion of such a policy was Charles de Gaulle, President of France after 1958. But de Gaulle had his counterparts in communist countries, where the 1960's saw cracks in the Stalinist monolith and concerted efforts in Czechoslovakia and Rumania to follow something like Tito's path toward genuine independence and neutralism. (See Chapter 16.)

The End of Empire

European imperial expansion had originally encountered resistance and provoked prenationalist stirrings throughout Africa and Asia. The experience of imperial rule did more to turn those stirrings into mature independence movements. Especially in Africa, colonial rule forced formerly disparate clans and groupings under a common administration and began to forge at least a degree of unity where none had existed before. Moreover, colonialism meant at least the partial Europeanization of the indigenous elite—exposure to European mores, education, and political ideas, especially nationalism. To the degree that European powers allowed or encouraged a European education for the local populations, they were preparing nationalist movements, whether they meant to or not.

Nationalist movements had already begun to develop in Asia and the middle east during the 1920's and 1930's, but World War II gave them a decisive impetus. The war temporarily weakened British and French control over their southeast Asian possessions during the period of Japanese occupation, and permanently weakened the western powers' ability to control a worldwide empire. At war's end, there was general, if vague, consensus in Britain and France that the old modes of imperial rule would give way before some greater or lesser degree of self-government.

The British had already made such a commitment eight years before the war. According to the Statute of Westminster, promulgated in 1931, the British government anticipated that its overseas possessions would ultimately achieve autonomous status within a Commonwealth bound together by common recognition of the crown and by certain mutually advantageous trade arrangements. In one sense, this agreement was only the elaboration of what had been imperial policy in the nineteenth century, when the mother country had granted self-government within the Empire to Canada and Australia. But the Statute of Westminster made a commitment in principle only; it did not establish a timetable for self-government nor did it prescribe specific conditions which colonial dominions would have to meet before being granted autonomy. Much depended, therefore, upon the play of political forces within Britain and within its respective possessions.

Probably the most important development in this regard was the fall of Churchill's Conservative government in July 1945. This astounding political reversal, coming at the victorious conclusion of the war, had resulted from the growing sense in the British electorate that the postwar period would have to bring substantial social and economic reforms. While the Conservatives were not totally averse to certain fundamental changes, the Labor party seemed the more likely candidate for leadership in these circumstances. Labor, under Clement Attlee, was a broadly based party with a socialist, but not revolutionary Marxist wing. Atlee's government proceeded to undertake substantial economic changes, including the nationalization of certain industries, the institution of a sweeping National Health Service, and drastic alterations in the tax structure. But the Laborites were also strongly committed to accelerating the process of decolonization, in part on principle, and in part because Britain's slender and shrinking economic resources no longer permitted the upkeep of a vast empire.

The first step came in the middle east, when Britain granted independence to little Transjordan * in 1946. The same year, Ceylon received virtual self-government, joining the Commonwealth as an independent nation in 1948. But the major step came in 1947, when the British relinquished what had been their most important imperial possession for nearly two centuries (and what had also become the world's second most populous country). Even though India had become increasingly self-governing prior to the war, the Conservatives had been reluctant to part with so major a possession before absolutely necessary, and even went so far as to jail militant nationalist leaders. The Labor government, however, was determined to grant complete independence as quickly as possible, especially as peaceful but troublesome agitation mounted under the guidance of Mahatma Gandhi, the skilled and revered practitioner of political nonviolence. First, Indian nationalists were bent upon creating a republic, which would have been in violation of the letter of the Statute

---

* Later enlarged at the expense of Palestine and renamed Jordan.

of Westminster. In order to keep India within the Commonwealth (to which Gandhi and his first lieutenant, Nehru, were amenable for economic reasons), the Statute had to be duly altered in order to allow the inclusion of republics. More troublesome was the religious conflict on the subcontinent between Hindus and Moslems. The vocal Moslem minority insisted upon an autonomous nation-state of its own, lest the newly independent India find itself plunged into civil war. Therefore, the British government carved sections out of northern India for the Moslem population which wished to center there, thus creating the wholly artificial but perhaps unavoidable state of Pakistan. These arrangements were finally concluded in 1947, and represented a major success for colonial nationalism everywhere.

By the time Churchill and the Conservatives returned to office in 1951, there was no way to halt the rush of decolonization. But now the focus shifted to Africa, where nationalist movements were also beginning to blossom. In 1957, the "model" colony of the Gold Coast received independence, whereupon it took the name of Ghana; it was followed in 1960 by Nigeria, both nations joining the Commonwealth. Still, the Conservatives were determined that they would *grant* independence; it would not be wrested from them. When a terrorist secret society known as the Mau Mau tried to force the British out of Kenya in the mid-1950's, colonial authorities responded with prompt repression. But once the Mau Mau movement had subsided, the British swiftly resorted to conciliation with what it regarded as the "responsible" Kenyan leaders and soon negotiated arrangements for independence.

Self-government in British colonial territories was promoted in part by a dose of political realism in the mother country and by recognition that world empire was no longer feasible for postwar Britain. But it was also facilitated by the style of British colonial administration. There had always been a strain of racism in European imperialism, but the British made certain attempts to overcome its worst effects by systematically training Africans and Asians in the skills necessary for autonomous rule. These efforts doubtless had a paternalistic flavor which native nationalists would find unpalatable. Yet when the British finally vacated their overseas territories, more often than not they left behind responsible and experienced leadership.

The French experience in decolonization was rather more painful and disruptive than the British. The postwar French government was far more reluctant to part with overseas possessions than the British Labor party. Although France had transformed its empire into a French "Union" which ostensibly had similar purposes to those of the British Commonwealth, in fact the machinery of the Union made self-government and independence far more difficult to achieve. Territories which the French had only recently acquired, such as Syria and Lebanon (held as mandates under the League of Nations after World War I), they swiftly relinquished in 1945. Older colonies, in Africa and southeast Asia, they clung to more tenaciously. Consequently, native nationalist movements stepped up their pressure, and in the long run the Union unraveled, with most of the former members seeking unqualified independence.

One area where French and British policy converged was in the Mediterranean. Britain held the territory of Palestine, which it had designated as early as 1917 as a future "national home" for European Jews. Throughout the interwar years, Jews migrated to Palestine in large numbers, a process which naturally continued after 1945. The British delayed on fulfilling their promise, however, since the prospect of a Jewish state in the heart of the middle east provoked angry threats from neighboring Arab nationalists as well as the Palestinian Arab population. Finally, in 1948, the state of Israel was born, and almost immediately besieged by Arab forces.

Seven years later, the British terminated their last major commitment in the area by ending their control over the Suez Canal, which they ceded to the group of European stockholders who "rightfully" owned it. The Egyptians, under their new president Gamal Abdel Nasser, understandably felt that the Canal belonged to them; it was flanked on both sides, after all, by Egyptian territory. In 1956, Nasser seized Suez. For Britain, joined by Israel, it was a convenient pretext for moving against aggressive and disruptive Arab nationalism. French interests were also involved, however, since the Egyptians were sending aid to the Arab rebels in the French colony of Algeria. Thus, in early November 1956, an Anglo-French expeditionary force parachuted into Suez, with the aim of not only reestablishing European control over the Canal but also of marching on Cairo and dispatching the Nasser government. Predictably, the Soviet Union—which had been trying to gain a toehold in the Mediterranean—came to the diplomatic defense of Egypt. But, in a rare display of agreement with its Cold War antagonist, the United States also took a firm stand against this recrudescence of nineteenth-century strong-arm imperialism. The French and British were forced to back down, and a United Nations international force assumed control of the Canal. If anything, the blatant European intervention further solidified nationalism—not only in the Arab world, but throughout Africa and Asia as well.

Decolonization and the Cold War

Colonial independence movements—whether Arab, sub-Saharan, or Asian—were almost always nationalist first of all. But, in the conditions of mid-twentieth century Europe, it would have been surprising had they not taken on at least some Marxist coloration. The major colonial powers, Britain and France, were both aligned with the western bloc in the Cold War, both identified with a capitalist economic tradition (in spite of the fact that they had each nationalized important industries after World War II). Marxism, which closely identified imperialism and capitalism, was the major ideological antagonist of the western democracies in Europe. Moreover, the economically underdeveloped nations of Africa and Asia were anxious to modernize as rapidly as possible. The socialist model of industrialization, exemplified by the centralized planning and swift progress in the Soviet Union, seemed to make more sense for these areas than the somewhat more nonchalant modernization of the capitalist countries. Besides, the Soviet Union—and later, Communist China—were usually ready both to aid incipient nationalist movements in western colonies and to give economic assistance to ideologically sympathetic governments. For all these reasons, it was more or less natural that colonial nationalists would attempt to graft Marxism onto their nationalist programs.

Decolonization was a difficult enough experience in itself. When Cold War conflicts cut across colonial conflicts, however, the whole process became dangerously explosive. While the British gave ground before nationalist agitation, they balked at withdrawing in the face of communist pressure. When a partially communist guerrilla movement tried to force them out of Malaysia in the 1950's, they responded with a vigorous military counterattack. In 1960, the Belgians abruptly withdrew from the Congo after having made few preparations for self-government. Congolese politics quickly deteriorated into chaos; a Marxist-Nationalist movement under Patrice Lumumba vied for influence with various pro-western forces. As soon as it became clear that both the Russians and the Chinese were fishing in these troubled waters, the United States quickly sought to counteract their influence (though American intervention was limited to aid and advisory personnel operating through United Nations channels).

The most troublesome case of postwar decolonization became inextricably entangled with Cold War politics almost from the very beginning. French involvement in Indo-China stretched back into the 1860's; by the end of the nineteenth century, the French had extended their influence throughout Vietnam, Laos, and Cambodia. During World War II, Japanese occupation of the region substantially weakened French authority. To complicate matters, the principal anti-Japanese partisan movement was led by a Vietnamese nationalist and communist, Ho Chi Minh. In 1945, it appeared as though the expulsion of the Japanese would be followed by a transition to Vietnamese independence under Ho's leadership, and the French even made some vague commitments to this effect. The

French began to drag their feet, however, and when Ho continued in 1946 to act as though he took prior French statements seriously, French forces in northern Vietnam tried to crush his movement with an armed attack.

Ho and his followers, known as the Viet Minh, retreated into the hinterland, but only to regroup for large-scale guerrilla activities. By combining hit-and-run military tactics with a cogent political appeal to Vietnamese nationalism (and against the European presence), the Viet Minh gradually extended their influence throughout the area. The French soon escalated the festering war into an affair of national honor and justified their growing commitments in Vietnam with Cold War arguments about holding back the red tide. Such arguments were increasingly persuasive as the east-west conflict spread to Asia, with the final success of Mao Tse-tung's revolution in China in 1949 and the outbreak of war between North and South Korea the following year. The United States government, stunned by the "loss" of China from the western camp, was ready to see the war in Vietnam as merely another dimension of the struggle which stretched from Korea around the globe to Berlin.

By 1954, the Vietnamese war had proceeded past the point where the French were not winning (and therefore in a sense were losing), to the point where Viet Minh victory was in sight. A major French force blundered into an indefensible position at Dienbienphu, where their enemy won a decisive victory. The armistice concluded shortly thereafter; and the peace negotiations whereby Vietnam was divided into a communist state in the north under Ho and a pro-western state in the south were widely viewed in the west as a major setback in the Cold War. But the Vietnamese war was by no means over. In the early 1960's, there developed in the south a coalition composed of communists, partisans of Vietnamese national unification, and various dissident factions which opposed the pro-western government of South Vietnam. This National Liberation Front, which ultimately received support from the north, began waging a civil war in the south which was really an extension of the struggle begun in 1946. France no longer held responsibility for affairs in the area, and it was left to the United States to attempt to stem what it saw as a tide of communist aggression. In early 1965, the Americans began massive infusions of troops into Vietnam, somehow hoping that they could win where the French had lost.

No postwar political event has set off greater reverberations than the Vietnamese war of 1946–73; for present purposes, the impact upon France deserves special attention. The French government which emerged from the liberation of 1944–45 was a parliamentary democracy, weakened by the absence of a decisive executive power and by a multiparty system which made durable coalition governments impossible. Cabinets rarely lasted beyond a few months, giving this Fourth Republic in France's history a decided air of instability and uncertainty. Defeat in the Vietnamese war was a major shock at a time when national pride was visibly fragile. Thus, when a nationalist revolt broke out in Algeria in 1954—the same year as Dienbienphu—there was a broad consensus in France that this oldest major French colony would remain a French colony.

Arab nationalism in north Africa was hardly confined to Algeria, and independence movements also bubbled up in Tunisia and Morocco. France relinquished these possessions in the mid-1950's; but Algeria was something else again. The French had begun to conquer Algeria in 1830 and to colonize it shortly thereafter. In the thin, rich strip of the country which ran along the Mediterranean, French *colons* (or colonists) quickly developed themselves into an elite which, after several generations, thought of itself as Algerian as much as French. The *colons* had of course dispossessed the Arabs not only of self-government, but of the richest land as well. By the mid-twentieth century, the Arabs constituted a classic example of an underclass. Consequently, Algerian independence was likely to mean the overthrow of the *colon* class as well as a blow to French prestige and national pride. When an Arab nationalist movement raised the banner of revolt, in the backwash of Dienbienphu, France fought back ferociously.

Wars of national liberation, in which nonwhite populations are fighting on their own soil for independence from white imperialists, afford few advantages to the Europeans. Guerrilla warfare is hard to stamp out, especially when the guerrillas can virtually disappear into an indigenous population which sympathizes with them. The French army thought that it had learned its lesson from Vietnam, depending upon mobile special forces units which employed many guerrilla tactics themselves. Even so, by the late 1950's, the war was not going well for France, and a powerful antiwar movement welled up among the mainland French. By 1958, the nation was polarizing dangerously, and the unstable republican government could neither deal with the war decisively nor command much confidence from its citizens. The crisis came to a head in May 1958, when French army units in Algiers—despairing of vigorous support from civilian authorities in Paris—took over the city and threatened what amounted to civil war. It was a moment when forceful leadership was essential, and a combination of desperate public opinion and secret political negotiations decided that such leadership was only to be found in Charles de Gaulle.

De Gaulle, a retired army general, had led the anti-Nazi and anticollaborationist French forces from abroad during World War II. With the Liberation, he returned to assume the Presidency of a Provisional Government. But his dislike of parliamentary (as opposed to executive) rule and his inability to work with the established parties in France's Fourth Republic led to his resignation in 1946. For twelve years, he languished in retirement from politics, periodically expressing his contempt for what he regarded as a spineless republican regime. His wartime exploits, however, made him as close to a living national hero as the French had; and his lack of affiliation with any of the traditional parties meant that he was not identified with the unpopular policies of the Fourth Republic. Therefore, de Gaulle assumed office as the last premier of the republic; shortly thereafter, he proposed a new constitution which created a Fifth Republic, with de Gaulle in the office of president.

The reemergence of de Gaulle in French politics turned out to have worldwide repercussions. In the first place, although de Gaulle had been the choice of French nationalists determined to hold on to Algeria, the President came to realize that the war was a losing proposition which could only further drain French national resources and tarnish its prestige. His decision to liquidate the war took time to evolve and brought him squarely into conflict with army leaders in Algeria, who (in alliance with *colon* elements) inspired several assassination attempts on de Gaulle and very nearly plunged France into civil war. But by 1962, de Gaulle had overcome resistance among his own countrymen, brought the war to an end, and granted Algeria complete independence. It was the last major struggle of decolonization involving a European power, and to all intents and purposes brought the age of European imperialism to an end.

De Gaulle's Algerian policy was born of expediency; it is doubtful if there has even been a more fervent French nationalist. In particular, he chafed at the subordinate role France played in international affairs to the United States. All of de Gaulle's sympathies in the Cold War were on the western side, yet he regarded that struggle as a means by which the Americans could treat the French as a third-rate power. Even before he had liquidated the Algerian war, de Gaulle set out on a foreign policy which would establish French—and, by extension, European—independence from American influence.

Converging with de Gaulle's efforts in this regard were the various approaches being made by continental Europe to some degree of cooperation in economic matters. The end of overseas empire and the Cold War had dwarfed the traditional European great powers. World War II proved beyond doubt that military supremacy lay with the United States and the Soviet Union. Once postwar reconstruction had been achieved, economic power seemed the most likely route back to status and influence in world affairs. Accordingly, the efforts to integrate the European economy and coordinate economic decision making took on the greatest importance.

16 / Integration and Coexistence

The Cold War and the decolonization of Europe threatened the eclipse of Europe. Two major developments of the postwar world—both still tentative and ongoing as of the 1970's—have given indications of reversing, or at least halting, that trend. The first is the groping efforts of the western European nations to move toward some degree of integration. The second is the appearance of cracks in the great Cold War monoliths, both east and west. If the western European nations could reestablish themselves as a collective economic power to be reckoned with, then they might stake out viable ground between the two superpowers. By the same token, as the Cold War blocs of the 1950's began to splinter, opportunities began to emerge for the European states to follow policies independent of the great antagonists. Before investigating these developments in greater detail, however, it is necessary to give some attention to the political and social framework in which the individual nations functioned.

People's Democracy and the Welfare State

"People's Democracy" was the rather grotesque euphemism given to the Soviet satellites of eastern Europe. Of the extent to which they were democratic, there can be little doubt. The governments of the communist states were all rigidly centralized dictatorships; politics was the affair of the bureaucracy, itself the creation of the only party recognized by law. Elections were a laughable charade. The press was an arm of the state. Any eastern Europeans harboring illusions about their political autonomy could contemplate the example of Hungary in 1956. Yugoslavia alone of the communist nations had been able to wriggle free of Moscow's suffocating grip; yet even Tito's government was not entirely free of domestic Stalinism.

On the other hand, Sovietization did bring profound socioeconomic changes to eastern and southern Europe. With the exception of parts of Czechoslovakia, these states were heavily agricultural, many of them dominated by massive estates concentrated in a few hands. Agrarian reform was the most pressing domestic issue in the postwar years, and the Communists met it head-on. Solutions varied from place to place—collectivization, the creation of cooperatives, outright grants to peasants of small farms which would be held as private property. Everywhere, however, the large landowners were expropriated and the *latifundia* broken up in one of the major social revolutions of modern times. At the same time, forced modernization of the economy took place; agriculture was mechanized; and industrial production vastly overhauled. Although these developing economies gave scant attention to the manufacture of consumer goods, they made every effort to provide a high rate of employment. The very worst sorts of poverty were eliminated, and while the standard of living achieved often fell short of modest by western standards, the government still assumed the responsibility for social services—basically, education, health, and general welfare. At the cost of political freedom, the People's Democracies made some strides toward answering the social needs of their peoples.

In noncommunist Europe, the early postwar era was a sort of heyday for parties of a reformist cast. Summer 1945 elections in Britain brought to power the Labor party, herbivorous socialists as distinguished from the carnivores of revolutionary communism. Labor's program did not exactly call for a classless society, but it did envisage total "social security": that is, the state would insure its citizens against the prohibitive costs of health care, disability, unemployment, accident, education, and old age. Government would guarantee that all persons would have access to these services with but a nominal outlay. The bill would be paid by restructuring the economy, the tax system, and the prevailing distribution of wealth. In its six years in power, Labor set about funding its social insurance programs by nationalizing a number of important industries (coal, steel, electricity, gas, railroads, airlines) and by sharply graduating taxes—especially inheritance taxes—so as to strike at the means by which the very wealthy perpetuated their status from generation to generation. Labor also argued that state operation would result in more stringent management and thus greater efficiency. As a result, the British worker found that he was buffered from extreme financial disaster—in the case, for example, of serious illness or disabling accident—while at the same time the government took a startlingly large bite out of his regular paycheck.

Of the major western powers, Britain's experiment with the so-called welfare state was the most ambitious. Continental socialists had similar dreams, but lacked Labor's decisive parliamentary majority. Frequently, they had to work in some sort of coalition with a new species of reformism, Christian Democracy. The Christian Democratic parties had sprung up largely during the wartime resistance movements, combining a vaguely leftist social platform with Christian moralism and resistance to fascism. As the enemy switched to "godless communism," Christian Democrats eased gradually to the right. In any event, they were an important centrist force in postwar politics, an attractive alternative to radical leftists and discredited conservatives alike. Independently in West Germany, and together with moderate socialists and communists in France and Italy, they helped construct social insurance programs on something like the British model, though rather less extensive. In most cases, these programs too entailed some measure of nationalization—at a minimum, the railways, airlines, and public utilities.* By the time that traditional conservative parties had reestablished substantial political influence, in the 1950's, the welfare state had become firmly rooted.

One of the first protests raised against the welfare state was that it amounted to socialism. It is true that state assumption of the responsibility for social services and the nationalization of hitherto private industry were parts of the socialist program. But it should also be noted that the European welfare state varied from place to place in its extent; nowhere was all industry nationalized. Moreover, the socialists who created these various programs were always of the moderate, democratic, nonrevolutionary variety; and their legislation was either supported or accepted (though sometimes reluctantly) by non- and antisocialists. Indeed, in retrospect, the welfare state looks less like "creeping socialism" than like a typical liberal response to pressure from the extreme left, granting partial reform in order to avoid full-scale revolution. Throughout western Europe, social insurance schemes have proved entirely consistent with the continuation of capitalism (unlike the case of the People's Democracies).

A government deeply engaged in administering far-flung social services and managing key industries will naturally find itself physically enlarging. One of the more controversial features of the welfare state was the expansion of the bureaucracy which it entailed and the implications of this process for life in a democracy. Increasing segments of government authority, that is to say, fell under the executive; more and more important decisions were being made by bureaucratic officials effectively (if not constitutionally) independent of the democratically elected legislature. It

* The most sweeping experiments in welfare statism took place in Scandinavia. In Sweden, for example, state expenditures on social security account for close to 20 percent of the total national income.

is something like what nineteenth-century scientism would have called a law of nature that bureaucracy, as it grows, becomes more rigid, less responsive to the persons it is supposed to serve, and concerned most of all with the preservation of its own power and prerogative. At the same time, the state administration finds its power growing, both because its jurisdiction spreads and because it employs such large numbers of people. The implications of the whole process have by no means revealed themselves, and the welfare state gives few signs of becoming as thoroughly bureaucratized as the People's Democracies. Still, it seems likely that the traditional politics of liberal parliamentary democracies will certainly be affected.

Reconstruction and Integration

World War II had thoroughly exhausted the economies of the European states, whether by German occupation (and expropriation) or, as in the case of Britain, the devotion of virtually all national resources to the war effort. In eastern Europe, economic reconstruction was a part of the broader programs of social revolution which the new communist governments instituted. A rash of five-year plans and the like, all proceeding from centralized planning agencies, aimed at the modernization of the industrial sector of the economy, where one existed, and the creation of such a sector where one did not. Heavy industry received the main emphasis, which meant employment—but also austerity—for the ordinary consumer: even if a person had a job, his modest wages could hardly purchase goods which were not being produced. Even so, the results of modernization were relatively impressive. East Germany, which had been primarily an agrarian area under conditions of unification, transformed itself into the world's tenth leading industrial power. Rumania, in 1945 counting 80 percent of its population as peasants, relied upon its extensive mineral resources to create a large industrial plant and the consistently highest industrial growth rate of the Soviet-bloc countries. Progress was uneven, and frequently Soviet industrialization took priority over that in the satellites. Nonetheless, a genuine transformation began in the late 1940's (and is still under way).

Reconstruction in the west largely awaited generous infusions of American capital via the Marshall Plan. Only in 1948 did western industrial production begin to approach prewar levels (which, by the 1950's, would be surpassed). But dollars alone did not bring the remarkable economic recovery of the parliamentary democracies, though recovery would probably have been impossible without them. State planning also played an important role.

The role of the state in the "mixed" economies of the west—that is,

those with a large privately owned sector and a smaller but still important public sector—has been rather different from that in the People's
Democracies. The first great experiment in democratic planning came in
France, where its chief advocate was Jean Monnet. The Monnet Plan,
which went into effect in 1946, did not call for dictatorial government
control of the economy. Rather, it envisaged the state and private ownership cooperating in the establishment of production goals, quotas, and
emphases which bore some rational relationship to total national needs.
The government had no powers to make adherence to the plan obligatory, unlike the case of eastern Europe. However, the state did have certain suasive powers and resources of influence which it could exploit to
keep private ownership within the confines of the plan. Chief among
these resources was credit: nationalization had brought certain savings
banks under public control, besides which state treasury officials had the
power to manipulate credit supplies and interest rates. When private industry showed an inclination to move in step with the Monnet Plan, its
managers would find that cheap credit opened up to them, not to mention preferential rates on the purchase of state coal, the use of the railways, and so forth.

The French style of planning has tended to be the norm in western
Europe. Private capitalists, to whom planning has traditionally been
anathema, have generally found it in their interest to accept these innovations. Not only could the state make life inconvenient for them if they
chose to defy planning, but the success of these procedures was their own
justification. Anything which improved the general economic climate improved it for the private sector as well. Five-year plans, formerly a part of
Stalinist rhetoric, began to crop up in such unlikely places as the Netherlands.

Opponents of planning like to point out that the most impressive economic advances of postwar Europe have been undertaken in relative freedom from government meddling. West Germany, the home of the
"economic miracle," had but a skeletal planning bureaucracy during the
period of its most phenomenal advances, which is apparently evidence for
something like the orthodox laissez faire position. On the other hand,
West Germany had—perhaps rather surprisingly—emerged from the war
with less damage to its industrial economy than was generally imagined.
Although people in the west were accustomed to photographs and news-
reels of Berlin reduced to rubble, allied bombing had actually done little
to smash the German industrial plants—which in its turn underwent a
sharp jump in production during the years 1943–45. Where destruction
did take place, the Germans were able to rebuild modern plants with
Marshall Plan aid. Wartime devastation may even have been a prod to
economic growth, particularly by producing a huge demand in the con-

struction and building trades. Besides not starting so far back as many persons supposed, the Germans *did* engage in economic planning. Most of it was conducted, however, by the private sector itself—by professional associations of the largest industrialists and banks which combined the same resources of suasion and influence as government elsewhere. The banks in particular played an important part, emphasizing their concern about where credit was going by appointing watchdog committees to oversee the operation of important private firms.

For better or for worse, and whether desired or not by its advocates, economic planning places increased (and increasing) authority in the hands of the planners, which in most cases has meant in the hands of government bureaucrats. The planning bureaucracy, like the welfare bureaucracy, has ballooned enormously in the past generation, and has created a whole new class of experts in such matters as investment, interest rates, and a variety of arcane technological matters. In the People's Democracies, where it has been an announced goal of public policy to eradicate an overpowerful bourgeoisie, the state bureaucracy has begun to move into the vacuum and to look increasingly like an elite class. In the west, government "technocrats" commanding critical specialized knowledge have seen their jurisdiction and power expand rapidly. Again, as with the growth of the welfare state bureaucracy, increasing numbers of important public decisions are being made not by democratically elected representatives, but by administrative "experts" in the executive branch.

The development of economic cooperation grew out of both the drive for economic reconstruction and the Cold War. As the eastern and western European blocs each drew together politically, diplomatically, and militarily, it was not entirely surprising when economic policy followed suit. In the Soviet bloc, what was viewed as the economic offensive embodied in the Marshall Plan led directly to the creation of COMECON (the Council of Mutual Economic Assistance) in early 1949. Prior to its establishment, the satellite countries had proceeded with their economic plans more or less independently. As a result, all manner of wasteful competition and overlap occurred, which it was part of COMECON's justification to eliminate. The Council, made up of delegates from all the member states,* sets national priorities and goals, and to a degree identifies areas of economic specialization for certain states. Interestingly enough, however, COMECON has no power to impose its plans upon member states, which remain fully independent to pursue their own individual plans. It remains largely a consultative body, putting forth sugges-

---

* USSR, Poland, East Germany, Czechoslovakia, Hungary, Rumania, Bulgaria; Albania, originally a member, dropped out after the development of the Sino-Soviet split, while Yugoslavia never joined.

tions and serving as a clearinghouse for information for states the great bulk of whose international trade is with one another.

In the western bloc, economic cooperation also began during the Marshall Plan era, when the American government—largely for political reasons—urged the beneficiaries of the program to hold down competition detrimental to the economic health of the parliamentary democracies. However, when certain visionaries like Monnet and his countryman Robert Schuman began talking of moving from "cooperation" to "integration," they received nothing but encouragement from the U.S.A. The first significant efforts at integration were prompted in part by foreign policy considerations. As a part of Cold War diplomacy, the Americans had determined to create a sizeable West German armed force within NATO. The idea of a rearmed Germany raised understandable apprehensions in France, which was nonetheless hardly in a position to obstruct the will of the United States. Instead, the French devised a scheme for drawing France and West Germany closer together, and thus hopefully averting antagonisms which might lead to war. Schuman proposed in 1950 to consolidate the French and West German coal and steel industries under a supranational administrative body called the High Authority, which would decide upon price levels and marketing independent of the governments involved. Within a year of its approval in 1951, the Schuman Plan had expanded to include Italy, Belgium, the Netherlands, and Luxembourg. The resultant European Coal and Steel Community was a modest but still remarkably successful foray into economic integration. The member states found that with a marginal concession of their sovereignty they could balance production, maintain acceptable price levels, and ensure adequate distribution.

The next step came in 1957, when the members of the ECSC (who had come to be known as the Six) agreed in the Treaty of Rome to form the European Economic Community. The first priority of the EEC has been to establish a free-trade community among the Six, while also raising tariffs somewhat against the imports of nonmembers. Signatories of the Rome Treaty could thus contemplate a future market, once internal trade barriers had in fact been reduced, of more than 170 million consumers.

It is difficult to know whether to be impressed by the extent of economic integration in western Europe or by the relative lack of progress which has been made since the late 1950's. The ECSC and the EEC, along with a number of minor international agencies which the Six have developed, certainly represent a substantial departure from the situation of the prewar years. On the other hand, the free-trade community envisaged by the Rome Treaty has not yet been achieved: the stated goal of the free circulation of labor, capital, and goods among the member states remains unrealized, though progress toward it goes on. Moreover, the Six have demonstrated a greater ability to agree in principle than to effect those agreements in practice. While there is general consensus, for example, that further economic integration makes little sense without monetary unity, no such policy has been forthcoming.

Part of the difficulty has been that the member states were by no means economic equals. While the elimination of tariffs opened up new markets to European industry, it also threatened to turn over the lion's share of those markets to the most industrially advanced power, West Germany. The specter of integration has also stirred deep nationalist sentiments and raised questions about whether or not a people would remain the masters of their own destiny. The chief spokesman of nationalism during the 1960's was French President Charles de Gaulle. An ardent French nationalist, de Gaulle had no wish to see French national identity submerged within some larger unit. He was deeply committed to the proposition that France could take its place once more as a leading power in the world, and not just be a dwarf in the shadow of the superpowers. Therefore, he tended to think more in terms of France leading a league of western European states than of integrating into some larger union. While de Gaulle was ready to use Europe as a counterbalance to what he regarded as stifling American influence, he was cautious about involving France in further progress toward European integration.

British nationalism and traditional isolation from continental affairs in time of peace also blocked the entry of Great Britain into the EEC. When the Six invited Britain to join their ranks, the Conservative party talked about the compromises to national sovereignty involved and worried about the possible severance of economic ties with the Commonwealth, while the Labor party feared competition from the cheaper continental work force would depress the wages of the British working classes. Instead, the British chose a customs union with Austria, Portugal, the three Scandinavian nations, and Switzerland. Yet the markets thus opened to British goods were less than one-fourth the size of those afforded by the EEC. However, by the time British opinion began to shift and sympathy for joining the EEC ran higher, continental politics themselves had begun to change. In particular, de Gaulle suspected that British entry was nothing more than a wedge for American influence over the EEC, and in January 1963 he vetoed the idea in a dramatic press conference. Only after de Gaulle's death was his more flexible successor, Georges Pompidou, able to negotiate British entry into the EEC, which was achieved in early 1973.

Polycentrism and Coexistence

European integration held out at least the promise that the western states might achieve economic independence from the United States. During the 1960's, political events likewise pointed to a certain loosening of the superpowers' dominance of Europe.

The Soviet grip on the People's Democracies was particularly onerous because it was so firm and so explicit. When efforts were made to shake it, as in Hungary during 1956, the Russian response was brutal and direct. None of the east European states possessed anything like the military resources to withstand Soviet intervention. The opportunity for change arose only when the USSR was confronted with a major challenge to its dominant position among communist states. The successful conclusion to the Chinese revolution in 1949 meant that the world's most populous state was henceforth ruled by communists. But while China and the Soviet Union maintained outwardly congenial relations, the political tone and style of the Maoist and Stalinist regimes differed markedly. Stalin's Russia was rigidly bureaucratized, an authoritarian police state whose highest priority was to keep the ruling authorities in power. Mao's China, facing massive difficulties in socializing and modernizing its economy, was a somewhat more dynamic society. Mao himself felt his people could only accomplish the great tasks before them by maintaining a sharp revolutionary edge and constantly renewing their commitment to sweeping change. Even after the de-Stalinization of the 1950's, it was perhaps inevitable that these styles would clash, that the Chinese would be jealous of their independence and suspicious of what they regarded as Soviet efforts to turn them into Asian satellites.

Maoist criticism of Soviet communism mounted in the 1960's to the point of denouncing the Russian regime as "revisionist," or not authentically revolutionary. It was not so much that this criticism picked up support in Europe; only tiny Albania openly aligned itself with the Chinese. Rather, the very fact of dissension and the inability of the Soviets to treat China as a mere client state suggested that some degree of independence might be possible also for the European People's Democracies, perhaps along the lines of Tito's Yugoslavia. At the same time, communist parties in the western states began to grow restless, to assert their autonomy from Moscow. The Italian communists announced the doctrine of "polycentrism," which simply argued that the communist movement was not a monolith controlled by the Russians. French communists followed suit, though rather less energetically.

The extent to which this restlessness over Soviet domination can proceed in the People's Democracies themselves remains to be seen. In the late 1960's and early 1970's, Rumania appears to be edging cautiously toward greater independence, and there are hints of similar desires in Hungary and Poland. But in 1968, just as in 1956, the Soviet leaders gave ample evidence of the limits of their patience. The Czechoslovakian government, under Alexander Dubcek, had been steadily liberalizing authoritarian rule and relaxing censorship, paying greater attention to consumer goods, and tentatively seeking enlarged contacts with the west. Emboldened by the popularity of these measures, Czech leaders talked increasingly of moving on an independent course toward the socialist future. In August 1968, however, the Soviet Union brought these illusions to an abrupt end: Red Army units marched into Prague, deposed Dubcek and the liberal faction, and installed a puppet regime which revoked many of the reforms. Although the intervention earned the Soviet Union widespread condemnation in world public opinion, Russian leaders were willing to withstand criticism in order to hold their western flank secure. The events of 1968 may not have quashed polycentrism in the other People's Democracies, but they must have given leaders there serious pause.

East European nationalism had its counterpart in the west, where American influence was by no means so direct but was still widely seen as pervasive. De Gaulle was the most abrasive advocate of greater European independence. When he had replaced the shaky Fourth Republic in 1958, American public opinion applauded the advent of a stable new government with a strong executive modeled on the American presidency. By the early 1960's, however, de Gaulle was criticizing the United States in terms regarded as nothing short of anti-American. Although he left no doubt of his ultimate commitment in the ideological conflict between communism and capitalism, he made no secret of his annoyance that American policy took its European allies for granted and treated them like so many very junior partners. He insisted upon France being treated like an equal, and as a symbol of that equality he plunged forward with the construction of an independent nuclear force (which in fact the French budget could ill afford). Later he expelled NATO headquarters, which had been set up outside Paris, from French soil. In terms of power relationships in the world, de Gaulle's actions merely tweaked Uncle Sam's beard rather than bloodying his nose. But they were symptomatic of a new spirit of independence in western Europe.

In part, that spirit of independence arose from the EEC's demonstrable viability, even if only as a customs union, and in part from the softening of Cold War tensions. Even after the Soviet intervention in Czechoslovakia, no one was seriously prepared to argue that Russian invasion of western Europe was a likelihood. The United States and the Soviet Union seemed to move away from violent confrontation after the Cuban missile crisis of 1962, and even began to engage in tentative negotiations to normalize their relationships.* As the world came to seem less like two armed camps facing one another, it became increasingly difficult for the Americans to exact strict foreign policy obedience from its western European allies. European support for the American war in Indo-China during 1965–72 was conspicuous by its absence; characteristically, de Gaulle was one of the chief noncommunist critics of American policy in southeast Asia. Events in the early 1970's only accelerated the process of the softening of Cold War tensions. American President Richard Nixon's forays into summit diplomacy in Moscow and Peking announced that even a politician whose career had been substantially built upon anticommunism was apparently prepared to seek an end to the Cold War. The shakiness of the American dollar as opposed to the robust strength of the German mark showed just how great European economic recovery and progress had been. In short, European emergence from the shadow of the superpowers depends at least as much upon the behavior of the superpowers as it does upon developments within Europe itself.

The Struggle with Affluence

The postwar economic recovery of western Europe was one of the more remarkable revolutions in modern history. From the ravages of war has emerged a modernized, industrialized, urbanizing, and increasingly prosperous civilization. For growing numbers of west Europeans, a degree of comfort—however modest—has become a reality rather than an ideal which hopefully one's children might achieve. For better or for worse, creature comforts which many Americans have taken for granted for a generation—a television set, an automobile, a refrigerator—may soon become commonplace for west Europeans (or at least those who dwell in cities). Correspondingly, the welfare state helps to buffer them from the most debilitating economic disasters. Just how Europeans will cope with this new affluence will probably be answered in the remainder of the twentieth century.

Many social critics feel that affluence has brought in its wake as many problems as it has solved. In the late 1940's, for example, Italian filmmakers like Roberto Rosselini and Vittorio de Sica unflinchingly depicted the poverty and misery of the immediate postwar world. By the early 1960's, the leading Italian filmmakers—such as Michelangelo Antonioni and

---

* One example is the Nuclear Non-Proliferation Treaty of 1965, which would have limited the development of nuclear weapons beyond those states currently possessing such devices (the USA, the USSR, and Great Britain). Significantly, both France and China underscored their determination to assert their independence of the superpowers by refusing to sign the treaty.

Federico Fellini—were probing the moral decay of middle-class society, the stagnation and despair of the spirit in a world of *things*. University students, most of whom came from comfortable middle-class surroundings, bitterly attacked the materialism of capitalist prosperity. Their most articulate spokesmen raged at an educational system which prepared one to be nothing more than technocrat, a cog in the impersonal machine of the welfare bureaucracy, a consumer manipulated by television advertisements, or a psychologist trained to manipulate consumers.

Much of this criticism originated on the political left, but rarely from the communist parties. Like the social democrats of the early twentieth century, the communists of contemporary Europe have discarded revolutionary tactics, if not revolutionary rhetoric. In essence, they are radical critics of the liberal parliamentary regimes who hope that their criticism will help them to extract some greater material benefits for the working classes. Just how conservative the communists have become was graphically demonstrated in France during the student riots and general strike of May–June 1968. Student radicals in Paris occupied a number of university buildings and engaged in running battles with the police. The French Communist party immediately dismissed the demonstrations as mere bourgeois highjinks, without political significance. But in fact the students were expressing a deep dissatisfaction with the Gaullist regime, its stuffy quasi-authoritarianism, its regressive wage policy, its inability to cope with inflation. Young communist workers in a number of factories openly sympathized with the students' anti-Gaullism and prompted a number of wildcat strikes. Eventually, to keep hold of their working-class rank and file, the communists had to join the movement, at least to the extent of declaring a general strike.

But the communists and the student radicals still harbored sharply different purposes, even though both groups hoped that somehow their agitation would bring down the Gaullist regime. The communists were interested first of all in raising the minimum wage and in winning a variety of other material concessions from management and from the government. The students had grander, though also foggier, goals. They urged doing away with "consumer society" and pleaded for a liberation of human creative instincts which were now being dulled by a world devoted mostly to selling and buying. The student regard remained low for the communists, whom they were liable to characterize as "Stalinist creeps."

De Gaulle was ultimately able to put down the student revolt and end the general strike, but at least two implications of the remarkable uprising were clear. First, for all the economic advances that had been made, there remained profound dissatisfaction, and it was located within the very heart of the middle classes—those who had materially benefited most from the advances. Second, the student riots and the general strike had virtually paralyzed France for weeks, leading to widespread speculation that the government would not be able to restore order (and would thus have to resign) and sharply reducing France's industrial production (thus momentarily reducing exports and delivering a severe blow to the currency and the trade balance). But this uprising had struck in what was almost universally regarded as the most stable of all west European governments. What regime, then, was safe? Was stability only an illusion? Historians make poor prophets. In confronting the human experience, their job is to face the other direction. Besides, though every moment in history is one of transition, the present in which this book is written is especially fragile. The political and economic developments which have molded contemporary Europe are still very much an ongoing process, the ends of which are by no means clear. The entire planet appears to be undergoing structural shifts in its economic life, with the dominance of the United States which has characterized so much of the century now in question. The Cold War is also at a delicate and uncertain juncture which is bound to have major implications not merely for Europe, but for all nations. How these and related issues will alter Europe and its place in the world remains to be seen.

This much, however, is clear: political conflict, economic change, and ideological ferment—the broad problems with which Europeans are now grappling—are the same sorts of problems which faced Europeans at the end of the eighteenth century. There are differences, obviously; but they are not so great as to render the study of the earlier era irrelevant to the understanding of the present one.

Suggestions for Further Reading

The following brief bibliographical notes are intended for students whose curiosity may have been stimulated somewhere in the preceding sixteen chapters and who wish to pursue certain subjects further. However, although all the books listed below are more specialized than the present book—dealing, that is, with narrower subjects in greater detail—few of them are technical treatises comprehensible only to specialists. Although most of them were written by professional scholars, they are also generally accessible to intelligent and interested nonhistorians. In most cases, the books contain bibliographies which list the highly specialized works on their subject. By and large, I have tended to favor in these lists the more up-to-date treatments, and have made no effort to offer anything like a "representative" historiographical survey.

Chapter 1 / FRENCH POLITICS

The best short general introduction to Europe in the eighteenth century is C.B.A. Behrens, *The Ancien Regime* (1967). R.R. Palmer's *Age of the Democratic Revolution,* 2 vols. (1959–64), argues, especially in volume one, for the similarity of European (and American) political development in this period. For France itself, Alfred Cobban's *A History of Modern France,* volume I (1963 edition), is still the most useful introduction to the Old Regime and the revolution; volume II carries on the story from 1799. Two excellent general studies of the revolution which go into greater detail than Cobban are Norman Hampson, *A Social History of the French Revolution* (1963), and J.M. Thompson, *The French Revolution* (1943), the latter of which ends with the fall of Robespierre. Georges Lefebvre's *The Coming of the French Revolution* (1947) has been something like a bible for a generation of American students on the origins of 1789; lately it has been challenged on a number of counts, and interested readers should consult Alfred Cobban, *The Social Interpretation of the French Revolution* (1964). On the terror, Robespierre, and the Committee of Public Safety, see George Rude, *The Crowd in the French Revolution* (1959); J.M. Thompson, *Robespierre,* 2 vols. (1936); R.R. Palmer, *Twelve Who Ruled* (1941).

Georges Lefebvre's *The French Revolution,* 2 vols. (1961–64), not only considers domestic events, but the impact of the revolution outside of France as well; Lefebvre's *Napoleon*, 2 vols. (1969), does the same job for the period 1799–1815. Other sources on the imperial interlude are Felix Markham's concise biography, *Napoleon* (1964); Robert Holtman's institutional analysis in *The Napoleonic Revolution* (1967); Pieter Geyl's historiographical study, *Napoleon: For and Against* (1949); and Owen Connelly's *Napoleon's Satellite Kingdoms* (1965).

On the peace of 1814–15 and its aftermath, in the absence of any thoroughly convincing synthesis, see Harold G. Nicolson, *The Congress of Vienna: A Study in Allied Disunity, 1812–1822* (1946), and Henry A. Kissinger, *A World Restored: Metternich, Castlereagh, and the Problems of Peace, 1812–22* (1957). For national histories in the early Restoration period, see the bibliography to chapter 4.

Chapter 2 / BRITISH MACHINES

The best introductions to the early industrial revolution in Britain are E.J. Hobsbawm, *Industry and Empire* (1968), and the second chapter of David S. Landes, *The Unbound Prometheus* (1969), the later chapters of which are valuable for the treatment of the spread and growth of industrial development throughout Europe. Also useful, and providing somewhat different perspectives upon this controversial subject, are T.S. Ashton, *The Industrial Revolution, 1760–1830* (1948), and Phyllis Deane, *The First Industrial Revolution, 1750–1850* (1965). For the social implications of British industrialization, see S.G. Checkland, *The Rise of Industrial Society in England, 1815–1885* (1964); F.M.L. Thompson, *English Landed Society in the Nineteenth Century* (1963); and the immensely exciting work by E.P. Thompson, *The Making of the English Working Class* (1963).

On continental developments, see (besides Landes) A.L. Dunham, *The Industrial Revolution in France* (1955); J.H. Clapham, *The Economic Development of France and Germany, 1815–1914* (1937 edition); W.O. Henderson, *The State and the Industrial Revolution in Prussia* (1958); the early sections of Theodore S. Hamerow, *Restoration, Revolution, Reaction: Economics and Politics in Germany, 1815–1871* (1958); William L. Blackwell, *The Beginnings of Russian Industrialization, 1800–1860* (1968).

Chapter 3 / THE ROMANTIC REVOLT

On eighteenth-century thought, the regnant synthesis is now Peter Gay's *The Enlightenment: An Interpretation*, 2 vols. (1966–69), with a massive bibliography. Many of the issues there discussed in detail may be studied in Gay's earlier and livelier book, *Voltaire's Politics: The Poet as Realist* (1959). There are some provocative inquiries into neoclassicism and romanticism in A.O. Lovejoy's *Essays in the History of Ideas* (1948); for a different sort of approach—one more convinced that the concept of romanticism is meaningful—see Jacques A. Barzun, *Classic, Romantic, and Modern* (1961), and Rene Wellek's *Concepts of Criticism* (1963). The following are studies of romanticism in the several arts: Harold Bloom, *The Visionary Company* (1961), which deals with English poetry from Blake to Keats; Kenneth Clark, *The Gothic Revival* (1963 edition), architecture; E.M. Tillotson, *Novels of the Eighteen-Forties* (1954); Jacques Barzun, *Berlioz and his Century* (1956), a condensation of the author's two-volume study (1950) of the greatest romantic composer; Marcel Brion, *Romantic Art* (1960). See also Josef L. Altholz, *The Churches in the Nineteenth Century* (1967); Crane Brinton, *The Political Ideas of the English Romanticists* (1926); and Hans Kohn, *The Idea of Nationalism* (1943) for an introduction to romanticism's impact beyond the arts.

Chapter 4 / LIBERALISM AND NATIONALISM

For a general introduction, see George Rude, *Debate on Europe, 1815–1850* (1972), and William L. Langer, *Political and Social Upheaval, 1832–1852* (1969). For France, there is G. de Bertier de Sauvigny, *The Bourbon Restoration* (1967); David H. Pinkney, *The French Revolution of 1830* (1972); and Douglas Johnson, *Guizot* (1963). The first two volumes of Elie Halevy's *A History of the English People in the Nineteenth Century* (1961 edition) are still helpful, but should be supplemented by the considerably different perceptions to be found in E.P. Thompson's *The Making of the English Working Class* (1963) and in the work of Norman Gash—*Mr. Secretary Peel* (1961) and *Politics in the Age of Peel* (1953). For Germany, the best study is still Theodore S. Hamerow's *Restoration, Revolution, Reaction* (1958), though Donald G. Rohr's *The Origins of Social Liberalism in Germany* (1963) is also of use.

All the revolutions of 1848 are treated in George Fasel, *Europe in Upheaval: The Revolutions of 1848* (1970); Robert W. Lougee's *Midcentury Revolution, 1848* (1972) deals only with France and the German states. Some of the more notable works on the individual revolutions are R. John Rath, *The Viennese Revolution of 1848* (1957); Stanley Z. Pech, *The Czech Revolution of 1848* (1969); P.H. Noyes, *Organization and Revolution: Working-Class Associations in the German Revolutions of 1848–49* (1966); Leo A. Loubere, *Louis Blanc* (1960); and two engrossing narratives by G.M. Trevelyan, *Garibaldi's Defence of the Roman Republic* (1908) and *Manin and the Venetian Republic* (1923).

Chapter 5 / SOCIALISM

Three indispensable studies on pre-Marxian socialism are Frank E. Manuel, *The Prophets of Paris* (1962), George Lichtheim, *The Origins of Socialism* (1969), and Carl Landauer, *European Socialism: A History of Ideas and Movements*, 2 vols. (Berkeley and Los Angeles, 1959); see also David Owen Evans, *Social Romanticism in France, 1830–1848* (1951). On the radical left under the Second Republic, no work in English has yet superseded the contemporary accounts by Alexis de Tocqueville, *Recollections* (1970), and Karl Marx, *The Class Struggles in France, 1848 to 1850* and *The Eighteenth Brumaire of Louis Bonaparte* (each in numerous recent editions). However, Georges Duveau's *1848: The Making of a Revolution* (1967) is still a useful supplement.

Isaiah Berlin's *Karl Marx* (1963 edition) remains the best biography, while George Lichtheim's *Marxism* (1965 edition) provides both an intellectual history and a lucid reading of the doctrine. Oscar Hammen's *The Red 48ers: Karl Marx and Friedrich Engels* (1969) follow the two revolutionaries through 1848. Robert C. Tucker has authored two interesting studies—*Philosophy and Myth in Karl Marx* (1961) and *The Marxian Revolutionary Idea* (1969)—and edited the best English-language collection of texts for beginners, *The Marx-Engels Reader* (1972).

The literature on the Paris Commune has vastly multiplied after the recent centenary; it remains to be seen what drastic changes these commemorative contributions will make. Of the earlier works, the best are probably Frank Jellinek, *The Paris Commune of 1871* (1937), and Roger L. Williams, *The French Revolution of 1870–71* (1969).

Chapter 6 / CONSERVATISM AND CONCESSION

The most highly regarded modern authority on Italian unification is Denis Mack Smith; see in particular his *Cavour and Garibaldi, 1860* (1954) and *Italy: A Modern History* (1959) for the immediate postunification period. On Bismarck and Germany, the best introductions are Otto Pflanze, *Bismarck and the Development of Germany: The Period of Unification, 1815–1871* (1963); Erich Eyck, *Bismarck and the German Empire* (1950), the condensation of a three-volume work; Theodore Hamerow, *The Social Foundations of German Unification*, 2 vols. (1969–72); and the relevant chapters of Gordon A. Craig, *The Politics of the Prussian Army, 1640–1945* (1956). David Thomson, *Democracy in France Since 1870* (1969 edition), is the best analytical study of the French Third Republic; Gordon Wright's *France in Modern Times* (1960) has some helpful narrative chapters. Robert Kann's *The Multinational Empire*, 2 vols. (1950–64), is still the English work to which one goes first on Habsburg politics during these years. There are first-rate biographies of Disraeli and Gladstone by, respectively, Robert Blake (1966) and Philip Magnus (1954). W.E. Mosse, *Alexander II and the Modernization of Russia* (1958), provides an interesting short introduction to the period of the great reforms; Hugh Seton-Watson's *The Decline of Imperial Russia, 1855–1914* (1952) goes into somewhat greater detail.

Chapter 7 / MAN OVER NATURE

W.O. Henderson's *The Industrialization of Europe, 1780–1914* (1969) contains some interesting observations on the European economy in the second half of the nineteenth century, but David Landes' *The Unbound Prometheus* (1969) remains the best introduction and bibliographical guide as well. On technology, see two volumes of collected articles: William L. Thomas, ed., *Man's Role in Changing the Face of the Earth* (1956), and Melvin Kranzberg and Carroll W. Pursell, Jr., *Technology in Western Civilization*, vol. I (1967). Lewis Mumford, *Technics and Civilization* (1934), is a lively critical interpretation. Of the massive literature on Darwin, one might begin with Loren Eiseley, *Darwin's Century: Evolution and the Men Who Discovered It* (1958); Gertrude Himmelfarb, *Darwin and the Darwinian Revolution* (1959); and, in the absence of a comprehensive study of European social Darwinism, Richard Hofstadter's *Social Darwinism in American Thought* (1955 edition). Positivism may be approached through W.M. Simon, *European Positivism in the Nineteenth Century* (1963) and D. G. Charlton, *Positivist Thought in France During the Second Empire, 1852–1870* (1959).

Chapter 8 / INDUSTRIAL SOCIETY AND CULTURE

Charles Morazé, *The Triumph of the Middle Classes* (1966), and Jurgen Kuczynski, *The Rise of the Working Class* (1967), are good introductions to the social history of the late nineteenth century. For a study of urban life, see Asa

Briggs's *Victorian Cities* (1965); the relevant sections of Lewis Mumford's *The City in History* (1961); and for an excellent case study, Francis Sheppard's *London, 1808–1870: The Infernal Wen* (1971). Readers interested in the subjects gathered in the text under the rubric "the quality of life" might begin by consulting something from the following list: John Burnett, *Plenty and Want: A Social History of Diet in England from 1815 to the Present Day* (1966); Richard N. Shryock, *The Development of Modern Medicine* (1947 edition); Raymond Williams, *Culture and Society, 1780–1950* (1958); K.S. Inglis, *Churches and the Working Class in Victorian England* (1963); J.A. and O. Banks, *Feminism and Family Planning in Victorian England* (1964). The social history of continental Europe during these years is largely confined either to specialized monographs or works in foreign languages; one happy exception is Gerhard Masur's *Imperial Berlin* (1971). Otherwise, one might consult the appropriate sections of Peter N. Stearns, *European Society in Upheaval: Social History Since 1800* (1967).

Chapter 9 / POLITICS IN INDUSTRIAL SOCIETY

The best guides to the social democratic parties are the works by Lichtheim and Landauer, cited in the bibliography to Chapter 5, and James Joll, *The Second International, 1889–1914* (1955). On revisionism, see Peter Gay, *The Dilemma of Democratic Socialism* (1952), and Carl Schorske, *German Social Democracy, 1905–1917* (1955). The essential introductions to anarchism are James Joll, *The Anarchists* (1965), and George Woodcock, *Anarchism* (1962). For national politics in pre-World War I Europe, see (in addition to the relevant titles suggested for Chapter 6): Douglas Johnson, *France and the Dreyfus Affair* (1966); Harvey Goldberg, *The Life of Jean Jaures* (1962); Alexander Gerschenkron, *Bread and Democracy in Germany* (1943); J. Alden Nichols, *Germany after Bismarck* (1958); G.M. Young, *Victorian England: Portrait of an Age* (1936); George Dangerfield, *The Strange Death of Liberal England, 1910–1914* (1935); Arthur J. May, *The Hapsburg Monarchy, 1867–1914* (1951); George Fischer, *Russian Liberalism from Gentry to Intelligentsia* (1958); T.H. von Laue, *Why Lenin? Why Stalin?* (1971 edition). The best general study and most recent bibliography is Oron J. Hale, *The Great Illusion, 1900–1914* (1971).

Chapter 10 / WORLD POWERS IN CONFLICT

Raymond F. Betts, *Europe Overseas: Phases of Imperialism* (1968), is a handy and reliable introduction. The works of Hobson (1902) and Lenin (1916) have been excerpted in any number of anthologies; Harrison M. Wright, ed., *The "New Imperialism": Analysis of Late Nineteenth-Century Expansion* (1961), reprints important passages along with selections from their critics. Among these latter, two in particular deserve note: Joseph A. Schumpeter, *Imperialism and Social Classes* (1951), and John T. Gallagher and Ronald I. Robinson (with Alice Denny), *Africa and the Victorians* (1961). On French imperialism, see Henri Brunschwig, *French Colonialism, 1871–1914* (1966); on Russia, B.H. Sumner, *Tsardom and Imperialism in the Far East and the Middle East, 1880–1914* (1942); on Germany, Hans-Ulrich Wehler, "Bismarck's Imperialism, 1862–1890," *Past and Present* (1970), pp. 119–55. On the European implications of imperial expansion, William L. Langer's treatments and bibliographies are indispensable: *European Alliances and Alignments, 1870–1890* (1956 edition) and *The Diplomacy of Imperialism, 1890–1902* (1960 edition). For one important issue of the post-1902 period, E.L. Woodward's *Great Britain and the German Navy* (1935) is still useful.

Chapter 11 / WAR AND REVOLUTION

Laurence Lafore, *The Long Fuse* (1971 edition), is a popular interpretive account of the origins of World War I. Luigi Albertini's *The Origins of the War of 1914*, 3 vols. (1952–57), goes into much greater detail; the first volume covers the period from 1878 to 1914, while volumes II and III examine the crisis of summer 1914. Erich Brandenburg, *From Bismarck to the World War* (1927), is especially concerned to exonerate Germany from "war-guilt" charges; Bernard Fay, *The Origins of the World War*, 2 vols. (1938 edition), also tends to allocate the blame among all the belligerents. Pierre Renouvin, *The Immediate Origins of the War* (1928), and Fritz Fischer, *Germany's Aims in the First World War* (1967), are harsh with the Central Powers. Barbara Tuchman's *The Guns of August* (1962) is already something of a classic account of the war's early weeks. A general military and political history of the war years is provided in A.J.P. Taylor, *A History of the First World War* (1963). "Life-in-the-trenches" memoirs are legion; none is better than Robert Graves, *Good-bye to All That* (1929).

The poles of argument on the peace of Versailles are John Maynard Keynes, *The Economic Consequences of the Peace* (1919), and Etienne Mantoux, *The Carthaginian Peace, or The Economic Consequences of Mr. Keynes* (1946). Harold Nicolson's *Peacemaking, 1919* (1935), is an intriguing first-hand account. On the peace in a larger setting, see Arno J. Mayer, *Political Origins of the New Diplomacy, 1917–1918* (1959) and *Politics and Diplomacy of Peacemaking* (1967).

On the Russian revolutions, there is an embarrassment of riches; see Adam B. Ulam, *The Bolsheviks* (1965); E.H. Carr, *The Bolshevik Revolution*, 3 vols. (1950–53); Leon Trotsky, *The Russian Revolution* (1959 abridged edition).

Chapter 12 / THE MODERN IMAGINATION: BEYOND SCIENTISM AND REALISM

The best starting point for a study of early twentieth-century thought is H. Stuart Hughes, *Consciousness and Society: The Reorientation of European Social Thought, 1890–1930* (1958). Readers interested in the laboratory sciences may wish to consult Carl T. Chase, *The Evolution of Modern Physics* (1947), and the illuminating study by Jeremy Bernstein, *Albert Einstein* (1973). On Freud, see Ernest Jones: *The Life and Work of Sigmund Freud* (1961 abridged edition), and Philip Rieff, *Freud: The Mind of a Moralist* (1959).

For an introduction to modern art, there are any number of convenient surveys: E.H. Gombrich, *The Story of Art* (1956); Herbert E. Read, *A Concise History of Modern Painting* (1959); Edmund Wilson, *Axel's Castle* (1931), on literature; Nikolaus Pevsner, *Pioneers of Modern Design* (1964 edition), on architecture; the relevant sections of T.M. Finney, *A History of Music* (1947 edition). On various "movements," see Renato Poggioli, *The Theory of the Avant-Garde* (1968); Hans Richter, *Dada* (1965); Patrick Waldberg, *Surrealism* (1965); Lotte Eisner, *The Haunted Screen* (1970 edition), on expressionism in the German cinema during the 1920's. There is an interesting collection of texts in Eugen Weber, ed., *Paths to the Present: Aspects of European Thought from Romanticism to Existentialism* (1960).

Chapter 13 / THE POLITICS OF EXTREMISM

Richard Pipes, *The Formation of the Soviet Union* (1964 edition), and T.H. von Laue, *Why Lenin? Why Stalin?* (1971), are helpful accounts of the early Soviet Union. Isaac Deutscher has written the best biography of Stalin (1949), but see also Robert Conquest, *The Great Terror* (1968).

Hans Rogger and Eugen Weber, eds., *The European Right* (1965), is an extremely important collection of articles. On fascism, see Eugen Weber, *Varieties of Fascism* (1964); Ernst Nolte, *Three Faces of Fascism* (1965); and the stimulating but more abstract essay by Arno J. Mayer, *Dynamics of Counterrevolution in Europe, 1870–1956* (1971). The best introductions to Italian fascism are Elizabeth Wiskemann. *Fascism in Italy: Its Development and Influence* (1969), and Ivone A. Kirkpatrick, *Mussolini* (1964). The authoritative study of Hitler remains Alan Bullock, *Hitler, A Study in Tyranny* (1964 edition). Of the massive literature on Nazi Germany, the following are particularly interesting: David Schoenbaum, *Hitler's Social Revolution* (1966); William S. Allen, *The Nazi Seizure of Power* (1965); Karl D. Bracher, *The German Dictatorship* (1970); Gerald Reitlinger, *The SS* (1957); Gordon A. Craig, *The Politics of the Prussian Army, 1640–1945* (1955); George Mosse, *Nazi Culture* (1966); Bruno Bettelheim, *The Informed Heart* (1960), on concentration camps; Hannah Arendt, *Eichmann in Jerusalem: A Report on the Banality of Evil* (1964 edition).

For the Popular Front and the interwar era, see Raymond J. Sontag, *A Broken World, 1919–1939* (1971). On the Spanish Civil War, there is Gabriel Jackson, *The Spanish Republic and the Civil War, 1931–1939* (1965).

Chapter 14 / THE END OF THE EUROPEAN ERA

A.J.P. Taylor's *Origins of the Second World War* (1962) is at the center of a huge controversy; the case for the opposition is best presented by Bullock in *Hitler, A Study in Tyranny* (1964 edition). Gordon Wright's *The Ordeal of Total War, 1939–45* (1968) is now the best introduction to the war itself, with an excellent bibliography. For various aspects of the struggle, see Alexander Werth, *Russia at War, 1941–1945* (1964); F.W. Deakin, *The Brutal Friendship: Mussolini, Hitler, and the Fall of Italian Fascism* (1962); J.C. Masterman, *The Double Cross System in the War of 1939 to 1945* (1972); H.R. Trevor-Roper, *The Last Days of Hitler* (1947); Robert O. Paxton, *Vichy France: Old Guard and New Order, 1940–1944* (1972).

The end of the hot war and the beginning of the cold one are just beginning to get a scholarly treatment, though the lack of access to official documents is obviously a serious difficulty. Some of the more useful accounts are Herbert Feis, *Churchill, Roosevelt, Stalin* (1957) and *Between War and Peace: The Potsdam Conference* (1960); Gar Alperovitz, *Potsdam Diplomacy* (1965); and Gabriel Kolko, *The Politics of War: The World and United States Foreign Policy, 1943–1945* (1968).

Chapter 15 / EUROPE IN THE POSTWAR WORLD

The post-1945 conflict between the Soviet and American blocs is well handled in John A. Lukacs, *A New History of the Cold War* (1966 edition), and in David Rees, *The Age of Containment* (1967). On specific incidents, see W.P. Davison, *The Berlin Blockade* (1958); Paul Zinner, *Revolution in Hungary* (1962) and, as editor, *National Communism and Popular Revolt in Eastern Europe* (1956); Joyce and Gabriel Kolko, *The Limits of Power: The World and United States Foreign Policy, 1945–1954* (1972); W.W. Kulski, *Peaceful Coexistence* (1959). Decolonization has yet to find its historian, and the connections between the end of European empire and the Cold War are only just beginning to emerge. Some suggestive work has been done by Raymond Betts, *Europe Overseas* (1968); John Strachey, *The End of Empire* (1959); Dorothy Pickles, *Algeria and France: From Colonialism to Cooperation* (1963); D.O. Mannoni, *Prospero and Caliban* (1956); John Marlowe, *Arab Nationalism and British Imperialism* (1961); Jean Lacouture, *Vietnam Between Two Truces* (1966); Margery Perham, *The Colonial Reckoning: The End of Colonial Rule in Africa in the Light of British Experience* (1961); Rupert Emerson, *From Empire to Nation: The Rise to Self-Assertion of Asian and African Peoples* (1960).

Chapter 16 / INTEGRATION AND COEXISTENCE

Maurice Crouzet, *The European Renaissance since 1945* (1970), is a splendid introduction to problems of economic reconstruction both east and west. On the People's Democracies, there are J.F. Brown's *The New Eastern Europe* (1966), Z.K. Brzezinski's *The Soviet Bloc* (1967 edition), and J.P. Nettl's enlightening *The Soviet Achievement* (1967). The west European countries may be approached through John Ardagh, *The New French Revolution* (1968); Philip M. Williams and Martin Harrison, *Politics and Society in De Gaulle's Republic* (1972); David Thomson, *England in the Twentieth Century* (1964); E.A. Johns, *The Social Structure of Modern Britain* (1965); Ralf Dahrendorf, *Society and Democracy in Germany* (1968); F. Roy Willis, *Italy Chooses Europe* (1971). See also the articles in Stephen Graubard, ed., *A New Europe?* (1964). The history of European economic integration is, like the subject itself, still in progress; but see H. Schmitt, *The Path to European Union* (1962); Miriam Camps, *European Unification in the Sixties* (1966); F. Roy Willis, *France, Germany and the New Europe, 1945–1967* (1968 edition). On the welfare state and its problems, consult P. Goldman, *The Welfare State* (1964); R. Millar, *The New Classes* (1966); Jacques Ellul, *The Technological Society* (1965); Stephen Spender, *The Year of the Young Rebels* (1969).

Index

9123